OXFORD HISTORICAL MONOGRAPHS

EDITORS

J. H. ELLIOTT
P. LANGFORD
H. M. MAYR-HARTING

M. H. KEEN
H. C. G. MATTHEW
A. J. NICHOLLS

SIR KEITH THOMAS

The Catholic Priesthood and the English Reformation

PETER MARSHALL

CLARENDON PRESS · OXFORD
1994

Oxford University Press, Walton Street, Oxford OX2 6DP

Oxford New York Toronto
Delhi Bombay Calcutta Madras Karachi
Kuala Lumpur Singapore Hong Kong Tokyo
Nairobi Dar es Salaam Cape Town
Melbourne Auckland Madrid
and associated companies in
Berlin Ibadan

Oxford is a trade mark of Oxford University Press

Published in the United States
by Oxford University Press Inc., New York

© Peter Marshall 1994

All rights reserved. No part of this publication may be reproduced,
stored in a retrieval system, or transmitted, in any form or by any means,
without the prior permission in writing of Oxford University Press.
Within the UK, exceptions are allowed in respect of any fair dealing for the
purpose of research or private study, or criticism or review, as permitted
under the Copyright, Designs and Patents Act, 1988, or in the case of
reprographic reproduction in accordance with the terms of the licences
issued by the Copyright Licensing Agency. Enquiries concerning
reproduction outside these terms and in other countries should be
sent to the Rights Department, Oxford University Press,
at the address above

British Library Cataloguing in Publication Data
Data available

Library of Congress Cataloging in Publication Data
Data applied for
ISBN 0–19–820448–5

1 3 5 7 9 10 8 6 4 2

Typeset by Graphicraft Typesetters Ltd., Hong Kong
Printed in Great Britain
on acid-free paper by
Bookcraft (Bath) Ltd.
Midsomer Norton, Avon

BX
1492
.M35
1994

For Ali

Acknowledgements

In researching and writing this book I have accumulated a good many debts. Its first incarnation was as a doctoral thesis, and I was more than fortunate to have as my examiners two exemplars of the historian's craft: Cliff Davies, who did much to encourage my research in its early stages, and John Bossy, whose writings on early modern religion have long been a source of inspiration. Susan Brigden has been involved with every stage of this book's evolution: as supervisor of the research on which it is based and, more recently, as sub-editor. Whatever merits it may be thought to possess owe a great deal to her judicious criticism and meticulous scholarship. Many thanks are due also to those friends and colleagues who have provided me with references, read over parts of the text, or simply taken time to discuss matters which were more probably of interest to me than to them: Christoph Hölger, Veronica Lawrence, Alexander Murray, Caroline Coster, John A. F. Thomson, Gillian Roberts, and Will Coster. I am equally indebted to those scholars who have allowed me to consult and to cite their unpublished theses, a debt which will be evident in the pages which follow.

The task of research was eased considerably by the efficient and dedicated service provided in the various libraries and record repositories where I have worked. I hope it will not be invidious to extend special thanks to the staff of the Bodleian Library in Oxford, and of the Borthwick Institute in York, where the director, Dr David Smith, dealt most patiently with my queries. Much of the final version of this book was written in the library of Ampleforth Abbey. I am grateful to the Abbot and community for this courtesy, and to the librarian, Fr. Anselm Cramer, for his many labours on my behalf. My teaching colleagues at Ampleforth College have been notable supporters of my work; I am particularly grateful to Peter Galliver for his tolerance and encouragement. Many thanks are due also to the staff of Oxford University Press, who have patiently guided a neophyte through the mysteries of publication.

My family, as ever, have been supportive throughout, and I am especially indebted to James and Margaret Bruce for providing me with a home at a critical stage of research, and with hospitality on countless subsequent visits to Oxford. My greatest debt is to Ali Marshall. Without her unfailing support and encouragement this book would never have been written, and I have dedicated it, with gratitude, to her.

P.M.
Ampleforth
June 1993

Contents

Abbreviations	x
Introduction	1
1. THE PRIEST AS CONFESSOR	5
2. THE PRIEST AS CELEBRANT	35
3. THE PRIEST AS TEACHER	86
4. THE PRIEST AS ANOINTED	108
5. THE PRIEST AS CELIBATE	142
6. THE PRIEST AS PASTOR	174
7. THE PRIEST AS NEIGHBOUR	194
8. THE PRIEST AS ENEMY	211
9. CONCLUSION	233
Bibliography	237
Index	261

Abbreviations

AC	*Archaeologia Cantiana*
ACC	Alcuin Club Collections
ARG	*Archiv für Reformationsgeschichte*
BIHR	Borthwick Institute of Historical Research
CAS	Cambridge Antiquarian Society
ChS	Chetham Society
CS	Camden Society
CW	The Yale Edition of the Complete Works of St Thomas More (New Haven, Conn., 1963–)
CYS	Canterbury and York Society
EETS	Early English Text Society
ES	Extra Series
EHR	*English Historical Review*
Foxe, *Acts and Monuments*	John Foxe, *Acts and Monuments*, ed. S. R. Cattley and G. Townsend, 8 vols. (1837–41)
GLRO	Greater London Record Office
Hale, *Precedents*	W. H. Hale (ed.), *A Series of Precedents and Proceedings in Criminal Causes, 1475–1640, extracted from act books of ecclesiastical courts in the diocese of London* (1847)
JBS	*Journal of British Studies*
JEH	*Journal of Ecclesiastical History*
Kentish Visitations	K. L. Wood-Legh (ed.), *Kentish Visitations of Archbishop William Warham and his Deputies, 1511–1512*, Kent Records (1984)
Latimer, *Sermons*	Hugh Latimer, Sermons, ed. G. E. Corrie, PS (1844) and *Sermons and Remains*, ed. G. E. Corrie, PS (1845)
Lincoln Visitations	A. H. Thompson (ed.), *Visitations in the Diocese of Lincoln, 1517–1531*, LRS, 33, 35 (1940–4)
LoRS	London Record Society

LP	J. S. Brewer *et al.* (eds.), *Letters and Papers, Foreign and Domestic, of the Reign of Henry VIII*, 21 vols. (1862–1932)
LRS	Lincoln Record Society
Lyndwood	J. V. Bullard and H. C. Bell (eds.), *Lyndwood's Provinciale* (1929)
More, *Dialogue*	Thomas More, *A Dialogue Concerning Heresies*, ed. T. M. C. Lawler, G. Marc'hadour, and R. C. Marius, *CW* 6 (1981)
NCCD	E. D. Stone and B. Cozens-Hardy (eds.), *Norwich Consistory Court Depositions, 1499–1512 and 1518–1530*, Norfolk Record Society (1938)
NS	New Series
OCRO	Oxford County Record Office
OED	*Oxford English Dictionary*, 2nd edn. (1989)
OS	Old Series
PCC	Prerogative Court of Canterbury
PP	*Past and Present*
PRO	Public Record Office
PS	Parker Society
SCH	Studies in Church History
SCJ	*Sixteenth Century Journal*
SRS	Somerset Record Society
SS	Surtees Society
Test. Ebor.	J. Raine (ed.), *Testamenta Eboracensia*, SS 53, 79, 106 (1869–1902)
TRHS	*Transactions of the Royal Historical Society*
Visitation Articles	W. H. Frere and W. M. Kennedy (eds.), *Visitation Articles and Injunctions of the Period of the Reformation*, 3 vols., ACC 14–16 (1910)
Wilkins, *Concilia*	D. Wilkins (ed.), *Concilia Magna Britanniae et Hiberniae . . . 446–1718*, 4 vols. (1737)
YAS (RS)	Yorkshire Archaeological Society (Record Series)

Note: Reference, unless otherwise stated, is to document numbers. Place of publication, unless otherwise stated, is London. Spelling has been modernized and punctuation standardized, and quotations from Latin documents have been translated.

Introduction

In Walter Scott's novel *The Heart of Midlothian* the reader makes the welcome acquaintance of the heroine's father, the stern Cameronian 'Douce Davie' Deans, of whom the author observes, 'highly as Douce Davie honoured the clergy, it was not upon each individual of the cloth that he bestowed his approbation'.[1] Though the setting is eighteenth-century Scotland, and the ecclesial context Presbyterian, this paradoxical attitude could probably be found in virtually all societies which have employed the services of a professional religious ministry. In early Reformation England, which provides the subject matter of this book, the attitudes of the people towards their priests and the priesthood were frequently informed by the same dichotomy, and no less a figure than Henry VIII was equally insistent that 'the excellency of the office doth not always in all points extol the dignity of the minister'.[2]

This dialectic of theory and practice, of priesthood and priest, is the starting-point of this study, which aims to elucidate what expectations English laypeople had of their priests in the first half of the sixteenth century, their reactions when these were unfulfilled, and their perceptions of the mutual obligations which underlay their relationship with the clergy. The period over which these features are to be observed, that from the latter years of Henry VII to the accession of Mary I, was one in which the concepts of priesthood and ministry were violently disputed by religious theorists, and in which new understandings of the implications of the clerical office were to receive growing institutional expression. Bishops and theologians of Protestant sympathies, whose influence was contingent in Henry VIII's reign, and paramount in that of Edward VI, saw the priesthood in terms of function rather than of essence: priests were conceived as faithful pastors and, most importantly, ministers of the Word of God. To Catholic traditionalists, the pastoral element was also important, but the quiddity of the priest was his inherent capacity to mediate grace via the sacraments, in particular those of the eucharist and

---

[1] W. Scott, *The Heart of Midlothian* (1967), 102.
[2] *The Records of the Northern Convocation*, SS, 113 (1907), 225.

penance.[3] As these rival conceptions were hammered out in the political developments of the 1530s, 1540s, and 1550s, ordinary lay men and women found their accustomed ways of dealing with the clergy challenged and tested, and they reacted in ways that seem to have ranged from idealism, to sophisticated self-interest, to simple confusion. In so far as shifts and constants in collective mentality can be discerned, they will be delineated and discussed in the chapters which follow.

The focus of this work is firmly on the parish clergy, those priests with whom the laity were in closest day-to-day contact, and of whom there were perhaps 20,000–25,000 in the first decades of the sixteenth century.[4] Lay attitudes to the upper reaches of the clerical hierarchy and to the religious orders have been considered only tangentially. After many years of ill-deserved neglect, the early sixteenth-century parish clergy have been well served by historians.[5] Little work has been done, however, on the more specific areas of relations between the secular clergy and their parishioners and of lay perceptions of the clerical office.[6] Recent writing on the concept of 'anticlericalism' with respect to the English Reformation, though stimulating and salient, presents only one aspect of a considerably more complex picture.[7] We have recently been warned against 'a nervous preoccupation with the Reformation, as if everything inevitably

[3] It has become fashionable among students of the early Reformation in England to discard the labels 'Catholic' and 'Protestant' as constrictive and anachronistic. In this book they are retained, but should usually be understood in a common-sense, non-technical way, the Catholics being those who preferred sacraments and the authority of an institutional Church to the greater scripturalism and individualism of the Protestants.

[4] For estimates of total clerical numbers, and the difficulties in making such estimates, see M. L. Zell, 'Economic Problems of the Parochial Clergy in the Sixteenth Century', in R. O'Day and F. Heal (eds.), *Princes and Paupers in the English Church 1500–1800* (Leicester, 1981), 21–3; R. O'Day, 'The Anatomy of a Profession: The Clergy of the Church of England', in W. Prest (ed.), *The Professions in Early Modern England* (Beckenham, 1987), 30; J. Youings, *Sixteenth-Century England* (Harmondsworth, 1984), 36. Christopher Haigh puts the total number of secular priests rather higher, at around 40,000: *English Reformations: Religion, Politics, and Society under the Tudors* (Oxford, 1993), 5.

[5] See P. Heath, *English Parish Clergy on the Eve of the Reformation* (1969); M. Bowker, *The Secular Clergy in the Diocese of Lincoln, 1485–1520* (Cambridge, 1968); J. C. H. Aveling, 'The English Clergy, Catholic and Protestant in the 16th and 17th Centuries', in W. Haase (ed.), *Rome and the Anglicans* (Berlin, 1982), as well as a host of local studies by the authors of postgraduate dissertations.

[6] An exception is the recent article by R. N. Swanson, 'Problems of the Priesthood in Pre-Reformation England', *EHR* 417 (1990), which from a late medieval standpoint addresses some of the same concerns as this present study.

[7] C. Haigh, 'Anticlericalism and the English Reformation', in Haigh (ed.), *The English Reformation Revised* (Cambridge, 1987); A. G. Dickens, 'The Shape of Anticlericalism and the English Reformation', in E. I. Kouri and T. Scott (eds.), *Politics and Society in Reformation Europe* (1987). See below, pp. 211–14.

led to this',[8] and in seeking to illustrate the totality of possible reactions and responses to priests and the priesthood, the emphasis will not be upon identifying the causes of religious change, but upon attempting to illuminate something of the nature of 'popular religion' in the early sixteenth century, and the impact of reform on the interaction of the ordinary Christian and his pastor.

The methodological difficulties inherent in such an attempt are considerable. The French historian, Philippe Ariès, identified two possible approaches to the study of *mentalités*. The first involved 'the quantitative analysis of homogeneous documentary series'. In the second, less objective but more comprehensive approach, 'the observer scans a chaotic mass of documents and tries to decipher . . . the unconscious expression of the sensibility of the age'.[9] Although in the pages that follow some attempts at quantification have been made, of necessity, and with due diffidence, the second approach has been followed. The attitudes, prejudices, and assumptions of the people of early-Reformation England can be reconstructed only with great difficulty and at the risk of doing violence to the idiosyncracies of the individual. Each category of possible source material provides its own pitfalls. Some of the conclusions of this book are based on an examination of some 5,500 wills, made by laypeople in the period 1500 to 1553, and representing most English counties.[10] It is notorious that such evidence has not always been handled with great care. Not only did will-making penetrate down the social scale to a markedly limited extent, but the circumstances under which such documents were produced may raise legitimate doubts as to the authenticity and normative value of the sentiments they display.[11] Theological and devotional works may sometimes reflect the preoccupations only of a religious élite, and may have been used or understood in ways that their authors did not intend. Judicial documents by their very nature record the socially

---

[8] N. P. Tanner, 'The Reformation and Regionalism: Further Reflections on the Church in Late Medieval Norwich', in J. A. F. Thomson (ed.), *Towns and Townspeople in the Fifteenth Century* (Gloucester, 1988), 129.

[9] P. Ariès, *The Hour of Our Death*, tr. H. Weaver (Harmondsworth, 1981), p. xiii.

[10] The sample comprises manuscript wills from the registers of the Prerogative Court of Canterbury for the counties of Kent, Hampshire, and Oxfordshire, as well as wills from most English counties in printed collections. Full details can be found in the Bibliography.

[11] For such caveats, see R. N. Swanson, *Church and Society in Late Medieval England* (Oxford, 1989), 265–8; M. L. Zell, 'The Use of Religious Preambles as a Measure of Religious Belief in the Sixteenth Century', *Bulletin of the Institute of Historical Research*, 50 (1977); J. J. Scarisbrick, *The Reformation and the English People* (Oxford, 1984), 10–12; R. O'Day, *The Debate on the English Reformation* (1986), 155–9; E. Duffy, *The Stripping of the Altars: Traditional Religion in England, 1400–1580* (New Haven, Conn., 1992), 504–23.

pathological. Crucially, the great majority of English men and women in this period remain silent and ultimately unknowable. None the less, by examining these and other kinds of contemporary evidence, and by remaining sensitive to nuance and context, it is possible to proceed in the conviction that connections and patterns will emerge that may do much to elucidate the inarticulate, the inchoate, and the assumed.

In structuring this book, eight paradigms of priestly 'function' have been identified, eight contexts within which lay perceptions of the priest and his office may have been formed. The early chapters deal with the changing soteriological role of the priest, his duties of hearing confessions, saying mass, and instructing his parishioners. The middle chapters discuss how these tasks mediated and reflected the 'otherness' of the priest, his unique and distinctive status *vis-à-vis* the laity. The final chapters examine the social and contextual interaction of priests and layfolk; its successes and dysfunctions. Within each chapter a broad chronological framework has been assumed, but the intention has not been to tell the story of the English Reformation, or to pass judgement on its success. Rather, it has been to study one aspect of a society which tended to assume its essential immutability just as it was undergoing irrevocable change, and to attempt to make sense of the stressful symbiosis of two of the most obvious groups within that society, the priests and the people.

1

The Priest as Confessor

THE PRACTICE OF CONFESSION

Nowhere in pre-Reformation England was the distinction between lay-man and priest more marked than in the theory and practice of auricular confession. The juxtaposition is striking both visually and symbolically: the priest sitting in judgement, the lay man or woman a kneeling peti-tioner. And yet the relationship of penitent and confessor remains an elusive historical theme. In a society which was deeply concerned with spectacle and display, confession was a secret, though not a visibly hid-den, activity, and one which has left few written records of its proceed-ings. Accounts of actual confessions which do survive document cases which are probably by definition exceptional. We can know what the authors of guides and manuals for confessors considered ought to have taken place between priest and penitent, but not what usually did take place. The sources tell us likewise how laypeople should have regarded the sacrament of penance and its ministers; what they might actually have felt is much harder to determine. Not surprisingly, historians have dis-agreed about the functions and failings of pre-Reformation confessional practice, and in recent years a number of important, though divergent interpretations have been advanced.[1]

In the hearing of confessions and in the pronouncing or withholding of absolutions, the confessor performed a quintessential priestly act, one that had undergone centuries of theological refinement and that was at once pastoral and sacramental.[2] It might seem that in attempting to reconstruct perceptions of the priest as confessor, we might capture something of the

[1] S. E. Ozment, *The Reformation in the Cities* (New Haven, Conn., 1975); T. N. Tentler, 'The Summa for Confessors as an Instrument of Social Control', in C. Trinkaus and H. A. Oberman (eds.), *The Pursuit of Holiness in Late Medieval and Renaissance Religion* (Leiden, 1974); *Sin and Confession on the Eve of the Reformation* (Princeton, NJ, 1977); J. Bossy, 'The Social History of Confession in the Age of the Reformation', *TRHS* 25 (1975); L. G. Duggan, 'Fear and Confession on the Eve of the Reformation', *ARG* 75 (1984).

[2] The development of penitential theory in the Middle Ages is traced by B. Poschmann, *Penance and the Anointing of the Sick*, tr. F. Courtney (Freiburg, 1964).

essence of the lay understanding of and commitment to the concept of
sacerdotalism as a whole. The equation, however, is uncertain, involving
a number of variables. For instance, did the mass of the population share,
or at least to some degree comprehend, the theologians' conception of the
purpose and value of sacramental penance? Were the conduct and consequences of individual confessions likely to elicit some definable response
to the sacramental action of the priest? It is easier to pose these questions
than to fashion answers to them. Perhaps the issues might be clarified by
addressing some contingent and more malleable lines of enquiry: by
assessing, for instance, the relative importance of confession in the religious life of the laity, and by reflecting on whether confession was likely
to contribute to a generally positive or to a negative image of the priests
who controlled and administered it.

It has been noted at the outset that it is impossible to discover what
really took place during the great majority of confessions. It is, none
the less, important to try to establish some kind of schedule of the most
likely pattern of pre-Reformation English confession.[3] To make his confession a penitent would kneel in front of or at the side of the priest in
some visible part of the church. This was usually either immediately
behind or in front of the rood screen, and although the closed confessional
box was unknown in pre-Reformation England, some churches had a
special faldstool or 'shriving pew' which was used for the purpose.[4]
Next, the penitent would probably request a blessing, 'benedicite', to
which the confessor would respond, 'Dominus sit vobiscum'.[5] After some
preliminary questions to enable the priest to determine the parochial,
social, and marital status of the penitent, the latter would proceed to his

[3] Evidence for this will be drawn in the main from three contemporary sources: the 15th-
c. *Instructions for Parish Priests*, compiled by John Mirc; a simple vernacular confessional
handbook, *The Boke of the Ghostly Father*, printed in the early 16th c. and drawing on Mirc;
and the Latin manual copied into his commonplace book by the London merchant, Richard
Hill. The latter work was almost certainly the *Modus Confitendi* of the early 15th-c. canonist,
Andreas de Escobar.

[4] F. Gasquet, *Parish Life in Medieval England* (1906), 200; A. E. Nichols, 'The Etiquette
of Pre-Reformation Confession in East Anglia', *SCJ* 17 (1986), 153; 'Churchwardens' Accounts of the Parish of St Mary Pattens, London', *The Sacristy*, 1 (1871), 259; J. E. Foster
(ed.), 'Churchwardens' Accounts of St Mary the Great, Cambridge', *CAS* 35 (1905), 6;
J. F. Williams (ed.), *The Early Churchwardens' Accounts of Hampshire* (1913), 11; H. Littlehales
(ed.), *The Medieval Records of a London City Church (St Mary at Hill) 1420–1559*, EETS
125 (1904), 198; E. G. Cuthbert and F. Atchley (eds.), 'On the Mediaeval Parish Records
of the Church of St Nicholas, Bristol', *Transactions of the St Paul's Ecclesiological Society*, 6
(1906–10), 63.

[5] Balliol College MS 354, fo. 180ᵛ; R. Whitford, *A Werke for Housholders* (1530), sig. F.iᵛ;
Friar Garard, *The Interpretacyon and Sygnyfycacyon of the Masse* (1532), sig. V.ivʳ.

confession.[6] It was then the responsibility of the priest to question him further about his sins, the methodology of the interrogation being supposed to reflect various theological taxonomies. Most common was for questions to be organized around the Seven Deadly Sins, with perhaps as many as twenty questions for each type of sin. Had the penitent sinned in pride by feigning sanctity, or by rejoicing in his skill at games or dancing? Had he envied the possessions of his neighbour, or taken pleasure in his misfortunes? Had he been slothful in coming to mass on Sundays and feast-days? Committed adultery, or desired to listen to lecherous songs?[7] John Mirc's arrangement expanded the format to include an examination on sins against the Ten Commandments, and on venial sins committed through the exercise of the Five Senses and in omitting the Works of Corporal Mercy. The *Modus Confitendi* which Richard Hill copied into his commonplace book had, in addition to the Seven Deadly Sins and Ten Commandments, the Twelve Articles of Faith, the Seven Sacraments, the Five Senses, and the Works of Corporal and Spiritual Mercy.[8] The examination might be concluded by some advice on avoiding sin in the future; then a direction to the penitent to repeat an act of contrition, followed by the pronouncement of absolution and the imposition of penance.[9]

In the performance of all this, two aspects are particularly stressed. In the first place, the manuals are stern in their insistence on a complete confession, the *Boke of the Ghostly Father* warning that sins kept from the confessor will be revealed to everyone by the Devil on the Day of Judgement.[10] Secondly, the confessor is required to discover all the circumstances attending the sin, though he is warned not to enquire after the names of others involved. Penitents would often say, for instance, 'I have sinned in lechery', but this was not sufficient.[11] Only with a complete knowledge of the circumstances could a confessor assess the gravity of the sin and be able to assign an appropriate penance.[12] It was, for

---

[6] J. Mirc, *Instructions for Parish Priests,* EETS 131 (1868), 25; Tentler, *Sin and Confession,* 84; *The Ordinary of crysten men* (1506), sig. Q.i[r]; G. A. J. Hodgett, *Tudor Lincolnshire* (Lincoln, 1975), 15. [7] *Boke of the Ghostly Father* (?1521), sigs. A.iii[v]–iv[r], B.ii[v], B.iv[r].

[8] Mirc, *Instructions,* 43–6; Balliol MS 354, fos. 179[v], 181[r–v]. Some confession manuals employed as many as 10 or 12 categories: Tentler, *Sin and Confession,* 135. Garard, *Interpretacyon and Sygnyfycacyon,* espoused no fewer than 19: sig. A.ii[v]–iii[v].

[9] Mirc, *Instructions,* 46–56; *Boke of the Ghostly Father,* sig. C.iii[v].

[10] Ibid., sig. B.vi[v]. See also Tentler, *Sin and Confession,* 109; J. Mirc, *Festial,* ed. T. Erbe, EETS es 96 (1905), 89; J. Hughes, 'The Administration of Confession in the Diocese of York in the Fourteenth Century', in D. M. Smith (ed.), *Studies in Clergy and Ministry in Medieval England* (York, 1991), 130. [11] *Boke of the Ghostly Father,* sig. C.i[v].

[12] Ibid.; Mirc, *Instructions,* 48–9; Balliol MS 354, fo. 179[v].

example, a more serious sin to strike a cleric than to strike a layman, worse still if the offence took place inside a church, and worse again if it occurred on a feast-day or holy day.[13]

Pronouncements on the nature of early sixteenth-century confession based upon confessors' manuals depend of course on the dual assumption that parish clergy possessed such manuals and made practical use of their directives. If they did not, and were forced to improvise, then the practice of penance may have been very different from that described tentatively above. It is perhaps particularly pertinent to ask if many ordinary parish priests possessed the elaborate *Summae* of confession described by T. N. Tentler, and which have been designated by him 'an instrument of social control'.[14] Clearly, some of them did. In 1504, William Rowkshaw, the rector of Lowthorpe in Yorkshire, bequeathed a 'summa confessorum' to be chained in the choir of his parish church, thus plainly intending it for pastoral use.[15] John Adeson, curate of Caldbeck in Cumberland in the 1530s, had, among his other books, copies both of the *Summa Anthonini* and the *Summa Angelica*.[16] The *Summa Angelica* was also bequeathed by Edmund Kingston, vicar of Southwell, in 1549.[17] In general, however, priests' wills suggest that penitential manuals were less prominent a feature of clerical libraries than devotional works like Ludolph of Saxony's *Vita Christi*, or homilectic aids of the *Sermones Discipuli* variety, and it is by no means certain that actual confessions always followed the prescriptions of the experts. Wills, however, are a notoriously unreliable means of ascertaining the extent of book ownership and penitential matters featured prominently in the many popular handbooks or manuals for the cure of souls which are known to have circulated widely both in manuscript and in print among the late medieval English parish clergy.[18] It seems

---

[13] Ibid.

[14] The author himself raises this possible objection to his thesis: Tentler, 'Summa for Confessors', 122.   [15] *Test. Ebor.* iv. 231.

[16] J. W. Clay (ed.), *North Country Wills*, SS, 116 (1908), 173.

[17] *Test. Ebor.* vi. 289.

[18] R. M. Ball, 'The Education of the English Parish Clergy in the Later Middle Ages, with Particular Reference to the Manuals of Instruction', University of Cambridge Ph.D. thesis (1976). The principal examples of the genre included William of Pagula's *Oculus Sacerdotis*, the *Pupilla Oculi* of John de Burgh, and, for the less erudite, works such as the *Manuale Sacerdotis* and Mirc's *Instructions for Parish Priests*. In this latter category, particularly in demand was Guy de Montrocher's *Manipulus Curatorum*, printed at least 9 times in England between 1498 and 1517. Ball, 'Education of Clergy', 7–11, 32; W. A. Pantin, *The English Church in the Fourteenth Century* (Cambridge, 1955), ch. 9. Such manuals are depicted as being used by priests in confession in the relevant panels on several late medieval East Anglian Seven-Sacrament fonts: E. Duffy, *The Stripping of the Altars: Traditional Religion in England, 1400–1580* (New Haven, Conn., 1992), 58.

probable that the pattern laid down by such works was to some degree normative, an impression that is partially confirmed by the evidence of a Kentish man in the early 1540s, declaring his intention to 'come to my ghostly father and show to him I have sinned in the Seven Deadly Sins and have broken the Ten Commandments, and misspent my five wits'.[19] This was precisely the text-book analysis of sin.

How, then, did this somewhat inquisitorial mode of confession affect those who were bound to submit themselves to it? Did it, as Steven Ozment has suggested in the context of Reformation Germany, lead to scrupulosity and a preoccupation with sin?[20] Or even, ultimately, to a semi-Pelagian despair of salvation? William Tyndale, admittedly not the most detached or impartial observer of the contemporary English scene, was convinced that it did: 'how sore a burden, how cruel a hangman, how grievous a torment, yea, and how painful a hell, is this ear-confession unto men's consciences.' Tyndale rehearsed the popular terror of dying unshriven and claimed that in the absence of a priest, sailors in peril would confess their sins to the mast of their ship.[21] Yet confession was also difficult and humiliating: 'a poor woman with child, which longed, and, being overcome of her passion, ate flesh on a Friday; which thing she durst not confess in the space of eighteen years, and thought all that while that she had been damned.'[22] Similar arguments were canvassed by Tyndale's fellow-Protestant, Miles Coverdale:

What great harm the strait confession hath brought to pass among the simple people. For seeing they think, that they cannot be saved except they confess everything as narrowly as the same shrift tradition bindeth, and yet leave it undone, sometime for shame and sometime through forgetfulness; no doubt they fall into despair, and are ever, yea, as long as they live, far from holy hope.[23]

That laypeople sometimes were hesitant or ashamed to make a full confession was admitted by the authorities.[24] Even Thomas More, whose commitment to the sacramental system was unshakeable, was prepared to concede obliquely that men and women could find confession onerous, making the 'Messenger' in his *Dialogue Concerning Heresies* declare that

---

[19] *LP* xviii (2), 310. See also the confession made by John Stanton in 1536, described in G. R. Elton, *Policy and Police: The Enforcement of the Reformation in the Age of Thomas Cromwell* (Cambridge, 1972), 28–30.

[20] Ozment, *Reformation in the Cities*, 22–8, 49–56.

[21] W. Tyndale, 'The Obedience of a Christian Man', in *Doctrinal Treatises*, ed. H. Walter, PS (1848), 245.   [22] Ibid. 246.

[23] M. Coverdale, *Remains of Myles Coverdale*, ed. G. Pearson, PS (1846), 482.

[24] *Boke of the Ghostly Father*, sig. B.vi^v; Mirc, *Instructions*, 28; *Visitation Articles*, ii. 22.

when presented with a variety of confessors 'yet I scant like one of them so well upon the sight, that I would tell any such tales to once in seven years, if I might choose'.[25]

Were priests as confessors, then, widely regarded as fearsome and inhumane judges in the tribunal of sin? It may have seemed so to Margery Kempe, who in the early fifteenth century described in her book how she had been prevented from confessing a sin which had long weighed on her conscience by the severity of her confessor.[26] The authors of the manuals went to some lengths, however, to try to ensure that this should not happen. The *Modus Confitendi* directed the confessor to comfort the penitent by reminding him that Christ died for our sins, and that although St Peter denied Christ, and Paul persecuted him, David committed murder, Mary Magdalen was a sinner, and the Canaanite woman was taken in adultery, all of them had been subsequently sanctified.[27] The *Boke of the Ghostly Father* likewise emphasized the boundless mercy of Christ, comparing it to an ocean in which the spark of man's sin is quenched.[28] Mirc thought that priests should encourage the diffident by saying that they themselves had sinned as badly, or perhaps worse. He recommended in addition that, where appropriate, light penances be imposed.[29] A good confessor was not to interrupt the penitent in the course of his confession, nor was he to stare him in the face, or to register disapproval of the sins about which he was being told.[30] Although thoroughness of examination was clearly regarded as the keynote of confessional practice, it may not be implausible to suggest that the catechetical format may have been welcome to some of the 'many' penitents who, as Richard Whitford found, 'come unto confession that could not tell how to do, or what to say there'.[31] Whether, in fact, this thoroughness was always applied in practice is open to question, and crucial to an assessment of lay attitudes to the confessor.

Overt hostility to confessors and confession was not, of course, unknown. It was a basic leitmotiv of Lollard anticlericalism that priests had no power to forgive sins, and that their absolutions availed nothing, though some heretics seem to have espoused the more characteristically Wycliffite position that it was only the ministrations of priests in mortal

[25] More, *Dialogue*, 349.

[26] M. Kempe, *The Book of Margery Kempe*, ed. S. B. Meech, EETS 212 (1940), 7.

[27] Balliol MS 354, fo. 179ᵛ.   [28] *Boke of the Ghostly Father*, sig. A.iiᵛ.

[29] Mirc, *Instructions*, 28, 50–1; *Ordinary of crysten men*, sig. Q.iiʳ.

[30] Balliol MS 354, fo. 179ᵛ; Tentler, *Sin and Confession*, 93.

[31] Whitford, *Werke for Housholders*, sig. F.iʳ.

sin that were inefficacious.[32] With others a materialistic and practical outlook seems to have characterized the objections. A fairly common Lollard attitude was that priests should not forgive penitents, but that the latter should seek the forgiveness of the offended party.[33] One fifteenth-century Bristol heretic denied the need for confession to a priest, but felt it was necessary to find a suitable person to impose a penance.[34] It is conceivable that some shades of popular opinion held the virtue of the sacrament to lie in its social and restorative aspects, rather than in those stressed by contemporary theologians who had reduced penance itself to a largely symbolic element, and emphasized contrition and absolution, thus underscoring the sacramental power of the priest. It would, however, be unwise to generalize from the evidence provided by heresy trials, which may merely reflect the esoteric views of radical separatists rather than provide echoes of more general concerns. It is true that, fearing detection for heresy, many Lollards shared in the sacramental life of the Catholic parish, and that from time to time some of them made successful converts to their views.[35] But this is very far from suggesting that parochial opinion would have concurred in finding the practice of confession oppressive and flawed. Here some further matters need to be brought into consideration.

In the first place the obligation on each Catholic to confess his or her sins to a priest, instituted by the Fourth Lateran Council in 1215 in its decree *Omnis utriusque sexus*, was only an annual one. Tentler is probably right in his assertion that the strength and importance sacramental confession drew from its vital position in the Christian calendar was likely to outweigh its relative infrequency.[36] None the less, it is difficult to believe that even the most reluctant of penitents found the rest of the year overshadowed and blighted by this sporadic requirement. This, of course, is to assume that because everyone was bound to confess once a year, everyone in fact did so. Laypeople were sometimes prosecuted by the

[32] Foxe, *Acts and Monuments*, iv. 133–4, 228, 231, 585, 698; v. 28, 33–4; J. A. F. Thomson, *The Later Lollards* (Oxford, 1965), 37, 44, 68, 71, 105, 134, 136, 183; A. Hudson, *The Premature Reformation* (Oxford, 1988), 152, 298, 469, 495; G. Leff, *Heresy in the Later Middle Ages* (Manchester, 1967), ii. 525.

[33] Hudson, *Premature Reformation*, 299, 469; Thomson, *Later Lollards*, 137.

[34] Ibid. 37. This attitude finds an interesting parallel in the idiosyncratic views of the late 16th-c. Italian miller Domenico Scandella, alias Menocchio, who defended his opinion that one might as well confess to a tree as to a priest on the grounds that 'if that tree could give the knowledge of penance, it would be good enough', since men only sought out priests 'because they do not know what penance has to be made for their sins'. C. Ginzburg, *The Cheese and the Worms*, tr. J. and A. Tedeschi (1980), 10.

[35] Hudson, *Premature Reformation*, 149, 495.   [36] Tentler, *Sin and Confession*, 81.

Church authorities for failing to confess in Lent, though this offence
seems to have been rare in comparison with other correctional matters
dealt with by the Church courts.[37] If all, or nearly all, parishioners were
confessed at least annually then this represents an impressive pastoral and
logistical achievement. A large parish might well have over 2,000 communicants: Plymouth had 2,500, Tewkesbury 2,600.[38] Though many rural
and some urban parishes were much smaller, many would still have had
several hundred penitents waiting to be shriven in Lent. The problem
was perhaps compounded by a tendency to wait right until the end of the
Lenten season: one fifteenth-century homilist complained that people
usually came to confession, not in the first, second, or third weeks, 'but
in the sixth week, and on Good Friday and on Pasch Day, more for
shame and custom-keeping than at stirring of compunction or contrition'.[39] In response, some parishes were forced to hire extra clerical
manpower at Easter time.[40] Others presumably managed with the priests
they had, but it is reasonable to suppose that in many places Holy Week
would have seen the entire clerical contingent of the parish, the incumbent, his deputy, as well as chantry, stipendiary, guild, and morrow-mass
priests engaged in the hearing of confessions.[41] Their efforts did not always pass unappreciated: in 1501, for example, a parishioner in Wells left
12*d.* each to 'the three chaplains who hear confessions in the . . . church
during the season of Lent'.[42] Yet in some parishes, the operation was less
diligently performed. In about 1530, the churchwardens of Haverhill in
Suffolk complained of the 'unthrifty demeanour' of the vicar, Simon
Taillour, who, amongst other offences, was accused of neglecting his duty
of hearing confessions. When the parishioners came to the church in
Lent 'to be shriven as true Christian people' they were forced 'to stand
in the church from morning to night having nobody there to shrive

[37] Hale, *Precedents*, 26, 28, 83; *Kentish Visitations*, 205; R. Houlbrooke, *Church Courts and the People during the English Reformation* (Oxford, 1979), 278–9; B. L. Woodcock, *Medieval Ecclesiastical Courts in the Diocese of Canterbury* (Oxford, 1952), 79–82.

[38] C. H. Thompson (ed.), 'Chantry Priests at Plymouth', *Devon and Cornwall Notes and Queries*, 18 (1935), 354; J. Gairdner (ed.), 'Bishop Hooper's Visitation of Gloucester', *EHR* 19 (1904), 105.

[39] E. H. Weatherley (ed.), *Speculum Sacerdotale*, EETS 200 (1936), 68.

[40] 'Ancient Churchwardens' Accounts of a City Parish, St Andrew Hobard, Eastcheap', *British Magazine and Monthly Register*, 33 (1848), 670; J. C. Cox and C. B. Ford, *Parish Churches* (1961), 36; M. L. Zell, 'The Personnel of the Clergy of Kent in the Reformation Period', *EHR* 89 (1974), 523–4.

[41] A. Kreider, *English Chantries: The Road to Dissolution* (Cambridge, Mass., 1979), 53; A. H. Thompson, *The English Clergy and their Organization in the Later Middle Ages* (Oxford, 1947), 144; W. Page (ed.), *Yorkshire Chantry Surveys, vol. i*, SS 91 (1894), 175.

[42] F. W. Weaver (ed.), *Somerset Medieval Wills, 1501–1530*, SRS 19 (1903), 17.

them'.[43] The parishioners of Pendle in Lancashire complained similarly in 1535 that their curate was absent and did not hear their confessions, while in 1543 those of Black Notley in Essex noted that 'divers times in the Lent last there was no priest to confess the parishioners'.[44] Aquinas had remarked that some priests would spend their whole lives doing nothing else if they were to shrive all their penitents, and while this observation may not encapsulate the English situation, it does seem probable that many priests found themselves severely stretched.[45] At Doncaster, for example, the chantry commissioners of Henry VIII reported that there were '2,000 houseling people and above within the said parish whereof the said incumbent and other seven priests now resident in the said church, can scant hear the confessions of the said parishioners from the beginning of Lent unto Palm Sunday'.[46] In the parish of St Mary Woolchurch in London in 1548, the parishioners claimed that at Easter 'all the priests we have do not suffice'.[47] The implications of cases like this are twofold. In the first place, one is tempted to wonder whether, in the pre-Easter rush, confessors could really have adhered to the full meticulous examination prescribed by the penitential authorities, or whether in the circumstances confessions were likely to become quicker, more formalistic, and perhaps less incisive and intrusive. The second implication is that in practice curates could not maintain the monopoly of hearing confessions to which they were entitled under ecclesiastical law.

CHOOSING THE CONFESSOR

In attempting to delineate lay responses to the action of the priest in confession, it is vital to ask whether some parishioners were themselves anxious to go to one confessor rather than to another, in spite of the identical sacramental powers that each possessed. The Fourth Lateran Council had allowed Catholics to confess to a priest other than their own curate only with the permission of the latter.[48] Yet when English men and

---

[43] PRO, STA. C. 2, 31/61.

[44] A. M. Cooke (ed.), *Act Book of the Ecclesiastical Court of Whalley, 1510–1538*, ChS 44 (1901), 175; Hale, *Precedents*, 126. See also A. Watkyn (ed.), *Dean Cosyn and Wells Cathedral Miscellanea*, SRS 56 (1941), 155.

[45] H. C. Lea, *A History of Auricular Confession and Indulgences in the Latin Church* (1896), i. 243.   [46] Page (ed.), *Yorkshire Chantry Surveys*, 175.

[47] C. J. Kitching (ed.), *London and Middlesex Chantry Certificates 1548*, LoRS 16 (1980), 24.

[48] J. T. McNeill and H. M. Gamer (eds.), *Medieval Handbooks of Penance* (1938), 413.

women were prosecuted in the church courts for failing to confess to
their curate at Easter time, they nearly always claimed to have been
shriven by another priest.[49] Sometimes one suspects that this was no more
that a specious defence to mitigate the consequences of a major spiritual
offence. When, for example, John Inglepage, a weaver of Blunham in
Bedfordshire, was interrogated in 1518 as to who had heard his confession in the previous Lent, he claimed to have been confessed in his parish
church, and the year before at Barford, but in neither case could he recall
by whom.[50] In other cases, however, one senses a genuine desire to be
absolved by a priest other than the penitent's curate, from whom it may
perhaps have been difficult or embarrassing to request a licence for the
privilege of exemption. Some parishioners apparently preferred the ministrations of the friars or of local monastic houses, and as late as 1537
Bishop Lee of Coventry and Lichfield was complaining that 'some fro-
ward persons, partly for malice and disdain, neglect their curates, and
such as have the cure and charge of their souls, and partly to cloak and
hide their lewd and naughty living, as they have used all the year before,
use at Lent to go to be confessed to the friars and such other religious
houses'.[51] Even after the dissolution of the monasteries and the disappear-
ance of the mendicant orders, the Bishop of London could deplore that
some people 'use at Lent to be confessed of other priests which have not
the cure of their souls'.[52] Confessors sometimes make an appearance in
contemporary wills, either as the recipient of a bequest to the testator's
'ghostly father', or as a witness to the will. These cases show that the
priest regarded by the maker of the will as his confessor or 'ghostly
father' was not necessarily the incumbent or curate of the parish where he
lived. In most instances the position occupied by the confessor cannot be
ascertained from the internal evidence of the will, but in a sample of 254
early sixteenth-century wills making mention of a ghostly father, there
are fifty cases where it is possible to do so. In twenty-one of these, the
confessor is the testator's vicar or rector, and in thirteen the curate. In

---

[49] Hale, *Precedents*, 16, 25, 87; J. T. Fowler (ed.), *Acts of the Chapter of the Collegiate Church of Ripon, 1452–1506*, SS 64 (1875), 186–7.

[50] M. Bowker (ed.), *An Episcopal Court Book for the Diocese of Lincoln, 1514–1520*, LRS 61 (1967), 62.

[51] *Visitation Articles*, ii. 21–2. This complaint was, by the later Middle Ages in England, a very familiar topos: see e.g. W. Langland, *Piers the Ploughman*, ed. J. F. Goodridge (Harmondsworth, 1966), 253; G. Cigman (ed.), *Lollard Sermons*, EETS 294 (1989), 102; Hughes, 'Administration of Confession in the Diocese of York', 90; R. N. Swanson, 'Problems of the Priesthood in pre-Reformation England', *EHR* 417 (1990), 858.

[52] *Visitation Articles*, ii. 85.

seven wills, however, the confessor, though his exact status is uncertain, is clearly not the incumbent; in a further five he is identified as a friar, in two as the parish priest, and he appears once as a soul priest and once as a fraternity priest. The figures may even exaggerate the proportion of named confessors who were vicars or rectors, as these were often described by name and parochial title in testamentary documents, and many of the 204 ghostly fathers whose status cannot be determined from the context of the will in which they appear may have been lower parish clergy or chantry priests. Either with or without the blessing of their curate, some parishioners seem to have expected and enjoyed a degree of latitude in their choice of confessor.

In theory, of course, it should have made no difference which priest heard one's confession. The priest was the minister of Christ's forgiveness; as the *Boke of the Ghostly Father* advised confessors to remind their penitents, he was there 'in God's stead'.[53] Yet in practice there were a number of reasons why a parishioner might wish to avoid a particular confessor, some of which received official sanction. These included a knowledge or suspicion that the priest would lead the penitent into sin, would be indiscreet with the confession, or might be incited to anger or vengeance by what he would hear.[54]

It would be unwise, however, to assume that all who sought some degree of choice in their relationship with a confessor did so for essentially negative reasons, to avoid dissension or embarrassment, to secure a lighter penance, or to express disapproval of their pastor. Some laypeople may have been seeking more expert or exacting spiritual direction, like those, who as Tyndale disdainfully noted, chose to shrive themselves 'at Syon, Charterhouse, or at the Observants'.[55] Those who took confession more seriously as a religious duty may have included the readers of Richard Whitford, himself a Brigittine of Syon, whose *Werke for Housholders* set out a short form of confession in the traditional pattern of deadly sins and Commandments, remarking, significantly, that 'there be

[53] *Boke of the Ghostly Father*, sig. B.ii^r.

[54] Mirc, *Instructions*, 26; Lea, *Auricular Confession*, i. 285–6; N. F. Blake (ed.), *Quattuor Sermones printed by William Caxton* (Heidelberg, 1975), 71; G. de Roye, *The Doctrinal of Sapyence* (1489), sig. K.v^r.

[55] W. Tyndale, *Doctrinal Treatises*, 337. The Brigittines of Syon, Carthusians, and Franciscan Observants were the strictest and best disciplined of the English regular clergy on the eve of the Reformation, and their popularity with the laity is attested to by the frequency with which bequests were made to them: J. A. F. Thomson, 'Piety and Charity in Late Medieval London', *JEH* 16 (1965), 189–90; S. Brigden, *London and the Reformation* (Oxford, 1989), 73; C. Harper-Bill, *The Pre-Reformation Church in England, 1400–1530* (1989), 42–3.

many forms of confessions in print set out at length'.[56] In this work, and in its sequel, *A Dialogue or Communicacion bytween the curate or ghostly father & the parochiane or ghostly chyld for a due preparation unto howselynge*, Whitford idealized the relationship between the confessor and the penitent, who will, as a matter of course, thank his 'ghostly father' for 'the charitable labours you took with me when I was last with you'.[57] This manner of quasi-paternal relationship may sometimes have been more than a literary stereotype; there clearly were Englishmen for whom it was important to have a 'ghostly father', and who went to him, not merely to confess their sins, but 'to desire him of his ghostly counsel'.[58] A number of sources imply that the phrase 'ghostly father' was not merely a descriptive label, but was used as a term of deferential address.[59] The resonances of the expression are significant: fatherhood implies love and solicitude but also demands obedience and respect, and priests were not slow to see in the injunction 'honour thy father and mother' a reference to their own position.

The importance of the ghostly father was probably most marked at the moment of passing from this life, as for many people the prospect of dying unconfessed was a grim one.[60] When priests were found wanting at visitation a common cause of complaint was that through their negligence they had allowed parishioners to die without 'shrift and housel'.[61] A deathbed confession lay at the centre of an intriguing case which came before the court of Chancery in the latter part of Henry VIII's reign, the executors of Richard Benson suing those of Roger Turner for the sum of £66, allegedly due for certain quantities of wood which Turner had purchased from Benson. The plaintiffs based their case on the claim that Turner had 'confessed and declared to John Lammot, his ghostly father, lying sick and in the mercy of Almighty God, a little before he departed out of

---

[56] Whitford, *Werke for Housholders*, sig. F.i^v.

[57] R. Whitford, *Dialogue . . . unto howselynge* (1537), sig. A.iii^v.

[58] *LP* xviii (2), 310.

[59] Whitford, *Werke for Housholders*, sig. F.iv^r; Elton, *Policy and Police*, 28. See also the 15th-c. English poem ascribed to Charles d'Orleans: 'My ghostly father, I me confess'. D. Gray (ed.), *The Oxford Book of Late Medieval Verse and Prose* (Oxford, 1985), 169.

[60] This is attested to e.g. by the popular story of St Gregory's Trental, which recounted how Gregory's mother, having died without making her confession, appeared to him in a vision of her great sufferings in purgatory: Balliol MS 354, fo. 139^{r-v}. See also B. Manning, *The People's Faith in the Time of Wyclif* (Hassocks, 1975), 31; Mirc, *Festial*, 281; Weatherley (ed.), *Speculum Sacerdotale*, 173; Kempe, *Book of Margery Kempe*, 7; Duffy, *Stripping of the Altars*, 310–13.

[61] See below, pp. 182–4. 'Shrift and housel' refers to confession and communion respectively.

this world' that he owed the money, but without written proof of the bargain Benson's executors were powerless at the common law. Since Lammot was 'a man of age and if he should die the truth of the matter . . . should not come to the knowledge', and exhibiting scant regard for the sacrosanctity of confession, the plaintiffs petitioned that he be summoned before the court and 'examined upon the whole matter and circumstance'.[62] The incident illustrates how sharply at variance attitudes towards the confessor could be between those who needed his imminent assistance in preparing to go to their Maker and those who, for some years at least, could afford to focus their anxieties on more pressing temporal concerns. Clerical moralists were quick to attack the attitude that there would be time enough to repent and be shriven.[63] For those who were in imminent danger of death, however, many may have reacted like Nicholas Samborne of Mapledurham in Berkshire, who sent at the last 'for my ghostly father, Sir Thomas Peythe, vicar of Mapledurham, and declared this aforesaid my will in his presence', or William Dyester of Bicester who as witness to his will had 'called unto me my ghostly father, Sir John Stanley'.[64] Some testators assigned to their confessor responsibility for funeral arrangements.[65] Others were anxious to allow them a role in the disposal of their goods. In 1509 the Yorkshire gentleman, Thomas Pykering, stipulated in his will that 'Friar Harvey, my ghostly father, which knoweth my conscience, will, and mind, be overseer' of the testament.[66] Richard Hall of Bucknall in Lincolnshire bequeathed a sheep to his curate in 1513 so that he might 'dispose it for the health of my soul as I have showed him in confession'.[67] Alice Pycke, of the parish of St John, Glastonbury, wanted her ghostly father, James Smith, to say masses for her soul, and left him 'a little ale cup, a featherbed, 2 pair of sheets, one of 3 leaves, and the other of 2 leaves, and 5 nobles'.[68] As late as 1551 a Hampshire widow might leave money and linen to her 'ghostly counsellor'.[69] These and similar bequests suggest a strong and long-standing bond between priest and penitent which survived to the grave, and

[62] PRO, C. 1, 945/31.   [63] Mirc, *Festial*, 91.

[64] J. R. H. Weaver and A. Beardwood (eds.), *Some Oxfordshire Wills Proved in the Prerogative Court of Canterbury*, Oxfordshire Record Society (1958), 91; PRO, PCC, Prob. 11, 4 Maynwaring.

[65] PRO, PCC, Prob. 11, 6 Porch (John Arderne); M. McGregor (ed.), *Bedfordshire Wills Proved in the Prerogative Court of Canterbury*, Beds. Historical Record Soc. (1979), 108.

[66] Clay, *North Country Wills*, 82.

[67] C. W. Foster (ed.), *Lincoln Wills Registered in the District Probate Registry at Lincoln, 1271–1526*, LRS 5 (1914), 50.

[68] F. W. Weaver (ed.), *Somerset Medieval Wills, 1531–1558*, SRS 21 (1905), 57.

[69] PRO, PCC, Prob. 11, 14 Bucke (Emma Henslowe).

indeed, beyond. Not all laypeople could draw on such a relationship. The witness to Elizabeth Cayling's will in 1526 was Thomas Hanson, 'my ghostly father, chosen at this present tyme'. Another Somerset testator in the same year left 8*d.* to the unspecified priest 'being my ghostly father at the time of my death'.[70] There do, none the less, seem to have been people for whom the advice and direction of a specific ghostly father was important, and who would have taken to heart the advice to seek out 'a good confessor . . . continuing with him without running from one to another, the which shall know his state and life'.[71] Such enthusiasts probably made their confession more frequently than the bare legal requirement of once a year. After all, English canon law recommended three confessions, and a work such as the *English Prymer* printed at Rouen in 1538 could suggest weekly shrivings.[72] The *Prymer of Salisbury Use* with its prefixed *maner to lyve wel / devoutly and salutartly every day for all persones of meane estate* likewise advised its readers: 'shrive you every week to your curate except ye have great let and beware ye pass not a fortnight except very great let'.[73] Common sense might seem to suggest, then, a fundamental divergence in attitudes and approach to the sacrament of penance and its ministers: on the one hand a pious and committed élite, who confessed relatively frequently and who laid great stress on the relationship with a particular confessor; on the other, the conformist majority. One fifteenth-century preacher claimed that only one in five penitents 'useth to come to confession with a true heart and very compunction of heart as they should'.[74] The reality of such a dichotomy is, however, difficult to establish positively. Wills which make mention of ghostly fathers are not, for example, markedly more forthcoming with charitable or pious bequests, nor, interestingly, are they any more likely to contain gifts to the clergy for mortuaries or 'tithes forgotten'. For virtually all laypeople the encounter with a priest in confession was a regular experience, and probably not for the most part an unduly painful one. Indeed, it was a service that may sometimes have been greatly appreciated. In this as in other areas of priestly ministration, however, much depended on the ability of the priest to marry successfully a theological construct of great profundity to the vagaries and difficulties of individual experience. It was a task to which he was not always equal.

[70] Weaver (ed.), *Somerset Medieval Wills, 1501–1539*, SRS 19 (1903), 257, 252.
[71] Garard, *Interpretacyon and Sygnyfycacyon*, sig. V.iii^{r-v}.
[72] *Lyndwood*, 154; F. Gasquet, *The Eve of the Reformation* (1900), 287.
[73] *Prymer of Salysbury Use* (Paris, 1531), 24.
[74] Weatherley (ed.), *Speculum Sacerdotale*, 69.

CONFESSION IN ACTION: FUNCTIONS AND DYSFUNCTIONS

At its best, confession was a forum where priests could play the role of
spiritual physician, and administer ghostly counsel to sick or troubled consciences.[75] It could also from time to time assume wider social functions.
The sacrament was designed not only to provide the individual sinner
with access to the infinite mercy of God, but to facilitate his reconciliation to Christ's Body, the Church, and its members.[76] A priest could
not in good conscience pronounce absolution on a penitent who proposed
to perpetuate hostile relations with his neighbours.[77] Coexistence in a
state of charity was a precondition of the communal reception of the eucharist at Easter, and the restoration of that state received symbolic public
expression in the ritual of the imposition of the priest's hands on the
absolved penitent.[78] The type of restitution which the re-establishment
of charity implied was sometimes disarmingly straightforward. It seems,
for instance, to have been common practice for priests to give public
notice of a theft, and to invite the return of the stolen items. These then
sometimes found their way back to their original owner by way of confession.[79] In cases where theft or wrongful possession was confessed, absolution may have been made contingent on the return of the pertinent
articles.[80]

Ideally, then, confession was a focus for unity and social harmony, and
the practice should have reflected credit on the priests who ministered it.
Yet there were circumstances in which the confessor, far from being the
agent of reconciliation, could divide and distress the community entrusted to his care. One way in which this might happen was if the

[75] This analogy was particularly favoured by writers on penitential matters: Tentler, *Sin
and Confession*, 103; *Boke of the Ghostly Father*, sig. A.iii^v; *Ordinary of crysten men*, sigs. Ff.iv^r–
Gg.i^r; de Roye, *Doctrinal of Sapyence*, sig. K.vi^r; Pantin, *English Church in the Fourteenth
Century*, 227; W. C. Hazlitt (ed.), *A Select Collection of Old English Plays* (1874), i. 134; Hughes,
'Administration of Confession', 118.
[76] This aspect of pre-Reformation confession has been notably illuminated by John
Bossy: 'Social History of Confession', *passim*, and *Christianity in the West, 1400–1700*
(Oxford, 1985), 46–8.
[77] Bossy, 'Social History of Confession', 25; Balliol MS 354, fo. 181^v.
[78] Nichols, 'Etiquette of Confession', 145; Bossy, *Christianity in the West*, 47. It was public
because it took place, as did confession itself, openly in the church.
[79] A. P. Moore (ed.), 'Proceedings of the Ecclesiastical Courts in the Archdeaconry of
Leicester, 1516–1535', *Associated Architectural Societies Reports and Papers*, 28 (1905), 607;
C. T. Martin (ed.), 'Clerical Life in the Fifteenth Century, as Illustrated by Proceedings of
the Court of Chancery', *Archaeologia*, 60 (1907), 361–2.
[80] Weatherley (ed.), *Speculum Sacerdotale*, 71; Hughes, 'Administration of Confession',
129.

secrecy of what passed between penitent and confessor was not, or did not seem to be, absolutely guaranteed. Grounded firmly by the theologians in natural and divine positive law, the 'seal of confession' was also essential to the practical working and day-to-day administration of the sacrament. A penitent came to his confessor on the clear understanding that what he had to say would remain inviolably hidden. The priest's obligation to secrecy was underpinned by the theologians' insistence that what he knew from confessions he had learned not as a man, but vicariously as the representative of Christ. In human terms he had no knowledge of the sin, and could under no circumstances be obliged to reveal it, Aquinas reasoning that a man can be called to witness only as a man, and could therefore with a clear conscience declare that he had no knowledge of something he knew only in his capacity as God's minister.[81] Thomas More reiterated the point, insisting that 'if a priest that had heard a man's confession were called before a judge and sworn for a witness, he might boldly swear he knew nothing of the matter', not simply for 'the common gloss' that the confession had been made to him as God's minister, but because to do otherwise was to create a precedent, that could not be allowed even to testify to a man's innocence.[82] The *Ordinary of crysten men* declared that a confessor should 'choose more sooner to die than ever to say or anything declare of the sin the which unto him hath been confessed', and indeed, hagiographical tradition provided an inspiring, if spurious, martyr to the seal, in the person of the Bohemian court chaplain, John Nepomuk.[83]

Not all this weight of theological ratiocination, moral exhortation, and legal sanction could, however, alter the fact that Christ's ministers were fashioned from human clay. It takes a commentator as unsympathetic to the pre-Reformation clergy as H. C. Lea to observe that 'human nature being what it is, there is a manifest impossibility in preventing priests from talking about the sins which they learn in confession',[84] yet in small and interdependent communities it must sometimes have been very difficult for the parish priest to have held aloof with his superior and secret knowledge. To confirmed Protestants it was a matter of faith that priests habitually betrayed the secrets of confession. Simon Fish, for example, in his anticlerical tirade *A Supplicacyon for the Beggars*, included the accusation that though priests get money from confessions 'yet they will keep

---

[81] *New Catholic Encyclopedia* (Washington, 1967), s.v. 'Seal of Confession', 134.

[82] More, *Dialogue*, 281–2.

[83] *Ordinary of crysten men*, sig. P.viii^v; D. Hay, *Europe in the Fourteenth and Fifteenth Centuries* (1970), 225.   [84] Lea, *History of Auricular Confession*, i. 448.

thereof no counsel'.[85] Miles Coverdale claimed that 'some of them openly told abroad the thing, that hath been committed to their fidelity in confession'.[86] Interestingly, however, these accusations were more commonly suggestive of grand conspiracy theory than of the garrulousness and indiscretion of individual confessors. In *The Burial of the Mass*, Wolsey is described as the 'general confessor' of the nobility, in so far as private chaplains reported to him the misdeeds of their masters.[87] Brinklow thought auricular confession had been invented 'to betray princes and other great men', so that the Pope could maintain his power over them, while Tyndale regarded confessors as spies for the prelates, and confession as a means whereby pope might know the thoughts of every king and emperor, and bishop learn 'the confession of whom he lusteth throughout all his diocese: yea and his chancellor commandeth the ghostly father to deliver it written'.[88] In *The Practice of Prelates* he included the more specific allegation that in the reign of Henry VII, Morton and Fox supplied the King with the confessions of as many lords as he wished.[89] These claims made ideal propaganda, being both faintly plausible and effectively impossible to refute; yet they do perhaps contain the implicit admission that the regular betrayal of confessions was not within the experience of the average parishioner.

Despite, or perhaps because of, the severe penalties prescribed for priests who broke the seal, the offence does not seem to have been a major problem of clerical discipline, comparable in extent with, say, sexual irregularity or unlicensed absenteeism.[90] This is not, of course, to claim that it did not ever happen. In 1512 a parish priest in Ipswich was supposed to have revealed the confession of Agnes Fastelinge, that she had had intercourse with her husband before they were married, and further instances of real or putative breaches of the seal can be found

[85] S. Fish, *A Supplicacyon for the Beggars*, ed. F. J. Furnivall, EETS ES 27 (1871), 2.
[86] Coverdale, *Remains*, 482.
[87] J. Barlow, *The Burial of the Mass*, in E. Arber (ed.), *English Reprints* (1871), 106. This claim might seem to derive a little credibility from the trial and execution of the Duke of Buckingham in 1521. Buckingham's chaplain, John Delacourt, revealed to the authorities the treasonous prophecies of the Carthusian, Nicholas Hopkins, despite being sworn to 'keep it secret under seal of confession', LP iii (1). 1284. One of the charges against the Countess of Salisbury in 1538 was that she had had a priest repeat to her what he had learned in confession about the attitude of her tenants. LP xiii (2). 817.
[88] H. Brinklow, *The Lamentacyon of a Christen Agaynst the Cyte of London*, ed. J. M. Cowper, EETS ES 22 (1874), 111; Tyndale, *Doctrinal Treatises*, 191, 281, 336–7.
[89] W. Tyndale, *The Practice of Prelates*, ed. H. Walter, PS (1849), 305.
[90] McNeill and Gamer, *Medieval Handbooks of Penance*, 416; *Lyndwood*, 150. By the 1540s these penalties do not always appear to have been strictly enforced: Hale, *Precedents*, 119; Houlbrooke, *Church Courts and the People*, 197.

scattered through the court records of this period.[91] The victims of clerical indiscretion often reacted forcefully to such abuses. When the parishioners of Pembury in Kent charged their vicar with having made public the miller's confession, one parishioner remarked that it would be preferable to be shriven by the lions at the Tower of London.[92] At All Hallows on the Wall in London, John Philcock called his confessor a 'naughty priest' and threatened to bring him before the bishop, 'for thou hast opened my confession'.[93] Understandably, parishioners whose sins had been publicized turned their wrath upon the 'ghostly father'. In 1521 the East Anglian priest, Sir Thomas Thrower, underwent a bruising encounter with one of his parishioners, William Corbett: 'Thou art a wretch, it is pity that ever thou was made priest, thou betrayest confessions.'[94]

In mitigation, it should be noted that instances of a supposed breach of the secrecy of confession sometimes come to our attention from legal cases brought by the supposed betrayer in an effort to clear his name. In the case just cited, for example, Thrower was suing Corbett for defamation in the Bishop of Norwich's Consistory Court, since, as a witness admitted, Thrower's good reputation had been much damaged by the accusation.[95] When, in the mid-1520s, John Bolton, the vicar of Shakerston in Leicestershire, sued John Reve for saying he had revealed his confession, Reve submitted to judicial penance, and was ordered by the judge to ask the vicar's pardon between matins and high mass in the presence of eight or ten parishioners.[96] When sins confessed were those of commission, rather than of omission, and of deed rather than of thought, they might often become public knowledge in a tightly knit village community, despite the discretion of the priest. Yet on finding himself the butt of ale-house jokes, or the staple of local gossip, an aggrieved and embarrassed parishioner might easily blame the confessor whom he regarded as the sole guardian of his secret.[97] Thomas More confidently claimed that

[91] *NCCD*, no. 169; PRO, STA.C. 2 26/15; Hale, *Precedents*, 119; S. Lander, 'The Diocese of Chichester, 1508–1558', University of Cambridge Ph.D. thesis (1974), 234; Houlbrooke, *Church Courts and the People*, 195; C. Harper-Bill (ed.), 'An Edition of the Register of John Morton, Archbishop of Canterbury, 1486–1500', University of London Ph.D. thesis (1977), 746; *LP* viii. 406.

[92] J. Davis, *Heresy and Reformation in the South-East of England, 1520–1559* (1983), 7–8.

[93] GLRO, DL/C/208, fo. 144ʳ.   [94] *NCCD*, no. 250.   [95] Ibid.

[96] Moore, 'Ecclesiastical Courts in the Archdeaconry of Leicester', 649. See also *LP* xiii (2). 817.

[97] Note here the illuminating comment of Alexander Murray, that in the late Middle Ages 'village amateurs at canon law could often surmise, from whom a person confessed to or what penance he or she performed, what had been said in confession'. The penances for

'no man letteth boldly to tell such his secrets, as upon the discovering or close keeping thereof his honesty commonly and often time his life also dependeth', and added optimistically that no man was ever found to 'take harm by his confession, or cause given of complaint through any such secrets uttered and showed by the confessor'.[98] Probably the evidence agrees with More that the indiscreet confessor was very much the exception rather than the rule. None the less, lay anxiety about this matter was resonant with dangers for the clergy, and might sometimes raise questions as to the value of sacramental penance. In 1540, for example, the vicar of Pawlett in Somerset, Thomas Sprent, had apparently remarked that one of his parishioners, John Gallampton, was 'a thief of his own confession and was worthy to be hanged fourteen years gone'. The following Lent, Gallampton taunted Sprent in the church: 'think thou to confess one this Lent, by God's Blood I had liever see thee hanged ... I had liever be confessed of a dog than of thee ... if my dog were or should be confessed of thee I would hang him up straight'.[99] Here, the language and attitudes of Lollardy might be employed to articulate a deeply felt personal grievance.

But if the revealing of confessions could generate such passion, it was, ironically, the very secrecy with which the operation of the sacrament was shrouded which could at other times cause difficulties, particularly where the confessions of women were concerned, and the article cited as heretical in 1538, that 'it was not convenient for a priest to hear the confession of a woman',[100] may from time to time have struck a chord in more orthodox breasts. The ecclesiastical authorities were ever anxious that no occasion should be given for scandal, and canon law directed that the confessions of women be heard in an open or public place, while some of the manuals emphasized that a priest should not look on a woman penitent's face during her confession, and that to this end she should kneel at his side rather than in front of him.[101] Some manuals recommended also that the imposition of hands be omitted in the case of female penitents, though there is iconographical evidence which suggests that this advice was not

adultery were particularly well known. A. Murray, 'Confession as a Historical Source in the Thirteenth Century', in R. H. C. Davis and J. M. Wallace-Hadrill (eds.), *The Writing of History in the Middle Ages* (Oxford, 1981), 283.

[98] More, *Dialogue*, 315.

[99] PRO, STA. C. 2, 31/20. A similar case, in which a personal quarrel led to a parishioner declaring 'he would rather be shriven by a dog' is cited by Thomson, *Later Lollards*, 136.   [100] *LP* xiii (2). 498.

[101] *Lyndwood*, 153; Mirc, *Instructions*, 27; Nichols, 'Etiquette of Confession', 150.

universally followed.[102] In spite of these safeguards it was not unknown
for some priests to attempt seductions in confession. One London curate
in 1493 'after he had shriven young women at Easter in the vestry, and
assoiled them, then he would common with them, and kiss and put his
hands under their clothes, and common with them to have pointed with
them, where he and they might meet to do sin'.[103] Another was noted in
1496 as 'a wicked counsellor of his parishioners, desiring them in confession to commit the crime of adultery'.[104] The vicar of Carleton, George
Wallay, was reported to have attempted to rape the wife of one of his
parishioners 'the same night that he did shrive her in the morning', while
Robert Crane of Suffolk complained that Thomas Cornwallis, rector of
Freston, had 'enticed provoked and turned the good wit and mind' of his
wife, Anne 'unto the most shameful sin of advowtry . . . as well under the
cloak of confession as other wise'.[105] Sexual relations between a confessor
and one of his penitents were viewed by contemporaries as a particularly
shocking offence, a kind of spiritual incest.[106]

Perhaps not surprisingly, angry reaction to this type of disreputable
behaviour on the part of some confessors could lead to the same kind of
quasi-heretical posturing we have noted in connection with breaches of
the seal. The fact that his wife was suspiciously familiar with the vicar
of Iver in Buckinghamshire seems to have incited Richard Carder to
declare that he might just as well confess himself to a post.[107] A young
Yorkshire shearman in the early 1540s maintained 'that he would not
show his offences to the priest, as if he had japed a fair woman, or such
like offence, for the priest would be as ready within two or three days
after to use her as he'.[108] This topic was also a staple of Protestant propaganda. According to Brinklow, priests used the knowledge acquired
in confession to blackmail female penitents into agreeing to their 'abominable desire'.[109] The Devon Protestant, Philip Nichols, suggested to his
readers that confession enabled priests to 'take their pleasure and secrets

[102] Nichols, ibid. 145. A woodcut illustrating penance, which appeared in several contemporary English works, shows clearly a woman receiving the imposition of hands: *The Traytte
of Good Lyvyng and Good Deying* (Paris, 1503), 44ʳ; *Boke of the Ghostly Father*, frontispiece;
Ordinary of crysten men, frontispiece.   [103] Hale, *Precedents*, 42.
    [104] Ibid. 58.   [105] PRO, STA. C. 2, 26/454; 24/20.
    [106] E. M. Elvey (ed.), *The Courts of the Archdeaconry of Buckingham, 1483–1523*, Buck-
inghamshire Record Society, 19 (1975), 77, 171; *Kentish Visitations*, 141–2; M. Bowker, *The
Secular Clergy in the Diocese of Lincoln, 1485–1520* (Cambridge, 1968), 34; R. M. Wooley
(ed.), *The York Provinciale put forth by Thomas Wolsey* (1931), 54.
    [107] Foxe, *Acts and Monuments*, iv. 231.
    [108] A. G. Dickens, *Lollards and Protestants in the Diocese of York* (1959), 48.
    [109] Brinklow, *Lamentacyon of a Christen*, 111.

with your wives and daughters'.[110] Because of the relative secrecy of confession, lascivious behaviour was a charge to which all priests remained sus-
ceptible. Even the pious Richard Whitford was threatened by Cromwell's
agent Thomas Bedyll in 1535 that 'he should be brought to the great
shame of the world for his irreligious life and for his using bawdy words
to divers ladies at the time of their confession, whereby . . . he might be
the occasion that shrift shall be laid down through England'.[111]

Yet the apprehension that women might be vulnerable to the sexual
attentions of their confessor was only one aspect of a more general suspicion of the influence that confession might enable priests to exercise over
men's wives, required by the Pauline ethic of the age 'to be subject in
everything to their husbands'. Replying to the demand of the South-
Western rebels in 1549 for the restoration of the Six Articles, Philip
Nichols included in his arguments against compulsory auricular confession the consideration that its abrogation had taken from the priests 'all
opportunity of moving men's wives to folly'.[112] What Nichols probably
had in mind was the practice of exhorting wives to refuse to sleep with
their husbands at certain holy times and seasons, principally during Lent,
advice that would not have gone down well with husbands, resentful of
clerical interference with their marital rights.[113] When, during the Henrician
Reformation, the stricter forms of Lenten observance could become associated with religious and political disaffection, such feelings might be
taken as matter for legitimate complaint. Among the articles compiled
against the conservative vicar of Faversham in 1543 was the charge that
he had commanded the wife of Newman, a tanner in his parish, not to lie
with her husband during Lent.[114] Two priests of Windsor found themselves accused by a reform-minded parishioner in 1538 of having made
improper inquiries of married women in confession. Significantly, the
version of one of the priests involved was that he had merely 'counselled
a woman to be guided by God's laws rather than by her husband'.[115]

Although all this might in one sense be regarded as a manifestation of

[110] N. Pocock (ed.), *Troubles Connected with the Prayer Book of 1549*, CS NS 37 (1884), 152.

[111] G. Williams, 'Two Neglected London-Welsh Clerics: Richard Whitford and Richard Gwent', *Transactions of the Honourable Society of Cymmrodorion* (1961), 26.

[112] Pocock, *Prayer Book Troubles*, 152, where the tract is erroneously ascribed to Nicholas Udall. For the correct attribution see A. Fletcher, *Tudor Rebellions*, 3rd edn. (1983), 118.

[113] W. Harington, *The Comendacions of Matrymony* (1528), sig. D.iv^r. Some priests seem to have gone further in advocating this type of abstinence than a reading of the penitential authorities really warranted: Tentler, *Sin and Confession*, 214; Bossy, *Christianity in the West*, 50. See also P. Benedict, *Rouen during the Wars of Religion* (Cambridge, 1981), 204.

[114] *LP* xviii (2). 243.   [115] *LP* xiii (1). 260.

fairly irrational domestic authoritarianism, there does seem to be some
substance to the notion that confessors could wield an influence over
their women penitents, which husbands might regard as inordinate. In
Germany, for example, where, as Steven Ozment has shown, the confessional became a special focus of the Protestant assault on traditional
religious practice, the reformer Jacob Strauss was able to claim that many
women were always running to confession, and were so submissive to
their confessors that they were home only at mealtimes. Strauss further
considered that the teaching they received not to sleep with their husbands on certain holidays and during Lent was driving thousands of men
to adultery.[116]

The axiom that women are inherently more religious than men is, of
course, only partially amenable to historical inspection. An examination
of the wills of some early sixteenth-century women does, however, open
some interesting avenues of thought. While 'ghostly fathers' and confessors are mentioned in under 5 per cent of the wills made by male testators,
they appear in the wills of women almost exactly twice as often.[117] It must,
of course, be borne in mind that female testators were usually widows, as
such perhaps more inclined to seek the consolations of religion, and the
spiritual direction of a male authority figure. It is also true, for example,
that women were more likely to designate a priest as executor of their
wills. None the less, it may be possible to suggest that the stereotypically
devout penitent, then as now, was a married or widowed woman.[118]

Another way in which the confessor's role might sometimes exacerbate
social tensions was if he himself became involved in disputes or quarrels
with his penitents. The hazards of a system mediating an objective assurance of forgiveness through a sacramental ritual performed by actual
neighbours is neatly illustrated by an exchange between Richard Grant,
chaplain of Houghton Conquest in Bedfordshire, and a parishioner,
Thomas Audley, in 1529. When Grant called Audley a 'false harlot', the
latter retorted, 'ye have been my ghostly father, and ye know whether I

---

[116] Ozment, *Reformation in the Cities*, 53.

[117] Between 1500 and 1547, 4.6% of the male testators in the sample mentioned a ghostly
father; 9.2% of females did so. The sample contains the wills of 645 women.

[118] In *The Territory of the Historian*, tr. B. and S. Reynolds (Hassocks, 1979), 238, E. Le
Roy Ladurie attributes the gender imbalance in religious observance in modern France to
an 1842 ruling by the Vatican Grand Penitentiary that while a husband sins in committing
a contraceptive act, his wife in submitting passively to his will commits no sin. One wonders
whether a similar perception of greater male culpability with regard to sexual sins within
marriage may have helped promote confession's apparently greater popularity with women
in the early 16th.c.

be a false harlot or no, and I be so, declare me'.[119] More intractable was the quarrel between the vicar of Charing in Kent, Henry Mastall, and the widow, Elyn Hatche. Hatche accused the vicar of having improperly acquired certain 'evidences' which had belonged to her husband, and of using them to challenge her rights to property. He had also denied the last rites to her dying husband, and had purloined the tapers she had placed around his hearse. In addition to this, he had at the previous Easter refused her the sacrament of the eucharist, having previously 'denied to assoil her when he heard her confession, and that only because she, willing to be in charity with him and every man, showed him in her confession that she had complained to my Lord of Canterbury against him, for reformations of such great wrongs and injustices as he hath done unto her'.[120] Equally serious was the putative behaviour of another Bedfordshire priest, who, having heard the confession of the parish constable's wife, 'because he was displeased with her, did openly in the church there at Chillington declare the same upon a Sunday'.[121] Sensibly, the authorities allowed penitents the right to make their confession elsewhere if personal rancour was liable to disturb its orderly ministration, and some parishioners were quick to take advantage of this concession. An inability to agree over privy tithes seems to have impelled Roger Hampton of Twickenham to confess to 'an honest priest of St Clement's' rather than to his vicar, Thomas Stanard, in 1524.[122] Disagreement over tithes may also have been behind the failure of William Lybbe, rector of Down St Mary in Devon, to retain the penitential allegiance of his parishioners in 1531. Lybbe was thought to be making unaccustomed and unreasonable demands, and was taking action in the spiritual courts against those who resisted him. Frustrated in this, he began slandering his parishioners, dropping hints that 'there were not above five or six honest men and women within the said parish'. In consequence, a number of his flock 'like Christian men, by authority of certain indulgences and pardons by them obtained have made resort sometimes to the friars and other confessors more meet and convenient for the hearing and concealment of their confessions'.[123] In confessing their sins, lay men and women made a substantial investment in the integrity of their parish priest. Where that confidence was found to be misplaced, a pastor's hold over his people could become increasingly untenable.

[119] E. Peacock (ed.), 'Extracts from Lincoln Episcopal Visitations in the Fifteenth, Sixteenth and Seventeenth Centuries', *Archaeologia*, 48 (1885), 261–2.

[120] PRO, STA. C. 2, 25/333.   [121] PRO, STA. C. 2, 26/15.

[122] GLRO, DL/C/207, fos. 287ᵛ–300ᵛ.   [123] PRO, C. 1, 900/34.

THE CRISIS OF CONFESSION

The potential that confession carried for exacerbating or focusing discord and dispute could only increase under the pressure of religious change. Although the Six Articles of 1539 declared auricular confession to be 'expedient and necessary to be retained and continued',[124] the government had reason to become increasingly suspicious of what some reformers regarded as 'the privy chamber of treason'.[125] In the late 1530s a number of reports reached the authorities that conservative priests were in confession encouraging disaffection with the religious changes.[126] In August and October 1538, Cromwell was apprised of the activities of certain priests in Salisbury who forbade the consumption of 'white meats' (dairy products and eggs) in Lent, the reading of the New Testament in English, and the company of people of the 'new learning', and who in general 'privily stirred the people in confession to the old fashion'.[127] In Faversham in 1543, the vicar was reportedly encouraging penitents to abandon saying the Pater Noster in English, since they 'knew not how soon the world would change'.[128] More serious still were the activities of another Kentish priest, John Bromfyld, who had been advising his penitents in confession, 'suffer awhile and ye shall see the Pope in as great authority as ever he was'.[129] These and similar cases could only come to light when the penitents involved felt shocked enough by what they were hearing to bring it to the attention of the authorities. If such covert resistance was more widespread, it may be that confession did much in the 1530s and 1540s to mitigate the effects on individual consciences of royal and episcopal attempts to reform religious 'abuses'.

A number of episodes illustrate the nervousness of the authorities about the potential of the confessor to inform political attitudes. In the aftermath of the Pilgrimage of Grace, in the instigation of which conservative priests had played a leading role, curates in the diocese of York were instructed to exhort their parishioners 'both in confessions and otherwise to conform themselves in all points to such order as it shall please the king's highness to take for the governance and quietness of this his realm'.[130] In 1538 Lord Mordaunt was suspected of treason for having made his Lenten confession to the dissident Friar Forest, and in the same

---

[124] H. Bettenson (ed.), *Documents of the Christian Church* (Oxford, 1943), 329.

[125] H. Brinklow, *The Complaynt of Roderyck Mors*, ed. J. M. Cowper, EETS ES 22 (1874), 46.   [126] Elton, *Policy and Police*, 27–30.

[127] *LP* xiii (2). 51, 235; PRO, STA. C. 2, 16/91.   [128] *LP* xviii (2). 293.

[129] *LP* xiv (1). 492.   [130] BIHR, D/C Misc.

year Robert Croucaer, rector of Dennington in Suffolk, was summoned before the Council for expressing the thoroughly orthodox opinion that a priest is bound to conceal treason revealed to him in confession. Croucaer averred that all priests would agree with him 'who have not utterly in contempt the cure of man's soul'.[131] Official suspicion of confession became even more marked after King Henry's death and the rapid acceleration of religious reform. In 1548 a royal proclamation complained that 'divers unlearned and indiscreet preachers and other priests, of a devilish mind and intent, hath . . . incited and moved his loving subjects, as well in confession as otherwise, to disobedience and stubbornness against his majesty's godly proceedings'.[132] A ballad composed in London after the collapse of the conservative rising in Devon and Cornwall in 1549 was explicit as to what had underpinned the rebellion:

> For under confession, these priests doth bind
> the simple people, most earnest of all
> on pain of damnation to follow their mind . . .
> To most rank treason they caused men to fall.[133]

If the religious and social purposes of confession were, from the late 1530s, being seen by some in authority as contingent to considerations of political expediency, the traditional focus of the sacrament was also being blurred in other ways that may perhaps have lessened the appeal of the ritual to a broad section of English society. Henry's Royal Injunctions of 1538 commanded curates to examine in Lent 'every person that comes to confession unto you, whether they can recite the Articles of our Faith, and the Pater Noster in English, and hear them say the same particularly; wherein if they be not perfect, ye shall declare to the same that every Christian person ought to know the same before they should receive the Blessed Sacrament of the Altar'. Lee's Injunctions for York Diocese the following year added the Ten Commandments and the Ave Maria to

---

[131] H. Miller, *Henry VIII and the English Nobility* (Oxford, 1986), 45; *LP* xiii (1). 234; Elton, *Policy and Police*, 346. In fact, a number of cases of treason were confirmed by priests who had heard reports of them under the seal of confession: A. G. Dickens, 'Sedition and Conspiracy in Yorkshire During the Later Years of Henry VIII' in *Reformation Studies* (1982), 3; *LP* v. 649. Katharine Howard warned her lover, Thomas Culpeper, that he should 'never shrive him of any such things as should pass betwixt her and him, for if he did, surely the King, being supreme head of the Church, should have knowledge of it'. L. B. Smith, *A Tudor Tragedy: The Life and Times of Catherine Howard* (1961), 130. See also B. Kurtscheid, *A History of the Seal of Confession*, tr. F. A. Marks (1927), 153–4.

[132] P. L. Hughes and J. F. Larkin (eds.), *Tudor Royal Proclamations* (New Haven, Conn., 1964), i. 421.   [133] F. Rose-Troup, *The Western Rebellion of 1549* (1913), 337.

the list, and instructed confessors to warn their penitents that 'they shall not be admitted to receive the Blessed Sacrament of the Altar at Easter till they can perfectly rehearse them'.[134] Thenceforth, royal and episcopal injunctions regularly required ghostly fathers to examine the extent of the religious knowledge of their parishioners in confession.[135] That these requirements were sometimes perceived to be burdensome and confusing is suggested by John Heywood's two epigrams, 'Of him that forgot his pater noster in Latin' and 'Of him that could not learn his pater noster in English'.[136] In fact, the didactic aspect of confession was not in itself an innovation.[137] Confessors' manuals directed priests to inquire if penitents knew the Pater Noster, Creed, Twelve Articles of Faith, and Ten Commandments, and if not, to exhort them to learn them.[138] A comic poem entitled *A lytell geste how the plowman lerned his pater noster*, printed by de Worde in 1510, tells how a wise confessor tricks an idle and greedy ploughman into learning the prayer and reciting it in confession.[139] To insist, however, on an abstract standard of religious knowledge, rather than on contrition and sincerity of intention to amend, as an essential precondition for the reception of the eucharist, was to break with the traditional understanding of the purpose of the sacrament of penance, and to seem to stress its utility rather than its integrity as a divine ordinance. In 1543 Kentish conservatives were shocked when the Archbishop's commissary ordered the clergy at a visitation at Sevington to refuse absolution to those who could not say the Pater Noster and Creed in English, but in fact his initiative reflected the logic of the new thinking.[140] In their turn, reformers were shocked when Catholic preachers continued to repeat the medieval *obiter dictum* that 'if Judas had gone to God and confessed his fault, saying Peccavi as he went in to the priests, he had not been damned'.[141]

In 1548 with the appearance of the new *Order of Communion*, the reformers' opposition to the tradition of mandatory confession secured its triumph. The *Order*, later incorporated into the 1549 Prayer Book, included an exhortation to be delivered by the curate, declaring that any with troubled consciences might confess to him secretly to receive comfort and absolution, and requiring

---

[134] *Visitation Articles*, ii. 37, 45.   [135] Ibid. ii. 106, 119, 178.

[136] B. A. Milligan (ed.), *John Heywood's Works and Miscellaneous Short Poems* (Urbana, Ill., 1956), 126.

[137] For the 13th-c. requirements in the diocese of Norwich, see *Visitation Articles*, ii. 37.

[138] Mirc, *Instructions*, 28; Balliol MS 354, fo. 179ᵛ.

[139] W. C. Hazlitt (ed.), *Remains of the Popular Poetry of England* (1864), i. 209 ff.

[140] *LP* xviii (2). 313.   [141] Ibid. 229; Weatherley (ed.), *Speculum Sacerdotale*, 120.

such as shall be satisfied with a general confession, not to be offended with them that do use, to their further satisfying, the auricular and secret confession to the priest: nor those also which think needful or convenient, for the quietness of their own consciences particularly to open their sins to the priest: to be offended with them that are satisfied with their humble confession to God, and the general confession to the church.[142]

This pious hope was not, however, likely to be realized: optional confession could serve to underline religious differences, and to affirm doctrinal partisanship. These divisions could at times receive open symbolic expression. In 1548 William Jackson, a parishioner of Deal in Kent, complained that on Maundy Thursday he had seen some of his fellow parishioners with the rector at confession, 'to whom immediately after he saw the said parson minister the bread whole, and to other that were not confessed he ministered the same broken'.[143] Some priests may not even have been prepared to go as far as this in compromising with the government's latitudinarian policy. In the early 1550s Bishop Hooper demanded to know if any of the priests in the dioceses of Gloucester and Worcester 'require and demand of such as come to communion, first to make their auricular confession to the curate, as they did in the time of papistry'.[144]

If, then, private confession was not actually forbidden by the English Church in 1548, it is important to attempt to assess how popular and widespread the practice remained in the years before the Marian regime briefly reintroduced the medieval obligation. Protestants, and of course their Lollard precursors, had long been opposed to it. Not only was the sacramental confession of individual sins clearly 'unnecessary' in the context of a solifidian soteriology, but Protestant preachers could find no mention of the practice in the Bible.[145] The Edwardian divine, John Bradford, marshalled eight principal reasons why auricular confession ought to be considered wicked and unlawful, including the practical objection that 'it requireth of itself an impossibility, that is, the numbering and telling of all our sins, which no man perceiveth, much less can utter'.[146] Yet reformers like Bradford, Latimer, and Ridley were not completely opposed to the confession of sin as such, and even Tyndale could remark of confession to a priest, 'that tradition, restored unto the right

[142] E. C. Gibson (ed.), *The First and Second Prayer Books of Edward VI* (1910), 217.
[143] C. E. Woodruff (ed.), 'Extracts from Original Documents Illustrating the Progress of the Reformation in Kent', *AC* 31 (1915), 96–7.   [144] *Visitation Articles*, ii. 302.
[145] *LP* xviii (2). 306, 311, 313.
[146] J. Bradford, *The Writings of John Bradford ... Letters, Treatises, Remains*, ed. A. Townsend, PS (1853), 119. The same opinion was held by George Joye: W. A. Clebsch, *England's Earliest Protestants, 1520–1535* (New Haven, Conn., 1964), 216.

use, were not damnable'.[147] Thomas Becon, in his *Potation for Lent*, also suggested that confession could be good, but only when 'they that sit in confession be men of gravity, sagacity, wisdom, discretion, sobriety, integrity'.[148] The ideal Catholic confessor was, of course, all of these things; the London merchant, Richard Hill, had hoped to find in him a collection of qualities virtually identical to Becon's list.[149] Yet to make the personal qualities of the confessor, rather than the powers inherent in priesthood, the hallmark of penitential practice was to invert the traditional logic of the sacrament and to remove the spiritual benefit derived by the penitent from an objective to a subjective plane. It is not clear, of course, to what extent arguments over the role of the confessor may have been absorbed or understood by the common people, just as it is not possible to say for certain how widespread private confession remained after 1548. What seems most likely, however, is that it entered a terminal decline. When George Lowes, a former mayor and Member of Parliament for Winchester drew up his will in 1553 he included an acknowledgement of sin under the traditional headings of Ten Commandments, Seven Deadly Sins, Seven Works of Mercy, and so on, while noting regretfully how 'auricular confession is not now with all men allowed and now little used'.[150] The testamentary evidence would seem to bear out Lowes's pessimism: references to a 'ghostly father' all but disappear from wills made in the Edwardian period: from 1547 only one in every two hundred of the wills in the sample mentions him. If this statistic truly represents the malaise of the practice, and it can only tentatively be suggested that it does, then it seems unlikely that Protestant conversion was the sole factor dissuading English laypeople from coming to confession. G. R. Elton's contention that 'by 1553 England was almost certainly nearer to being a Protestant country than to anything else' would probably not now command acceptance among most Reformation historians of a moderately 'revisionist' outlook.[151] Patrick Collinson's suggestion, that the real Protestant breakthrough came in the 1570s, perhaps more closely reflects the

---

[147] *Visitation Articles*, ii. 298 n.; K. Thomas, *Religion and the Decline of Magic*, Peregrine edn. (1978), 187; T. W. Drury, *Confession and Absolution: The Teaching of the Church of England as Interpreted and Illustrated by the Writings of the Reformers of the Sixteenth Century* (1903), 111. Some Elizabethan Protestants espoused the same view: P. Collinson, 'Shepherds, Sheepdogs and Hirelings: The Pastoral Ministry in Post-Reformation England' in W. J. Sheils and D. Wood (eds.), *The Ministry: Clerical and Lay*, SCH 26 (Oxford, 1989), 218.   [148] T. Becon, *Early Works*, ed. J. Ayre, PS (1843), 100.

[149] Balliol MS 354, fo. 179ʳ.

[150] G. J. Mayhew, 'The Progress of the Reformation in East Sussex, 1530–1559: The Evidence from Wills', *Southern History*, 5 (1983), 44.

[151] G. R. Elton, *Reform and Reformation: England 1509–1558* (1977), 371.

present consensus.[152] The decline in attendance at confession may have owed more to semi-official discouragement, apathy, and a pusillanimous attitude to an occasionally onerous religious duty, than to ideological conviction. That death-bed confession may have been becoming less of a soteriological imperative, however, is suggested by the dramatic decline in the percentage of wills naming a priest as a witness; from a constant of over 72 per cent in the reign of Henry VIII to just under 52 per cent in that of Edward, though here again such an interpretation of neutral statistics must be advanced with caution.

With the possible exception of a devout and introspective élite, auricular confession may not have been regarded by many otherwise orthodox lay people as a central and indispensable component of an adequately spiritual life. There appears to be little other way to account for its apparently sudden and ignominious demise. More difficult to assess is how the abrogation of mandatory confession may have altered perceptions of the function and duties of the priest, and of the nature of priesthood itself. Lollards and Protestants virulently opposed the institution of compulsory confession because it seemed to them paradigmatic of the unwarranted prerogatives of a privileged priestly class, and was as such incompatible with the teaching of the Gospel. In so far as the clergy at all possessed the ability to bind and to loose from sin, this was through the proper preaching of God's Word, which alone wielded the power claimed by the Catholic priesthood and the papacy.[153] Catholic thinkers, of course, saw the practice of confession as being central to God's plans for the sanctification and salvation of man, and as growing out of the very essence of sacramental priesthood itself. As we have seen, penitents were encouraged to think of the confessor as the representative of Christ, sitting in the seat of judgement 'in God's stead'. But the appealing simplicities of this theoretical starting-point were tempered by the reality that the hearing of confessions was also in practice a pastoral undertaking which could be performed well or performed badly and which either way reflected on the standing of the individual confessor, and perhaps indirectly on that of the priesthood as a whole. The interplay between a sacramental theology which accorded to priests both elevated status and great responsibility, and the practical way in which their ministry was performed and received must have generated rather ambivalent attitudes.

---

[152] P. Collinson, *The Birthpangs of Protestant England* (1988), ix.
[153] C. C. Butterworth and A. G. Chester, *George Joye 1495?–1553* (Philadelphia, 1962), 79; R. Barnes, *The Reformation Essays of Dr Robert Barnes*, ed. N. S. Tjernagel (1963), 53–61; P. E. Hughes, *The Theology of the English Reformers* (1965), 183.

The tensions produced by the system could be creative, expressive of the desire for reform and renewal, or (from the clerical perspective) destructive, seeking the abolition of forms which maintained corrupt priestly domin-ance. The penitential practice of the Church encapsulated that paradox as readily as any of the confluences of clerical and lay, and yet it is difficult to generalize about how reactions to confession may have been constitutive to wider perceptions of the nature and functions of the priesthood. The historian is a prisoner of his written sources, and much of the above has inevitably concentrated on the disputes and hostilities which have a genius for generating documentation. The many thousands who may have appreciated the opportunity to unburden themselves to a sympathetic confessor, or who merely accepted with resignation the necessity of regular confession, have left little or no record of their satisfac-tion or acquiescence. If the abolition of obligatory confession removed for some a reason to fear, distrust, or resent the priest, it could represent for others a loss of valued contact and raise questions as to the social and fiscal status of the priest in the parish community. Penance, replete as it was with the profoundest of theological implications, tended perhaps in any case to be more a preoccupation of the intelligentsia of both religious camps than of the common people. It was otherwise with the other great sacramental task of the priest: the celebration of the mass.

2

The Priest as Celebrant

THE SPECTACLE OF THE MASS

'Ye come unto your altar as a game-player unto his stage.'[1] Among mid-Tudor English Protestants, Thomas Becon was not alone in discerning a distinct theatricality adhering to the Catholic mass and to the priest's role within it. William Turner thought that priests had replaced the sacrament of Christ's body and blood with 'a mere man's invention, a certain popish play', while to John Bale, priests made mockery of Christ's people 'in all your juggling plays'.[2] In rather more homely fashion Hugh Hilarie observed that 'Brandon the juggler had never goodlier knacks than ye have at your mass.'[3] Such comments enshrined the essential Protestant critique of the mass: that it was profoundly unscriptural, that in it the people's communion had been deformed into a priestly sacrifice at which the laity were reduced to helpless and ignorant spectators. The theatrical metaphor seemed an appropriate way to express the hypocrisy and lack of substance they believed the mass to exemplify. Yet to Catholics, the mass could legitimately be conceived of as a kind of drama, its subject the life and death of Jesus Christ. Framed by the chancel screen, and before a backdrop of altar and reredos, priests and their assistants performed the 'drama' daily to an audience of Catholic layfolk.

Contemporary writers who attempted for the English laity a vernacular exegesis of the mass sought to show 'how in the ceremonies of the mass we may find meditations of the holy passion of our Lord Jesu'.[4] In other words, if the mass was a drama, then the mode of dramatic expression it

---

[1] T. Becon, *The Displaying of the Popish Mass*, in *Prayers and Other Pieces of Thomas Becon*, ed. J. Ayre, PS (1844), 259.

[2] W. Turner, *A new Dialogue wherein is conteyned the examinatio[n] of the Messe and of that kind of priesthode, whiche is ordeyned to say messe* (1548), sig. A.iii^r. J. Bale, *An answere to a papystycall exhortacyon*, in H. Huth and W. C. Hazlitt (eds.), *Fugitive Tracts* (1875), unpaginated. See also J. Bale, *The Vocacyon of Johan Bale to the Bishoprick of Ossorie in Irelande* (1553), fo. 30^v; J. F. Davis, *Heresy and Reformation in the South-East of England 1520–1559* (1983), 85; J. Strype, *Ecclesiastical Memorials* (Oxford, 1822), i (2). 264.

[3] H. Hilarie, *The Resurrecion of the Masse* (Strasbourg, 1554), sig. B.iv^r.

[4] W. Bonde, *The Pylgrymage of Perfeccyon* (1531), fo. 259^r.

employed was that of allegory. This manner of explaining the mass belonged to a long and venerated tradition, which derived in large measure
from the *Liber Officialis* and other works of Amalarius, Bishop of Metz in
the early ninth century. Attempting to meet the requirements of a laity
now largely unable to comprehend the official liturgical language,
Amalarius, and those he later influenced, wished to demonstrate how
every facet of the ceremonial of the mass could be shown to bear a
meaning pertinent to Christian concepts of eschatology and soteriology.[5]
Although Amalarius's allegorical exposition of the mass never acquired
complete legitimacy in the eyes of theologians,[6] commentators in late
medieval England developed the technique with enthusiasm, intending
their writings both as an aid to devout meditation during the time of
mass, and as a means of impressing into the popular mind the intimacy
of the connection between the sacrifice of the mass and Christ's sacrifice at Calvary.[7] Every item of the Church's sacred equipment, every gesture or movement of the celebrant, was regarded as able to present some
theological verity or episode from the incarnation and passion of Christ.
For example, the altar might signify the cross; the chalice, Christ's sep-
ulchre; and the paten, the stone that covered it.[8] The various liturgical
cloths known as the corporas, sudary, and sindon were identified with the
materials in which Christ was wrapped in the tomb.[9] The allegory was
not, however, merely static and depictive, confined to the spiritual significance of these various ritual objects. The Brigittine, William Bonde,
exemplified the contemporary fashion when he insisted that 'the process
of the mass representeth the very progress of Christ to his passion'.[10] The
Interpretacyon and Sygnyfycacyon of the Masse posited a three-part division

---

[5] Y. Brilioth, *Eucharistic Faith and Practice, Evangelical and Catholic*, tr. A. G. Herbert
(1961), 83; O. B. Hardison, *Christian Rite and Christian Drama in the Middle Ages* (Baltimore,
1965), ch. 2; J. A. Jungmann, *The Mass of the Roman Rite*, tr. F. A. Brunner (New York,
1951), i. 107–16.   [6] J. Martos, *Doors to the Sacred* (1981), 265–6.

[7] The following account of the allegorical exposition of the mass has been compiled in
the main from these works: Langforde, *Meditatyons for goostly exercyse in the tyme of the
masse*, in J. Wickham Legg (ed.), *Tracts on the Mass*, Henry Bradshaw Society, 27 (1904),
which is largely a transcription of Bonde, *Pylgrymage of Perfeccyon*, 259ʳ ff.; *The Storie of the
Masse*, appended to Caxton's 1483 edn. of Jacob de Voragine's *Golden Legend*; *Dives and Pauper*
(1534); C. S. Cobb (ed.), *The Rationale of Ceremonial, 1540–1543*, ACC 18 (1910); Friar
Garard, *The Interpretacyon and Sygnyfycacyon of the Masse* (1532). This last work was a
translation of *Dat Boexken van der Missen* by the Flemish Observant, Gherit van der Goude,
which first appeared on the Continent in 1506. See P. Dearmer, *Dat Boexken van der Missen*,
ACC (1903), which reproduces the illustrations omitted from the Eng. edn.

[8] Langforde, *Meditatyons*, 19; Bonde, *Pylgrymage of Perfeccyon*, 259ʳ.

[9] Langforde and Bonde, ibid.; Garard, *Interpretacyon and Sygnyfycacyon of the Masse*, sig.
I.iiʳ.   [10] Bonde, *Pylgrymage of Perfeccyon*, 259ʳ.

of the mass, corresponding to the supposedly tripartite nature of the life of Christ. Up to the Sanctus, the mass related the story of His life until the entry into Jerusalem; the canon and the priest's communion represented the passion and the entombment, while the final section from the priest's emptying of the chalice (the empty tomb) to the final blessing represented the resurrection and ascension. In all, this work listed thirty-three 'articles' of the mass, each relating an incident from the life, death, and resurrection of Christ, and, of course, corresponding to the traditional thirty-three years of the incarnation.[11] No feature of the ceremonial of the mass was considered too trivial to be endowed with a deeply symbolic significance: 'the priest doth not say one word, nor doth not move his hand in the mass: but it doth signify some thing of the life of our Lorde.'[12]

It will be apparent that the logical coherence of the mass as a vehicle for intelligible allegory depended very largely on the identification of the celebrant with the person of Christ. In the mass the priest signified or betokened Christ, just as the altar signified the cross, or the empty chalice the empty tomb.[13] More precisely, 'the priest at the altar doth signify our Lord upon the cross'.[14] Of course, the idea that an ordained priest became in some sense an *alter Christus* was central to the very theology of orders, but in the mass this was seen as being so in a special sense. As the author of the popular fifteenth-century work, *Dives and Pauper*, expressed it, 'as oft as the priest singeth his mass, he representeth the person of Christ that died for us all upon the tree'.[15] The priest's vesting symbolized the incarnation, Christ's taking upon Him our human nature.[16] In Caxton's version this was symbolized by the priest's kissing of the altar, though to Bonde/Langforde this kiss represented the marriage between the Son of God and the Church.[17] The connection was maintained up to and beyond the point when, at the consecration and elevation of the eucharistic elements, the priest made a dramatic presentation of the crucifixion and death of Jesus Christ. Nearly all commentators agreed that the vestments worn by the priest to celebrate mass themselves bore witness to the passion story, and that the laity should take care to understand 'the moral

---

[11] Garard, *Interpretacyon and Sygnyfycacyon of the Masse*, sigs. K.ii^r–O.iii^r.
[12] Ibid. E.iv^v.
[13] Langforde, *Meditatyons*, 19; Bonde, *Pylgrymage of Perfeccyon*, 259^r.
[14] Garard, *Interpretacyon and Sygnyfycacyon of the Masse*, sig. I.ii^r.
[15] *Dives and Pauper*, 287^r.
[16] Garard, *Interpretacyon and Sygnyfycacyon of the Masse*, sig. K.iii^r; Langforde, *Meditatyons*, 20. [17] *Storie of the Masse*, 435^r; Langforde, *Meditatyons*, 20.

meaning of that ghostly armour'.[18] The amice represented the blindfold put on Christ by the Jews; the alb, the white garment with which Herod mockingly clothed Him; the fanon, stole, and girdle, the various bonds with which Christ was tied at His scourging; and the chasuble, the purple robe in which He was mockingly clad by Pilate's soldiers.[19] The vestments also carried a second layer of allegorical significance, representing the virtues with which Christ bore his passion. The amice could signify ghostly strength; the alb, innocence; the stole, cleanness from sin; and the chasuble, charity.[20] The virtues of faith, chastity, humility, strength, and charity were also associated with the various vestments by the fifteenth-century poem *The Vertue of the Masse*, which went on to employ the chivalric metaphor of

> A priest made strong with this armour
> Afore the altar as Christ's champion.[21]

The author of *Dives and Pauper* advanced similar views touching the symbolic import of the vestments, and suggested that if priests celebrated mass without true devotion to Christ's passion, they bore false witness, 'for it is not with them inward as the tokens do show outward'.[22] The committee of bishops, charged in the early 1540s with providing a rationale for the ceremonies still used in the English Church, developed this idea further, explaining each item of the vestments as 'partly representing the mysteries that were done in the time of the passion, partly representing the virtues that he himself ought to have that celebrateth the mass'.[23] Thus, the alb would signify the innocence and purity 'the which he ought to have especially when he singeth the mass'; the girdle 'the continent and chaste living or else the close mind which he ought to have in prayer when he celebrates'; and the stole, the yoke of patience which the minister must bear as the servant of God.[24] In short, the public representation of Christ carried with it great responsibility as well as great honour. To a Protestant like Thomas Becon, however, the linen alb declared how well priests loved women, especially other men's wives; the stole signified their desire to persecute and strangle those who opposed them; while the

---

[18] J. Lydgate, *The Minor Poems*, ed. H. N. MacCracken, EETS 107 (1911), 87.

[19] Langforde, *Meditatyons*, 21–2; Bonde, *Pylgrymage of Perfeccyon*, 259ʳ; *Dives and Pauper*, 287ʳ; Garard, *Interpretacyon and Sygnyfycacyon of the Masse*, sigs. I.iiᵛ–iiiʳ; Cobb (ed.), *Rationale of Ceremonial*, 16–18.   [20] Langforde, *Meditatyons*, 20.

[21] T. F. Simmons (ed.), *The Lay Folk's Mass Book*, EETS 71 (1879), 167–8; *The Vertue of Yᵉ Masse* (?1520), sig. A.ivʳ.   [22] *Dives and Pauper*, 287ᵛ.

[23] Cobb (ed.), *Rationale of Ceremonial*, 16.   [24] Ibid. 16–17.

chasuble, their 'fool's coat, gaily gauded, signifieth your pleasant fineness and womanly niceness, and your delectation in the verity or change of Venus' pastimes'.[25] The allegorical meaning of the vestments was satirized at length because it was a concept that mattered to thinking Catholics. The aura of sanctity with which mass vestments were surrounded explains the relative frequency with which lay people bequeathed money or cloth for them in their wills, and the desire of some donors to have their arms emblazoned upon them, thereby publicly associating the donor with the holy mystery which the vestments both commemorated and enabled to take place.[26] Women sometimes bequeathed expensive gowns to their parish churches so that these could be made into vestments.[27]

By its very nature, of course, the meaning of allegory is seldom self-evident, and it is worth asking what, if anything, this complex interweaving of themes may have meant to the ordinary worshipper. For a start, it must be admitted that there was no absolutely uniform tradition of allegorical interpretation. To one writer, the priest's going to the left corner of the altar to read the Gospel might signify the declaration of the mystery of faith to the Gentiles; to another it represented the return of the infant Christ from exile in Egypt.[28] Moreover, the central allegory of the priest representing Christ might not in itself be entirely consistent. The exigencies of a coherent allegorical 'narrative' might necessitate on occasion the presentation of the priest as the Church, as the angels, even as Pilate or as the two thieves crucified with Christ.[29] Even where it remained consistent the allegory could be confusingly esoteric. It is doubtful, for example, if many laypeople who were not conversant with the appropriate devotional works could have been aware that when the priest returned to the right-hand corner of the altar after reading the Gospel, he was giving notice of how at the end of the world the Jews would be converted, or that the five turnings of the priest towards the congregation in the course of the mass signified the five appearances of Christ after the resurrection.[30] One is entitled to wonder how the majority of ordinary worshippers could gain access to such ideas, assuming they were capable of assimilating them, at a time when religious instruction was likely to be

---

[25] Becon, *Displaying of the Popish Mass*, 259.

[26] See e.g. PRO, PCC, Prob. 11, 16 Porch (John Wilshire); 5 Porch (William Abell); 12 Maynwaring (Robert Thornburghe).

[27] PRO, PCC, Prob. 11, 8 Pynnyng (Elizabeth Goldon); 11 Pynnyng (Isabell Flemyng).

[28] Langforde, *Meditatyons*, 20; Garard, *Interpretacyon and Sygnyfycacyon of the Masse*, sig. L.i[v]; Jungmann, *Mass of the Roman Rite*, i. 116.

[29] *Storie of the Masse*, 438[r]; Langforde, *Meditatyons*, 22; Garard, *Interpretacyon and Sygnyfycacyon of the Masse*, sig. M.iii[r], iv[r].   [30] Langforde, *Meditatyons*, 20, 28–9.

confined to the essentials of the faith. Although the literate might be seen 'taking the office of Our Lady with them' to mass,[31] and although 'devotional literacy' was almost certainly becoming more common at the close of the Middle Ages,[32] it seems probable that, in the countryside at any rate, an informed and reflective eucharistic piety would still be very much the exception rather than the rule.

On the other hand, the allegorical 'impersonation' of Christ undertaken by the priest in the mass was not always as abstruse as the examples cited above might suggest. Few could mistake the reference to the crucified Christ when, after the elevation of the host and chalice, the priest stood at the altar with his arms outstretched.[33] It also seems likely that many ordinary laypeople would have sought to establish the meaning of the priest's tonsure. According to one fifteenth-century homilist, this was precisely the sort of thing that priests were likely to be asked, and a view was current that it was designed to call to mind the crown of thorns.[34] Most importantly, of course, from the section of the mass beginning *qui pridie*, the priest mimicked the actions of Christ at the Last Supper, and here the identification between celebrant and Saviour became particularly close. In a late medieval sermon for the Feast of the Purification, a devout woman is unselfconsciously portrayed as having a vision in which mass is celebrated by Christ himself, vested as a priest and with angels for his altar servers.[35]

If Catholics understood nothing else about the mass, they knew that during it Christ was made present among them, and that this miracle could come about only through the agency of a priest. It is questionable whether the physical presence of the 'real' Christ after the consecration was likely to reinforce or to undermine the dramatic impersonation of Christ by the officiating priest. What is clear is that with the declining frequency of lay communion over the course of the Middle Ages, this appearance of Christ, the moment at which the congregation knew Him to be really present, had developed into the apotheosis of popular devotion.

---

[31] C. A. Sneyd (ed.), *A Relation or Rather a True Account of the Island of England . . . about the Year 1500*, CS, 1st ser. 37 (1847), 23.

[32] M. Aston, *Lollards and Reformers: Images and Literacy in Late Medieval Religion* (1984), ch. 4.

[33] Simmons (ed.), *Lay Folk's Mass Book*, 42, 144; Langforde, *Meditatyons*, 25; Cobb (ed.), *Rationale of Ceremonial*, 25; Hardison, *Christian Rite and Christian Drama*, 65.

[34] Garard, *Interpretacyon and Sygnyfycacyon of the Masse*, sig. I.iiiᵛ. An alternative theory was that priests shaved their heads so that nothing should come between them and God: J. Mirc, *Festial*, EETS ES 96 (1905), 125–6.

[35] Mirc, ibid. 61; E. H. Weatherley (ed.), *Speculum Sacerdotale*, EETS 200 (1936), 27–8.

As the German liturgical historian J. A. Jungmann expresses it, 'the *eucharistia* has become an *epiphania*'.[36]

THE PASTORAL ROLE OF THE CELEBRANT

For the worshippers what gave existential meaning to the presence among them of the risen Christ was the elevation of the eucharistic elements, made by the priest immediately after their consecration. This had come to be associated so closely with the actual consecration of the bread and wine that in England the elevation was referred to as the 'sacring', while the second elevation of the consecrated elements at 'per ipsum et cum ipso et in ipso' at the end of the canon was known as the 'second sacring'.[37] For those who witnessed it the elevation was a moment of unique experience; one might aptly borrow a phrase from T. S. Eliot, and describe it as a 'point of intersection of the timeless with time'. In the sanctuary itself a 'sacring bell' was rung to mark the solemnity of the moment, while at the same time the church bells were tolled to enable those out working in the fields to be suitably reverential.[38] Additionally, various practical steps could be taken to facilitate the people's adoration of the consecrated host.[39] In some churches a black cloth or curtain was spread behind the host to make it more visible to the onlookers.[40] If this was insufficient more drastic action could be taken: in 1502 the churchwardens of Wooton in Kent were ordered to whitewash the walls of the church, as these were 'so dingy that the parishioners sitting in the nave can scarcely see the sacrament of the altar'.[41] In London and in York, wealthy testators left money for candles to be lit at the moment of the elevation.[42] One eccentric alderman of Hull bequeathed £10 in 1502 for

[36] Jungmann, *Mass of the Roman Rite*, i. 117.

[37] Becon, *Displaying of the Popish Mass*, 277.

[38] T. W. Drury, *Elevation in the Eucharist* (Cambridge, 1907), 126. E. Duffy, *The Stripping of the Altars: Traditional Religion in England, 1400–1580* (New Haven, Conn., 1992), 95–8.

[39] The chalice, of course, was elevated as well, but does not seem to have rivalled the host as an object of devout contemplation. This was due probably to the invisibility to the onlookers of the consecrated wine, and to the circumstance that fear of spillage inhibited priests from making as flamboyant an elevation with the chalice as with the host.

[40] Wickham Legg (ed.), *Tracts on the Mass*, 234.

[41] C. E. Woodruff (ed.), 'An Archidiaconal Visitation of 1502', *AC* 47 (1935), 48.

[42] C. Pendrill, *Old Parish Life in London* (Oxford, 1937), 37; S. Brigden, *London and the Reformation* (Oxford, 1989), 16, 33, 107; BIHR, Prob. Reg. 11, fo. 250ᵛ (John Mason); M. Rubin, *Corpus Christi: The Eucharist in Late Medieval Culture* (Cambridge, 1991), 61–2.

an elaborate machine by which angels would descend from the church roof at the elevation.[43]

Ironically, the very eagerness of the laity to see and worship the consecrated host could sometimes disturb the solemnity of the occasion. Some worshippers apparently ran about the church, or jostled with their neighbours in order to get the best possible view.[44] Others might come to church just in time to see the elevation, and then leave again immediately afterwards. One late fifteenth-century German preacher spoke incredulously of people fleeing from the church after the elevation as though it was the Devil they had just seen.[45] An English anecdote which similarly illustrates the great appeal of the sacring, and which suggests something of the relative popularity of contemporary devotional forms, is provided by William Thorpe's complaint in the early fifteenth century that at the ringing of the sacring bell the audience abandoned his sermon and rushed off to view the elevation in another part of the church.[46] An episode in John Rastell's *Book of C Mery Talys* suggests that in the early sixteenth century it may not have been unusual to come to church 'even at the sacring time'.[47] For many English men and women the chance to view the elevated host was the main, sometimes perhaps the sole reason for coming to mass, and an inquisitive Lincolnshire merchant who had travelled to Germany in 1528 was clearly astonished that 'there was no sacring' at the Lutheran service he had attended.[48]

Protestants scoffed at the intensity (or as they saw it, the superstitious folly) of the people's devotion to the consecrated host. 'I have lost sacring, a vengeance on it', a Catholic is made to exclaim in Michael Wodde's *Dialogue or familiar talk betwene two neighbours* (1554).[49] Cranmer and Becon both described how worshippers would habitually run from altar to altar, shouting to their neighbours to 'stoop down before', since they could not be merry unless they saw their Maker at least once a day.[50] Their account

[43] Rubin, ibid. 62.

[44] Garard, *Interpretacyon and Sygnyfycacyon of the Masse*, sig. E.i'; H. Thurston, 'The Elevation', *The Tablet* (2 Nov. 1907), 685.

[45] P. Browe, *Die Verehrung der Eucharistie im Mittelalter* (Freiburg im Breisgau, 1967), 68.

[46] R. N. Swanson, *Church and Society in Late Medieval England* (Oxford, 1989), 276.

[47] H. Oesterly (ed.), *Shakespeare's Jest Book* (1866), 134.

[48] E. Peacock (ed.), 'Extracts from Lincoln Episcopal Visitations', *Archaeologia*, 48 (1885), 257.

[49] Drury, *Elevation in the Eucharist*, 95. Michael Wodde was the pseudonym of John Day.

[50] T. Cranmer, *An Answer unto A Crafty and Sophistical Cavillation devised by Stephen Gardiner*, in J. E. Cox (ed.), *Writings and Disputations of Thomas Cranmer relative to the Sacrament of the Lord's Supper*, PS (1844), 229. Becon, *Displaying of the Popish Mass*, 270. Becon's account is heavily dependent on Cranmer's.

of the people's shouting to 'Sir John' to 'hold up, heave it a little higher' (if it can be credited), hardly suggests a reverential attitude on the part of those worshippers to the sacramental status of the celebrant as *alter Christus*, or a proper response to the notion that 'the priest is not there before the altar as Sir John, but he is there as the son of God [that] hath hanged upon the cross'.[51] It does, however, remind us that at the moment of the elevation the laity were utterly dependent upon the clergy for the fulfilment of their deepest religious needs. Popular devotion to the elevation is well illustrated by the bequest of William Hampden of Hartwell in Buckinghamshire in 1521: 'my body to be buried within the chancel of Hartwell before the midst of the high altar so that the priest may stand upon my feet in the sacring of the mass.'[52] Viewed from this perspective, priests in elevating the host were performing an essentially pastoral work. On the Continent various mass books had had to forbid extended, idiosyncratic, or repeated elevations, and to discourage priests from making the elevation at 'per ipsum' as high as that at the consecration itself.[53] John Foxe sardonically included among the essential duties of a Catholic priest 'to lift up fair', while in a Protestant satire of 1554, a Catholic character expresses satisfaction with his curate by describing him as 'as fair a lifter as any is within Hampshire'.[54] Conversely, Robert Conyng, rector of Grayingham in Lincolnshire, greatly offended his parishioners in the late fifteenth century when he set up an image in the parish church which impeded their view of the elevation.[55] At Minster Lovell in Oxfordshire in 1519, where the detached piers beneath the tower obstructed the view of the congregation, the parishioners complained that the vicar (who was technically in the right) would not allow them into the chancel to see the elevation.[56] Pastoral duty notwithstanding, it is perhaps not entirely fanciful to see in the elevation of the host the epitome of the priestly presentation of Christ. At the moment when in the eucharist symbol merged with reality, the stretching movements of the priest suggested an image of heroic self-immolation, a posture redolent of a Gothic crucifix.

Another 'pastoral' activity priests could perform in the mass was their final blessing of the kneeling congregation, an action which the allegorists

---

[51] Garard, *Interpretacyon and Sygnyfycacyon of the Masse*, sig. H.iii[v].

[52] E. M. Elvey (ed.), *The Courts of the Archdeaconry of Buckingham, 1483–1523*, Buckinghamshire Record Society, 19 (1975), 344.　　　[53] Browe, *Verehrung der Eucharistie*, 63–4.

[54] B. L. Manning, *The People's Faith in the Time of Wyclif* (Hassocks, 1975), 39; Wickham Legg (ed.), *Tracts on the Mass*, 256.

[55] C. T. Martin (ed.), 'Clerical Life in the Fifteenth Century, as Illustrated by Proceedings in the Court of Chancery', *Archaeologia*, 60 (1907), 366.

[56] *Lincoln Visitations*, i. 132.

identified with Christ's blessing and taking leave of his disciples on the
Mount of Olives at the ascension.[57] The *Interpretacyon and Sygnyfycacyon
of the Masse* attached great importance to this blessing, suggestive, perhaps, of the practice's widespread popular appeal as much as of its assertion
of clerical privilege. In the Old Testament, children were blessed by their
fathers, and so 'we do receive with all humility the blessing of the priest
at the end of his mass, for his hands be much more holy than were the
hands of the old fathers: and by the blessing of the priest we be made
worthy of the blessing of our Lord God in heaven'.[58] As if this were not
persuasive enough, a couple of instructive exempla followed. One concerned a carpenter, whose lucky escape from a serious fall was attributed
by his neighbours to the fact that he had been 'well blessed this day'.
Another told of two merchants, 'of the which the one received always the
blessing of the priest, and the other never did regard nor care for it'.
Predictably enough, when a ferocious thunderstorm interrupted their
journey, the latter was struck dead by lightning, while his companion
returned alive.[59] Some contemporary Continental illustrations show the
final blessing being administered by the priest with the paten or with the
host, a clear identification of the efficacy of the priest's blessing with his
unique custodianship of the body and blood of Christ.[60] In the
Interpretacyon and Sygnyfycacyon of the Masse, the connection was made
explicit: 'O man, remember what virtue the blessing which the priest
doth give after the mass is, for his hands have ministered at the altar the
blessed body of our Lord Jesu Christ.' The careless carpenter attributed
his good fortune to 'the blessing which the priest gave after the masse,
whose hands had touched the body of our Lord'.[61]

THE STATUS OF THE CELEBRANT

The priest, quintessentially, was the man empowered to make, and perhaps scarcely less importantly, to *touch* the body of Christ Jesus. Laypeople,
even when communicating, were not permitted to touch the host with
their hands, but priests did so daily. The unique status that this implied

[57] Langforde, *Meditatyons*, 28; Bonde, *Pylgrymage of Perfeccyon*, 261ʳ; J. H. Blunt (ed.),
The Myroure of Oure Ladye, EETS ES 19 (1873), 332.
[58] Garard, *Interpretacyon and Sygnyfycacyon of the Masse*, sig. G.iiiʳ⁻ᵛ.   [59] Ibid. G.ivʳ.
[60] W. H. Frere (ed.), *Exposition de la messe*, ACC 2 (1899), pl. 17; Dearmer (ed.), *Dat
Boexken van der Missen*, no. 33.
[61] Garard, *Interpretacyon and Sygnyfycacyon of the Masse*, sig. G.iiiᵛ. See also *The Vertue
of Yᵉ Masse*, sig. B.iiʳ.

allowed free rein to the encomiasts of priesthood. In his famous sermon to the fathers of Canterbury Convocation in February 1512, John Colet suggested that the dignity of priests was superior to that of kings or emperors; it was equal to that of angels.[62] Others had fewer inhibitions about claiming more than a mere parity with the status of the angels, and late medieval English preachers may regularly have reminded their congregations that no angel had ever been granted the privilege of saying mass.[63] Even if a man were 'as holy as our Lady, the mother of God', he could not say mass unless he had been first ordained.[64] Such rhetoric permeated the religious culture of late-medieval Europe. The pious readers of the perennially popular *Imitation of Christ*, which appeared in numerous editions in early sixteenth-century England, were reminded that not even the purity of an angel could make them worthy to touch the sacrament, unless, of course, they were a priest.[65]

These concepts were anathema to the first generation of Protestants, many of whom were clerics who had voluntarily surrendered their claim to such exalted status. In a sermon of 1541, Luther recalled how reverence for the priests' function of saying mass had ranked them above Mary and the angels: 'For the angels and Mary could not celebrate Mass—only a priest could do that. And a new priest and his first Mass was a matter for heartfelt joy; and blessed was the woman who was the mother of a priest.'[66] Priestly status predicated upon a theory of eucharistic particularity was clearly a 'damnable abuse', and it was with bitter sarcasm that William Tyndale referred to 'that high power of priests above all angels'.[67]

None the less, the view that their unique commission placed priests

---

[62] J. H. Lupton, *Life of John Colet*, 2nd edn. (1909), 297.

[63] Mirc, *Festial*, 169; F. Clark, *Eucharistic Sacrifice and the Reformation* (Chulmleigh, 1981), 548.

[64] Garard, *Interpretacyon and Sygnyfycacyon of the Masse*, sig. E.iv^v. See also W. C. Hazlitt (ed.), *A Select Collection of Old English Plays* (1874), i. 132–4; Catherine of Siena, *The Orchard of Syon* (1519), sig. r.v^v–vi^r; W. O. Ross (ed.), *Middle English Sermons*, EETS 209 (1940), 280–2; W. Melton, *Sermo Exhortatorius Cancellarii Eboracensis hiis qui ad sacros ordines petunt promoveri* (c.1510); D. Bagchi, ' "Eyn Mercklich Underscheyd": Catholic Reactions to Luther's Doctrine of the Priesthood of all Believers', in W. J. Shiels and D. Wood (eds.), *The Ministry: Clerical and Lay*, SCH 26 (1989).

[65] E. J. Klein (ed.), *The Imitation of Christ from the First Edition of an English Translation Made c.1530 by Richard Whitford* (New York, 1941), 232.

[66] Clark, *Eucharistic Sacrifice*, 113. This high conception of priesthood could on occasion go to priests' heads. In 1537 William Mynstreley was apparently preaching in Calais that since priests ranked above the angels 'they ought to have no temporal prince over them nor pay any thing to them', A. Kreider, *English Chantries: The Road to Dissolution* (Cambridge, Mass., 1979), 142.

[67] A. Marcourt, *A Declaration of the Masse* (1547), unpaginated; Tyndale, *Doctrinal Treatises by William Tyndale*, ed. H. Walter, PS (1848), 380.

'higher than the angels' was common currency in the pre-Reformation Church.[68] But what practical expectations did this inflationary language create or reflect? Did it mean that all priests were supposed to emulate the ethereal purity of those whose estate they theoretically eclipsed? Some contemporaries had little difficulty in picturing to themselves the ideal priest that the privilege of celebrating mass seemed to imply or demand. The *Imitation of Christ*, in the translation attributed to Richard Whitford, maintained that

a priest ought to be adorned with all virtues and to give others example of good life; his conversation should not be in the common way of the world; but with angels in heaven, or with perfect men in earth that be most disposed to serve God ... When a priest sayeth Mass he honoureth God; he maketh angels glad; he edifieth the church; he helpeth the people that be living, and giveth rest to them that be dead, and maketh himself part-taker of all good deeds.[69]

The gap that existed here between ideal and reality could not but be glaringly apparent to all but the most naïve observer. There were, to recall an expression attributed to J. A. Froude, a great many 'unpleasing priests' in early sixteenth-century England, and the grandly poetic conceptions of priesthood had in some way to accommodate the fact that the great mystery and miracle of the mass was in the main brought about by the agency of often very ordinary and imperfect men. Some learned contemporaries found the contradictions inherent in this difficult to reconcile. Erasmus complained that many priests treated the celebration of masses as a mere occupation, and were bringing the sacrament into disrepute through their behaviour: 'Nowadays when the celebration is over, the man who has offered the sacrifice adjourns to drinking parties and loose talk, or to cards or dice, or goes hunting or lounges in idleness. While he is at the altar, angels wait upon him, when he leaves it he seeks the refuse of mankind.'[70] Erasmus's friend, Colet, while reminding priests of 'how clean, how scoured, how fresh' and 'polished inwardly' they ought to be if they presumed to handle the sacrament of the Lord's body, reserved even stronger condemnation for 'the abominable impiety of those miserable priests, of whom our age contains a great multitude, who fear not to rush from the bosom of some foul harlot into the temple of the Church, to the altar of Christ, to the mysteries of God!'[71] In slightly more

---

[68] This topos will be examined further in Ch. 4.

[69] *Imitation of Christ*, 233–4. The attribution to Whitford has been questioned by G. Williams, 'Two Neglected London-Welsh Clerics', *Transactions of the Honourable Society of Cymmrodorion* (1961), 30–2.   [70] Quoted in Cobb (ed.), *Rationale of Ceremonial*, p. xvii.

[71] Lupton, *Life of Colet*, 71.

restrained tones, the distinguished common lawyer, Christopher St German, argued that the eucharist itself was dishonoured by the behaviour of priests who immediately after saying mass 'dispose themselves to worldly company and outward pleasure'.[72]

Humanist reformers and anticlerical lawyers might be expected to air such attitudes, but there is evidence that the disparity between the sacral quality of the mass and the disposition of the priests who sometimes celebrated it could be equally perplexing to those of much more humble station. The parishioners of Wooton in Oxfordshire expressed disquiet to the authorities in 1520 that their curate, Thomas Philipps, habitually went straight from tending his sheep in the field to celebrating mass in the church.[73]

Such perplexity inevitably evoked a question of overwhelming importance: could priests who were wicked and impious, or even merely worldly and uninspiring, minister the sacraments of the Church, in particular the eucharist, as validly and securely as priests of the most supernal virtue? This dilemma had been exercising Christian minds and consciences since the Donatist controversy of the fourth century. In the Middle Ages the question simply refused to go away, and the neo-Donatist argument that sinful priests could not perform the sacraments became a staple of heretical thought.

On this point informed orthodox opinion was apparently unanimous. In its sermon for Corpus Christi, the *Festial* asserted that each priest had identical powers from Christ's gift 'be he better, be he worse. For that sacrament is so high and holy in himself that there may no good man amend it, nor no evil man impair it.'[74] In discussing the prerogatives of priesthood in his *Dialogue Concerning Heresies*, Thomas More likewise insisted that, however vicious and impenitent a priest might be

yet that sacred sacrifice and sweet oblation of Christ's holy body offered up by his office, can take none impairing by the filth of his sin, but highly helpeth to the upholding of this wretched world from the vengeance of the wrath of God, and is to God as acceptable and to us as available for the thing itself, as though it were offered by a better man.[75]

---

[72] C. St German, *Salem and Bizance*, in J. Guy *et al.* (eds.), *The Debellation of Salem and Bizance, CW* 10 (1987), 379. [73] *Lincoln Visitations*, i. 131.

[74] Mirc, *Festial*, 169. See also Simmons (ed.), *Lay Folk's Mass Book*, 132, 279, 374; T. Hoccleve, *Minor Poems*, ed. F. J. Furnivall, EETS ES 61 (1892), 18–19; *Storie of the Masse*, 438ᵛ; Garard, *Interpretacyon and Sygnyfycacyon of the Masse*, sig. B.ivᵛ; *Orchard of Syon*, sig. r.iʳ.

[75] More, *Dialogue*, 299. See also F. Manley *et al.* (eds.), *Letter to Bugenhagen, Supplication of Souls, Letter against Frith, CW* 7 (1990), 254.

No Christian should really, then, have had cause to doubt in the matter, but the very regularity with which the assurance was made suggests that for many people, questions regarding the ministrations of unworthy priests may have been a real worry. Significantly, the author of the *Doctrinal of Sapyence* believed an exemplum was needed to correct the views of a 'simple man that would not take the sacrament of such priests as he supposed to be evil'.[76] Such anxieties need not have been confined to the laity. When the fifteenth-century English Carthusian Nicholas Love wrote a *Short treatise of the Highest and Most worthy sacrament of Christ's Blessed Body and the Marvels therof*, he included an account of St Hugh of Lincoln's supposed encounter with a French curé, who, having sought ordination at a time when he was 'agreeing neither in years nor manners to that worthy degree', had fallen into mortal sin, yet continued to say mass without seeking confession and absolution. This priest told the holy bishop how, while consecrating the host at mass, his sin had come forcefully to mind, and he had been tempted to wonder 'whether that precious body in flesh and blood of my Lord Jesu . . . is now made, treated and received verily by me, so foul and abominable a sinner'. At the fraction of the host, however, a segment turned to bloody flesh in his hand, and terrifyingly confounded his disbelief.[77] Perhaps not too much emphasis should be laid on a didactic exemplum in a devotional work, but a genuine, and extremely poignant, example of clerical scrupulosity is provided by the case of the young Luther, who was apt to flee from the altar in terror when reflecting on his own unworthiness, and who was 'so fearful in conscience' that he would attend confession several times before saying mass.[78]

In England these questions had received greater urgency from the religious controversies set in motion in the late fourteenth century by John Wyclif. Among the propositions from Wyclif's works, condemned as heretical by the Blackfriars Council of 1382, was that 'a bishop or priest in mortal sin does not ordain, consecrate or baptize'.[79] In fact, Wyclif's attitude may have been more equivocal, at times denying any power to wicked priests, at others conceding that the ministrations of the sinful might sometimes be beneficial.[80] Among Wyclif's Lollard followers, many evinced an even more fundamental antisacerdotalism, rejecting

---

[76] G. de Roye, *The Doctrinal of Sapyence* (1489), sig. I.i^r.

[77] N. Love, *The Mirror of the Blessed Life of Jesu Christ*, ed. a monk of Parkminster (1926), 309–10.   [78] Clark, *Eucharistic Sacrifice*, 113.

[79] Hudson, *Premature Reformation*, 316.

[80] G. Leff, *Heresy in the Later Middle Ages* (Manchester, 1967), i. 526.

the very concept of a priesthood as an instrument of grace, but others were closer to the Waldensian attitude which linked spiritual power to personal sanctity. In the fifteenth century the proposition that 'a priest in mortal sin does not consecrate the body of Christ' was a regular feature of English heresy trials.[81] Particularly graphic was the insistence of the Kentish heretic, Thomas Cooper, in 1454 that he would 'no more wish to hear the mass of a bad priest than that of a barking dog'.[82] The canine motif was reprised by the Londoner, Elizabeth Sampson, who in 1509 was reported to have said 'I will not give my dog that bread that some priests doth minister at the altar when they be not in clean life.'[83] In the 1520s in London, the belief that bad priests had no power to consecrate might be held by those who supposed themselves to be Lutherans,[84] while Coverdale's translation of Calvin's *Treatise on the Lord's Supper* expressed indignation that the Catholic Church expected him to believe that 'a priest (being never so ungodly in his living, never so much subject unto sin, never so much the devil's member), is the minister of God, and that his prayer and sacrifice in the mass is acceptable to God'.[85]

Ultimately, of course, an institutional Protestant church which admitted the concept of sacraments could no more allow doubt in this matter than had its Catholic predecessor. In 1550 Bishop Ridley's visitation articles for London enquired 'whether any sayeth that the wickedness of the minister taketh away the effect of Christ's sacraments', an indication of the concern the Protestant authorities were feeling about the activities of Anabaptist sectaries, who had adopted the ancient heresy.[86] Article 27 of the 42 Articles promulgated in 1553 was designed specifically to refute the notion that the shortcomings of the minister might vitiate 'the effectual operation of God's ordinances'.[87]

In one sense it is paradoxical to wonder if the attitudes of Thomas Cooper or Elizabeth Sampson might have been shared by orthodox

[81] K. B. McFarlane, *Wycliffe and English Non-Conformity* (Harmondsworth, 1972), 110, 116; Thomson, *Later Lollards*, 28, 37, 39, 45, 79, 181; J. F. Davis, 'Lollardy and the Reformation in England', *ARG* 73 (1982), 223.   [82] Thomson, *Later Lollards*, 181.

[83] P. I. Kaufman, 'John Colet's *Opus de sacramentis* and Clerical Anticlericalism: The Limitations of "Ordinary Wayes" ', *JBS* 22 (1982), 1.

[84] *LP* iv (1). 885; iv (2), 1945; S. Brigden, 'Religion and Social Obligation in Early Sixteenth-Century London', *PP* 103 (1984), 80.

[85] M. Coverdale, *Writings and Translations of Myles Coverdale*, ed. G. Pearson, PS (1844), 530.   [86] *Visitation Articles*, ii. 239.

[87] C. Hardwick, *A History of the Articles of Religion* (1890), 324. Basically unaltered this became no. 26 of the 39 Articles: E. J. Bicknell, *A Theological Introduction to the Thirty-Nine Articles of the Church of England*, 3rd edn. (1955), 353.

believers; the opinion that only good priests could consecrate validly was by definition heretical. It is, none the less, perhaps worth considering just how far doubts and anxieties about the sacramental functions of unworthy priests, though probably never rationalized in any propositional way, may have informed the outlook of those who emphatically did not share the essentially antisacerdotal views of the Lollards. Such inchoate and unarticulated attitudes would, of course, be very difficult for the historian to reconstruct. A recent historian of the pre-Reformation clergy has asserted that, given the persistent failings of that group, 'the road to Donatism lay temptingly open', but he accepts that it is a difficult phenomenon to identify and interpret.[88] One way to cast some light upon the problem, however, might be through a detailed examination of the wills of lay people. Frequently in this period these asked for masses to be said for the testator's soul, a task for which, of course, the services of a priest were essential.

The theological rationale of this phenomenon was the belief that the fruits of the mass, which was itself the application in space and time of the merits of Christ's redemptive passion, could, through the intention of the celebrant, be applied for the needs of individuals. An unsympathetic, yet substantially accurate, account of the belief was given by the Edwardian Protestant, John Bradford: 'The mass is called and had for a sacrifice propitiatory and that such a one as fetcheth pardon *a poena et a culpa* ('from punishment and from guilt') for the quick and the dead, and for whom Sir John will.'[89] More particularly, men and women believed that votive masses could assist the souls of the departed suffering in purgatory, and, on the understanding that each mass supplied but a limited application of the fruits of the passion, the multiplication of masses came to be seen as the essential means of shortening the soul's 'stay' there. Testamentary bequests might therefore provide some insight into what the mass may have meant to the ordinary (if comparatively wealthy) layperson at the expectation of death, particularly as here people were generally thinking of the mass *per se*, independent of its wider social functions or position in the liturgical cycle of the Church. Some testators had clear views on the type of priest who was to celebrate the masses on their behalf, and it is this which is of primary interest here.

In the years 1500 to 1546, just over one third of English testators

[88] R. N. Swanson, 'Problems of the Priesthood in Pre-Reformation England', *EHR* 417 (1990), 861.

[89] J. Bradford, *The Writings of John Bradford ... Letters, Treatises, Remains*, ed. A. Townsend, PS (1853), 313.

requested masses to be said for their souls.[90] In Edward VI's reign, in the context of advancing Protestantism and official hostility to the concepts of purgatory and intercession, only just over 3 per cent did so. These bequests were more common in the earlier part of this period. Up to 1529, 44.1 per cent of wills contained them; between 1530 and 1546, this fell to 24.3 per cent. The bequests could, of course, take very different forms: some testators established chantries, which, they assumed, would ensure for them an eternal source of intercessory prayer, though far more common was the habit of requiring a limited number of masses, or of stipulating a limited period during which masses were to be said. Testators might institute an 'obit', an annual service to be celebrated on the anniversary of the testator's death, or they might ask for one or more 'trentals', a series of thirty requiem masses, often felt to be endowed with a particular efficacy. Most commonly, however, testators left money for a priest to celebrate masses for a defined period of time, which might be three months, a year, seven years, or up to twenty years and beyond. For our purposes, the crucial point is to examine what testators thought about the priests who were to administer these services, and the focus of interest will be those cases where testators stipulated that masses were to be said by a specific individual, or by a priest endowed with a number of specific attributes. This comprehended a very significant proportion of the total. Of the 1,707 wills in the sample which contained explicit requests for masses in the period 1500–46, 510 (29.9 per cent) wanted some or all of the masses to be said by a certain type of priest, while 203 (11.9 per cent) requested the services of a specified individual. In addition, 45 (2.6 per cent) wanted masses only from the regular clergy, of these, the great majority (37) favoured the friars.

The wills which required a particular type of priest did not do so in any absolutely uniform or stereotypic way, a circumstance which suggests that this feature was generally a matter of genuine individual inclination, and not a scribal or formulaic convention. Overwhelmingly, however, the attribute testators sought for in the priest was 'honesty'. The simple desire for 'an honest priest' to say the masses expressed the wishes of 58 per cent of the testators who imposed conditions on the type of priest

---

[90] This figure, 34.3% of the wills in the sample, includes only those which made specific provision for masses to be said, and does not take into account other forms of intercessory benefaction, such as requests for prayers, pilgrimages, and alms-giving; nor does it take account of the substantial number of testators who left the residue of their estate for the 'wealth of their soul' and clearly expected their executors to arrange for some form of intercession.

who was to celebrate for them. What precisely contemporaries understood by the designation 'honest' is clearly crucial to establish, and it
would be an etymological fallacy to assume that its meaning and associations have passed unchanged into twentieth-century usage. In this context, honesty was probably largely associated with sexual conduct,[91] though
it cannot be regarded purely as a synonym for 'chaste'. The term seems
to have embraced a number of values including honour and respectability
as well as probity and candour.[92] It was shorthand for all the virtues one
would expect, or hope, to find in a priest, though testators sometimes
linked the phrase with other desirable attributes, expressing the wish for
a priest who was 'honest and discrete', 'honest and well disposed', 'honest
and virtuous', or 'honest and of good conversation'. Other popular requirements were that the priest be 'of good name and fame', 'sad' (i.e.
serious and steadfast), 'convenient', 'able', 'sufficient', and 'suitable' (in
Latin, *idoneus*). These attributes were considered far more important than
experience or scholarly learning, and the sample contains only one example of a specifically educational qualification being imposed.[93] There were,
however, several testators who wanted their priest to be 'a good choirman'
and to have ability in plainsong. A few others (six in all) wanted an
Oxford or Cambridge scholar. About twenty merely requested a secular
priest, though one should be wary of reading an antifraternal implication
into this, as such wills often included gifts to the friars as well. Some
others may have taken the opportunity to exercise posthumous patronage,
by insisting on a priest who was 'not beneficed'. The Yorkshireman, John
Holme, left money in 1513 for a trental to be said by 'a poor priest being
out of service'. In Oxfordshire in 1544 George Longford simply wanted
'a priest that is without wages', perhaps because such a priest would not
lack time to devote himself to his intercessory duties.[94]

Admittedly, what testators and their executors regarded as rendering
an applicant 'sufficient' or 'convenient' may not be immediately obvious
to us. It was, nevertheless, rare for a testator to describe a hoped-for
priest without including some unmistakably moral qualification.[95] Even if

---

[91] See below, pp. 161–2.   [92] See *OED*, 2nd edn. (1989).

[93] In 1504 Robert Wedon of Buckinghamshire requested a suitable chaplain 'scienciam habenti'. Elvey (ed.), *Courts of the Archdeaconry of Buckingham*, 196.

[94] *Test. Ebor.* v. 44; PRO, PCC, Prob. 11, 32 Pynnyng.

[95] The question of the significance of such testamentary formulae was first raised in the 1930s by the French historian, Pierre Janelle, who had little doubt that they reflected popular anxiety about the validity of the masses of unworthy celebrants. However, his reliance on a narrow range of printed sources means his contention that the practice was particularly prevalent in the north of England can be discounted. P. Janelle, *L'Angleterre catholique à la veille du schisme* (Paris, 1935), 33–4.

we exclude the designations 'lawful', 'fit', 'able', 'sufficient', 'suitable', and 'convenient' as having no explicitly moral connotations (which is extremely unlikely), then over 80 per cent of the testators who imposed conditions on the choice of their priest seem to have been concerned about his virtue and standards of behaviour.

It is in a sense harder to elucidate the motives of testators who wanted masses to be said for them by a named individual. Sometimes the priests concerned were their relatives, and the bequests might reflect a sense of family loyalty or obligation. In 1505, for example, John Philippes of Eston in Hampshire left money for his son's exhibition to Oxford, as well as to celebrate masses for his father's soul; in 1510 Henry Savile willed that his son should celebrate for him for a year when he became a priest.[96] In other cases one can surmise that the priest named was a personal friend of the deceased, and that the bequest was, at least in part, concerned with rewarding and favouring that individual. Sometimes, however, testators added the stipulation that 'some other honest priest' was to be chosen if their preferred candidate was unable or unwilling to meet the commitment. This does not, of course, exclude the possibility that people were eager to reward their friends and relations, but it does imply that in many cases the primary motivation for naming a specific individual might be that the testator knew that priest to be honest. The relative infrequency with which testators seem to have asked for their kinsmen to celebrate for them (and there could have been few Tudor English men and women who did not have some relation in holy orders) perhaps supports this interpretation: testators did not automatically expect or want their cousins or nephews to be their sacramental advocates.

It is perhaps acceptable, then, to add together the testators who specified the attributes of the priest with those who asked for an individual, and to suggest that over 40 per cent of mass-bequests may have been in some way concerned with the *quality* of the priest involved. If we include those who asked for masses only from friars and monks, the percentage grows even higher. Interestingly, this was not a constant throughout the early Tudor period. Prior to 1530, 49 per cent of bequests for masses fall into this category; between 1530 and 1546 the figure is 35.1 per cent. It would be unwise to suggest with any assurance that this represented a declining preoccupation with the personal qualities of the priest. It could be that it reflected a change in the type of bequests favoured by testators. There seems after 1530 to have been a rise in relatively short-term endowments

[96] PRO, PCC, Prob. 11, 40 Holgrave; J. W. Clay and E. W. Crossley (eds.), *Halifax Wills 1389–1544* (Halifax, 1904), 37.

at the expense of more lavish and long-term benefactions. Before 1530, for example, 20.5 per cent of the mass-bequests in the sample were for trentals, whereas this rose to 28.9 per cent after 1530. There seems, in fact, though one should not overemphasize the principle, to have been a corollary between the length of the endowment and the likelihood of the testator's specifying the attributes or identity of the priest. In the period 1500–46, only 2.8 per cent of the testators instituting obits bothered to 'define' the celebrant; with trentals this rose to 27.8 per cent. When masses were to be said for a period up to and including a year, the figure was 59.3 per cent; up to 6 years, 61.2 per cent; up to 19 years, 66.7 per cent, and 20 years and over, 68 per cent. Curiously, only just over half the testators in the sample who endowed perpetual chantries evinced this concern. Perhaps this reflected a feeling that in the long term things would work themselves out, or that in the case of a permanent appointment executors would be more careful (or perhaps simply the inadequacies of the sample). In general, however, the principle seems clear: those testators who were both anxious and wealthy enough to make long-term provision for the health of their souls were much more likely to insist upon a good moral character in the priest who was to be hired.

There were some testators who seem to have looked to the quantity rather than the quality of clerical ministrations. In 1526 Richard Leke, a brewer of Oxford, left 200 groats for no less than 200 priests to say mass and *dirige* on the day of his burial, and wanted the event duplicated on his 'month's mind' and 'year's mind'. Hiring clerics on this scale was exceptional, but even in the mid-1540s a Durham tanner, Robert Biddic, expected thirty priests to say mass at his funeral and it was by no means uncommon for testators to leave a small sum to every priest prepared to come to their burial and month's mind and to say a mass.[97] Other testators placed their trust in the efficacy of certain masses or groups of masses, in particular the 'trental of St Gregory', with its legendary associations of being able to secure a speedy release from purgatory.[98] Also requested were masses of the Holy Ghost, of the Five Wounds, of the Name of Jesus, of the Holy Trinity, of Our Lady, or the recitation during the mass or at other times of the psalms *De profundis*, and *Miserere mei deus*. Sometimes testators exhibited a concern with the very punctuation

---

[97] PRO, PCC, Prob. 11, 9 Porch; J. C. Hodgson (ed.), *Wills and Inventories from the Registry at Durham*, SS 112 (1906), 1; PRO, PCC, Prob. 11, 3 Alenger.

[98] This was requested by 13 testators in the sample. For the trental of St Gregory, see Clark, *Eucharistic Sacrifice*, 57–8; N. P. Tanner, *The Church in Late Medieval Norwich, 1370–1532* (Toronto, 1984), 102–3; Duffy, *Stripping of the Altars*, 293–4, 370–6.

of what we might term their 'liturgical literacy'. William Millet of Dartford in Kent stipulated in 1500 that his priest, in addition to his mass, was to say for five days the psalm *Miserere mei deus*, 'and when he beginneth to say it let him say these words "miserere mei deus" five times with casting up heart and eyes to Almighty God as heartily as he can'.[99] An Essex contemporary laid down that the priest saying the St Gregory trentals for him begin the exequies every day about the second hour after *nones*, starting mass about the ninth hour, and that he should maintain a strict fast on every Friday throughout the year without fish or milk products.[100] As late as 1545 a testator in Kent insisted that between the feasts of the Annunciation and St Michael the Archangel, mass was to begin at 8 o'clock, and at other times of the year at 9, that Mass of Jesus be sung every Friday, and that every weekday in Lent an anthem be sung in the parish church.[101]

It is probably wrong, however, to view the testators (comparatively few in number) who insisted on special masses or services as having an especially or extreme 'mechanistic' view of the salvific role of the mass, a stronger belief in what Weber regarded as its function of 'coercing' the deity. These testators were just as likely to insist upon moral qualifications for their officiating priests, and there is no necessary inconsistency in bequests like that of Sir John Fitzjames in 1538 which combined quantity, quality, and liturgical nicety in requesting 'fifteen masses of the Five Woundes of our Lord by fifteen most honest priests'.[102] Works like the *Interpretacyon and Sygnyfycacyon of the Masse* might encourage the notion that the recitation of seven so-called 'golden masses' could lead to souls 'flying out of purgatory as thicke as sparks of fire', but the *sine qua non* was still the participation of a 'devout priest'.[103]

All of this raises, of course, considerable interpretative difficulties. Can one really regard those testators who expressed a preference for 'honest priests' as quasi-Donatists, sharing, albeit partially or unconsciously, in the Lollards' contemptuous rejection of the masses of sinful priests? Noting similar features in the wills of laymen in late medieval Norwich, Norman Tanner has suggested that 'such requirements probably express the wish that deserving priests find employment rather than the belief that the value of a mass comes "ex opere operantis" not "ex opere

---

[99] PRO, PCC, Prob. 11, 18 Moore.
[100] G. M. Benton (ed.), 'Essex Wills at Canterbury', *Transactions of the Essex Archaeological Society*, 21 (1937), 261.   [101] PRO, PCC, Prob. 11, 33 Pynnyng (John Bisshop).
[102] F. W. Weaver (ed.), *Somerset Medieval Wills, 1531–1558*, SRS 21 (1905), 48.
[103] Garard, *Interpretacyon and Sygnyfycacyon of the Masse*, sig. C.i{{v}}.

operato"'.[104] Clearly, something of that impulse must be present, but one wonders whether the two motives had necessarily to be mutually exclusive, or indeed whether such a clear and radical distinction between these two modes of sacramental action could have existed within the popular lay mind.

As we have seen, religious writers insisted on the validity of a mass celebrated by an unworthy and sinful priest, but this does not necessarily imply that we have to posit a fundamental dichotomy of 'popular' and 'official' belief regarding the issue. No writer was so bold as to assert that the manner of life of priests celebrating the mass was a matter of little or no importance, and the lay people we have been discussing formulated their testamentary wishes in the context of a climate of thought which held that when unworthy priests celebrated the mass they were acting at best ambiguously, and at worst, literally, damnably. The dilemma in which the orthodox found themselves was exposed neatly by 'the Messenger', the relentless questioner of traditional values who participates in More's *Dialogue Concerning Heresies*. The Messenger affected to marvel at the suggestion that it would be better to have fewer and better priests, 'For if their masses be so good for us, be themselves never so nought, then seemeth it better for us to make yet more though they were yet worse, that we might have more masses.'[105] The solution to this conundrum, More suggested, was that although God might accept the oblation for the sake of others, 'yet he is with that priest's presumption highly discontented'. The proper Christian attitude was to be prepared to forgo the benefit of a mass rather than to suffer God to be offended by any such 'odious minister'.[106] This issue was one on which More felt deeply and he returned to it in his *De Tristitia Christi*, arguing with reference to Christ's betrayal by Judas that 'Christ is also betrayed into the hands of sinners when His most holy body in the sacrament is consecrated and handled by unchaste, profligate, and sacrilegious priests.'[107] Yet horror at the idea of sinful priests celebrating the mass was not an idiosyncratic quirk of Thomas More but a concept deeply enmeshed in contemporary religious culture. *The Traytte of Good Lyvyng and Good Deying*, printed in Paris in 1503, laid down as axiomatic that 'any minister of holy church may not give nor administer the sacraments, he being in deadly sin, but he sins deadly', and the stern judgement of canon law was that the masses of sinful and unshriven priests were best described as 'execrations and cursings'.[108]

[104] Tanner, *Church in Late Medieval Norwich*, 109.   [105] More, *Dialogue*, 299.
[106] Ibid.   [107] T. More, *De Tristitia Christi*, ed. C. H. Miller, *CW* 14 (1976), 351.
[108] *The Traytte of Good Lyvyng and Good Deying*, 36ᵛ; *Lyndwood*, 153; B. Cooke, *Ministry to Word and Sacraments: History and Theology* (Philadelphia, 1977), 582.

While stressing the worship of the angels that virtuous priests would accumulate by saying mass, the Corpus Christi sermon in a contemporary collection warned that 'he that is an evil liver, and wot himself in deadly sin, and is in no purpose to amend him, be he sure for to have a perpetual confusion of fiends in hell, and be under them in everlasting pain'.[109]

The problem, however, went deeper than the irreverence and disrespect for the sacrament implicit in such priests' behaviour. Posing the question of whether 'it be more for the soul's health to hear mass of a devout and virtuous priest than of an evil priest', the *Interpretacyon and Sygnyfycacyon of the Masse* reported the opinion of 'devout doctors' that the mass could be considered under three heads: in terms of the real presence, in terms of the votive purpose of the mass, and in terms of the prayers said by the priest during the mass. The reality of Christ's presence was not, of course, affected by the virtue or otherwise of the priest, though 'nevertheless the evil priest being in sin doth receive it to his damnation'. Nor could the unworthiness of the celebrant impair the application of the fruits of the mass 'if it be said . . . for other persons and not for himself'. But in the third case, 'touching the prayers and orisons, the which the priest sayeth in the mass time . . . then the mass said of a good and devout priest is more better than of a sinner and an evil priest'.[110] The idea that the prayers of an unworthy priest were ineffectual was not unique to this work, but had long been current in devotional writing.[111] One is entitled to wonder, however, whether all laymen would have understood the distinction apparently being drawn here between the votive value of the mass as a propitiatory sacrifice, and the intercessory value of the mass as prayer articulated by the priest. The intention could surely not have been to refer only to the private mental prayer which the priest might, or might not, make during the course of the mass, but to his public and liturgical role. In the canon of the mass the priest was directed to pray both for the living and the dead, asking God to remember them, yet if the priest were a wicked one, these petitions might be null and void.[112] Doubtless there were those who could follow the technical distinctions involved, and who recognized that the mass of any ordained celebrant was in essence equally efficacious, but the impression had nevertheless been conveyed that the mass of a sinful priest was somehow less

[109] Mirc, *Festial*, 169.

[110] Garard, *Interpretacyon and Sygnyfycacyon of the Masse*, sig. B.iv[v].

[111] Manning, *People's Faith in the Time of Wyclif*, 72; Simmons (ed.), *Lay Folk's Mass Book*, 374; de Roye, *Doctrinal of Sapyence*, sig. I.i[r]; More, *Dialogue*, 299; Rubin, *Corpus Christi*, 220; Duffy, *Stripping of the Altars*, 365–6.

[112] F. E. Warren (ed.), *The Sarum Missal in English* (1911), 43, 47.

powerful than that of a virtuous one, and the desire of testators to secure 'honest priests' to sing for their souls becomes more understandable and more pressing. When Richard Aylef of Hampshire requested in 1540 that an honest priest should celebrate for him, he added a codicil in which a note of anxiety is clearly discernible: 'I charge my executors and overseers of my testament upon their conscience to see the ability and sufficiency of the priest that shall sing for me.'[113] Nor is it surprising that some testators envisaged the removal and replacement of their intercessors if their behaviour fell from the prerequisite standards of moral rectitude. Nicholas Talbot of Bury St Edmunds left money in 1501 for a good and virtuous priest to celebrate for seven years, and added 'if he be not virtuous, I pray you that be my executors, let him be changed'.[114] In 1529 in Leicestershire Sir John Digby endowed an 'able' chantry priest, but stipulated his replacement 'if the said priest be worthy to be put from his said service by reason of any incontinence of living or misbehaviour', while in 1533, Edmund Robyns, a yeoman of Appledore in Kent, showing great sensitivity to the personal conflicts that often marred village life, provided that if 'five or six of the honest and indifferent persons of the said parish of Appledore shall have cause without malice borne by them to the said priest' to complain that he was not 'of honest condition and behaviour', and if after one warning he was not 'thenceforth . . . of good behaviour as a priest ought to be', then the executors were to dismiss him and to hire another honest priest.[115]

The natural corollary to the suggestion that the prayers, even the liturgical prayers, of wicked priests were virtually nugatory, was to place an inflated value on the imprecations of supposedly saintly priests, a tendency that may have been encouraged from the fourteenth century by the mendicants' claims to especial holiness and power.[116] The *Interpretacyon and Sygnyfycacyon of the Masse*, while accepting the idea that 'the holy sacrament consecrate of the priest is in all masses and of all priests of like power and might, as touching the holy sacrament', nevertheless sought to advance the notion that the first mass of a newly ordained priest was unusually efficacious, 'for in the first mass the priests be wont to prepare themself more devoutly: than at another time, and therefore their prayers

[113] PRO, PCC, Prob. 11, 24 Alenger.

[114] S. Tymms (ed.), *Wills and Inventories from the Registers of the Commissary of Bury St Edmunds and the Archdeacon of Sudbury*, CS 49 (1850), 88.

[115] A. Clark (ed.), *Lincoln Diocese Documents, 1450–1544*, EETS 149 (1914), 139; PRO, PCC, Prob. 11, 3 Hogen. See also Swanson, *Church and Society*, 61; C. Platt, *The English Medieval Town* (1976), 169.   [116] Manning, *People's Faith in the Time of Wyclif*, 70.

be then more acceptable, devout, and fervent to pray for them that do hear their first masses for to obtain grace'.[117] This may explain Thomas Waldyng of Pontefract's eagerness in 1507 for 'two priests which shall newly sing their first mass to be elect at the discretion of my executors to sing for the health of my soul for one year'.[118]

PREPARING TO CELEBRATE

Given the apparent strength of feeling regarding the intolerable admixture of the holy and the unholy that the sacramental functions of unworthy priests seemed to imply, the Church had to find some *modus vivendi*, some way of reconciling the exalted claims of priesthood with the harsh realities of sin and failure. It was all very well for Thomas More to advance the slogan of fewer priests and better, but, as J. R. Lander has reminded us, this remained an impossible solution as long as both popular and educated piety demanded the provision of so many masses.[119] At the very least it might be expected that priests, though, like other men, ineluctably fallible in their daily lives, should seek in some way to sanctify themselves before embarking on the celebration of the sacred mysteries. Sarum and York missals provided special prayers for the priest to say before mass, asking to be freed from sin and made worthy to offer sacrifice. The latter work asked rhetorically, 'what must be the reverence and veneration, what must be the chastity of body and purity of soul with which man ought to celebrate this divine and heavenly sacrifice . . . who can worthily celebrate this rite unless thou, who art God almighty, make him worthy to offer?'[120] In the mass itself the *lavabo* and the accompanying rite symbolized the priest's intention to wash away his sinful nature, before starting the consecration. The laity, so often considered totally passive bystanders, were invited to participate in this process of preparation. The so-called *Lay Folk's Mass Book* instructed its readers to say during the office

> . . . Lord thou save
> the priest, that it shall say,
> from great temptation this ilka day
> that he be clean in deed and thought

---

[117] Garard, *Interpretacyon and Sygnyfycacyon of the Masse*, sig. B.iv^r.

[118] R. B. Cook (ed.), *Early Pontefract Wills*, Thoresby Society, 26 (1924), 342.

[119] J. R. Lander, *Government and Community: England, 1450–1509* (Cambridge, Mass., 1980), 129.   [120] Clark, *Eucharistic Sacrifice*, 552; Warren (ed.), *Sarum Missal*, 17–19.

                          that evil spirit noy him nought
                          to fulfil this sacrament . . .[121]

Lydgate's *Merita Missae* likewise advised laypeople to pray for the priest
at the start of mass

                          Thou for him, and he for thee,
                          And that is a deed of charity.[122]

Indeed, after the offertory and the washing of hands, the priest was
specifically to ask the people to pray for him in the *orate fratres*.[123]
    More important than any of this, however, was the duty of any priest
in mortal sin to avail himself of the sacrament of penance before saying
mass: this was an explicit requirement of canon law, and without absolution validly conferred no such priest was in theory allowed to celebrate.[124]
According to the *Speculum Sacerdotale*, 'it behoveth priests for to be
cleaner cleansed of sin by confession and penance more than another
man, for their privilege in that they the ofter receiveth the body of
Christ'.[125] There is evidence that some priests perhaps did habitually
confess in preparation for mass. When, in about 1518, Richard Carder of
Iver in Buckinghamshire confronted his wife with her suspicious friend-
ship with the vicar, she retorted, 'how could he be evil with her, seeing
he sayeth mass every day, and doth confess himself before?'[126] In a case
which came before the Court of Requests in 1532, a priest claimed to
have been violently disturbed as he 'kneeled in confession' in the chancel
of his parish church 'preparing himself to mass'.[127] Evidence as to the
manner and regularity of priestly confession is, however, sparse. Certainly,
provincial canons had complained of its infrequency, and the authorities
had attempted to rectify the situation with the appointment of special
confessors in each deanery.[128] Yet Thomas Becon was able to write sarcastically of priests celebrating mass, having 'given yourself absolution,
for lack of a ghostly father'.[129] There must, moreover, have been certain
priests whose very lifestyle effectively barred them from the forgiveness
of sin guaranteed by the confessional. A concubinary, for example, with
no intention to separate from his partner, could not validly have been
granted absolution, and, as we have noted, his status as celebrant of the

---

    [121] Simmons (ed.), *Lay Folk's Mass Book*, 5.   [122] *Vertue of Y^e Masse*, sig. A.viii^v.
    [123] J. Wickham Legg (ed.), *The Sarum Missal* (1916), 219.   [124] *Lyndwood*, 149.
    [125] Weatherley (ed.), *Speculum Sacerdotale*, 86.
    [126] Foxe, *Acts and Monuments*, iv. 231.   [127] PRO, Req. 2, 7/38.
    [128] *Lyndwood*, 146, 152–3; R. M. Wooley (ed.), *The York Provinciale put forth by Thomas
Wolsey* (1931), 56.   [129] Becon, *Displaying of the Popish Mass*, 263.

mass would have remained highly ambivalent. In the fifteenth century Thomas Hoccleve had reproached his readers by insisting that no man could know the state of another's soul, and even implied that it was unlikely a priest in mortal sin would dare undertake to say mass.[130] Too often, one suspects, experience would have taught otherwise.

The very least that laypeople could expect was for a priest to be in charity with his neighbours before embarking on the mass, itself the symbol of perfect charity. To be in charity was considered by contemporaries a precondition for the reception of the body of Christ, and priests were instructed to deny the eucharist to anyone still bearing a grudge.[131] Priests did in fact sometimes refuse communion to those who could not agree with their neighbours, an action which may have been unpopular with the objects of the sanction, but which undoubtedly provided an effective practical demonstration of the Church's understanding of the significance of the eucharist.[132] Most laypeople, however, received the body of Christ only once a year; priests received His body and blood daily, and for them the need to be in charity might seem particularly acute. The *Vertue of Yᵉ Masse*, attributed to Lydgate, carried the stern warning,

> Beware ye priests when ye mass sing
> That love and charity be not far absent,[133]

while in the *Interlude of Youth* (*c.*1514), the personification of charity is made to exclaim,

> And all priests that be
> May sing no mass without charity;
> And charity to them they do not take,
> They may not receive him that did them make,
> And all this world, of nought.[134]

Among the many complaints catalogued against Thomas Kyrkeby, the parish priest of Halsall in Lancashire in 1531, was the charge that after having on various occasions threatened and insulted some of the poor people of the parish, calling them 'knaves and other ungodly names', he had 'gone on straight way' to say mass and other divine service.[135] A more appropriate, though in pastoral terms perhaps equally problematic,

---

[130] Hoccleve, *Minor Poems*, 19.

[131] Balliol MS 354, 180ʳ. See also Brigden, 'Religion and Social Obligation', 73–4; Mirc, *Festial*, 131. [132] See below, pp. 185–6.

[133] *Vertue of Yʳ Masse*, sig. A.viiiᵛ.

[134] I. Lancashire (ed.), *Two Tudor Interludes* (Manchester, 1980), 104.

[135] H. Fishwick (ed.), *Pleadings and Depositions in the Duchy Court of Lancaster, Time of Henry VII and Henry VIII*, Lancashire and Cheshire Record Society, 32 (1896), i. 199.

response was evinced by Ralph Willett, parish priest of Shirland in Derbyshire in around 1536. On a certain Sunday he had met and quarrelled with the young John Revell and his friend Leonard, who were returning from breakfast together. When Willett told Revell that 'the devil was in him', Revell's answer was to take a 'piece of pudding' from his friend Leonard's hand, and to thrust it into the priest's mouth, 'wherewith the said Sir Ralph, being in great fury said no masses that day'.[136]

It was, of course, extremely difficult for a priest to remain in charity with all of his parishioners, all of the time. Perceived inadequacies of pastoral care, squabbles over tithes and mortuaries, and, increasingly from the 1530s, over religio-political questions, or simply personal incompatibilities; all could sour relations within a parish, and cast their shadow over the celebration of the eucharist itself. In June 1511 Richard Loose of Wissett in Suffolk was cited before the Norwich Consistory Court for the ostensibly Lollard utterance that 'he had as lieve see an oyster shell betwixt the vicar's hands at the sacring of the mass as the blessed sacrament'. But Loose, who apparently 'could not brook' the vicar of Bramefield, claimed that he had 'spoken in passion', because abusive words had been exchanged between the vicar and him.[137] When relations between a priest and one of his parishioners became badly strained, the latter might also refuse to receive their 'houseling' from the former, a gesture which could be construed as a pungent comment on the priest's worthiness to consecrate and distribute the body of Christ. In the late 1540s, Robert Abell, rector of Tendring in Essex, was in dispute with a parishioner, John Sadler, over the latter's tithes, and complained that Sadler would not be confessed by him at Easter, and 'refused to receive the said blessed sacrament at his hand'.[138] The monumental quarrel of John Gallampton and Thomas Sprent, vicar of Pawlett in Somerset, reached its symbolic climax at Easter 1541 when Gallampton (or so at least Sprent claimed) sought to keep the parishioners from coming to communion, and declared openly that he 'had liever receive the sacrament at a dog's mouth than of . . . [Sprent's] hand'.[139] In October 1550 it was reported of Reginald Broke, the vicar of Newington in Kent, that a number of his parishioners found that 'the said vicar's hand is so sore divers times in the year that they could not find it in their hearts to receive the communion at his hands'.[140]

---

[136] PRO, STA. C. 2, 26/194.   [137] *NCCD*, no. 117.
[138] PRO, C. 1, 1077/1.   [139] PRO, STA. C. 2, 31/120.
[140] C. E. Woodruff (ed.), 'Extracts from Original Documents Illustrating the Progress of the Reformation in Kent', *AC* 31 (1915), 98. The witness who supplied this information

The mass, it has been suggested, was of immense importance to Catholic laypeople, both as a manifestation of God's presence in their lives, and as a means of succouring them after their deaths. Popular and learned sentiment seemed to agree that only men of the highest moral calibre should be entrusted with its administration, but it was equally apparent to all that this was not always the case. The resultant incongruity, whereby the essential sanctifying office of the Church might seem to be entrusted to the sinful, the wrathful, or the lustful, was a source of considerable disquiet. In the mass the celebrating priest was identified with Christ, the great High Priest, and as such was presented to the people as a type of the perfection of mankind. Moreover, in the mass the priest handled, broke, and consumed the really present Christ in a manner to which even the most pious laymen could never aspire. Yet there was no guarantee that priests were necessarily more virtuous than laypeople. Practical efforts to resolve these antinomies might appear fragile and contingent. Was, then, this approximation of the imperfect to the perfect hypocritical, blasphemous even, or could the apparent paradox be resolved in any other emotionally and theologically satisfying ways? This question will be more directly addressed in due course, but for the moment it is necessary to consider the antithesis of the proposition, the Protestant ideas concerning the mass and priesthood which began entering England from the early 1520s.

THE HERETICAL CRITIQUE; THE ORTHODOX RESPONSE

To Protestants, the mass was almost the quintessence of blasphemy, an idolatrous caricature of the scriptural sacrament of the Lord's Supper, 'the most abominable and damnable idol that ever Satan with all his craft could invent'.[141] At the root of the malaise, Protestants discovered the exclusivity of the mass as a priestly sacrifice: if priests were men of but common virtue (and some Protestant propagandists suggested they were almost invariably vicious, vengeful, and licentious), how could God have intended the means of salvation to be concentrated so closely in their

admitted, however, that he had received communion from the vicar and 'felt no evil savour thereat', an equally revealing instance of how attitudes to the eucharist might be conditioned by the priests who ministered it.

[141] *The v. abominable Blasphemies conteinid in the Masse* (1548), quoted in N. Pocock, 'The Condition of Morals and Religious Belief in the Reign of Edward VI', *EHR* 39 (1895), 419.

hands? The priest celebrated the mass at an altar away from the people, separated from them physically by the rood screen and the space of the chancel, and mentally by the use of a special liturgical language. The congregation, claimed Protestants, 'understand nothing at all', their sole contribution was to exercise themselves in a mechanical and essentially vacuous ritualism: 'when ye rehearse the name of Jesus, they learn to make solemn courtesy; and so, a piece of the gospel being once read, they stroke themselves on the head and kiss the nail of their right thumb, and sit down again as wise as they were afore'.[142] Thomas Becon detected in the pattern of the mass a deliberate reviling of the laity: 'the massmonger, altogether unhonestly and ungently turning himself from the people, standeth at an altar after the manner of Aharon, the unclean parts of his body turned to the people'.[143] Most offensive of all, however, was the fact that the priest alone communicated. Whereas Christ had fed his disciples at the Last Supper, priests 'like swinish beasts . . . eat and drink up all alone yourselves'.[144] Protestant feeling on this issue was exemplified in the poignant image of the priest's blessing the people with an empty cup.[145]

It was true, of course, that most worshippers could not understand the Latin texts of the mass, that preaching at the mass was generally intermittent and of doubtful quality, that except at Easter, priests usually communicated alone. Even the works which were designed to promote a better devotional attitude among the laity, such as the primers, or books of hours, and the 'allegorical' works cited from above, provided nothing approximating to a translation of the texts of the liturgy; rather, they sought to promote devotions independent of and parallel to those performed by the priest.[146] The *Interpretacyon and Sygnyfycacyon of the Masse* cited canonical authority for its opinion that it was enough merely to be present at mass, irrespective of whether any of the words could be heard or understood; it was, significantly, 'sufficient if he do see the priest'.[147] Stephen Gardiner was later to argue that 'it was never meant that the

---

[142] Hilarie, *Resurrecion of the Masse*, sig. A.iv^r; Becon, *Displaying of the Popish Mass*, 257.

[143] Becon, *A Comparison between the Lord's Supper and the Pope's Mass*, in *Prayers and Other Pieces*, ed. Ayre, 356.

[144] Becon, *Displaying of the Popish Mass*, 268. The concept of priestly 'gluttony' in the mass was a recurrent feature of Protestant criticism. See Coverdale, *Writings and Translations*, 530; Hilarie, *Resurrecion of the Masse*, sig. B.iii^v; Bradford, *Writings*, 315; N. Ridley, *The Works of Nicholas Ridley*, ed. H. Christmas, PS (1843), 108; F. Rose-Troup, *The Western Rebellion of 1549* (1913), 336.

[145] Becon, *Displaying of the Popish Mass*, 268; Hilarie, *Resurrecion of the Masse*, sig. B.iv^r; Bradford, *Writings*, 316.

[146] Aston, *Lollards and Reformers*, 122; Manning, *People's Faith*, 8; Brilioth, *Eucharistic Faith and Practice*, 83.   [147] Garard, *Interpretacyon and Sygnyfycacyon of the Masse*, sig. C.i^r.

people should indeed hear the mattins or hear the mass, but be present there and pray themselves in silence'.[148]

Such attitudes were guaranteed to rouse Protestant writers to the pinnacle of scornful invective, yet when, in his *New Dialogue wherein is conteyned the examinatio[n] of the Messe*, William Turner made his Catholic apologist, Porphyrius, declare the mass to be 'such a high and inscrutable mystery, that no lay man ought to resolve or dispute of it', he was scarcely caricaturing a certain type of orthodox attitude.[149] The reform-conscious bishops who drew up the 'Rationale of Ceremonial' in the early 1540s might maintain that the canon of the mass was recited secretly as a token of reverence and to facilitate devotion, and 'not because it is unlawful to be heard, read or known of the people', but this was by no means the unanimous conclusion of late medieval English Catholicism.[150] A particular concern was that if laypeople were to learn phrases that occurred in the canon, and especially the words of institution, then they might attempt to use them for magical or irreverent purposes.[151] The *Storie of the Mass* in Caxton's edition of the *Golden Legend* typified this concern, and provided an apposite exemplum: in ancient times when most people knew the words, some shepherds took bread and, laying it on a stone, recited the words of institution over it. The bread was miraculously converted into flesh, but 'soon after by the will of God, fire descended from heaven upon them and they were all combusted and burnt' for their presumption.[152] Other expositions of the mass for the laity were happy to provide a detailed account of the actions of the celebrant, but tended to leave out the words of consecration, 'that no man but a priest should read'.[153] An episode recounted by John Foxe suggests something of the jealousy with which priests were perceived to guard their monopoly of these arcane matters: when, in around 1520, a Buckinghamshire man spoke slightingly of the real presence before his wife's brother, a priest, the latter retorted that 'it was not meet for any layman to speak of such things'.[154]

Some recent writing on the pre-Reformation mass has suggested, plausibly enough, that though formal liturgical participation by the laity in

[148] S. Gardiner, *The Letters of Stephen Gardiner*, ed. J. A. Muller (Cambridge, 1933), 355.

[149] Turner, *Examination of the Messe*, sig. B.ii^r.

[150] Cobb (ed.), *Rationale of Ceremonial*, 23.

[151] J. Bossy, 'The Mass as a Social Institution, 1200–1700', *PP* 100 (1983), 33.

[152] *Storie of the Masse*, 438^r. The work did go on to give an English paraphrase of the consecration, but referred coyly to 'five words sacramental' spoken by the priest.

[153] Simmons (ed.), *Lay Folk's Mass Book*, 147.

[154] Foxe, *Acts and Monuments*, iv. 234.

the celebration of the mass may have been minimal, laypeople did not necessarily feel ostracized or excluded. They could, for example, contribute to the offertory, and participate actively in the ceremonies of the *pax* and of holy bread.[155] More importantly, perhaps, they would have believed that the essential purpose of the mass was for Christ to be made present for them, and shown to them at the elevation. None the less, all of this had to coexist with a keen awareness of the prerogatives of the priest. Laymen, unlike priests, were not permitted to touch the consecrated host; when they received it, it was placed directly in their mouths. In addition they never received the eucharist under the form of wine, though this was an essential aspect of the priest's communion. The withdrawal of the wine from lay communicants in the course of the Middle Ages had been occasioned by a fear that the sacred species might be spilt or mishandled, and was justified theologically by the doctrine of concomitance, the belief that the entire Christ was present under either form. A consequence of this prohibition was that the chalice itself came to be seen as a ritual object which the laity was forbidden to touch or handle in any way. Even the devout lay server was to take care 'that he do not touch the chalice, paten, or corporas, for if he do he doth offend'.[156] Foxe provides an account of how a Protestant might try to ridicule or undermine this dictum. Robert Man, a servant who abjured in London diocese in 1531, was apparently in the habit of asking priests 'whether a man were accursed, if he handled a chalice, or no?' On the priest's affirming it to be so, he would then ask 'if a man have a sheep-skin on his hand . . . he may handle it' (i.e. a pair of gloves). When the priest again agreed, Man would then triumphantly complete the syllogism by announcing 'ye will make me believe, that God put more virtue in a sheep-skin than he did in a Christian man's hand, for whom he died'.[157] This striking juxtaposition may have been a commonplace of Protestant objections to clerical ascendancy over the laity. In 1545 the heretical vicar of Streatley in Bedfordshire, John Carter, was accused before the Bishop of Lincoln of noting the incongruity of men being unable to touch the chalice with the hand God made, but permitted to do so with a towel or a 'rotten sheep's skin'.[158]

---

[155] Bossy, 'Mass as a Social Institution', 35–6; J. J. Scarisbrick, *The Reformation and the English People* (Oxford, 1984), 43–4. Moreover, as Eamon Duffy has recently reminded us, by no means all late medieval masses were performed at the distant high altar. Many laypeople attended weekday 'low' masses where the liturgical celebration was of necessity more intimate and accessible: *Stripping of the Altars*, 111–13.

[156] Garard, *Interpretacyon and Sygnyfycacyon of the Masse*, sig. H.iii[r].

[157] Foxe, *Acts and Monuments*, v. 33.

[158] J. Fines (ed.), *A Bibliographical Register of Early English Protestants . . . 1525–1558, part 1* (1981), s.v. Carter.

The issue was more than a minor detail of liturgical etiquette; it spoke eloquently of the respective rights and responsibilities of clerical and lay, and some priests were highly reluctant to surrender their prerogative in this matter. In 1550 Reginald Broke, the vicar of Newington in Kent, was reported to the authorities for the, by now, 'superstitious opinion' that 'the chalice handled by a temporal man's hand was prophaned, and that he would sing with none such'. Whoever presumed to take the chalice in his hands 'sought his own damnation'.[159] In view of the vehemence with which the prohibition was sometimes affirmed, it is perhaps surprising that it was not unknown in Henry VIII's reign for lay men or women (whom we have no reason to believe to be Protestants) to take hold of, or even to confiscate the chalice when they wished to prevent a priest from celebrating mass. The rector of Hutton Wandesley in Yorkshire, Leonard Constable, claimed, for example, in a bill submitted to Star Chamber, that a number of men had entered his church as he stood at the altar ready to celebrate mass, and 'violently came and took the chalice from the altar where your said subject was standing, and said, "thou poll-shorn priest, thou shalt not say mass here"'.[160] Robert Whytt, the priest of Our Lady's chantry in the parish of Alfreton in Derbyshire was similarly used in 1533 when Dame Anne Meryng and her adherents came to the parish church as Whytt was 'preparing himself to God to mass'. After addressing 'malicious words' to him, saying he should say no mass in that church, she then 'took the chalice which belongeth to the said chantry . . . and with violence unreverently put the same chalice into the case and took it with her', saying that if she had him outside the church 'she would reckon otherwise with him'.[161] In 1530 or 1531 John Veysey, the rector of Lytchett Maltravers in Dorset, was apparently dragged from his church by William Parham and Edmund Bullak, who were acting on the instructions of a local JP, and who proceeded to take the key of the church and the chalice into their custody.[162] A London chantry priest, William Barton, encountered similar opposition at Easter 1540. He claimed that a group of nineteen men entered his chantry in the parish church of St Olave Old Jewry and 'commanded the chalice to be taken . . . and would have disturbed and interrupted him from the saying of his said mass, whereby divers parishioners there, that were then ready to have received their Maker at the said mass, was by them and their means kept back from the same'.[163]

[159] Woodruff (ed.), 'Progress of the Reformation in Kent', 98.

[160] PRO, STA. C. 2, 10/153. The bill is undated, but Constable certainly held the benefice in 1535: *Valor Ecclesiasticus temp. Henrici VIII*, ed. J. Caley and J. Hunter, Record Commission (1810–34), v. 30.   [161] PRO, STA. C. 2, 27/41.

[162] PRO, Req. 2, 7/38.   [163] PRO, STA. C. 2, 3/199.

What is one to make of these cases? Should they be interpreted as overt demonstrations of defiance of clerical prohibitions and contempt for clerical prerogatives? In the case of Leonard Constable, the absence of any answer to his bill of complaint makes it difficult to ascertain the motives of his opponents, but Constable claimed that he was attacked at the instigation of Sir Oswald Wyllestrop, knight, and Robert Wayd, clerk, and that these had also expelled him from his parsonage and installed another rector there. For whatever reasons, it was clearly believed that Constable had no right to hold the benefice or to celebrate mass there.[164] A similar paucity of documentation attends our second case, that of Robert Whytt. John Veysey, however, seems to have been a priest who invited trouble. In 1520 he had quarrelled with the patron of the benefice, the Earl of Arundel, over the rights of nomination to a chantry in the parish.[165] Some time after this he seems to have been deprived by the Bishop of Salisbury, though he refused to vacate the benefice, blaming his deprivation on the machinations of the Bishop's chancellor, Dr Hilley, and James Troublefeld, the priest who was appointed to succeed him.[166] By the time Veysey introduced his bill into Star Chamber, he had been excommunicated, and the Council dismissed his suit, awarding twenty shillings' costs to the defendant.[167] William Barton, the chantry priest of St Olave Jewry was an equally disreputable character. He had been suspected of sedition, and some of the parishioners had complained to the Bishop of London that he scarcely said one mass a week, preferring on feast-days to be in the alehouse rather than the church. When he refused to mend his ways he was imprisoned for a while in the Counter at the instigation of the parish priest. At Easter, Barton was apparently in the habit of saying mass at five in the morning, with his friend the barber-surgeon Richard Smyth as the only communicant, before adjourning with him to breakfast, neglecting the many parishioners who wished to receive at the mass, and for this reason the churchwardens ordered the parish clerk to take away the chalice. This at any rate was the rather more plausible version of events supplied by Barton's opponents, who disclaimed any other motive than to 'reconcile the said complainant and to cause him to do his duty according unto the will of the founder of the said chantry'.[168]

In certain circumstances, then, when the behaviour of a priest was felt

---

[164] PRO, STA. C. 2, 10/153.   [165] PRO, STA. C. 2, 18/290; 24/66; 26/251.
[166] PRO, STA. C. 2, 32/20.   [167] PRO, Req. 2, 7/38.
[168] G. R. Elton, *Policy and Police* (Cambridge, 1972), 7, 12; PRO, STA. C. 2, 3/200. Similar cases are recorded in Fishwick (ed.), *Pleadings and Depositions in the Duchy Court of Lancaster*, ii. 106; R. Whiting, *The Blind Devotion of the People: Popular Religion and the English Reformation* (Cambridge, 1989), 33.

to be intolerable, and his position untenable, laymen might intervene physically to prevent him from saying mass. The most effective way to ensure this was to remove the chalice, an act that at once deprived the priest of the necessary means to say the mass, and at the same time, by openly breaching what clerics at least felt to be a powerful taboo, challenged the boundaries that marked his superior status. Taking hold of the chalice was not necessarily indicative of resentment at the privileges of the priesthood, but it was a powerful symbol of rejection of an individual priest. Indeed, implicitly, it impugned his priesthood.

Where the sacrament of the eucharist was concerned, the position of the priest could be vulnerable in many ways. His holy orders carried with them the privilege of saying mass, but much lay opinion hoped and expected to find more than this technical qualification. An unsuitable priest was better not to celebrate the mass at all, while the very extent to which the administration of the sacrament was so exclusively a concern of the clergy seemed to underline the necessity for worthiness and virtue in the celebrant.

The monopolistic role taken by the priest in the celebration of the mass was not, however, without its logic, a logic which might have answered the anxious, and gone some way towards resolving the problem of unworthy celebrants. Concurrent with the conceptions of the priest in the mass as representing Christ, or as a mediator between God and man, was the equally important idea that in celebrating mass the priest stood for and embodied the whole Christian community. The *Rationale of Ceremonial* prefaced its discussion of the ceremonies used in the mass with the observation that 'the priest is a common minister in the name and stead of the whole congregation'.[169] Sixty years earlier, while providing a gloss on the use of the first person plural, *offerimus*, at the offertory, the *Storie of the Masse* noted that 'the priest speaketh not in his own person, but in the person of Holy Church'. The corollary of this was that 'there is none so wicked and evil after that he is priest but he may consecrate the precious body of our Lord Jesus Christ'.[170] A similar approach was taken by a vernacular work produced in the fifteenth century for the use of the Brigittine nuns of Syon, the *Myroure of oure Ladye*, on the use of *oremus* to introduce the Pater Noster. This indicated that the congregation ought to hear the priest and to pray quietly with him: among the Greeks the Pater Noster was sung by all the people, 'but amongst us the priest alone singeth it in the name of all'.[171]

---

[169] Cobb (ed.), *Rationale of Ceremonial*, 15.   [170] *Storie of the Masse*, 438[v].
[171] Blunt (ed.), *Myroure of oure Ladye*, 330.

A further implication of the priest's celebrating the eucharist in this capacity was that when he received the consecrated elements he did so not only for himself, but in the name, and to the benefit, of all present.[172] Protestants might reject as false the claim that the priest's sole communicating benefited any but himself, in their opinion one could no more receive communion for another than be baptized for him.[173] But orthodox opinion took the concept seriously: the priest 'receives to the health of all Catholic people'.[174] From this perspective, the priest's receiving of the eucharist under both kinds was essentially a corollary of the vicarious aspect to his communion, and not the exercise of a privilege inherent in priesthood *per se*. Richard Whitford, while stressing to his lay readers that the priest made the sacrifice not for himself alone, but for all Christians, reminded them that 'if the same priest should another time out of mass be communed and houseled as you be, he should receive as you do and none other than you do'.[175] The so-called 'King's Book' of 1543, defending the sufficiency of communion under one kind, pointed out that 'not only lay men but also priests (saving when they consecrate) use to receive this sacrament none otherwise'.[176]

Parallel to the idea of the priest's communion being for all, was the significant concept of 'spiritual communion'. Although most laypeople might receive the sacrament only three times, or more probably, once, in the course of a year, it was taught that a sincere desire to receive, expressed in devout aspiration focused upon the priest's communion, could secure for the supplicant the same effusion of grace as if he or she had actually communicated. For such occasions an appropriate prayer was provided by the *Myroure of oure Ladye*, 'Give us such faith and charity and devotion in our souls that thereby we may receive every day the bread of thy holy sacrament of the altar that is Lorde Jesu thyself in the unity of thy church, though we receive it not every day with our bodily mouths.'[177] This was not an aspect of piety whose appeal was restricted to pious nuns. The *Merita Missae* poem ascribed to Lydgate instructed laypeople

---

[172] Jungmann, *Mass of the Roman Rite*, i. 364; Strype, *Ecclesiastical Memorials*, i. (2), 261.

[173] Bradford, *Writings*, 315; Becon, *Comparison between the Lord's Supper and the Pope's Mass*, 375; *Visitation Articles*, ii. 274; E. C. Messenger, *The Reformation, the Mass and the Priesthood* (1936), i. 435; W. R. D. Jones, *William Turner: Tudor Naturalist, Physician and Divine* (1988), 152.

[174] Garard, *Interpretacyon and Sygnyfycacyon of the Masse*, sig. B.i^v. See also Cobb (ed.), *Rationale of Ceremonial*, 26; Blunt (ed.), *Myroure of oure Ladye*, 330; Whitford, *Dialogue or communicacion bytwene the curate ... & the parochiane*, sig. H.iv^r.

[175] Whitford, ibid. sig. H.v^r.

[176] T. A. Lacey (ed.), *The King's Book, 1543* (1895), 46.

[177] Blunt (ed.), *Myroure of oure Ladye*, 75.

to pray while the priest was communicating that the sacrament would work its effect in them also,

> And if ye be in charity,
> Ye be houseled as well as he.[178]

More's *Treatise on the Passion* insisted that in the mass the priest offered on behalf of all, and 'although that only himself receive it sacramentally . . . yet as many of them as are present at it and are in clean life, receive it spiritually'.[179] It was even possible that a lay man or woman hearing mass devoutly 'shall obtain more grace than the priest which doth it, for the priest is not always equally disposed, and so may the man every day receive the holy sacrament spiritually'.[180] The idea of a possible spiritual reception of the eucharist by worshippers was a subtle one, predicated upon an essential unity of purpose among congregation and priest, and one that implied a more sophisticated understanding of the eucharistic function and significance of the priest than that of theophanic thaumaturge.

These concepts, which seemed to qualify the imperious clericalism Protestants objected to in the mass, could receive further confirmation from the strongly Christological strand in sacramental theology which emphasized the centrality of Christ as primary cause in the consecration of the eucharistic elements. That the priest was essentially an agent of Christ, the real worker of the eucharistic miracle, was an Augustinian concept which became deeply rooted in the theological consciousness of the Middle Ages.[181] At a more accessible level it was promulgated by fourteenth-century clerical manuals such as the *Manipulus Curatorum*, and by the insistence of the *Imitation of Christ* that in the mass 'God is there the principal doer and the invisible worker'.[182] In his *Answer to a Poisoned Book*, Thomas More contended that 'when the priest ministereth us this meat [the eucharist], let us not think that it is he that giveth it us; not the

---

[178] Simmons (ed.), *Lay Folk's Mass Book*, 151.

[179] T. More, *Treatise on the Passion, Treatise on the Blessed Body, Instructions and Prayers*, ed. G. E. Haupt, *CW* 13 (1976), 176.

[180] Garard, *Interpretacyon and Sygnyfycacyon of the Masse*, sig. I.iv'. See also Bonde, *Pylgrymage of Perfeccyon*, 260ʳ; Langforde, *Meditatyons*, 26; Rubin, *Corpus Christi*, 64, 150.

[181] B. Gogan, *The Common Corps of Christendom: Ecclesiological Themes in the Writings of Sir Thomas More* (Leiden, 1982), 21; R. Rex, *The Theology of John Fisher* (Cambridge, 1991), 146; Jungmann, *Mass of the Roman Rite*, i. 186; C. G. Jung, 'Transformation Symbolism in the Mass', in J. Campbell (ed.), *Pagan and Christian Mysteries* (New York, 1963), 93.

[182] C. W. Dugmore, *The Mass and the English Reformers* (1958), 80; Clark, *Eucharistic Sacrifice*, 551; Klein (ed.), *Imitation of Christ*, 233. See also Hoccleve, *Minor Poems*, 19; G. Cigman, *Lollard Sermons*, EETS 294 (1989), 51, a passage which does not appear notably heterodox.

priest I say whom we see, but the Son of Man, Christ himself, whose own flesh not the priest there giveth us, but as Christ's minister delivereth us'.[183] To employ a modern political analogy, the celebrant was more delegate than representative. When Bishop John Hilsey wrote an *Instructio[n] of the maner in hearing of the masse*, to be included in Cromwell's 1539 Primer, he spoke of the mass as 'this sacrament consecrated (not by the power of the minister the priest) but by the power of God working in his word spoken of the priest'.[184] Although circumscribed by the lapidary orthodoxy of the recent Act of Six Articles, Hilsey may have wished to accent his own reformist sympathies, but there is no doubt that the position he advanced here was one of impeccable Catholic orthodoxy. On the Continent, the argument that Christ was the true priest of the mass became prominent in the polemical armouries of Catholic propagandists such as Cochlaeus, Murner, and Eck.[185]

It might appear, then, that all the materials were to hand to enable contemporaries to construct a truly 'ministerial' view of the eucharistic celebrant, one which, while recognizing, of course, the desirability of purity and virtue in the minister, could accommodate the unfortunate realities of weakness and sin, both by presenting the priest as the embodiment of the entire Christian community, and by uniting his depiction of the suffering Christ at the level of dramatic allegory with an awareness of how his action *in persona Christi* involved not an appropriation or transfer of Christ's powers, but a wholly vicarious exercise of them, taking place whenever the minimal conditions of sacramentality were met. All this was, as we have seen, implicit in the Church's teaching, but there may have been a basic psychological inability to grasp its real significance. At the level of the religious élites an almost fundamentalist clericalism, exemplified perhaps by Colet—who considered wicked priests to be worse than heretics, and who had even suggested that God might not uphold the ordination of a priest who forfeited his place among the righteous—was unwilling to allow that a priest's function and purpose in and for the Christian community ultimately might transcend the personal standing and prestige which staked his public claim to that function, while at the popular level many people were understandably hesitant

---

[183] T. More, *The Answer to a Poisoned Book*, ed. S. Foley and C. H. Miller, *CW* 11 (1985), 29.

[184] Hilsey, J., *The manual of prayers, or the prymer in Englysh & Laten, set forth by Ihon Bysshope of Rochester at the comaundemente of Thomas Cromwell* (1539), sig. Ii.ii^v. The point was also stressed by Lacey (ed.), *The King's Book*, 60.

[185] Clark, *Eucharistic Sacrifice*, 337–8.

about the idea that personal virtue was not in some way inextricably linked with spiritual power.[186] It may be also that the contemporary horror of what might be construed as hypocrisy perhaps hindered the formation of a more comprehensively ministerial outlook.[187]

The concept of the priest acting in the mass on behalf of and representing before God the entire Christian people could not but become increasingly problematic as the mass itself came to divide rather than to unite English Christians. To Protestants the mass was an abomination. When a copy of Caxton's *Golden Legend* with its appended 'noble history of the exposition of the mass' came into the hands of a mid-century Protestant, the new owner corrected the title to read 'the most abominable history of the exposition of the popish mass, most to be abhorred of all Christians'.[188] Some of the objections Protestant writers held against the theory and practice of the mass have been referred to above, and as the reign of King Henry progressed, and Protestant ideas began to circulate and in certain quarters find acceptance, these objections received vocal expression. In 1538, for example, Foxe tells of a Suffolk man confronting his priest in church with the charge that 'after he had drunk up all the wine alone, he afterwards blessed the hungry people with the empty chalice'.[189] In London, the epicentre of popular Protestantism, in the aftermath of the Six Articles, people might mock priests preparing for mass: 'Ye shall see a priest now go to masking.'[190] An apprentice of the parish of St Mildred, Bread Street, declared that he would 'rather hear the crying of dogs' than services sung by priests.[191] At St Giles, Cripplegate, four parishioners advanced the argument, much favoured by Protestant polemicists, that the mass 'was made of pieces and patches'.[192] The sacrament of the altar was referred to by John Mayler, a grocer of St Botolph, Billingsgate, as 'the baken god', and he suggested that the mass was abroad called 'miss' because all was amiss in it.[193] Protestants might, moreover, pour scorn on the piety of their Catholic neighbours. Eleanor Godfrey, of Great Marlow in Buckinghamshire, laughed openly at Thomas Collard, whom she termed

---

[186] Lupton, *Life of Colet*, 298; Kaufman, 'Colet's *Opus de sacramentis*', 14.

[187] It is notable that Catholic characters are named Hypocrisy in the works of many Reformation writers, and that in Girolamo da Treviso's allegory of the English Reformation the evangelists are shown stoning 'Hypocrisy' along with the Pope. J. N. King, *English Reformation Literature* (Princeton, NJ, 1982), 157; C. Lloyd, *The Queen's Pictures* (1991), 56–7.   [188] *Storie of the Masse* (Bodleian Library, Arch. G.b.2), p. 435ʳ.

[189] Foxe, *Acts and Monuments*, v. 253.   [190] Ibid. 443.   [191] Ibid. 444.

[192] Ibid. 445; Becon, *Displaying of the Popish Mass*, 266; Bradford, *Writings*, 310; J. Mardy, *A breife recantacion of maystres missa* (1548), sig. A.iiʳ.

[193] Brigden, *London and the Reformation*, 345; Foxe, *Acts and Monuments*, v. 447.

a 'pope-holy hypocrite' for his assiduity in kneeling and crossing himself at mass.[194]

In particular, the elevation of the consecrated host, once the epitome of concord, now came to symbolize the divergence of religious attitudes. Whereas Catholics marked the moment with prayerful reverence, Protestants could register their dissent by not removing their hats, by not looking up, or by ostentatiously studying a book.[195] At the London parish of St Martin Outwich in 1540 some parishioners paraded with their caps on around the church, and at Thomas the Apostle no fewer than thirteen parishioners were presented for giving 'small reverence at the sacring of the mass'.[196] Some Protestants preferred to indulge in more active irreverence, Robert Testwood calling out sarcastically at the elevation 'what, wilt thou lift him so high? What yet higher? Take heed, let him not fall.'[197] Anthony Peerson preached at Wingfield in Wiltshire in 1541 that just as Christ had been hanged between two thieves 'even so, when the priest is at mass, and hath consecrated and lifted him up over his head, there he hangeth between two thieves', adding the important proviso 'except he preach the word of God truly, as he hath taken upon him to do'.[198] A few years later the Ipswich Protestant, John Ramsey, reinforced the image in his corrosive satire *A Plaister for a galled horse*:

> Then make they God with words enough,
> And hang him up between thieves twain.[199]

It is instructive that the allegorical tradition might inform even the attitudes of those who opposed the mass and the traditional understanding of the priest, particularly in view of the fact that the image of the hands of the priest as the two thieves had featured in the *Interpretacyon and Sygnyfycacyon of the Masse* in 1532.[200] In the polemical atmosphere of mid-sixteenth-century England, orthodoxy could be contextual as much as propositional.

Confronted with growing evidence of disbelief in the real presence, some priests might be drawn to desperate measures to restore their credibility. In 1544 the London *Grey Friars' Chronicle* reported how a Kentish priest had been punished 'for cutting of his finger and making it to bleed on the host at his mass for a false sacrifice', a faked eucharistic miracle

---

[194] Foxe, ibid. 454.   [195] Ibid. 444–5, 454.
[196] Brigden, *London and the Reformation*, 406.
[197] Foxe, *Acts and Monuments*, v. 488.   [198] Ibid. 487.
[199] J. Ramsey, *A Plaister for a galled horse* (1548), unpaginated.
[200] Garard, *Interpretacyon and Sygnyfycacyon of the Masse*, sig. M.iv[r].

corresponding to the pattern familiar to the sermon literature and popular iconography of the Middle Ages.[201] The vehemence of the conservatives' assertion of a real *physical* presence of Christ in the sacrament mirrored the evangelical refusal to accept that this was so. Dr Johnson was later to respond characteristically to a query of Boswell's about the idolatry of the mass: 'Sir, there is no idolatry in the mass. They believe God is there, and they adore him.'[202] Such relativism would have made no sense to early Tudor Protestants, who considered the adoration of the elevated host to be idolatrous because they were convinced God was not really there, at least in the sense Catholics believed. Although English Protestants evinced a great variety of eucharistic belief, many, no doubt, like Archbishop Cranmer, holding different views at various times, all were united by their rejection of transubstantiation and detestation of Catholic eucharistic piety. To John Marbecke, a musician of the Chapel Royal, the elevation of the sacrament was 'the similitude of setting up of images of the calves in the temple builded by Jeroboam', while to Thomas Becon it seemed to '[provoke] the people that are present to commit most detestable idolatries. For the people take it to be their God.'[203] Scepticism regarding the real presence could be expressed in ways that embraced and amplified the problems of belief faced by those disappointed or perplexed by the apparent unworthiness of the clergy. In 1541 William Hart of Great Brickhill in Buckinghamshire posed his neighbours a thought-provoking question: 'thinkest thou that God Almighty will abide over a knave priest's head?'[204]

Not all Catholics accepted with equanimity this assault on their traditional beliefs. At the start of Edward VI's reign, Thomas Hancock alienated many of his new parishioners in Poole, Dorset, by his forthright preaching against the real presence and the supposed idolatry in the mass. When he suggested that 'that which the priest lifteth over his head is not God, for you do see it with your bodily eyes', it was too much for some of them, and the merchant Thomas Whyghtt tried to inspire a walk-out, saying, 'come from him, good people; he came from the devil, and teacheth unto you devilish doctrine'. Another parishioner told Hancock, 'it shall

---

[201] J. G. Nichols (ed.), *Chronicle of the Grey Friars of London*, CS 53 (1851), 48. For eucharistic miracles, see P. Browe, *Die eucharistischen Wunder des Mittelalters* (Breslau, 1938); Rubin, *Corpus Christi*, 108–29.

[202] J. Boswell, *Life of Samuel Johnson*, ii. 101, quoted in N. Love, *Mirror of the Blessed Life of Jesu Christ*, 301 n.

[203] Foxe, *Acts and Monuments*, v. 490; Becon, *Displaying of the Popish Mass*, 270.

[204] Foxe, *Acts and Monuments*, v. 454.

be God when thou shalt be but a knave'.[205] At Northampton, Protestant teaching against the presence of Christ in the elevated host provoked a similarly forthright reaction. When the former Dominican, John Godwyn, told Richard Morton that what he had seen that day between the priest's hands was not God 'but a similitude', some onlookers were so incensed that 'they would have thrust their daggers into him, if it had not been for their prince's displeasure'.[206] Yet such passionate traditionalism could do nothing to avert the inexorable movement towards eucharistic reform once Henry VIII was dead.

PRIESTS WITHOUT THE MASS

The defeat of Norfolk and Gardiner in the power struggle which preceded Henry's death led to the formation of an avowedly Protestant administration to guide the young Edward VI. In the atmosphere of expectant reform agitation against the mass increased. In 1548 alone, thirty-one tracts were published which condemned the mass and lent weight to the proposed introduction of a new liturgy.[207] At a popular level things had gone so far, in London at least, that in the new Parliament of 1547 an act was passed which, as well as sanctioning communion in both kinds for the laity, sought with fines and imprisonment to repress so-called 'revilers of the sacrament', noting that the sacrament 'hath been of late marvellously abused'. Later that year a royal proclamation was issued to address the same problem.[208] Meanwhile Cranmer's long-cherished proposal for liturgical reform was coming to fruition. In March 1548 a vernacular *Order of Communion* was inserted into the Latin rite, and early in the next year a complete overhaul of the liturgy was agreed to by Crown and Parliament. Although regarded by some Protestants as an insufficient measure, the promulgation of the new Prayer Book represented a radical change in the way English men and women were to experience public worship. Textually, the new Book of Common Prayer had much in common with the preceding Sarum rite. To the opponents of reform Cranmer was to riposte, 'it seemeth to you a new service, and indeed it is none other but the old. The selfsame words in English which were in Latin, saving a few things taken

[205] J. G. Nichols (ed.), *Narratives of the Days of the Reformation*, CS 77 (1859), 77–8.
[206] Peacock (ed.), 'Extracts from Lincoln Episcopal Visitation', 265.
[207] King, *English Reformation Literature*, 89; Dugmore, *Mass and the English Reformers*, 117.   [208] Dugmore, ibid. 116.

out.'[209] Yet to contemporary layfolk it must have seemed, for good or ill, a portentous change.

The authors of the new liturgy envisaged a new theological relationship between clergy and laity, and in the light of their efforts, laypeople may have been forced or persuaded to reassess their perceptions of the officiating priest. The most striking change was that, in theory, the congregation could now hear and understand what the priest was saying. The canon of the mass, or to give it its new title 'the Supper of the Lord and the Holy Communion commonly called the mass', was no longer a secret and powerful invocation of the deity dependent on the special professional knowledge of priests, but a public prayer to which the congregation was expected to give devout attention and intellectual assent. Other less drastic changes marked the shifts in emphasis. Vestments were simplified. The celebrant was to wear only 'a white alb plain, with a vestment or cope'.[210] No longer did the priest bear upon his person a complete typology of the passion. In 1552, when the Second Prayer Book was promulgated, the priest was directed to wear a surplice only.[211] The offertory rite of the priest's requesting the prayers of the people was abolished, probably because of its sacrificial context.[212] Protestants may have been sceptical about the value of a rite in which the priest 'turneth himself from the altar and speaketh unto the people in an unknown tongue saying *Dominus vobiscum, orate pro me*',[213] but, as we have suggested above, the rite may have promoted a sense of identification with the endeavours of the priest. No longer either did the rubrics instruct the priest to adopt the cruciform posture after the consecration, and the sign of the cross was removed from the final blessing, a circumstance that one suspects may have affected the perception of its efficacy in the popular mind.

Most significantly, the priest was no longer to lift up the consecrated host and invite the congregation to adore it. The words of consecration were to be said 'without any elevation or showing the sacrament to the people'.[214] The Second Prayer Book of 1552 carried no rubric to this effect, perhaps an indication that the practice was thought to have been eradicated fairly successfully, but it did seek to exclude any possibility of adoration of the bread by placing the communion directly after the

---

[209] Foxe, *Acts and Monuments*, v. 734.
[210] E. C. Gibson (ed.), *The First and Second Prayer Books of Edward VI* (1910), 212.
[211] Ibid. 347.
[212] The form of words had been 'Orate fratres [et sorores] ut meum pariterque vestrum acceptum sit domino deo nostro sacrificium.' Wickham Legg (ed.), *Sarum Missal*, 219.
[213] Ridley, *Works*, 108.   [214] Gibson (ed.), *Prayer Books of Edward VI*, 223.

consecration.[215] The banning of the elevation, as well as removing a public and dramatic function of the priest, must have been a bewildering development to the many English men and women who had grown up with the practice at the centre of their devotional lives. The change was accompanied by other measures designed to undermine the perception of the consecrated bread as a talismanic object. In 1549 the hosts were directed to be 'without all manner of print, and something more larger and thicker than it was', and to be distributed in broken pieces. From 1552 the bread was to be no other than 'is usual to be eaten at the table with other meats'.[216] Perhaps more significant for lay perceptions of the clergy was the thorough reform of the etiquette of communion which accompanied the introduction of the new rite. The chalice, once jealously reserved for the celebrant, was made available to the laity with the institution of communion in both kinds, a move which, it had long been recognized, carried with it serious implications for the status of the priestly office.[217] In 1552 another long-standing taboo was broken when the priest was directed to deliver the bread to the people in their hands.[218]

The common people were not, of course, invited to pass judgement on the process of reform, and it is difficult to assess the cumulative effect on them of the changes. The most notable instance of overt hostility to the new religious regime is provided by the South-Western Rebellion of 1549. In Devon the tumult began in the village of Sampford Courtney, where the parishioners, apparently horrified by the new service they had attended on Whitsunday, the next day forced their rector, William Harper, to put on his full set of vestments (his 'old popish attire' as an unsympathetic contemporary termed it), and to say mass in Latin.[219] In so far as the articles later formulated by the rebels touched upon the mass, they represented a demand for a return to the *status quo ante*. The fact that the new service was in English was viewed as particularly objectionable, making it seem 'but like a Christmas game'. The commons wanted 'the mass in Latin, as was before, and celebrated by the Priest without any man or woman communicating with him'. The laity should continue to communicate but once a year, and then in one kind only. In addition,

[215] Ibid. 389.   [216] Ibid. 230, 392.   [217] Rubin, *Corpus Christi*, 35.

[218] Gibson (ed.), *Prayer Books of Edward VI*, 389.

[219] Rose-Troup, *Western Rebellion of 1549*, 131–4; J. Cornwall, *The Revolt of the Peasantry, 1549* (1977), 64–5. Hostility to the new liturgy was almost certainly a factor in precipitating the simultaneous risings in the South Midlands and Yorkshire: A. Vere Woodman, 'The Buckinghamshire and Oxfordshire Rising of 1549', *Oxoniensia*, 22 (1957); A. G. Dickens, 'Some Popular Reactions to the Edwardian Reformation in Yorkshire', in *Reformation Studies*, 21–39.

every priest should pray at his mass for the souls in purgatory.[220] Historians are probably correct in assuming that the articles were drawn up by traditionalist priests, but there seems no reason to doubt that they articulated genuinely popular sentiments. All Tudor rebellions grew from a variegated matrix of motives, and some recent historical writing has emphasized secular and economic elements in this so-called 'Prayer Book Rebellion'.[221] Joyce Youings in particular has expressed some incredulity that 'men and women who had used vernacular prayers as long as they could remember, who must have listened to many a sermon in English, and some of whom had seen English bibles in their churches for more than a decade, now took up arms and left their homes just before the harvest to protest about the new English prayer book'.[222] Yet it may be that the people of the South West rejected the new Prayer Book not so much because they were instinctive reactionaries who would resent any innovation, but because, theologically naïve though they may have been, they understood the mass, the centre-piece of their spiritual lives, in a way that seemed fundamentally to be contradicted by the new liturgy. Their articles envisaged a return to a mass conducted by the priest alone. They did not want liturgical dialogue, or participation in common prayer, rather, one might suggest, they wanted an objective assurance of the presence of the sacred, guaranteed by the priest's use of Latin, and, other than at the great commensal feast of Easter, ritually exemplified by the priest's sole communicating, and by the priest's showing of Christ to the people.[223] Hugh Latimer was later to remark only half-ironically to Ridley that 'this is the matter: so long as the priests speak Latin, they are thought of the people to be marvellous well-learned'.[224] The point is a telling one. The Latin mass was thought to offer tangible spiritual benefits, and it almost certainly guaranteed at least a modicum of respect for the priests who celebrated it. With the new English Prayer Book the clergy were proffering an unknown quantity.

The aim of the reformers was, however, to promote a new understanding of the eucharist and of the position of the priest regarding it. The mass or Lord's Supper was not to be seen as a priestly sacrifice, but as a

---

[220] The demands of the rebels are printed in A. Fletcher, *Tudor Rebellions*, 3rd edn. (1983), 115.

[221] Whiting, *Blind Devotion of the People*, 34–6; J. Youings, 'The South-Western Rebellion of 1549', *Southern History*, 1 (1979). [222] Ibid. 104.

[223] It is perhaps rather surprising that a reinstatement of the elevation does not appear as a separate demand in the surviving version of the rebels' articles. It is probable, however, that the practice was so taken for granted that it was naturally subsumed in the demand for 'the mass in Latin, as was before'. [224] Ridley, *Works*, 109.

communal meal, a sacrifice only of praise and thanksgiving. For this reason the rubrics both in 1549 and in 1552 stipulated that there was to be no celebration of the communion unless a number of parishioners were willing to communicate with the priest. In other words, the celebrant was not to be seen as having communion rights or duties distinct from those of the laity. No particular *numerus clausus* was fixed in 1549, but in 1552 the requirement was said to be 'a good number', defined, rather ambitiously perhaps, as three or four in a parish of not more than twenty potential communicants.[225] Yet it is probable that no fundamental revision of general attitudes could have taken place in the few years allotted to the Edwardian regime, and that the deeply ingrained custom of infrequent communion died hard. This problem was anticipated by the 1549 Book, which provided a special exhortation to be read 'if upon the Sunday or holy day the people be negligent to come to the communion'.[226] In fact, the exhortations provided by the two liturgies may have been as likely to deter as to encourage potential communicants, dwelling as they did on the dangers of unworthy reception, and the Pauline concept of eating and drinking one's own damnation.[227] Naturally, the same preoccupations had characterized the pre-Reformation teaching, but the sacrament of penance had at least provided an objective guarantee of eucharistic eligibility. Now communicants were expected 'to search and examine your own consciences' rather than to rely on the inquisitorial skills of a priest. Not only had auricular confession been declared optional (and therefore by implication irrelevant) as an adjunct of worthy reception, but for those who felt no assurance that they were at peace with the world, 'neither the absolution of the priest, can any thing avail them, nor the receiving of this holy sacrament doth any thing but increase their damnation'.[228] The likelihood is that some parishes may have gone long periods without a Sunday communion, though the 1552 rite insisted that laypeople should now communicate at least three times a year.[229]

A more alarming tendency from the viewpoint of reformers was the apparent eagerness in some churches to 'counterfeit the popish mass' within the framework of the reformed liturgy, by retaining much of the eucharistic etiquette of the Catholic rite—the priest kissing the table, washing his fingers, crossing himself with the paten, or breathing on the bread and chalice—by using unauthorized vestments, and placing candles

[225] Gibson (ed.), *Prayer Books of Edward VI*, 392.   [226] Ibid. 216.
[227] Ibid. 214, 385.   [228] Ibid. 216–17.
[229] Ibid. 392; F. Procter and W. H. Frere, *A New History of the Book of Common Prayer*, 3rd edn. (1905), 502–3.

before the altars, by ringing 'sacring bells' and persisting with the elevation, by chanting the liturgy in the old manner or by having more than
one celebration a day, and by calling the services the 'high communion'
after the high mass, the 'Communion of the Apostles', or the 'Communion of the Virgin'.[230] One cannot say for certain whether such practices
reflected merely the conservative tendencies of many parish priests, or
whether their congregations may have encouraged and expected them to
act in this way. It is not impossible that in some cases priests and people
colluded to defeat the expectations of the ecclesiastical authorities, though
noting the rarity with which priests were cited for contravening the new
liturgies in the diocese of Ely, Felicity Heal suggests that non-observance
of the new forms 'would have required a conspiracy of silence between
parishioners and incumbent which would have been difficult to maintain
in many parishes'.[231] As Protestant realists had to recognize, however, the
mass 'hath taken such a root in the hearts of the simple and ignorant
people, that it can not easily be plucked away'.[232] Some layfolk may even
have begun exercising 'consumer choice' in matters of religious observance, in a manner not dissimilar to the practice of some modern Anglicans (and indeed, Catholics). Hooper's Visitation Interrogatories for the
dioceses of Gloucester and Worcester in 1551–2 wanted to know if any
condemned or were slow to come to the new services, and whether 'any
of them refuse their own parish, and frequent and haunt other, where the
communion is more like a mass than in his own'.[233]

   That the status of priests with the common people was bound up
intimately with their celebration of the mass had long been recognized by
Protestant writers; these foresaw a humbling of priests as a consequence
of the abolition of the mass, and rejoiced in the prospect. This notion is
a dominant theme of *The Burial of the Mass*, the most famous of the early
Protestant English anticlerical satires. This work supposed that the
'papistical sect' had gained great pre-eminence and dignity through 'their
false and crafty bringing up of the blasphemous mass, which principally
is their hold, stead, and defence'. Though corrupt prelates like Wolsey
may have been hated by the people, 'yet in the mass they put much
confidence . . . Priests also they have in reverence'. The hapless clergy

---

[230] *Visitation Articles*, ii. 191–3, 241–2, 276, 296, 299; Messenger, *The Reformation, the
Mass and the Priesthood*, i. 414–16; H. Robinson (ed.), *Original Letters Relative to the English
Reformation*, PS (1847), ii. 547.
[231] F. Heal, 'The Parish Clergy and the Reformation in the Diocese of Ely', *CAS* 66 (1977),
152.
[232] J. Veron, *Certayne litel treatises set forth . . . for the erudition and learnyng, of the symple
& ignorant peopell* (1548), sig. E.vii[v].   [233] *Visitation Articles*, ii. 292.

lament the demise of the mass, which in their time had made them 'lords and kings over all',

> Among all the people we went afar,
> By pretence of our fained holiness
> They reputed us for half gods and more
> Through the mass's beneficialness.[234]

Later writers harnessed the same theme. John Mardy's *breife recantacion of maystres missa* has the mass confess that she was created so that priests might 'increase their riches, and fill their coffers, and [that] me, Sir John Lacklatin, that could do nothing but mumble up matins [and] sing a mass, was had in as much reputation as a right honest and well lerned man'.[235] In Hilarie's *Resurrecion of the Masse*, the mass boasts of its labours on behalf of 'idle-bellied priests',

> I make them to be had in reputation,
> I make them to be called Sirs every one,
> I make them worshipful and honourable . . .
> I make the order of priesthood honourable,
> I only am the stay of all mass-mongers.
> It is I that make the mass priests able
> To match with the best and to be called masters.[236]

Becon thought that priests proclaimed the excellence of their 'new baken little great god, that by this means ye may be had in admiration among the foolish simple idiots, and be nourished of the sweat of other men's brows'.[237]

What these and other writers wanted was not, of course, the abolition of a professional clergy as such, but a radical redefinition of priestly status, predicated not upon a supposedly sacramental character conferred at ordination, but on standards of personal godliness, and above all on the willingness and ability to preach the Word of God. The mass, in their opinion, was 'but a fained thing to win money with to the idle priests that can not preach'.[238] Here, however, their aspirations may have extended beyond the feasible. While the mass could, as it were, disappear with a stroke of Cranmer's pen, a full preaching ministry could not so easily be established. As late as 1586 it was estimated that only a fifth of parishes

---

[234] J. Barlow, *Burial of the Mass*, in E. Arber (ed.), *English Reprints* (1871), 23, 26, 30, 33, 34.   [235] Mardy, *Recantacion of maystres missa*, sig. A.iii^v.

[236] Hilarie, *Resurrecion of the Masse*, sig. A.viii^{r-v}.

[237] Becon, *Displaying of the Popish Mass*, 261.

[238] Turner, *Examination of the Messe*, sig. A.vii^{r-v}.

had preachers.[239] While the clergy in the Edwardian period was declared to be primarily a Ministry of the Word, to many it must have looked an emasculated priesthood, whose sacramental powers were either (in the case of penance) drastically curtailed, or (in the case of the new communion service) rendered, at least to some onlookers, doubtful and ambivalent.

The contention has been implicit throughout this chapter that, theologically inconsistent though it may have been, many felt differently about priests in the context of their celebrating the mass. That this could raise tensions and pose intellectual and emotional problems has been noted. On the one hand the sacredness of the mass could focus attention on clerical weakness and inadequacies, but on the other, the mass explained the necessity for having a priesthood at all, and among those who affirmed it, may have inhibited the formation of truly anticlerical as opposed to critical or reformist attitudes. In the mass people left their ordinary lives and entered into 'sacred time' structured by the liturgy, and into 'sacred space', a building set aside and separated from profane use.[240] The Sacred responded to and reflected a different order of causation, attested to most powerfully by the transubstantiation of bread and wine, but also by other possible intrusions into the natural order, the so-called 'meeds' of the mass.[241] It would have been surprising if there had been no

---

[239] C. Haigh, 'The Church of England, the Catholics and the People', in C. Haigh (ed.), *The Reign of Elizabeth I* (1984), 206. The situation was much worse in the first half of Elizabeth's reign: Haigh, *English Reformations, Religion, Politics, and Society under the Tudors* (Oxford, 1993), 268–9.

[240] These concepts are discussed in M. Eliade, *The Sacred and the Profane*, tr. W. R. Trask (New York, 1959), and the articles by J. P. Brereton, B. C. Sproul, and T. W. Jennings on 'Sacred Space', 'Sacred Time', and 'Liturgy', in M. Eliade (ed.), *The Encyclopedia of Religion* (New York, 1987). It might be objected that this seems to postulate a more radical distinction of the Sacred and the Profane than that comprehended in the mental categories of early Tudor Englishmen. Admonishments about unsuitable behaviour in church are a feature of several contemporary works: Simmons (ed.), *Lay Folk's Mass Book*, 4, 136–9; Mirc, *Instructions*, 9; Garard, *Interpretacyon and Sygnyfycacyon of the Masse*, sig. G.ii^r; W. A. Pantin, 'Instructions for a Devout and Literate Layman', in J. G. Alexander and M. T. Gibson (eds.), *Medieval Learning and Literature* (Oxford, 1976), 399. Against this one should note the apparent readiness of the laity to bring charges against fellow-parishioners for these offences. See *Kentish Visitations*, 160, 200; Tanner, *Church in Late Medieval Norwich*, 10. John Bossy has suggested that the devotional attitude of the congregation would probably have changed profoundly at the onset of the canon, called in Germany *Stillmesse: Christianity in the West*, 68.

[241] Belief in these temporal benefits attendant on hearing mass is well attested to. See Simmons (ed.), *Lay Folk's Mass Book*, 131, 366–73; Mirc, *Instructions*, 10; *Festial*, 169; Garard, *Interpretacyon and Sygnyfycacyon of the Masse*, sigs. E.ii^r, I.i^r–K.i^v; J. R. Lumby (ed.), *Ratis Raving and other Moral and Religious Pieces*, EETS 41 (1876), 113–14; Harington, *Comendacions of Matrymony*, sig. E.iii^v; John Audelay, *Poems*, ed. E. K. Whiting, EETS 184 (1931), 67; J. Lydgate, *Minor Poems*, ed. H. N. MacCracken, 112–14.

accompanying impulse towards a 'sacralization' of the priest, a feeling that the priest vested for mass must conform with this sense of otherness, of separation from the ordinary things of the world. In a devotional work entitled *The floure of the commaundements of god*, an exemplum tells of a virgin attending mass who witnessed the transfiguration of the priest at the moment of communion. She 'saw the body of the priest so pure and clear that she saw the body of god as by a phial of crystal'. When the mass was over the body of the priest was seen 'little and little [to] thicken and return in the first form'.[242]

It is instructive to note how priests, generally insistent on their dignity at the best of times, were especially sensitive to insult or injury while they were still clad in their vestments. John Veysey, for example, described in detail to the Lords of Star Chamber how in July 1520 he had been importuned by messengers sent by the Earl of Arundel, 'his alb not being off his back'.[243] In 1529 Thomas Botefeld, the vicar of Ness in Shropshire, claimed nearly to have been assaulted 'while he was vested for mass'.[244] In June 1547 the parish priest of Nether Fonthill in Wiltshire was reported to have been forcibly taken from the parish church 'with his surplice upon his back, and his stole about his neck'.[245] 'Vested for mass' the celebrant could be a vital 'functional' element of popular religion, which even some of those who routinely rejected or disliked priests might find hard to ignore. In 1518 a Buckinghamshire woman was cited for heresy for claiming that she was 'as well-learned as the parish priest, in all things except only in saying of mass'.[246] Others might be driven to adopt a truly dichotomous attitude, which seemed to avoid the cognitive dissonance implicit in the outlook of those orthodox believers who disliked the pretensions of priests. In 1501 a man was brought before the Consistory Court of Canterbury for his view that 'a priest was only a priest at the time of celebrating mass'.[247] This striking opinion was not unique: in 1485 Richard Hilman had been persecuted at Coventry for his opposition to tithes and images and for saying, 'That a priest, while he is at mass, is a priest, and after one mass done, till the beginning of another mass, he is no more than a layman, and hath no more power than a mere

---

[242] *The floure of the commaundements of god*, tr. A. Chertsey (1521), 204ʳ.
[243] PRO, STA. C. 2, 18/290.   [244] PRO, STA. C. 2, 5/130.
[245] PRO, STA. C. 3, 4/74. See also STA. C. 2, 14/60.
[246] Foxe, *Acts and Monuments*, iv. 231.
[247] B. L. Woodcock, *Medieval Ecclesiastical Courts in the Diocese of Canterbury* (Oxford, 1952), 80.

layman.'[248] Another heretic, William Carpenter of Newbury in Berkshire, in 1491, thought of priests as scribes and pharisees, and suggested that 'when they be revested to mass they be as angels, and when they be unrevested they be as black brands of hell'.[249] These heterodox laymen seemed to have resolved to their own satisfaction the tense interplay of sacred and profane made manifest by the imperfection of priests. In a different way, the Edwardian Prayer Books and later 'Anglican' liturgies may have gone some way towards resolving the same tension. By 'desacralizing' the rite itself, in so far as they placed it within the compass of vernacular comprehension, reinterpreted the nature of Christ's presence in the eucharist, and shifted the focus of the action from a distant high altar to a simple communion table placed near the people, they may have diminished the emotional and psychological need for a priesthood worthy to meddle with mysteries of unbearable holiness. In so doing they could not, however, have left intact the exalted reputation enjoyed by the pre-Reformation clergy. The liturgical experiments of the mid-sixteenth century raised many questions about the functions and status of an ordained ministry that could not be settled quickly or painlessly.

[248] Foxe, *Acts and Monuments*, iv. 135. Somewhat inconsistently, he also seems to have held that the sacrament of the altar was but bread.

[249] D. P. Wright, *The Register of Thomas Langton, Bishop of Salisbury 1485–1493*, CYS 74 (1985), 79. Even if intended ironically, the remark attests to its author's perception of public attitudes.

3

The Priest as Teacher

The idea that a parish clergyman ought primarily to be a celebrant of the mass and hearer of confessions, a priestly dispenser of sacramental grace, was a perverse doctrine to those who had embraced the teachings of Luther and his successors. In their eyes, the paramount priestly duty was rather the preaching of the Word of God, the instruction and encouragement of the laypeople in the faith which alone could save them. A non-preaching priest was scarcely worthy of the name. According to Luther he was 'as much a priest as a picture of a man is a man',[1] and this striking metaphor was echoed by English Protestants. Thomas Becon regarded a priest or bishop who did not preach as no more genuine than a 'Nicholas' or boy-bishop, an idol, 'and indeed no better than a painted bishop on a wall'.[2] The author of an anonymous supplication to Henry VIII saw them as 'images and idols, having and bearing only the name and outward appearance of a bishop or pastor'.[3] The common people were deluded if they trusted to be saved by the ministrations of any 'mass-monger'. Justification through faith alone placed knowledge of the scriptures at the centre of all spiritual endeavour, and Latimer epitomized the dynamic of the new soteriology when he remarked that 'we cannot be saved without hearing of the word, it is a necessary way to salvation . . . there must be preachers, if we look to be saved'.[4] In this scheme the preaching office was of necessity 'the office of salvation, and the only means that God hath appointed to salvation'.[5]

This conviction had, of course, to co-exist with the central Protestant insight that each believer came to salvation through his own faithful acceptance of the passion of Christ, independent of any human mediator.

---

[1] M. Luther, *The Babylonian Captivity of the Church*, in A. R. Wentz (ed.), *Luther's Works*, xxxvi. *Word and Sacrament* (Philadelphia, 1959), 115.

[2] T. Becon, *The Catechism of Thomas Becon*, ed. J. Ayre, PS (1844), 320.

[3] J. M. Cowper (ed.), *Four Supplications, 1529–1553*, EETS ES 13 (1871), 32.

[4] H. Latimer, *Sermons*, ed. G. E. Corrie, PS (1844), 200.

[5] Ibid. 291, 306, 349, 418.

Yet the priesthood of all believers did not obviate the need for a distinct and well-educated body of men appointed to preach the word of God and instruct the faithful in the faith. Indeed, this conviction could be expressed in ways that might make a preaching ministry seem just as much a channel of salvation as a sacramental priesthood. If patrons promoted curates who were unable to preach, they were causing 'the death and damnation of the souls committed to the charge of all such unlearned priests'.[6] Henrician conservatives might continue to deny that the office of a priest 'is only to preach, as some men untruly do say', but Protestants were firm in their insistence that 'to preach the Gospel . . . is the true vocation and office of all godly bishops, parsons, vicars, and of other shepherds'.[7]

According to this view the Catholic Church had shamefully neglected the office of preaching. Catholicism was indicted not simply because under its tutelage preaching had been undervalued and intermittent, but because such preaching as there was was of the wrong sort; saints' lives and miracle stories rather than the pure word of God. Jerome Barlow blamed the friars not for failing to preach, but for preaching 'fables of their conjecture' rather than holy scripture.[8] Becon contrasted true preaching with clerical 'narrations out of English *Festival*, saints' lives out of *Legenda Aurea* and sermons out of *Dormi Secure*'.[9] The Yorkshire Protestant poet, Wilfrid Holme, evinced similar contempt for the preachers whose homilectic inspiration came from *Dormi Secure, Sermones Parati,* and *Sermones Discipuli,* all collections popular with the late medieval parish clergy.[10]

The notion that the preaching of priests was usually contemptible had strong Lollard antecedents. Richard Hilman, who was persecuted for his beliefs at Coventry towards the end of the fifteenth century, owned an English book containing the Lord's Prayer and the Creed, and contended that 'no priest speaketh better in the pulpit than that book'.[11] In 1511 the Londoner, Joan Baker, said that 'she could hear a better sermon at home

[6] Cowper (ed.), *Four Supplications*, 39.

[7] R. Smith, *A Defence of the Blessed Masse* (1546), sig. I.v^{r-v}; Cowper (ed.), *Four Supplications*, 51.

[8] J. Barlow, *The Burial of the Mass*, in E. Arber (ed.), *English Reprints* (1871), 73.

[9] T. Becon, *Prayers and Other Pieces*, ed. J. Ayre, PS (1844), 199–200. *Dormi Secure* was a popular sermon collection of the early 16th c., so called because possession of these prepared homilies guaranteed the preacher a sound and untroubled sleep on Saturday night.

[10] A. G. Dickens, *Lollards and Protestants in the Diocese of York* (1959), 123. Thomas More was also critical of preachers who relied on prepared material: E. F. Rogers (ed.), *St Thomas More: Selected Letters* (New Haven, Conn., 1961), 39.

[11] Foxe, *Acts and Monuments*, iv. 135.

in her house than any doctor or priest could make at Paul's Cross or any other place'.[12] Thomas Man, who was burned at Smithfield in 1518, maintained that pulpits were but 'priests' lying stools'.[13]

Such hostile comments argue at least for a familiarity with the priest in his role as preacher, and the notion that preaching was almost totally neglected by priests in the late Middle Ages is almost certainly a false one.[14] A basic minimum was required by canon law. Archbishop Peckham's constitution of 1281 required all priests with cure of souls to declare to their parishioners in English four times a year the Articles of Faith, Commandments, Gospel precepts, and the Seven Works of Mercy, Deadly Sins, Virtues, and Sacraments, or to procure some other priest to fulfil the obligation. Another canon exhorted rectors and vicars diligently to preach the Word of God lest they be accounted 'dumb dogs'.[15] Later authorities sought to reinforce these requirements. In the mid-fifteenth century Archbishop George Nevill reiterated Peckham's constitution for the northern province, and in the early sixteenth century conscientious diocesans like Fox of Winchester and West of Ely put great effort into trying to ensure the provisions were observed.[16] Certainly there is nothing to suggest that educated opinion in the late medieval Church under-valued the priest's duties of teaching and preaching. The author of the *Quattuor Sermones*, printed by Caxton in 1483, regarded the deposit of faith as that 'which we that have the cure of souls be bound to teach . . . our parishioners on pain of damnation of our souls'.[17] The fifteenth-century author of *Dives and Pauper*, whose essential orthodoxy is not really in doubt, regarded curates who failed to preach in almost proto-Protestant fashion as 'manslayers ghostly' and insisted that it was more profitable for a man's soul to hear a sermon than to attend mass.[18] In this opinion he was seconded by the impeccably orthodox Richard Whitford:

[12] A. Hudson, *The Premature Reformation* (Oxford, 1988), 199–200.

[13] Foxe, *Acts and Monuments*, iv. 208.

[14] For a survey of late medieval preaching, see G. R. Owst, *Preaching in Medieval England* (Cambridge, 1926); *Literature and Pulpit in Medieval English*, 2nd edn. (Cambridge, 1961); H. L. Spencer, 'English Vernacular Sunday Preaching in the Late Fourteenth and Fifteenth Century', University of Oxford D.Phil. thesis (1982).

[15] *Lyndwood*, 20–1, 26.

[16] R. M. Wooley (ed. and trans.), *The York Provinciale put forth by Thomas Wolsey* (1931), 8; R. Houlbrooke, *Church Courts and the People during the English Reformation* (Oxford, 1979), 199–200; F. Heal, 'Parish Clergy and the Reformation in the Diocese of Ely', *CAS* 66 (1977), 149.

[17] N. F. Blake (ed.), *Quattuor Sermones printed by William Caxton* (Heidelberg, 1975), 19. See also G. de Roye, *The Doctrinal of Sapyence* (1489), sig. I.i^v.

[18] *Dives and Pauper* (1534), 176^{r-v}.

'let them ever keep the preachings rather than the masse, if (by case) they may not hear both'.[19]

Priests were encouraged to take their duty of preaching seriously, and many of them surely did so. An examination of the books found in a sample of around 370 early sixteenth-century priests' wills reveals that, service books aside, volumes of sermons accounted for the largest category of named titles. Particularly popular were the *Sermones Discipuli* of Johannes Herolt, a book which was bequeathed more frequently than the Bible.[20] Not all priests may have relied on pre-prepared collections of this sort, but John West, vicar of Ringwood in Hampshire, was clearly exceptional in bequeathing 'all my sermons written with mine own hand'.[21] It is probable, then, that many ordinary parishioners, regularly if not necessarily frequently, had the opportunity to experience a priest as preacher, as well as a minister of the sacraments. Evidence as to how they might have evaluated the priest in this role is, however, sparse and indirect, and this account will inevitably involve the uncertain expedient of arguing from silence. If it can be shown that lay expectations in this regard were high, that laypeople wanted sermons, and sermons of a certain standard, then perhaps the religious upheavals of the mid-sixteenth century may have seemed to them more explicable and acceptable. If not, then the new insistence of religious authority that priests devote their energies primarily to preaching, may well have seemed a strange and unwelcome innovation.

At St Botolph's, Aldgate, in London in 1508, Michael Mawnford called upon the curate to 'leave thy preaching, for it is not worth a fart'. The consequent damage to the priest's reputation as a preacher was judged sufficient to enable him to sue Mawnford for defamation in the church court.[22] Recorded examples of lay evaluations of a priest's sermon

[19] R. Whitford, *A Werke for housholders* (1530), sig. D.iv^r. This order of priorities seems to have been an axiom of some Catholic reforming opinion, and was upheld in the 15th c. by Bernadino of Siena: B. Manning, *The People's Faith in the Time of Wyclif* (Hassocks, 1975), 18.

[20] Similar conclusions have been reached by C. Cross, 'Priests into Ministers: The Establishment of Protestant Practice in the City of York', in P. N. Brooks (ed.), *Reformation Principle and Practice* (1980), 209; Heal, 'The Parish Clergy and the Reformation in the Diocese of Ely', 146; P. Heath, *English Parish Clergy on the Eve of the Reformation* (1969), 88. It is unlikely that wills can provide a complete picture of clerical book ownership: some volumes were probably bequeathed by hand before the will was drawn up, and we have no guarantee that the remainder would be faithfully catalogued in the will. Indeed, it could be argued that the more books a cleric possessed, the less likely he would be to describe and bequeath the volumes individually.

[21] PRO, PCC, Prob. 11, 6 Pynnyng.

[22] R. M. Wunderli, *London Church Courts and Society on the Eve of the Reformation* (1981), 77.

are rare in the pre-Reformation period, but there are scattered indications that Mawnford's impatience with the pulpit was probably not unique. It was a common complaint of medieval preachers that their audiences were often inattentive, talking or sleeping during the sermon. The Dominican John Bromyard claimed that the English were the worst sermon-goers in the world, and the Franciscan Nicole Bozen asserted that 'many are more grieved by a short homily than by six week-days of labour and bodily affliction'.[23] Professional practitioners such as these were perhaps over ready to believe that their art was undervalued, but the charge is confirmed by other sources. In the late medieval examinations of conscience designed to assist in preparation for confession, a neglectful or contemptuous attitude to preaching was frequently listed among the matters to be confessed. *The Traytte of Good Lyving and Good Deying* impressed upon its readers that they should hear the Word of God willingly 'and should not go from the said preachings'.[24] The clerical handbook known as the *Exornatorium Curatorum* instructed curates to ask their parishioners whether they had been 'slothful to hear the Word of God preached'.[25]

Given the penitential context, such examples are not necessarily evidence for the prevalence of the attitudes of which they complain. A more useful source for these purposes is the visitation record, revealing as it does the matters which were a source of particular parochial concern.[26] Occasionally preaching features explicitly in this material. In 1481, for example, it was reported to the visitors in the parish of Bishophill in Yorkshire that 'when the Word of God is declared in the said church, and the said parishioners hath warning to come hear it, the most part of them cometh not at all, and especially those that be in the country, and that is the cause that there be so few sermons as is'.[27] In Bishophill, it seems, preaching came low in the scale of popular priorities. In other visitation records the silence of the parishioners is more revealing. Complaints

---

[23] Owst, *Preaching in Medieval England*, 173 ff., 179.

[24] F. A. Gasquet, *The Eve of the Reformation* (1900), 282, 285.

[25] *Exornatorium Curatorum* (1520), sig. B.iii^r. The *floure of the commaundements of god* (1521) included among its improving exempla one 'of the parishioners of a curate, the which would never hear the predication and commandments of the Church', 128^r.

[26] The value to the historian of visitation presentments undoubtedly needs to be qualified. They were made usually by the churchwardens, whose concerns probably reflected those of a parochial élite, and much depended on the thoroughness and preoccupations of the visitors, as is suggested e.g. by the great disparity in the number of parishes reporting *omnia bene* between the Lincoln visitations of 1518–19 and 1530. None the less, as a barometer of what respectable parish opinion held to be unbearable abuses, visitation material remains an indispensable source.

[27] J. Raine (ed.), *The Fabric Rolls of York Minster*, SS 35 (1858), 258.

about the behaviour and morals of parish priests, and their various
derelictions of duty were commonplace at early sixteenth-century visitations. All these matters featured prominently, for example, during Archbishop Warham's Canterbury visitation of 1511. Yet there was here no
suggestion that priests were failing to preach the Word of God. It is
possible that all priests were preaching as they ought to, but given the
highly variable standards of pastoral care which the visitation revealed,
this seems unlikely. A more probable explanation is that laypeople were
not sufficiently concerned by the absence or inadequacy of preaching to
bring the matter to the attention of the visitors. The sole *compertum* to
mention preaching complained of the behaviour of a certain Thomas
Fuller who 'forsaketh the church at the time of preaching and sitteth in
the church porch, talking and reasoning the words of the preaching
inordinately at alehouses'.[28] Fuller was more probably a parish trouble-
maker than an impassioned amateur theologian, but he was probably not
alone in complaining about sermons in the alehouse. The Henrician
preacher, Roger Edgeworth, clearly regarded the tavern as the enemy of
the pulpit: 'when you be on your ale bench or in your bankets . . . then
have at the preachers'.[29] The common lament of later Puritan preachers,
that men preferred ale to sermons, was probably not unknown among
their pre-Reformation predecessors.[30]

The visitations undertaken by the Bishop of Lincoln and his deputies
in 1517–31 suggest a similar lack of enthusiasm for preaching. A few
complaints were made: at St Michael's in Oxford the curate was reported
since 'he does not preach to us the Word of God'. At Westwell in
Oxfordshire it was noted that no one had preached there for a year, and
a couple of other parishes complained that the General Sentence had not
been read or the Articles of Faith declared. In 1530 it was said that the
vicar of Ashwell in Hertfordshire had not preached for ten years.[31] Perhaps, then, some modicum of preaching was expected, but it seems unlikely that from over a thousand parishes these were the only ones where
the hierarchy's instructions were not being fulfilled to the letter.

There were, of course, some who took the priest's preaching duties
very seriously. Erasmus noted with approval the attentiveness of Thomas
More's daughters at sermons and the discrimination with which they

[28] *Kentish Visitations*, 205.

[29] J. W. Blench, *Preaching in England in the Late Fifteenth and Sixteenth Centuries*
(Oxford, 1964), 237–8.

[30] P. Collinson, *The Religion of Protestants: The Church in English Society 1559–1625*
(Oxford, 1982), 203–7.   [31] *Lincoln Visitations*, i. 139, 132, 67; ii. 18.

listened. They were able to 'recite almost the whole sermon in its correct order . . . and if the priest has babbled something foolish, something impious or something otherwise improper for a preacher—which we see happening frequently nowadays—they know whether to laugh, or to ignore it or to express their indignation'. But Erasmus believed such ability to be extremely rare: too many women, he claimed, returned from sermons unable to say a sensible word about what they had heard.[32] Perhaps more typical was the attitude exhibited by Robert Revell in Derbyshire in 1538. The priest 'being in the pulpit very long declaring the gospel', Revell instructed his chaplain to tell him to 'make an end' (*fac finem*).[33] If we can accept the testimony of Henry Gold, arch-conservative rector of Hayes in Middlesex, and admittedly hardly a typical parish priest, some men would habitually enquire on arriving at church whether there was to be any sermon that day. If this was affirmed, they would leave the church again, saying that they would rather miss matins and mass than be forced to listen to the Word of God.[34]

Inevitably, the course of the Henrician Reformation placed a heavier preaching burden on to ordinary parish priests and explicitly accentuated their role as preachers and teachers of the Word of God. From 1534 the clergy were required to preach regularly in support of the royal supremacy and in derogation of the authority of the Pope. The royal injunctions of 1536 laid on priests the duty of declaring the Ten Articles and preaching the abrogation of superfluous holy days, as well as using sermons to teach their congregations the Pater Noster, Ten Commandments, and Articles of Faith in English, a provision reiterated by episcopal injunctions. In 1538 priests were to ensure that at least once a quarter they could 'purely and sincerely declare the very Gospel of Christ'. Some bishops pegged the number of sermons to be delivered annually to the value of the benefice. In 1547 the Edwardian injunctions finally stipulated the reading of homilies every Sunday.[35]

It is conceivable that these developments may have encouraged a perception in the parishes that priests ought to preach, or at least that they ought to do what authority expected of them, and from about 1540 onwards complaints about the neglect of preaching seem to become more frequent in visitation returns and other sources.[36] It is, however, difficult

[32] R. Marius, *Thomas More* (1985), 224.   [33] PRO, STA. C. 2, 26/194.
[34] *LP* vii. 523 (4).   [35] *Visitation Articles*, ii. 3–6, 37, 45, 47, 128–9.
[36] H. Salter (ed.), 'A Visitation of Oxfordshire in 1540', *Oxfordshire Archaeological Society Reports*, 75 (1930), 292, 294, 296, 300; Hale, *Precedents*, 112, 121, 127; PRO, C. 1, 1108/51; Houlbrooke, *Church Courts and the People*, 200.

to say whether this is primarily a reflection of changing popular aspirations, or of growing official interest in the clergy's proper performance of these duties. As late as 1543 a visitation of the diocese of Worcester could produce no complaints of lack of preaching, and the archdeaconry of Norwich provided hardly any in the 1540s.[37] Where a stronger impetus to uncover delinquency came from above the difference is marked: after the Protestant Bishop John Ponet's visitation of the diocese of Winchester in 1551, twenty-one parishes admitted that the incumbent had failed to provide quarterly sermons.[38]

At the same time positive dislike of preaching continued to cause concern to the authorities. In 1542 Bishop Bonner of London complained that many young people in his diocese 'doth use upon the Sundays and holy days in time of divine service, and preaching the word of God, to resort unto ale-houses, and there exerciseth unlawful games, with great swearing, blasphemy, drunkenness, and other enormities'.[39] In the archdeaconry of Norwich in 1548–9 the institution of weekly homilies seems to have led to a marked increase in the number of persons presented for absenting themselves from church; one woman was reported for walking out while the homily was being read.[40] In 1552 a statute complained of the 'great number of people in divers parts of this realm' who abstained from coming to church 'where common prayer, administration of the sacraments and preaching of the word of God is used'.[41]

A valuable witness to the popular attitude towards preaching in the late 1540s is the conservative prelate, Stephen Gardiner. In a letter of 1547, Gardiner sought to convince Cranmer that ordinary English people 'cannot abide to be long a teaching', a circumstance which he charitably ascribed to the quickness of their wits rather than to indolence or dullness. If priests were to read from the newly published Book of Homilies the people would hear them in the same way they heard matins, that is, they would be preoccupied with their own devotions and pay little attention to the priest. Gardiner went on to describe his own experience of a parish church where there was regularly good preaching 'and yet of all this town there may be percase sometime not above twenty at a sermon'. Nor could be Bishop of Winchester resist reminding his correspondent that in Cranmer's own cathedral church a sermon had attracted only

---

[37] S. Thompson, 'The Pastoral Work of the English and Welsh Bishops, 1500–1558', University of Oxford D.Phil. thesis (1984), 100; Houlbrooke, *Church Courts and the People*, 200. [38] Houlbrooke, ibid. 201.
[39] *Visitation Articles*, ii. 86. See also ibid. 56, 187–8, 244.
[40] Houlbrooke, *Church Courts and the People*, 243–4. [41] 5 & 6 Edward VI, c. 1.

about 100 listeners; even when Ridley preached 'there were not for all Canterbury many more'. In an earlier letter Gardiner had also argued that sermons generally made little impression on people, except with a minority 'that enterprising a knowledge above their capacity . . . will take upon them to travail in everything they hear'. The ineffectualness of sermons was compounded 'when they be not handsomely uttered'. At Cambridge, Gardiner claimed, there was a parish church where it commonly transpired that 'when the vicar goeth into the pulpit to read that [he] himself hath written, then the multitude of the parish goeth straight out of the church home to drink'. None of this can of course, be taken at entirely face value. Gardiner was desperate to resist the propagation of the solifidian theology of the 1547 Book of Homilies. Somewhat disingenuously, in view of his defence of the *Golden Legend* and the *Festial*, he argued that priests would not be esteemed were they to 'rehearse a homily made by another'.[42] Yet we should perhaps hesitate before dismissing Gardiner's insights as no more than the calculated persuasions of a partisan. Preachers of differing religious persuasions themselves sometimes complained of the ineffectiveness of their preaching. Bishop Longland, for example, asked rhetorically: 'what result follows from so many sermons? How few who wish to amend their lives in accordance with our preaching.'[43] In 1550 Latimer lamented 'we be many preachers here in England, and we preach many long sermons yet the people will not repent nor convert'.[44] The expectation that the bulk of parishioners would attend church services in order to pay devout attention to a sermon was still something of a hopeful one in the England of Edward's reign, perhaps even of Elizabeth's.[45]

It would be wrong, of course, to be overly dismissive of the significance of preaching in this period. In the 1530s and 1540s controversial preaching whether from conservatives or radicals had the potential to divide whole communities, and the sermons delivered at St Paul's Cross in London regularly attracted large audiences.[46] In 1517, according to Polydore Vergil, a Dominican and a canon regular 'quickly stirred up a multitude

---

[42] S. Gardiner, *The Letters of Stephen Gardiner*, ed. J. A. Muller (Cambridge, 1933), 355–6, 311, 314–15.   [43] Blench, *Preaching in England*, 237.

[44] Latimer, *Sermons*, i. 240.

[45] C. Haigh cites considerable evidence for the unpopularity of preaching in Elizabeth's reign in his article 'The Church of England, the Catholics and the People', in C. Haigh (ed.), *The Reign of Elizabeth I* (1984), 207–9.

[46] G. R. Elton, *Policy and Police* (Cambridge, 1972), 14, 17, 19–20, 23, 35, 37, 40, 101–2, 113, 139–41; *LP* xviii (2). 546; M. Maclure, *The Paul's Cross Sermons, 1534–1642* (Toronto, 1958).

of people by their sermons', leading directly to the 'Evil May Day' riots against foreigners.[47] Even more importantly, it seems to have been an impassioned sermon by the vicar of Louth, Thomas Kendall, that precipitated the Lincolnshire rising in 1536.[48] Yet dramatic and emotionally charged occasions such as these were by definition exceptional. Whether the preaching ideal could have become fully incorporated into the popular perception of the priestly vocation in this period remains highly doubtful.

Requests for priests to preach did, however, occur periodically in laypeople's wills. In 1515 Bertram Dawson of York left 3s. 4d. to 'the doctor that shall show the Word of God at my eight day'.[49] Edward Stanley, Lord Monteagle, endowed a funeral sermon in 1523, as did John Witdecombe of Martock in Somerset in 1527, and James Spire of Sherborne in Hampshire in 1533.[50] Such bequests were not necessarily indicative of proto-Protestantism. Witdecombe also left money for trentals from the regular and secular clergy, Monteagle endowed a chantry, and Spire expected the full panoply of intercessory benefaction. As late as 1545 John Bryngborne of Faversham in Kent could provide both for two sermons to be said at and after his burial, and for a priest to sing for his soul for six months.[51] The vogue for funeral sermons does, however, seem to have been the prerogative of the social élite: Dawson was an alderman and former mayor of York,[52] Bryngborne a merchant, and Witdecombe is described in his will as a gentleman.

In Edward's reign bequests for sermons were more likely to appear unequivocally Protestant. In 1549 John Lytell of Queenborough in Kent left no money for masses but provided for a sermon to be said in the parish church of Gravesend 'to the ghostly feeding of the parishioners'; at the place of his death he intended that 'some learned man of the best shall preach unto the people some godly sermon wherby the people may be spiritually fed'.[53] In 1550 William Pykes, a mercer of Bristol, followed the explicitly Protestant preamble of his will with a bequest for 'some

---

[47] Vergil, P., *The Anglia Historia of Polydore Vergil, AD 1485–1537*, ed. D. Hay, CS 74 (1950), 243.

[48] C. S. L. Davies, 'Popular Religion and the Pilgrimage of Grace', in A. Fletcher and J. Stevenson (eds.), *Order and Disorder in Early Modern England* (Cambridge, 1985), 71.

[49] *Test. Ebor.* v. 61.

[50] F. W. Weaver (ed.), *Somerset Medieval Wills 1501–1530*, SRS 19 (1903), 262; PRO, PCC, Prob. 11, 12 Hogen; J. W. Clay (ed.), *North Country Wills*, SS 116 (1908), 111.

[51] PRO, PCC, Prob. 11, 29 Pynnyng.

[52] A. Raine (ed.), *York Civic Records*, iii, YAS (RS) 106 (1942), 35–7.

[53] PRO, PCC, Prob. 11, 9 Bucke.

well-learned man to declare the most pure sincere and lively word of God
to the Christian congregation'.[54] In 1552 Giles Levyt of Suffolk wanted a
priest at his burial to make 'a small collation of scriptures desiring all
people I have offended to forgive me'.[55] It should be noted, however, that
compared to the volume of endowment for intercessory masses, these
bequests fade into statistical insignificance. Only about one in 700 of the
testators in the sample left money for funeral sermons, whereas over a
third endowed masses, and others requested the prayers of priests and
religious. Clearly, to most of those faced with the prospect of imminent
death, the priest was significant not as exponent of the word of God, but
as mediator and intercessor.

THE LEARNING OF THE PRIEST

In the bequests for funeral sermons there was usually no expectation that
they would be performed by the local parish clergy as part of the normal
course of their duties. The testators stipulated a university graduate or
some 'learned man'. Those with the ability to preach or to preach well
were evidently regarded as a group separate and distinct from the mass of
the parochial clergy. This perception was very probably correct. Medieval incumbents had been obliged only to provide quarterly sermons, not
necessarily to preach them themselves, and the duty was often carried out
by monks and friars from neighbouring religious houses.[56] In 1535
Archbishop Lee of York could claim that he did not know of more than
twelve secular priests in his diocese that were able to preach.[57] Many parish
priests did not preach, one can safely assume, because they were too
ignorant to do so properly. Priestly ignorance has long headed the historical indictment of the medieval parish clergy, yet modern research has
suggested that standards of clerical education on the eve of the Reformation were not so dire as was once imagined. The number of graduates
appointed to church livings had, for example, been rising since the fifteenth century, and in the early sixteenth century graduates seem to have
accounted for on average around 20–25 per cent of all appointments, a

[54] J. P. Wadley (ed.), *Notes or Abstracts of the Wills contained in the volume entitled The
Great Orphan Book and Book of Wills in the Council House at Bristol*, Bristol and Gloucestershire Archaeological Society (1886), 187.

[55] Tymms (ed.), *Wills and Inventories from . . . Bury St Edmunds*, CS os 49 (1850), 140.

[56] J. R. Lander, *Government and Community England, 1450–1509* (Cambridge, Mass., 1980),
111.

[57] H. Ellis (ed.), *Original Letters Illustrative of English History*, 3rd ser. (1846), ii. 338–9.

figure that was higher in the vicinity of the universities.[58] At the same time educational opportunities for non-graduates may also have been increasing, through the expansion of grammar and elementary schooling.[59] In addition, the ecclesiastical authorities could take direct steps to maintain basic standards, bishops examining candidates for ordination and refusing admission to benefices to the notoriously ignorant. In 1520, for example, the Dean of York rejected Lord Clifford's nominee to a benefice on the grounds that he had seen 'few priests so simple learned in my life'.[60] Concern about clerical ignorance may have been manifested more intensely by some of the Edwardian bishops, but the efforts and achievements of their predecessors are not to be despised.

The extreme ignorance of many parish priests was, nevertheless, a theme which featured prominently in the writings of both Protestants and humanists in the early sixteenth century.[61] John Skelton pilloried the deficiencies of his fellow priests in poems like *Speke Parrot* and *Colin Clout*, while in his *Dialogue between Pole and Lupset*, Thomas Starkey made the cardinal complain of the scandal whereby unlearned men filled the place of those who should preach the word of God and teach the people 'for commonly you shall find that they can no thing do but patter up their matins and mass, mumbling up a certain number of words no thing understood'.[62] His analysis scarcely differed from that of Tyndale, who suggested that most curates 'wot no more what the new or old Testament meaneth, than do the Turks: neither know they of any more than that they read at mass, matins and evensong, which yet they understand not'.[63] This type of priest was an easy subject for satire, characterized by Robert Crowley as 'thou that art lewd without learning whom men commonly call Sir John'.[64] Whether or not unlearned priests were addressed in this way by their parishioners, the appellation clearly formed part of a literary tradition which Protestant writers could employ for their own ends. The Edwardian preacher, John Bradford, depicted 'blind buzzard Sir John' and 'Sir John Masser', while Hugh Latimer suspected the

---

[58] P. Marshall, 'Attitudes of the English People to Priests and Priesthood, 1500–1553', University of Oxford D.Phil. thesis (1990), 135 n.

[59] J. A. H. Moran, *The Growth of English Schooling 1340–1548* (Princeton, NJ, 1958), 141; Lander, *Government and Community*, 131–2.

[60] Thompson, 'Pastoral Work of the English and Welsh Bishops', 34, 181–2; A. G. Dickens (ed.), *Clifford Letters of the Sixteenth Century*, SS 172 (1962), 84.

[61] H. M. Smith, *Pre-Reformation England* (1938), 40–3.

[62] J. Scattergood (ed.), *John Skelton: The Complete English Poems* (Harmondsworth, 1983), 230–78; T. Starkey, *A Dialogue between Pole and Lupset*, ed. T. F. Mayer, CS 37, 4th ser. (1989), 88.   [63] W. Tyndale, *Doctrinal Treatises*, ed. H. Walter, PS (1848), 146.

[64] R. Crowley, *Select Works*, ed. J. M. Cowper, EETS ES 15 (1872), 70.

existence of a papist plot to keep the people in ignorance 'lest their ignorant Sir Johns should be had in less estimation or despised'.[65] In his sermons on the Lord's Prayer, Latimer contrasted his ideal of a 'faithful painful preacher' with the type of priest patrons often advanced: 'a Sir John, which hath better skill in playing at tables, or in keeping of a garden, than in God's word'.[66] The alleged inability of such priests even to conduct formal services, let alone preach, was reflected in the fuller designation 'Sir John Lack-Latin'.[67] According to Francis Bigod, pluralists often placed in their livings 'a Sir John Lack-Latin that can scarce read his porteaus'.[68]

Sir John Lack-Latin was despised by Protestant reformers and humanist intellectuals; a more intriguing question is that of whether he was held in equal contempt by the laypersons entrusted to his care. Certainly the question of educational standards does not seem to have weighed very heavily with those lay patrons who appointed unlearned priests to benefices, or the lay rectors who put in ignorant curates. It was these rather than the priests themselves who were often the prime object of Protestant censure.[69] It is notable that lay patrons tended to promote fewer graduates to the livings in their gift than did the bishops, and that despite the risk of a *quare impedit* suit from the patron, bishops in at least twelve dioceses in this period either refused to admit, or admitted only conditionally, unsuitable nominees to benefices.[70] If the influential laymen who exercised ecclesiastical patronage were not infrequently careless about standards of clerical learning, one can perhaps expect little from the members of largely illiterate rural congregations. The Protestant divine, Thomas Lever, spoke hopefully in 1550 of the 'rude lobs of the country, which be too simple to paint a lie' complaining of how the curate 'minisheth God's sacraments, he slubbers up his service, and he can not read the humbles [homilies]'.[71] Yet it is striking that the evidence for clerical ignorance tends to come from literary sources such as this, rather than from genuine

---

[65] J. Bradford, *The Writings of John Bradford . . . Letters, Treatises, Remains*, ed. A. Townsend, PS (1853), 43, 324; N. Ridley, *Works*, ed. H. Christmas, PS (1843), 104.

[66] Latimer, *Sermons*, i. 317.

[67] Ibid. ii. 28; J. Pilkington, *Works*, ed. J. Scholefield, PS (1852), 20, 160, 271.

[68] A. G. Dickens (ed.), *Tudor Treatises*, YAS 125 (1959), 52.

[69] Cowper (ed.), *Four Supplications*, 38–9; Latimer, *Sermons*, i. 317; ii. 28; H. Brinklow, *The Complaynt of Roderyck Mors*, ed. J. M. Cowper, EETS ES 22 (1874), 33–4.

[70] M. Bowker, *The Secular Clergy in the Diocese of Lincoln, 1485–1520* (Cambridge, 1968), 45; S. J. Lander, 'The Diocese of Chichester 1508–1558: Episcopal Reform under Robert Sherburne and its Aftermath', University of Cambridge Ph.D. thesis (1974), 204; Thompson, 'Pastoral Work of English and Welsh Bishops', 30, 34–5.

[71] T. Lever, *Sermons 1550*, ed. E. Arber, *English Reprints* (1870), 65.

parochial protest. Visitation returns are usually silent on the question of priests' educational abilities. In 1519 the Prior of Spalding in Lincolnshire was criticized by parishioners for placing curates in the parish who were unsuitable and ignorant, and at Wrawby in Leicestershire the curate was similarly said to be ignorant, but these complaints are unique among the Lincoln material.[72] Claire Cross has discovered a fascinating case from Marian York in which a curate was criticized by three parishioners for grammatical errors in reading the Latin liturgy. Yet significantly it seems to have been the priest's habitual drunkenness rather than his ignorance which prompted the parish to take action against him.[73] In general, parishioners seem either not to have thought themselves competent to pass judgement on their priest's educational abilities, or else to have considered the matter as being of relative unimportance so long as the cure was served conscientiously and the sacraments ministered regularly and validly. The many priests who were found by the Edwardian chantry commissioners to be only 'meanly learned' or 'indifferently learned' but 'of honest conversation and qualities' seem to have been valued by their lay neighbours.[74] In any case, as students of the early sixteenth-century clergy have not been slow to recognize, a more uniformly graduate clergy would probably have done little to improve the quality of pastoral care in the parishes. Graduate priests tended to be absentees, and even if they chose to reside in the benefice, the university curriculum made no concessions to the kind of practical knowledge a parish clergyman would require.[75] So long as the mass was said regularly and without obvious error, it probably mattered little if the celebrant was a less than perfect latinist. To a Protestant such as Henry Brinklow it might seem an abomination to be expected to 'go pour out my vices in the ear of an unlearned buzzard', but the fact remains that such a priest was able to give an absolution as secure and valid as that of any other.[76] If the moral standing of the priest could

[72] *Lincoln Visitations*, i. 61; Bowker, *Secular Clergy in the Diocese of Lincoln*, 56.

[73] C. Cross, 'Lay Literacy and Clerical Misconduct in a York Parish during the Reign of Mary Tudor', *York Historian* (1980).

[74] A. Hussey (ed.), *Kent Chantries*, Kent Archaeological Society Records Branch, 12 (1936), 254; J. Raine (ed.), *The Injunctions and other Ecclesiastical Proceedings of Richard Barnes, Bishop of Durham 1576–1587*, SS 22 (1850), lxxviii–lxxxvii; C. J. Kitching (ed.), *London and Middlesex Chantry Certificates, 1548*, LoRS 16 (1980), 4–6.

[75] C. Harper-Bill, 'Dean Colet's Convocation Sermon and the Pre-Reformation Church in England', *History*, 73 (1988), 204; F. Heal, 'Economic Problems of the Clergy', in F. Heal and R. O'Day (eds.), *Church and Society in England, Henry VIII to James I* (1977), 106; Lander, *Government and Community*, 131.

[76] H. Brinklow, *The Lamentacyon of a Christen Agaynst the Cyte of London*, ed. J. M. Cowper, EETS ES 22 (1874), 111.

at times act as the barometer of something like a popular quasi-Donatism, the same does not seem to have been true to anything like the same extent of his educational standards. People wanted virtuous and honest priests to say masses for their souls, not skilled and learned graduates; it was lasciviousness, drunkenness, and idleness that aroused the wrath of parishioners, not educational mediocrity.

This is not to claim, of course, that no layperson showed any interest in clerical education. Some testators sought positively to encourage study in candidates to the priesthood by leaving money for the purpose in their wills, and such bequests may have been on the increase in the latter part of the fifteenth century.[77] Most frequently, the recipients of these bequests were the sons of the testators, and their parents were doubtless aware of the career opportunities education might open to the aspirant cleric.[78] Occasionally, however, testators displayed an appreciation of the value of clerical learning for its own sake. In 1530 William Pratt of Lenham in Kent made a bequest of twenty shillings yearly for seven years to a young friar in Aylesford 'if he so long live and be of good rule and will and may apply his learning or else to some other young friar of that house disposed to learning'.[79] In 1521 Thomas Everston of Buckinghamshire bequeathed forty shillings *per annum* to Andrew Page for his exhibition to Oxford. The money was to continue after Page was ordained, provided he continued as a scholar.[80] In some cases it is difficult to decide whether the funding of scholars represents concern for the renewal of the church, or a more traditional preoccupation with the accumulation of merit through the performance of 'good works'.[81] Perhaps the distinction is in most cases a meaningless one, but there seems to be a clear element of social concern in the insistence of William Swanne of Southfleet in Kent in 1533 that one of the two stipendiaries celebrating for his soul be 'a cunning learned man that may and can teach grammar and latin and to teach freely as a free school as many scholars as well poor children as other as shall resort and come to him'.[82] Swanne anticipated by only a few years the common episcopal injunction that chantry priests should instruct the children of the parish to read, though this duty may already

[77] Tanner, *Church in Late Medieval Norwich*, 31; J. A. F. Thomson, 'Clergy and Laity in London, 1376–1531', University of Oxford D.Phil. thesis (1960), 188–90.

[78] PRO, PCC, Prob. 11, 40 Holgrave (John Phillippes); Weaver (ed.), *Somerset Medieval Wills, 1501–1530*, 211.　　　　　　　　　　[79] PRO, PCC, Prob. 11, 12 Hogen.

[80] E. M. Elvey (ed.), *The Courts of the Archdeaconry of Buckingham 1483–1523*, Bucks. Record Society, 19 (1975), 387.

[81] See e.g. the wills of John Byncoll (1500) and Thomas Tremayll (1508), in Weaver (ed.), *Somerset Medieval Wills*, 6, 116.　　　　　　　　[82] PRO, PCC, Prob. 11, 16 Hogen.

have been widely undertaken in the Middle Ages.[83] Yet even among those testators who expressed an interest in clerical education, a minimal standard may sometimes have been considered sufficient. In 1535 a Yorkshire woman stipulated, for example, that her son 'be found at school till he can write and read and if he will be priest'.[84] There can have been no expectation that such a candidate for orders would have developed into a great doctor or learned divine: a little knowledge sufficed.

THE PRIEST AND RELIGIOUS INSTRUCTION

Modest though his accomplishments may have been, the village curate was still expected to be able to instruct his parishioners in the rudiments of the faith. How universally this obligation may have been honoured is difficult to say; certainly the poor showing of the Gloucester clergy in 1550 when half of those examined were unable to recite the Ten Commandments, does suggest that these priests had not been teaching them to their parishioners in English as they were required to do.[85] Most layfolk may have had little time for long discursive sermons, or may not have felt that preaching constituted an indispensable part of a parish priest's duties, yet there is some scattered evidence to suggest that parishioners had a genuine desire to be taught the basic facts of their religion, and did expect some information from their curate. At Kirkby Malzeard in 1500 the quarterly instruction prescribed by canon law was clearly not taking place and the parishioners petitioned the visitor 'to have our belief showed four times in the year as ye say we should have'.[86] In around 1511 it was noted that the neglect by its incumbent of the parish of Sezincote in Gloucestershire meant that there was no one to say mass or matins 'nor to inform or instruct the parishioners there as ought to be by the law of God'.[87] At Penrith in Cumberland during the Pilgrimage of Grace, four priests were appointed by the rebels as 'chaplains of poverty', and required on pain of death to instruct the commons in the faith.[88]

Only two years after this the reformer George Constantine was complaining: 'how loth be our priests to teach the commandments, the articles

[83] *Visitation Articles*, ii. 17, 63, 85; Moran, *Growth of English Schooling*, 178.
[84] Moran, ibid. 140.
[85] D. M. Barratt, 'The Condition of the Parish Clergy between the Reformation and 1660, with Special Reference to the Dioceses of Oxford, Worcester and Gloucester', University of Oxford D.Phil. thesis (1949), 118 n.
[86] Raine (ed.), *Fabric Rolls of York Minster*, 264.   [87] PRO, STA. C. 2, 35/68.
[88] *LP* xii (1). 687 (2).

of the faith, and the Pater Noster in English! Again how unwilling be the people to learn it. Yea they jest at it, calling it the new Pater Noster and new learning.'[89] This attitude seems to reflect deep conservatism rather than Philistinism or unbelief. It is the requirement to learn the Pater Noster in English rather than vernacular instruction as such which is the object of derision. Lay reservations about the new curriculum were encouraged by some conservative priests. One Kentish curate in the 1540s only very grudgingly taught the Pater Noster in English, likening it to the hard shell of a nut 'and the Pater Noster in Latin to the sweet kernel', and at least one Kentish layman obstinately refused to learn the English version of the prayer.[90]

A concern for the traditional content of religious teaching is also present in the demand of the South-Western rebels in 1549 that the clerics Dr Moreman and Dr Crispin be released and sent to them 'to preach among us our Catholic faith'.[91] As vicar of Menheniot in the previous reign, Moreman had kept a school and been active in catechetical instruction.[92] By the late 1540s the Lord's Prayer in English may have become more generally acceptable, but the kind of religious opinions the presence of a vernacular Bible encouraged clearly were not: the rebels demanded that 'the whole Bible and all books of scripture in English . . . be called in again, for we be informed that otherwise the clergy shall not of long time confound the heretics'.[93] That this clause was inserted at the instigation of 'obscurantist' priests seems evident, but the wording suggests that leaders among the laity were equally concerned at the implications of freer religious expression, and that their conception of religious instruction was wholly traditional in emphasis.

A mirror image to the concerns of the Devon and Cornwall rebels in 1549 were those of Kett's followers in East Anglia. Here a distinctly Protestant tinge marked the demands touching religion. The Norfolk rebels requested that any priest or vicar 'that be not able to preach and set forth the word of God to his parishioners' be put from his benefice, that all priests should be resident, 'whereby the parishioners may be instructed with the laws of God', and that incumbents of a benefice worth £10 or more should either themselves or by proxy teach the poor children of the

[89] T. Amyot (ed.), 'Transcript of an Original Manuscript, Containing a Memorial from George Constantyne to Thomas Lord Cromwell', *Archaeologia*, 23 (1831), 59.

[90] *LP* xviii (2). 546, pp. 296, 300.

[91] A. Fletcher, *Tudor Rebellions*, 3rd edn. (1983), 116.

[92] P. Tudor, 'Religious Instruction for Children and Adolescents in the Early English Reformation', *JEH* 36 (1985), 411.   [93] Fletcher, *Tudor Rebellions*, 115.

parish the catechism and the primer.[94] In their different ways both protests evinced concern for the priest's duty of instructing his parishioners,
and it may be that the doctrinal uncertainty of the late 1540s, linked with
more than a decade of firm insistence on the didactic function of the
priesthood, was working an effect on popular attitudes in both religious
camps.

LAY LITERACY AND 'UNWRITTEN VERITIES'

It is conceivable that growing standards of lay literacy in the sixteenth
century, coupled with the erosion of religious uniformity, may have encouraged a more questioning and critical attitude on the part of some
parishioners, and have led them to demand more from their priests in
the way of a reasoned rationale of the Christian faith. Some historians
have seen in the growing literary and devotional interests of the English
laity a cause for the breakdown of the traditional relationship between
priestly *literatus* and 'lewd' layman, and the source of a tension which
may indirectly have encouraged the spread of Protestantism.[95] Margaret
Bowker has argued that the traditional standards of learning of the clergy
were becoming increasingly inadequate as the advent of printing and
Lutheranism opened up the parish to outside influences, and has com-
mented that 'the church could afford this second-hand knowledge only
for as long as there were no probing questions from parishioners'.[96] Probing
questions from parishioners were surely not a novelty in the sixteenth
century. John Mirc had warned clerical readers of his *Festial* that it was
common for laypeople 'proud in their wit' to ask questions in Lent about
the significance of aspects of the Church's service 'and gladly such priests
as can not make a grave answer . . . for to put him to shame'.[97] Nevertheless,
the expansion of devotional literature for the laity, and the interest in
liturgical and spiritual works evidenced by the contents of some laypeople's
wills, may reflect the aspirations of a growing constituency of educated
lay Christians, potentially dissatisfied with the prevailing standards and
attitudes of the clergy.[98] It is important with such suggestions, however,

---

[94] Ibid. 121–2.
[95] M. Aston, *Lollards and Reformers, Images and Literacy in Late Medieval Religion* (1984),
131; Moran, *Growth of English Schooling*, 208, 224, 226.
[96] Bowker, *Secular Clergy in the Diocese of Lincoln*, 60.   [97] Mirc, *Festial*, 124.
[98] For the expansion of devotional works for the laity, see J. Rhodes, 'Private Devotion
in England on the Eve of the Reformation', University of Durham Ph.D. thesis (1974); for
the testamentary evidence of lay interest in liturgical and devotional writings, Moran,
Growth of English Schooling, ch. 7.

to retain a sense of perspective. The great mass of laypeople remained illiterate, and there is no sense in which the educational standards of the clergy could have been falling behind those of the laity in any absolute way, as priests and laypeople benefited equally from the expansion in educational opportunities.[99]

None the less, the idea that literacy and learning were or ought to be merely co-extensive with priestly orders was clearly under threat. Both in theory and in practice Protestantism was particularly corrosive of this notion. In William Turner's *New Dialogue wherein is conteyned the Examination of the Masse*, the judge accepts the credentials of the mass's prosecutors, commenting 'must they now be unlearned, because they are no priests?'[100] Sending a copy of Tyndale's New Testament to his mother in 1534, Robert Plumpton instructed her not to worry about understanding it 'for God will give knowledge to whom he will give knowledge of the scriptures, as soon to a shepherd as a priest'.[101]

It was probably here, in the demand for a vernacular Bible, that priestly sensitivities and the aspirations of some laypeople came into sharpest conflict. Protestant propaganda argued that the clergy tried to keep the Bible in English from the laity to prevent them making the invidious comparison between the lives of the present-day clergy, and those of Christ and his followers. Barlow's *ABC against the Spiritualty* declared:

> Might men the scripture in English read
> We secular people should then see indeed
> What Christ and the apostles' lives were.[102]

In 1531 Thomas Bennet castigated the clergy of the South-West for their suppression of the word of God: 'Ye bear such a goodwill to it that ye keep it close, that no man may read it but yourselves.'[103] The attack on the clergy for their refusal to countenance a Bible in the vernacular was tackled head-on in Thomas More's *Dialogue Concerning Heresies*. Priests, so alleged More's fictional Lutheran, kept from the people all knowledge of Christ's Gospel 'except so much only as the clergy themselves list now

---

[99] D. Cressy, *Literacy and the Social Order* (Cambridge, 1980), 176–7, posits a literacy rate in 1500 of around 10% for men and barely 1% for women, figures which had not risen markedly by 1550. These figures are admittedly estimates. Lander, *Government and Community*, 131–2.

[100] J. N. King, *English Reformation Literature* (Princeton, NJ, 1982), 287–8.

[101] T. Stapleton (ed.), *Plumpton Correspondence*, CS os 4 (1839), 232.

[102] E. G. Rupp, *Studies in the Making of the English Protestant Tradition* (Cambridge, 1947), 59.   [103] R. Whiting, *The Blind Devotion of the People* (Cambridge, 1989), 196.

and then to tell us'. All translations were damned 'as though a lay man were no christian man', and the priests' sole justification was their concept of 'unwritten verities', the claim that 'God taught his disciples many things apart, because the people should not hear it'. More did not attempt to refute the essential truth of this concept, but reiterated instead the traditional idea that the people should not meddle with mysteries that are too great for them, and quoted St Paul to the effect that God has ordained some to be teachers and others learners, and that misfortune follows 'when the one part meddleth with the other's office'.[104]

The notion that there was knowledge which pertained solely to the clergy, the result of direct transmission from Christ, was for many priests an attractive one, and one which was to endure despite the growing official hostility to such an attitude.[105] As late as 1547 the conservative theologian, Richard Smith, insisted, for example, that the prayers used by the priest at mass came from 'the holy tradition of Christ's apostles' and that it was not appropriate for the laity to learn them or to read them in translation.[106] The essential proof-text of such attitudes was to be found in Matthew 7: 6—'do not give dogs what is holy; and do not throw your pearls before swine'—a passage which was held to constitute a mandate for the withholding of a vernacular Bible. This text was very much in the mind of Henry Gold, rector of Hayes, in a sermon on St Luke's Gospel, the notes for which were later confiscated when Gold was arrested for his part in the Nun of Kent affair. Gold imagined a charged exchange between a priest and a parishioner: 'vicar, why speak thou not? Man, I cannot speak. Canst thou not speak? Why goest thou into the pulpit if thou canst say nothing?' The vicar justified his silence by reference to Matthew 7: 6, and maintained that God 'hath given a straight commandment to all such as be preachers of his holy laws . . . to preach not the holy gospels unto such men as hath poison'.[107]

Gold was not alone in preaching this doctrine of extreme economy in the face of an unsettled laity. In the late 1530s the vicar of Aylesbury, Dr Lush, was found to possess a number of suspect sermons written in his own hand, one of which condemned the translation of scripture into

[104] More, *Dialogue*, 29, 293, 334.
[105] H. C. Porter, 'The Gloomy Dean and the Law: John Colet, 1466–1519', in G. V. Bennett and J. D. Walsh (eds.), *Essays in Modern English Church History* (1966), 28; Aston, *Lollards and Reformers*, 132.
[106] R. Smith, *A briefe treatys settyng forth divers truthes* (1547), 52ᵛ.
[107] PRO, SP 1/83, fo. 147.

English, 'and in another sermon despising serving men and craftsmen for looking of the New Testament in English'.[108] The royal injunctions of 1538 expressly instructed the clergy 'that ye shall discourage no man privily or apertly from the reading or hearing of the said Bible, but shall expressly provoke, stir, and exhort every person to read the same'.[109] Yet to some priests this concept remained anathema. Thomas Cowley, vicar of Ticehurst in Sussex, rebuked those who read the English Bible, saying 'you butchers, bunglers, and cobblers which have the Testament in their keeping, ye shall deliver it to us gentlemen which have studied there- fore'.[110] In 1541–2 the parson of Swynnerton in Staffordshire, John Nowell, was reported for removing the Bible from the parish church saying 'it is not meet that the bible should remain within the same church so that the people might look upon the same'.[111] The *Supplication of the Poore Com- mons* complained in 1546 that priests were often removing Bibles from the body of the church and placing them in the choir 'where poor men durst not presume to come'.[112] In Edward's reign the view that laypeople ought not to read the Bible continued to be expressed. In 1548 Roger Harman, rector of Deal in Kent, sought to discourage a parishioner from reading the scripture in English telling him 'you oughteth not to read it, it doth pass your capacity, it is fit for such men as be learned'. The vicar of Godmersham was accused of having said in the pulpit 'that no layman ought to dispute, teach or hold opinion in the Gospel except a Master of Arts or a spiritual man admitted by the ordinary'.[113] It is not by any means self-evident, however, that all laypeople would have disagreed with these sentiments, or have felt that the clergy were unjustly retaining a mono- poly of vital religious knowledge. The Edwardian Book of Homilies noted in its sermon on the Holy Scripture that some laypeople were diffident about reading the Bible because they felt that 'the hardness thereof is so great, that it is meet to be read only of clerks and learned men'.[114] Yet by the 1540s there clearly were laypeople who through their reading of scripture judged themselves competent to assess and if need be condemn the interpretations offered by their curates. In 1542, for example, Richard Harvey and Robert Marshall presented Edmund Streteham, vicar of

---

[108] Ellis, *Original Letters*, iii. 70. Official policy was soon to swing in Lush's direction: in 1543 an Act of Parliament limited Bible reading to substantial merchants, nobles, and gentry. A. G. Dickens, *The English Reformation*, 2nd edn. (1989), 213.

[109] *Visitation Articles*, ii. 36.   [110] *LP* xiii (1). 1199.

[111] PRO, STA. C. 2, 29/181.   [112] Cowper (ed.), *Four Supplications*, 67.

[113] C. E. Woodruff (ed.), 'Extracts from Original Documents Illustrating the Progress of the Reformation in Kent', *AC* 31 (1915), 101–2.

[114] J. Griffiths (ed.), *The Two Books of Homilies* (Oxford, 1859), 11.

Kelvedon in Essex, for heresy, after quarrelling with him over the merits of a sermon. Harvey approved of the preacher and maintained that he had preached nothing but the Gospel, to which Streteham had retorted 'trust thou well to the Gospel and thou shalt go to the devil'. The vicar went on to elaborate his theory of how the faith would be taken from the Gentiles and returned to the Jews. To these esoteric utterances Marshall countered 'Master vicar, ye be far wide, for by the Gospel and the merits of Christ's passion, and by his blood shedding we all shall be saved.'[115]

Only a minority of English men and women would have been able or prepared to condemn a priest's teaching in this way. Most laypeople in the mid-sixteenth century were not seeking in the Gospel an alternative source of religious authority to that personified by their parish priest. To the majority of Englishmen and women, those who had not adopted the mentality and concerns of Protestantism, the didactic function of priests was probably a secondary one. The primary duty of the priest was to sing mass, rather than to preach or teach. In the programme of the South-Western rebels, the implied concern for religious teaching was clearly subsidiary to the various articles demanding 'the mass in Latin, as was before'.[116] John Hooper might insist that the office of priests was 'to be preachers of God's word and ministers of Christ's sacraments; not to sacrifice for dead nor live, nor to sing or mass, or any such like', or Thomas Becon might argue that 'one faithful preacher . . . is better than ten thousand mumbling massmongers', but it is doubtful whether a majority of their contemporaries would have concurred.[117] Perhaps the last word on this subject may be left to Hugh Latimer, here encapsulating what seemed to him the warped sense of popular priorities: 'If a priest should have left mass undone on a Sunday within these ten years, all England should have wondered at it: but they may have left off the sermon twenty Sundays, and never been blamed.'[118]

---

[115] Hale, *Precedents*, 131–2.   [116] Fletcher, *Tudor Rebellions*, 115.
[117] E. C. Messenger, *The Reformation, the Mass and the Priesthood* (1936), i. 435–6; Becon, *Prayers and other Pieces*, 160.   [118] Latimer, *Sermons*, i. 203.

4

The Priest as Anointed

ORDINATION AND VOCATION

When seeking for a proof-text to validate their position, early sixteenth-century upholders of clerical status and privilege frequently fell upon Psalm 105, with its stern admonition to 'touch not mine anointed'. The text declared to contemporaries both the unique dignity of priests and the obligations towards them of other Christians. Commonly these words were taken to justify the immunity of clerics from judgement in the secular courts, and it was on this text that the Abbot of Winchcombe, Richard Kidderminster, preached at St Paul's Cross in 1515 at the height of the public controversy over the legal immunity of clerks in minor orders which followed upon the Hunne case.[1] Contemporaries argued, sometimes fiercely, over the proper scope of 'benefit of clergy', but the essential principle it involved, the belief that priests at least had a right to special treatment under the law, was rarely challenged, and the attempts to restrict benefit of clergy in the late fifteenth and early sixteenth centuries were designed to confine the privilege to those actually in major orders, rather than to deny the principle altogether.[2]

The divide between ordained clergy and laity was held to be fundamental, and a distinct manner of life properly belonged to each estate. When John Colet had the opportunity to preach to the fathers of Canterbury Convocation in February 1512, he took as his theme St Paul's words 'be you not conformable to this world' and applied them to the priests and bishops of his day. In Colet's view the source of all evil in the church lay in 'priests not living priestly but secularly'.[3] To Colet and those who

---

[1] J. D. M. Derrett, 'The Affairs of Richard Hunne and Friar Standish', in J. B. Trapp (ed.), *The Apology*, *CW* 9 (1979), 228. For other contemporary appeals to this text, see Catherine of Siena, *The Orchard Of Syon* (1519), sigs. r.i', r.ii'; J. H. Lupton, *Life of John Colet* (1909), 303. John Fisher was unusually perspicacious in recognizing that the words referred not just to priests, but to the whole Jewish people: *The Defence of the Priesthood*, tr. P. E. Hallett (1935), 125.

[2] J. H. Baker (ed.), *The Reports of Sir John Spelman*, Selden Soc. 94 (1978), ii. 326–34; J. G. Bellamy, *Criminal Law and Society in Late Medieval and Tudor England* (Gloucester, 1984), ch. 6.

[3] Lupton, *Life of Colet*, 294, 299.

shared his ideals, the priest was one who had died to the world, who had taken upon him to live in nearer approximation to Christ and the apostles. To move from being a mere layman to becoming a priest was to undergo a radical ontological change, a change effected and symbolized by the sacrament of holy orders. The ritual of this sacrament comprised the imposition of hands by the bishop, investiture of the candidate in stole and chasuble, the anointing of the new priest's hands, and the 'tradition of the instruments', the presentation with bread and paten and chalice, symbolic of the priest's power to offer and consecrate the bread and wine.[4] This process was held to have imparted a new sacramental 'character', enabling the candidate to perform the uniquely priestly functions of saying mass and hearing confessions.[5] Having been 'priested', the 'otherness' of the ordinand was underlined in various ways. He had, for example, received the tonsure, a shaving of the upper part of the head, which Aquinas saw both as a symbol of 'royal' dignity and a pledge of separation from temporal concerns.[6] He was expected to dress distinctively and to remain celibate, and as a mark of his new standing he was now, like a secular knight, addressed with the courtesy title of 'Sir'. Although later to acquire pejorative undertones in the Protestant stereotypes of 'Sir John' and 'Sir John Lack-latin', this form of address must have served as a constant reminder to contemporaries of the status claimed by the priesthood. A bill presented to the Court of Chancery in the 1520s by the merchant William Annes is punctilious in describing a former business associate, Michael Godffrey, as 'now being a priest and called Sir Michael Godffrey, clerk'.[7]

The case reminds us that given the great number of priests in early sixteenth-century England, there were probably few laypeople who did not know someone, relative or friend, who had been ordained. One recent estimate points to the secular priesthood alone accounting for more practitioners than any occupation bar agriculture, and another suggests that priests may have amounted to as much as 4 per cent of the total male

---

[4] D. N. Power, *Ministers of Christ and His Church: The Theology of Priesthood* (1969), 92–3; F. Clark, *Eucharistic Sacrifice and the Reformation* (Chulmleigh, 1981), 192–4.

[5] Thomas Aquinas, *Summa Theologica*, Eng. edn. (New York, 1948), iii. 2694; A. Nichols, *Holy Order: The Apostolic Ministry from the New Testament to the Second Vatican Council* (Dublin, 1990), 60; Power, *Ministers of Christ*, 121.

[6] Aquinas, *Summa Theologica*, iii. 2702.

[7] PRO, C. 1, 458/3. Some late medieval writers drew on the analogy with secular knighthood to endow the priesthood with a chivalric aura: *The Vertue of Y[e] Masse*, sig. A.iv[r], regarded vestments as 'armour', and priests as Christ's 'champions'. To William Langland, priests ideally were 'knights of God': *Piers the Ploughman*, ed. J. F. Goodridge (Harmondsworth, 1966), 136.

population.[8] Inevitably, there were those who failed to be impressed by an acquaintance's reception of holy orders. One recent ordinand of the 1520s described pitifully his continued harassment by a creditor despite having 'taken upon him the order of priesthood', and his consequent inability to 'quietly serve God as he is bound to do'.[9] None the less, there is evidence that many laypeople sought positively to encourage acquaintances in their vocation to the priesthood, and bequests to intending ordinands are a recurrent feature of early sixteenth-century wills.[10] Some testators even provided the promise of secure employment after ordination. In requesting masses for his soul in 1506 Thomas Lamsyn of Heron in Kent stipulated that 'if my servant John Clerk be a priest and of good conversation, that then he to be preferred and deputed before any other priest to sing for the souls of me and of my friends'.[11] In 1519 Joyce Perry of Aldborough in Yorkshire wanted Edward Holme to celebrate for her for ten years 'if God fortune him to be a priest'.[12]

No doubt such testators hoped they were encouraging a devout vocation to the priesthood. That a deep sense of calling and commitment should have motivated candidates for the priesthood was axiomatic. Though it is, of course, impossible to assess the private motives of ordinands, it must seem highly doubtful that this was always the case. The desire for material prosperity, or at least for a secured future, may have weighed heavily with some candidates, and early sixteenth-century humanists were agreed that too many ordinations were producing too few dedicated priests.[13] Certainly, the prevalence of non-residence suggests that not all priests were intent upon a life of service in the cure of souls, and the fact that secular priests seem to have moved through the three major orders of subdeacon, deacon, and priest more quickly than did regulars has been pointed to as perhaps indicating a more career-orientated mentality on the part of recruits to the secular clergy.[14] Entry into major orders was unlikely to have been always a matter of pure personal vocation. One recent historian of the sixteenth-century clergy goes so far as to suggest

---

[8] J. Youings, *Sixteenth-Century England* (Harmondsworth, 1984), 36; C. Haigh, *English Reformations: Religion, Politics, and Society under the Tudors* (Oxford, 1993), 5–6.

[9] PRO, C. 1, 533/3.

[10] Marshall, 'Attitudes of the English People to Priests and Priesthood', 153–4.

[11] PRO, PCC, Prob. 11, 15 Bennett.

[12] J. W. Clay (ed.), *North Country Wills*, SS 116 (1908), 104.

[13] Lupton, *Life of Colet*, 300; T. More, *Dialogue*, 295, 301; T. Starkey, *A Dialogue between Pole and Lupset*, ed. T. F. Mayer, CS 37 (1989), 93.

[14] L. M. Stevens, 'The Durham Clergy of the Early Sixteenth Century 1494–1540', University of Durham MA thesis (1979), 80.

that 'most often it was thought of in a matter-of-fact way, decided by superiors, landlords or parents'.[15] This analysis would have been applauded by William Tyndale, who derided Thomas More's claim that every man had a choice as to whether he would be a priest or not; in Tyndale's view parents all too frequently 'compel their children, and sacrifice them to burn in the pope's chastity . . . so that they think by the merits of their children's burning, after the pope's false doctrine, to please God and to get heaven'.[16] On this point Tyndale receives the unlikely support of the Brigittine monk, Richard Whitford, who alleged that parents sometimes forced their children to enter religion in order to have the honour of a priest for a son.[17]

If parents did commonly apply such pressure, they were showing little regard for the notion that orders, like marriage, was a sacrament which should only be received voluntarily. But just as parents sometimes sought out marriage partners for their children, they were sometimes instrumental in deciding that their sons should enter the church. The apologia of Tristram Revel, in trouble in 1536 for translating a heterodox book, contains the revelation that 'his father would have had him a priest, to which he was not inclined'.[18] A few years earlier, a former mayor of Newcastle, Edward Baxter, is found writing to Cromwell urging him to use his influence with Wolsey to secure a living for one of his sons. It seems that the boy was not yet ordained, but one senses his father's eagerness that he should become 'God's servant and a man of Church'.[19]

Examples of parental pressure on sons to enter the priesthood are also to be found in wills. In 1529 Agnes Buknall of Thimbleby in Lincolnshire arranged that her elder son Robert would support his younger brother Henry at school till the latter was of an age to enter the Church: 'if so be Henry will not be a priest, then I will Robert to be discharged of him, and the said Henry to take his own chance'.[20] John Holdsworth of Halifax was also eager that his son, John, should take holy orders: in 1535 he left his

[15] J. C. H. Aveling, 'The English Clergy, Catholic and Protestant, in the 16th and 17th Centuries', in W. Haase (ed.), *Rome and the Anglicans* (Berlin, 1982), 61.

[16] W. Tyndale, *An Answer to Sir Thomas More's Dialogue*, ed. H. Walter, PS (1850), 161.

[17] J. Rhodes, 'Private Devotion in England on the Eve of the Reformation', University of Durham Ph.D. thesis (1974), 27. [18] *LP* x. 371.

[19] H. Ellis (ed.), *Original Letters Illustrative of English History* (1846), i, 332, *LP* iv (3). 5169. Another example of a child being directed towards a career in the Church apparently irrespective of his wishes in the matter is that of Lord Lisle's stepson, James Basset: M. St Clare Byrne (ed.), *The Lisle Letters* (Chicago, 1981), iv. 508–10.

[20] C. W. Foster (ed.), *Lincoln Wills 1505 to 1530*, LRS 10 (1918), 114.

executors instructions to finance and supervise his education 'and also find him honest apparel and books, and at his singing for to array him as I arrayed Sir Richard, my [other] son'.[21] Grandparents, too, might seek to have their say. In 1508 Thomas Howden of Biddenham in Bedfordshire left 6s. 8d. to his grandson Robert 'provided he is made a priest, but if he does not proceed to that order, he shall have nothing'.[22]

It is no surprise to come across ambitious and domineering parents in the early sixteenth century who, whether out of piety or strategy, directed younger sons towards the Church. Yet the same testamentary evidence reveals that a much greater number of parents seem to have recognized at the last that entry into the priesthood should have been a matter of genuine personal choice. Bequests to sons with a nascent vocation usually allowed the possibility of a contrary decision—'if he will be a priest'—and sometimes forbore even to present a preference in the matter. In 1529 Thomas Ilande of Tenterden in Kent set aside £20 for his son Christopher to support his education if he decided to become a priest 'and if he be not disposed to be a priest then I will the said £20 be paid to him when he cometh to the age of 22 years'.[23] Geoffrey Cantlowe of Ewell in Surrey left £20 to his ward Geoffrey Parker in 1509 irrespective of whether 'he will be a priest or a temporal man'.[24] Surprisingly perhaps, in view of what has been said regarding parental pressure on sons to enter the priesthood, a number of wills contained positive financial disincentives, providing that if a son to whom lands had been bequeathed were to become a priest, the estate should pass to other children.[25] This should not be regarded as indicative of hostility to the priesthood; these testators often made other more modest financial provision for sons who entered the Church. Rather it was a recognition that a priest should be able to support himself, and would be unable to provide heirs for the family estate. For some ordinands, then, a decision to enter the priesthood was against their immediate financial advantage. For these at least there may have been a stronger vocational element involved in becoming a priest than the constitutional cynicism of historians is sometimes prepared to allow.

[21] J. W. Clay and E. W. Crossley (eds.), *Halifax Wills 1389–1544* (Halifax, 1904), 100.
[22] P. Bell (ed.), *Bedfordshire Wills 1480–1519*, Bedfordshire Historical Record Society, 45 (1966), 90.   [23] PRO, PCC, Prob. 11, 11 Jankyn.
[24] PRO, PCC, Prob. 11, 16 Bennett. Further examples of this type of bequest are given in N. P. Tanner, 'The Reformation and Regionalism: Further Reflections on the Church in Late Medieval Norwich', in J. A. F. Thomson (ed.), *Towns and Townspeople in the Fifteenth Century* (Gloucester, 1988), 137; A. L. Rowse, *Tudor Cornwall*, 2nd edn. (1969), 155.
[25] The sample contains 11 examples of this type of bequest.

CONCEPTS OF PRIESTHOOD

If it is usually impossible to know for certain why individuals offered themselves for ordination, it is equally hard to ascertain what intending priests understood by their new sacramental status, what it meant to them to be a priest. Like other aspects of the Church's sacramental system, the theory of orders had undergone several centuries of theological fine-tuning, yet it seems certain that the conclusions of the schoolmen remained largely unknown to the mass of English parishioners.[26] Virtually the only pre-Reformation laymen from the non-literary classes whose views on the nature of priesthood have been recorded are those Lollard heretics who rejected, or wished to modify radically, the sacerdotal system itself. The perceptions of their more conformist neighbours can only be recovered obliquely. In the attempt to reconstruct what ordinary lay men and women thought the priesthood to represent, one is forced to turn to the sources illustrative of popular teaching on the sacrament of orders, bearing in mind the dictum that such teaching may not always be received or understood in the way its authors intended.

Since the late thirteenth century, all curates were bound to teach their parishioners about the seven sacraments, and works designed to help priests with this duty often contained some explication of the sacrament of orders.[27] Often the account provided was minimal in the extreme. The so-called *Lay Folk's Catechism*, a teaching aid for the clergy promulgated by Archbishop Thoresby of York in the mid-fourteenth century, explained merely that the sacrament gave power to sing mass and to minister the other sacraments.[28] Another didactic work which circulated widely among the pre-Reformation parish clergy, the *Exornatorium Curatorum*, was content to note that holy orders 'giveth authority to minister above the sacraments of holy Church'.[29] The account given in a late fifteenth-century work now known as the *Quattuor Sermones* was hardly fuller, remarking that orders gave power 'for to make the sacrament of Christ's

---

[26] For developments in the theology of Orders in the Middle Ages, see B. Cooke, *Ministry to Words and Sacraments: History and Theology* (Philadelphia, 1977); J. Leclercq, 'The Priesthood in the Patristic and Medieval Church', in N. Lash and J. Rhymer (eds.), *The Christian Priesthood* (1970); J. B. Brosnan, 'Episcopacy and Priesthood according to St Thomas', *American Ecclesiastical Review*, 121 (1949); Nichols, *Holy Order*, Power, *Ministers of Christ*. [27] *Lyndwood*, 21.

[28] T. F. Simmons and H. E. Noloth, *The Lay Folk's Catechism*, EETS 118 (1901), 69. The claim that one of the surviving manuscripts of this treatise represents a Lollard version has been refuted by A. Hudson, 'A New Look at the Lay Folk's Catechism', *Viator*, 16 (1985).

[29] *Exornatorium Curatorum* (?1520), sig. A.v.

flesh and blood and for to minister other sacraments to the people'. It noted that priests 'must have their crown shaved, their head tonsured, and their clothes honestly shapen as falleth to their estate'. It went on to detail some of the duties of priests and their need to be of good behaviour.[30]

Admittedly, some works of instruction were rather less laconic. *The Traytte of Good Lyvyng and Good Deying* described orders as 'a godly tokening and sign imprinted in the soul of him which receives it, to the which spiritual might and office is given to him which is ordained'.[31] Like the *Traytte of Good Lyvyng*, works of instruction for parish priests like the *Manipulus Curatorum* and the *Cura Clericalis* followed Hugh of St Victor in describing orders as a sign conferring spiritual power, the latter work elaborating somewhat in mentioning that the sacrament conferred an indelible spiritual 'character' which was imprinted on the soul.[32] On the whole, however, such works were technical rather than theological in their outlook. The *Manipulus Curatorum*, perhaps the most popular of the handbooks on offer to the late medieval clergy, laid most emphasis on the details of ordination itself: none was to be ordained without first receiving the tonsure; candidates had to be male, legitimate, of honest life, and had to have acquaintance with the scriptures.[33] The *Cura Clericalis* conveyed the technical information that 'matter', 'form', and 'intent' were needed for the valid administration of a sacrament and in the case of orders established these: the imposition of hands and the words spoken by the officiating bishop.[34]

Conspicuously absent from all these accounts of what priests could do and how priests were made, was any thorough exploration of the quintessence of priesthood, any explanation of why it was necessary or proper for a body of men to be sanctified and set apart, and entrusted with the supervision of religious worship. Nor was much attempt made to examine the biblical and apostolic origins of the priesthood. Of course, works such as these were concerned with the purveyance of basic religious instruction and it would be superfluous to criticize them for lacking theological sophistication. Yet it may have been difficult for the layperson instructed on the basis of such teaching to have formulated any very clear

[30] N. F. Blake (ed.), *Quattuor Sermones printed by William Caxton*, Middle English Texts, 12 (Heidelburg, 1975), 42–3.

[31] *The Traytte of Good Lyvyng and Good Deying* (Paris, 1503), 49^r.

[32] G. de Monte Rocherii, *Manipulus Curatorum* (1509), 48^v; *Cura Clericalis* (1532), sigs. A.ii^{r-v}, A.v^r.   [33] de Monte Rocherii, *Manipulus Curatorum*, 50^r–51^v.

[34] *Cura Clericalis*, sigs. A.v^v–vi^r.

understanding of what the priesthood meant, to have had more than the shakiest grasp of its Christological significance, or to have been aware at all of its function of representing the Christian community before God.

Such vagueness may in part have reflected a policy of deliberate obscurantism. It is notable that, in its section providing a programme of instruction for the laity, the *Oculus Sacerdotis* passed over the sacrament of orders, remarking that this was no business of the laity.[35] Even laypeople who evinced an interest in such matters may have had to be satisfied with the most jejune of data. When the Norfolk churchwarden, Robert Reynes, came to add a section on the sacraments to his fifteenth-century commonplace book, he was content to note that there were seven, and that orders, like baptism and confirmation, could not be repeated.[36] In short, the account of the Christian ministry which the pre-Reformation laity was offered and, we must assume, to a degree assimilated, was an eminently functional one, which made sense as long as the basic premises of the sacramental worship of the late medieval Church remained unchallenged. As we shall see, laypeople may have heard much about the dignity of priests and the honour and reverence due to them, but confronted, say, with the objections of an antisacerdotal heretic, most laypeople would probably have found it difficult or impossible to argue for the existence of priesthood from first principles.

As the Henrician Reformation progressed, however, long-held assumptions about the nature of the priestly office were to come under increasingly close scrutiny, and a much more detailed exposition of the clerical ministry was provided by the doctrinal formularies of 1537 and 1543, the *Bishops' Book* and the *King's Book*. Though there are important differences between the two works—the section on the jurisdictional powers of the clergy in the 1537 book was, for example, thoroughly revised in 1543 at Henry's instigation—the two books are broadly in agreement on the spiritual functions of the priesthood.[37] Orders, it is noted, were instituted by Christ and the apostles, and priests received commission

to preach and teach the Word of God unto his people: to dispense and administer the sacraments of God unto them: and by the same to confer and give the graces of the Holy Ghost: to consecrate the blessed body of Christ in the sacrament of

[35] L. E. Boyle, 'The *Oculus Sacerdotis* and some other Works of William of Pagula', *TRHS*, 5th ser., 5 (1955), 92.

[36] C. Louis (ed.), *The Commonplace Book of Robert Reynes of Acle* (New York, 1980), 180–1.

[37] E. G. Rupp, *Studies in the Making of the English Protestant Tradition* (Cambridge, 1947), 144.

the altar: to loose and absoyle from sin all persons which be duly penitent and sorry for the same: to bind and excommunicate such as be guilty in manifest crimes and sins . . . to order and consecrate others in the same room, order and office . . . and finally to feed Christ's people like good pastors and rectors (as the apostle calleth them) with their wholesome doctrine and by their continual exhortations and admonitions to reduce them from sin and iniquity as much as in them lieth and to bring them unto the perfect knowledge, the perfect love or dread of God, and unto the perfect charity of their neighbours.[38]

It is symptomatic of the influence that reformist ideas were exercising on some of the bishops that the primary duty of the priest is specified as 'to preach and teach the Word of God'. In the Middle Ages the constant teaching had been that it was primarily for the eucharistic ministry that priests were ordained, Aquinas arguing that all the other powers and tasks of the priest stemmed from this central duty.[39] Given that these sections of both the *Bishops' Book* and the *King's Book* were concerned fundamentally with upholding the royal supremacy and denying the power of the Bishop of Rome, it is unsurprising that they made little attempt to exalt the dignity of the clerical estate. It is notable, for example, that they treat merely of 'orders', not of 'holy orders', an omission which Professor Scarisbrick has seen as indicative of the fundamental anticlericalism of the King himself.[40] The *Bishops' Book* stresses further that the power of priests is a 'moderate' not a 'tyrannical' power.[41] In their condemnation of Donatism, both works emphasized that priests were merely the instruments of God, who himself was the sole worker of the sacraments. The *King's Book* declared that priests

be not the principal causers, nor the sufficient, or of themselves the efficient causers or givers of grace, or of any other spiritual gift which proceedeth and is given of God by his word and his sacraments; but God is the only principal, sufficient and perfect cause of all the efficacy of his word and his sacrament.[42]

For this position St Ambrose was cited as an authority: 'the priest layeth his hands upon us, but it is God that giveth the grace; the priest layeth upon us his beseeching hands, but God blesseth us with his mighty

---

[38] C. Lloyd (ed.), *Formularies of Faith put Forth by Authority during the Reign of Henry VIII* (Oxford, 1825), 101–2. The 'King's Book' had in its list as the final duty of priests that of praying for the Church of Christ and their own flock: T. A. Lacey (ed.), *The King's Book, 1543* (1895), 58.   [39] Aquinas, *Summa Theologica*, iii. 2692.

[40] J. J. Scarisbrick, *Henry VIII* (1968), 417.

[41] Lloyd (ed.), *Formularies of Faith*, 102.   [42] Lacey (ed.), *King's Book*, 60.

hand'.[43] This was in a sense sound Catholic theology, with a pedigree stretching back to St Augustine, but at the same time it could be read in this context as a subtle denigration of the dignity of the priest, in so far as it failed to mention the importance of the human intent of the minister of sacraments, and appeared to make him into a mere cypher.[44] Neither was there emphasis on the priest's acting *in persona Christi*, of the high dignity of the clerical office.

Yet it was precisely this, the great honour and excellence of priesthood that most earlier commentators had thrust to the fore. A few writers, notably Fisher and More, had, under the pressure of religious controversy, attempted a more fundamental appraisal of the priesthood. Fisher, for example, had adduced six practical reasons why 'it is reasonable, in matters concerning the salvation of souls, that some men be set apart to act in the name of and bear responsibility for, the whole multitude'. These sprang from six special dangers to which the laity were exposed and from which they were in constant need of protection. Laypeople needed a pastor to prevent them falling from faith, a teacher to stimulate the natural dullness of their minds, a monitor to prevent their falling into sin, and to combat their inherent sluggishness to do good. Priests were also necessary to stir people to defend themselves against diabolic temptation, and to guard them from the poisonous error of false teachers.[45] In his last unpublished polemical work Fisher precociously employed the techniques of comparative religion to argue that all societies have a 'convenient portion of men' set apart to oversee religious worship.[46] Thomas More was equally concerned to demonstrate that even pagans and Jews had always had priests.[47]

If a few thinkers were prepared to subject the role of priests in society to a thorough analysis, most popular writers of the late fifteenth and early sixteenth centuries contented themselves with eulogizing priesthood and its attributes, often suggesting, as we have seen, that priests were to be considered 'higher than the angels' since they could perform actions, saying mass and granting absolution, that even the angels could not do. This laudatory rhetoric perhaps reached its apotheosis in a book extremely popular with parish priests on the eve of the Reformation, the *Sermones Discipuli*. According to this work, the priest was 'higher than kings, more

---

[43] Ibid.; Lloyd (ed.), *Formularies of Faith*, 106–7.
[44] Nichols, *Holy Order*, 60, 79.   [45] Fisher, *Defence of the Priesthood*, 24–8.
[46] PRO, SP 6/11, fo. 215ʳ ff., discussed by J. J. Scarisbrick, 'Fisher, Henry VIII and the Reformation Crisis' in B. Bradshaw and E. Duffy (eds.), *Humanism, Reform and the Reformation: The Career of Bishop John Fisher* (Cambridge, 1989), 164–5.
[47] T. More, *Supplication of Souls*, CW 7 (1990), 165.

blessed than angels, the maker of his Maker'. In its sermon for the fourteenth Sunday after Trinity the *Sermones Discipuli* drew an extended comparison between priests and the Virgin Mary: Mary had conceived Christ with five words (*fiat mihi secundum verbum tuum*) just as the priest consecrates with five words (*hoc est enim corpus meum*); Mary carried Christ in her hands and lifted Him and laid Him down, the priest raises Him after the consecration; Mary was sanctified in her womb before she conceived, priests are ordained before they can consecrate. The sermon further adduced nine reasons why priests were to be honoured above angels.[48] This passage was later to be singled out by horrified Protestant writers, but it was in fact common for writers of sermons and devotional works to present themselves as enthusiastic encomiasts of priesthood.[49] In a chapter entitled *Of the dygnyte of prestes* the late fifteenth-century *Doctrinal of Sapyence* characterized them as

fathers ghostly of all Christian people. They be the light of the world, the which for the office that is committed to them and for the holiness that they ought to have in them be called the angels of our Lord . . . and as touchyng to absoiling or to give absolution they do that the angels may not do.[50]

In the popular early sixteenth-century morality play, *Everyman*, when the eponymous hero is summoned by God to give a final account of himself, he is abandoned by his allegorical companions, Fellowship, Kindred, Goods, and Riches. His new patrons, Knowledge and Five Wits, advise him that his only hope lies in receiving the sacraments from a priest, for as they explain

> Good priesthood exceedeth all other thing;
> To us holy scripture they do teach,
> And converteth man from sin heaven to reach;
> God hath to them more power given
> Than to any angel that is in heaven:
> With five words he may consecrate
> God's body in flesh and blood to take,
> And handleth his Maker between his hands,
> The priest bindeth and unbindeth all bands

---

[48] J. Herolt, *Sermones Discipuli* (1510), 152^{r-v}.

[49] John Jewel, *Works*, ed. J. Ayre, PS (1847), ii. 773. The durability of this rhetoric in its Catholic milieu perhaps deserves comment: in Joyce's *A Portrait of the Artist as a Young Man*, the Jesuit seeking to awaken a vocation in the young Stephen Dedalus remarks that 'No king or emperor on this earth . . . no angel or archangel in heaven, no saint, not even the Blessed Virgin herself has the power of the priest of God.'

[50] G. de Roye, *The Doctrinal of Sapyence* (1489), sig. H.vii^v.

Both in earth and in heaven;
He ministers all the sacraments seven:
Though we kiss thy feet, thou wert worthy
Thou art the surgeon that cureth sin deadly,
No remedy may we find under God,
But all only priesthood.
Everyman, God gave priests that dignity,
And setteth them in His stead among us to be;
Thus be they above angels in degree.[51]

Such a paean was not unique. According to the *Orchard of Syon*, priests were the 'anointed people' of God, his 'special anointed servants and ministers', 'lanterns in the mysterial body of holy church', 'more than angels'.[52] Indeed, what was said of priests in this work bore distinct affinities to the contemporary theory of image-worship, whereby reverence done to the image redounded to the prototype: 'Every reverence that is done to them is not done to them but to Me, by virtue of the blood that I have given to them for to minister.' The priest is thus regarded here as a kind of walking icon: no matter how priests behaved 'the reverence of them should never be minished, for when they [the laity] minish it, they offende Me'.[53] In his *Life of Pico*, Thomas More seems to have been thinking in a similar vein when he insisted on the reverence due to 'the quick relics, the ministers of His Church'.[54]

It went without saying that priests were obliged to be better than the laypeople; that sin in a priest was far more reprehensible than in a layman, 'because though the thing be equal, they be not equally bound thereto'.[55] In September 1530 the humanist monk, Robert Joseph, warned the vicar of Ombersley in Worcestershire that in his parish he would be watched carefully from all sides, and should therefore do nothing that could not be made public:

Remember what Juvenal says: the greater the sinner the greater the sin. When a vicar or rector is among his parishioners, how he ought to shine with innocence, since he is called by Christ the salt of the earth, a city set on a hill. In a vicar or parish priest the least failing like anger is worse than a crime like perjury in an ordinary man.[56]

[51] W. C. Hazlitt (ed.), *A Select Collection of Old English Plays* (1874), i. 133–4.
[52] Catherine of Siena, *Orchard of Syon* (1519), sigs. r.ii^v, r.v^v–vi^r, t.iv^v.
[53] Ibid. sigs. r.i^v–ii^r.
[54] T. More, *The Workes of Sir Thomas More Knyght . . . wrytten by him in the Englysh tonge* (1557), 30.   [55] T. More, *The Apology*, ed. Trapp, *CW* 9 (1979), 48.
[56] R. Joseph, *The Letter Book of Robert Joseph*, ed. H. Aveling and W. A. Pantin, Oxford Historical Society, NS 19 (1967), 110.

The *Lyfe of Prestes* agreed that for a clerk 'it behoveth to be more spiritual and virtuous than a layman, for as St Jerome sayeth, it is the most vehement destruction of the Church when laymen be better disposed then clerks'.[57] A favourite text of late medieval homilists was Hosea's prophecy of doom should society become 'like people, like priest'.[58] It was incumbent upon priests to be palpably better than laypeople. This was so not merely because priestly dignity demanded it, but because the salvation of the laity was widely seen to depend not only on the objective sacramental functions of the priest, but on his positive example. A pre-Reformation set of bidding prayers from the diocese of London calls for grace to be granted to all priests 'that it may be the salvation of their souls and of all Christian folk'.[59] 'They ought to induce the lay people by their example', insisted the *Lyfe of Prestes*, and a number of writers and preachers warned of the danger of priests giving a bad example to their flocks.[60] In the early sixteenth-century interlude, *Hickscorner*, the figure of pity is made to lament:

> And yet one thing maketh me ever mourning
> That priests lack utterance to show their cunning
> And all the while that clerks do use so great sin
> Among the lay people look never for no mending.[61]

In his treatise on the seven Penitential Psalms, John Fisher made the same point, if rather less pithily:

All fear of God, also the contempt of God cometh and is grounded of the clergy, for if the clergy be well and rightfully ordered giving good example to other of virtuous living, without doubt the people by that shall have more fear of almighty God. But contrarywise if the clergy live desolately in manner, as they should give

---

[57] Dionysius Carthusianus, *The Lyfe of Prestes* (c.1533), 104ʳ.

[58] G. R. Owst, *Preaching in Medieval England* (Cambridge, 1926), 249; *Literature and Pulpit in Medieval England*, 2nd edn. (Cambridge, 1961), 268, 277; Lupton, *Life of Colet*, 297; G. G. Coulton, *The Medieval Village* (Cambridge, 1926), 259; M. P. Tilley, *A Dictionary of the Proverbs in England in the Sixteenth and Seventeenth Centuries* (Ann Arbor, Mich., 1950), 556.

[59] Henderson (ed.), *Manuale et Processionale ad Usum Insignis Ecclesiae Eboracensis*, SS 63 (1874), 89.

[60] Dionysius Carthusianus, *Lyfe of Prestes*, sig. C.iiiʳ; J. Mirc, *Festial*, ed. T. Erbe, EETS ES 96 (1905), 192; G. R. Owst, *The Destructorium Viciorum of Alexander Carpenter* (1952), 15, 21; Owst, *Literature and Pulpit in Medieval England*, 248, 259, 265; Catherine of Siena, *Orchard of Syon*, sig. f.iiᵛ; C. Brooke, 'Chaucer's Parson and Edmund Gonville: Contrasting Roles of Fourteenth-Century Incumbents', in D. M. Smith (ed.), *Studies in Clergy and Ministry in Medieval England* (York, 1991), 18–19; PRO, SP 6/4, fo. 71ʳ; Hazlitt, *Select Collection of Old English Plays*, i. 134.   [61] Hazlitt, ibid. 153.

no account of their life past and done before, will not the lay people do the same? It is to be thought they will, and what followeth? Truly, then they shall set little or nought by almighty God. Therefore, by us of the clergy dependeth both the fear of God and also the contempt of God.[62]

The same theme was a major preoccupation of Colet's sermon to convocation in 1512, the Dean of St Paul's expressing there his conviction that reform of society must begin with reform of the clergy: 'wherefore, if priests that have the cure of souls be good, straight the people will be good.'[63] Nearly twenty years later Colet's views were appealed to by an embattled Thomas More: 'if the clergy be nought we must needs be worse, as I heard once Master Colet . . . preach'.[64] This topos was recycled constantly in contemporary Catholic thinking, and many years after More's death conservative English churchmen were insisting that 'as long as there be disorders in the clergy, it will be hard to bring the people to good order'.[65] Even the anticlerical lawyer, Christopher St German, followed this line of argument: 'if priesthood be whole, all the Church flourisheth, and if it be corrupt, the faith and virtue of the people fadeth also and falleth away.'[66] When contemporaries sought for a metaphor to express their ideal of the priest, they pictured him as a mirror wherein the laity could see a perfect reflection of how they ought to behave.[67] Moreover, Christ's metaphors of the Sermon on the Mount, 'the salt of the earth', 'the light of the world', 'the city on a hill', were widely understood as referring to the priesthood.[68]

All this tended of course to exalting the status of priests, to insisting that laypeople should reverence and respect them. It would be surprising indeed if it could be shown that these were all so many wasted words, that the office of priest was not at all esteemed by the laity. A fifteenth-century critic of the clergy referred to 'the common people, which be valiant in regard of priests', and even an implacable opponent of the Catholic priesthood like Jerome Barlow could admit of the laity, 'priests

---

[62] John Fisher, *The English Works*, ed. J. E. Mayor, EETS es 27 (1876), 179.

[63] Lupton, *Life of Colet*, 302.   [64] More, *Dialogue*, 298.

[65] R. Smith, *Of Unwritten Verities* (1548), sig. A.vii[r].

[66] C. St German, *A treatise concernynge the division betwene the spirytualtie and temporaltie*, in *CW* 9 (1979).

[67] Dionysius Carthusianus, *Lyfe of Prestes*, sig. G.iv[v]; J. Audelay, *Poems*, ed. E. K. Whiting, EETS 184 (1931), 32. See also R. H. Skaife (ed.), *The Register of the Guild of Corpus Christi in the City of York*, SS 57 (1872), 269.

[68] Joseph, *Letter Book*, 210; Lupton, *Life of Colet*, 294; More, *Dialogue*, 298; Herolt, *Sermones Discipuli*, 103[r]; S. Thompson, 'The Pastoral Work of the English and Welsh Bishops 1500–1558', University of Oxford D.Phil. thesis (1984), 95–6.

also they have in reverence'.[69] To some extent it could hardly be otherwise, given that the salvation of the laity depended so narrowly on the
spiritual ministrations of the clergy. As celebrant of the mass and absolver
of the penitent sinner, the priest possessed what the theologians had
come to regard as a twofold power; over Christ's natural body and over
his mystical body the Church, a power from whose implications no orthodox lay man or woman could escape.[70] In Berkshire in 1491, Thomas
Tailour of Newbury clearly shocked his neighbours by his heretical
opinions, having 'said and manifestly showed before divers in despite of
priesthood that the order of priesthood was never ordained nor made by
God'. Tailour had also spoken against the sacraments of baptism and
penance, but admitted that 'oft times . . . I have been questioned with:
what were a man at his first beginning and his later ending without the
help of a priest?'[71] Thomas Crabbe of Axminster in Devon countered the
heretical views of his neighbour Philip Gammon in 1536 by asserting that
'every man must needs have a priest at his coming into the world, and a
priest at his departing'.[72]

To orthodox Catholics, the vehement antisacerdotalism espoused by
such as Tailour and Gammon was quite clearly incomprehensible. Yet
even Lollard heretics could on occasion exhibit an oblique respect for the
priesthood and its practitioners. In 1528, for example, John Tyball of
Steeple Bumpstead in Essex set out to convert two priests to his heretical
views, feeling that if he were able to do this 'he were sure and strong
enough'.[73] Ten years earlier another Steeple Bumpstead Lollard, Robert
Hemstead, confessed that he had learned his unorthodox beliefs from his
curate, Sir Richard Fox, in the course of confession. Initially, claimed
Hemstead, he had been reluctant to accept Fox's Lollard teaching, but
eventually 'because he was priest, this respondent thought and believed
that in the blessed sacrament of the altar is not the very body of Christ'.[74]

To a great extent the very nature of the available sources ensures that
references to popular respect for the priesthood and deference towards
priests will be few and scattered. Defamatory words, assaults on priests,
or heretical utterances about the priesthood might all have their sequel in
the ecclesiastical or secular courts, but it is often only by chance that we

[69] G. Cigman (ed.), *Lollard Sermons*, EETS 294 (1989), 24; J. Barlow, *Burial of the Mass*,
in E. Arber (ed.), *English Reprints* (1871), 27.
[70] Aquinas, *Summa Theologica*, iii. 2686–7; Power, *Ministers of Christ*, 120; Nichols, *Holy
Order*, 127.
[71] D. P. Wright (ed.), *The Register of Thomas Langton, Bishop of Salisbury, 1485–1493*,
CYS 74 (1985), 70.   [72] PRO, STA. C. 2, 2/267.
[73] J. Strype, *Ecclesiastical Memorials* (Oxford, 1822), i (2). 52.   [74] Ibid. 61.

catch a glimpse of the other side of the coin. It would appear, for example, that the 'oath of a priest' may have struck a particular resonance with contemporaries.[75] A vicar providing a testimonial in the late fifteenth century, for a parishioner who had been unjustly accused of being Scottish, invited the reader to 'bear witness of my priesthood'.[76] It appears also to have been common for laypeople drawing up their last testaments to have appointed priests as executors or overseers.[77] In 1516 we hear of a criminal in Lincolnshire who was reported to have been 'conveyed in a priest's gown over the water there called Trent, out of Lincolnshire into Nottinghamshire'.[78] In October 1536, at the outbreak of the Lincolnshire Rising, Lord Hussey travelled from Sleaford to Nottingham similarly disguised as a priest.[79] The choice of disguise probably reflected the belief that a priest on his travels was less likely to be troubled than a layman. Even in the tense conditions of war and conquest there were Englishmen who hoped the proper attitude towards the clergy would be maintained: during Henry VIII's invasion of France in 1513 the troops were instructed that French priests going about their ordinary duties were not to be attacked or taken prisoner.[80]

It was possible, of course, to retain a healthy respect for the office of priest while heartily disapproving of the behaviour of individual clerics. In 1534 Gilbert Burton, rector of North Waltham in the diocese of Winchester, wrote to Lady Lisle to inform her that he had dismissed his curate, Thomas Gilbert 'by reason of divers and many great offences whereof some I will not write for the honour of priesthood'.[81] This type of attitude was perhaps natural in the clergy, but was by no means confined to them. It is interesting to note the reaction to James Harrison, a Lancashire priest, who in the early 1530s was a forthright partisan of Katherine of Aragon, and who wished to know 'who made that whore, Nan Bullen, Queen?' A local gentleman, William Dalton, retorted 'Hold thy peace, thou wots not what thou sayest; and, but that thou art a priest I should punish thee that other should take example.'[82] Wills can provide further evidence of respect for the priesthood. Aside from bequests for priests to say masses, gifts to the clergy were common, and many testators

---

[75] PRO, C. 1, 475/3.
[76] J. Raine (ed.), *English Miscellanies Illustrating the History and Language of the Northern Counties of England*, SS 85 (1890), 41.
[77] See below, 208.   [78] PRO, STA. C. 2, 17/26.
[79] H. Miller, *Henry VIII and the English Nobility* (Oxford, 1986), 149.
[80] C. Cruickshank, *Henry VIII and the Invasion of France* (Stroud, 1990), 110.
[81] St Clare Byrne (ed.), *Lisle Letters*, ii. 35–6.
[82] N. Pocock (ed.), *Records of the Reformation* (Oxford, 1870), ii. 567.

expressed the hope that a large number of priests would attend their funeral, often bequeathing a small sum to every priest who did so. One Somerset testator in 1539 insisted, for example, 'that there be at the least five priests to pray for my soul' at her burial.[83] John Pers of Faccombe in Hampshire requested in 1528 that at his dirige and mass, his trental and his anniversary, 'there be at the least every day of the same ten priests'.[84] In making bequests to members of the religious orders it was common to give a larger sum to those who were priests than to the lay brothers. In 1511 Richard Brekenden of Maidstone in Kent left 3s. 4d. to every monk in the monastery of Roberde, Sussex 'being a priest' and only 12d. to every monk not a priest.[85] Richard Seman of King's Langley in Hertfordshire wrote in his will in 1531 that 'to every friar that shall be at my burial being a priest, I bequeath 6d. and to every young friar being no priest, I bequeath 4d.'[86] There is clearly sufficient evidence to establish that priesthood was, in varying degrees, held in reverence by many of the laity of early sixteenth-century England. But the picture traced so far is a rather two-dimensional one. To negotiate the evidence concerning lay attitudes to the clergy across a specious dichotomy of pious acquiescence versus unremitting anticlericalism is to ignore a number of key variables generated by the theological and sociological interaction of pastors and people, which served to redefine, and sometimes to disorientate, lay responses to priests and the priesthood.

PERCEPTIONS OF PRIESTHOOD: PROBLEMS OF ORIENTATION

As we have seen, many writers and homilists in the pre-Reformation Church put considerable effort into exalting the status of priests, yet these same authorities put a tremendous burden of responsibility on to the clergy. In declaring the spiritual health of the laity to depend on the clergy's example, priests were indirectly made responsible for all the ills of society, and a necessary concomitant of high clericalism was a furious denunciation of wicked priests, a theme clearly discernible, for example,

[83] F. W. Weaver (ed.), *Wells Wills (Serel Collection)*, Somersetshire Archaeological and Natural History Society Proceedings, 1 (1916), 93.

[84] PRO, PCC, Prob. 11, 32 Porch. See also A. K. McHardy, 'Careers and Disappointments in the Late Medieval Church: Some English Evidence', in W. J. Sheils and D. Wood (eds.), *The Ministry: Clerical and Lay*, SCH 26 (Oxford, 1989), 120.

[85] PRO, PCC, Prob. 11, 3 Holder.

[86] L. M. Munby, *Life and Death in King's Langley: Wills and Inventories 1498–1659*, King's Langley Local History and Museum Society (1981), 9.

in Colet's convocation sermon of 1512.[87] The *Doctrinal of Sapyence* declared that priests who gave evil example to others should be grievously punished and tormented 'for if they live in deadly sin they be horrible and stinking before God and his saints and damn themselves villainously'.[88] In similar fashion the *Orchard of Syon* balanced its fulsome praise of righteous priests with an almost hysterical denunciation of the wicked: sinful priests betray the great trust and dignity placed in them and are servants of the Devil rather than of God. An evil priest is no more or less than a 'wicked sprite and fiend of hell'.[89] The *Stella Clericorum* neatly encapsulated this view of the priest by remarking 'if he lives in chastity of body and soul and with humility, he is an angel; if he lives otherwise he is worse than a devil'.[90] The consequence of such remarks was inevitably to suggest that a wicked priest was somehow less than a priest. In an Oxford lecture on Paul's Letter to the Romans, Colet had even suggested that God would not uphold the ordination of a priest who had forfeited his place among the righteous.[91] Colet's sensitivity to clerical weakness was perhaps an extreme case, but there was no shortage of Catholic clerics prepared to go with him down the well-worn medieval path of castigating the wickedness of fellow priests. In 1487, for example, Archbishop Morton had been forced to take action against preachers who railed against the sins of ecclesiastics in their sermons to the laity at Paul's Cross.[92] This kind of attitude is less properly described as anticlericalism than as an extreme form of clericalism: no mercy was to be shown to those who by their misconduct had disgraced the clerical order. Taken to extremes, this outlook could become theologically highly ambivalent. Wyclif had revived in late medieval England a view of ministry which bore affinities to the ancient Donatist heresy, and the evidence of heresy trials over the hundred years preceding the break with Rome shows that the opinion that wicked priests had no power to consecrate or to grant absolution was among the commonest of Lollard beliefs.[93] With this in mind, orthodox commentators invariably insisted that the sacraments, the sacrament of the altar in particular, were in no way dependent on the moral standing of the celebrant. Yet in the years before the Reformation the

---

[87] Lupton, *Life of Colet*, 293–304.   [88] de Roye, *Doctrinal of Sapyence*, sig. I.ii[r].

[89] Catherine of Siena, *Orchard of Syon*, sigs, s.v[v], t.vii[r], t.iii[r].

[90] *Stella Clericorum* (1531), sig. C.iii[v].

[91] P. I. Kaufman, 'Colet's *Opus de sacramentis* and Clerical Anticlericalism', *JBS* 22 (1982), 14.

[92] C. Harper-Bill (ed.), 'An Edition of the Register of John Morton, Archbishop of Canterbury, 1486–1500', University of London Ph.D. thesis (1977), 194–5.

[93] See above, 10–11, 48–9.

opportunity to broaden this out into a more reasoned case for the ministerial and vicarious character of sacramental priesthood was by and large
ignored. As we have seen, the same commentators who upheld the principle
of *ex opere operato* also suggested that the masses of notoriously wicked
priests were better not attended, that by saying mass in a state of sin
priests were ensuring their own damnation, and that though the sacrament
itself may have been validly performed, priestly prayers said during the
mass were worthless and rejected by God.[94]

Few priests can consistently have attained the standard expected of
them by the moralists. In many cases there may have been a profound
dissonance between, on the one hand, the content of quasi-official teaching
regarding the office and dignity of the priest, and on the other, the laity's
practical experience of the way in which that office was generally performed.
If the Church was encouraging laypeople to expect too much from priests,
was generating hopes that were consistently disappointed, then lay attitudes towards the priesthood may have been marked by a distinct am-
bivalence.

The assumptions of the moralists regarding clerical dignity were predicated on the proposition that priests should be distinct and separate,
that they should not, as Colet put it, 'live plainly after the lay fashion'.[95]
Yet as every clear-thinking contemporary should have been aware this
was to a large extent an unattainable ideal. The model of a parish priest
separated from his flock by a distinctive uniform, by distinctive education and outlook was to be the achievement of the Counter-Reformation
and of the 'Puritan' colleges of Elizabethan Cambridge. There were in pre-
Reformation England no seminaries to foster such a separatist mentality.
The late medieval clergy, it has been argued, did not in any sense com-
prise a 'profession', could not develop a true sense of group identity.[96]
The theoretically distinct spheres of clergy and laity, spiritualty and
temporalty, were fused together in a number of ways. Priests often acted,
and were seen to act, in an essentially lay capacity, at the higher levels
working as royal civil servants and ambassadors, lower down the social
scale acting as stewards to lay landowners, as farmers, tradesmen, or
craftsmen.[97] Priests who were employed as private chaplains to lay families
were frequently used on secular business, and sometimes acted as men of

---

[94] See above, 56–7; de Roye, *Doctrinal of Sapyence*, sig. I.i^r; Herolt, *Sermones Discipuli*, 153^r.
[95] Lupton, *Life of Colet*, 297–8.
[96] R. O'Day, *The English Clergy: The Emergence and Consolidation of a Profession, 1558–1642* (Leicester, 1979), 234. See also the review of this work by P. Heath in *JEH* 32 (1981).
[97] Aveling, 'The English Clergy', 61.

affairs for their masters, a notable example being the Paston family chaplain, Sir James Gloys. Such men may have on occasion appeared indistinguishable from the secular servants of their masters. The records of the court of Star Chamber are, for example, replete with examples of priests accompanying and abetting their lay employers in cases of riot and forcible entry. Lay and clerical society remained closely interpenetrated at all levels. Parish priests were often local men and remained in close touch with their families.[98] A rector or vicar who spent much of his time tilling his glebe land must have had much in common with his rustic lay neighbours. The strict apartheid of secular and spiritual that Colet and others longed for was never a realistic goal in the conditions of early sixteenth-century England. One recent writer has even suggested that 'there is not much evidence . . . that men thought in terms of distinct categories of laity and clergy, and that priests were identified as a homogeneous caste'.[99] Without significant qualification, such a conclusion may well be too extreme. If this was really the case, then the high clericalist ideal purveyed by the moralists must have meant little to most ordinary laypeople. If, on the other hand, the laity did discern a distinct clerical identity with its consequent rights and responsibilities, then the evident failure of priests to hold themselves aloof from secular affairs must have constituted another cause of tension between the ideal and the reality. The question of whether lay men and women did have a clear conception of the priest *per se*, and did expect him to remain separate and detached from things secular, is a crucial one, and will be considered more closely below. But for the moment a related question intrudes itself, that of whether such a unified conception was at all feasible in the face of the extreme differentiation manifested by the late medieval clerical body.

In a sense, the status of all priests was theoretically equal. All were empowered to say mass and hear confessions and to minister the other sacraments, and the trend of contemporary theology was even to minimize the distinction between priest and bishop.[100] Yet the levelling tendency inherent in ordination was mitigated by the profoundly hierarchical character of the pre-Reformation Church. The English clergy, even the parish clergy, comprehended a vast range of types, graduate and non-graduate, from richly beneficed rectors to poor salaried stipendiaries,

---

[98] See below, 194–6.

[99] C. Haigh, 'Anticlericalism and the English Reformation', in C. Haigh (ed.), *The English Reformation Revised* (Cambridge, 1987), 69–70.

[100] E. C. Messenger, *The Reformation, the Mass and the Priesthood* (1936), i. 74; Power, *Ministers of Christ*, 116; Nichols, *Holy Order*, 49–50, 80.

taking in curates, chantry, and fraternity priests along the way. While the sacramental status of priests was firmly established, their social status was extremely contingent, and it must have been difficult for laypeople to have maintained a consistent attitude towards priests when some of them were their social superiors, and others, perhaps, their social inferiors. It is instructive that when Polydore Vergil came to recount how a cleric had nurtured Lambert Simnel in Henry VII's reign, he described him as lowborn and could classify him unselfconsciously as a 'mere priest' (*unius praesbyteris*).[101] It has been suggested that an exacerbating factor in Richard Hunne's acrimonious dispute with the clergy in 1511–14 was that while Hunne, as an affluent merchant, enjoyed high social standing, the London parish clergy were commonly of much lower social status.[102]

Priests, as we have seen, could be honoured for the sake of their office alone, but it is unlikely that they could rely solely on their possession of holy orders to overawe the laity. One area in which this seems evident is in the hostility which was sometimes shown to foreign priests. In 1511, for example, the parishioners of Seasalter in Kent complained that 'they have appointed a Scot to sing for William Smelt, that willed in his testament a priest to sing for him half a year'.[103] The parishioners of Waldershare complained that the benefice was held by an Irishman, and a similar objection was raised to the curate of Moore in Oxfordshire in 1530.[104] No doubt these feelings were fuelled by the traditional xenophobia of the English; many contemporaries would have shared the sentiment of the Londoner who remarked in 1511 that 'it is great pity such whoreson Scots be suffered within the parish'.[105] During the war with Scotland in 1513, the London Church courts even held that it was defamatory to accuse someone of being Scottish.[106] Yet accusations of this sort featured periodically in verbal attacks on priests. Richard Alen, vicar of Colaton Raleigh in Devon, was called 'whoreson Scot' by Henry Copleston in 1518.[107] In 1539 John Gallampton of Pawlett in Somerset called his vicar

---

[101] P. Vergil, *The Anglia Historia of Polydore Vergil AD 1485–1537*, ed. D. Hay, CS 74 (1950), 16–17.

[102] R. J. Schoeck, 'Common Law and Canon Law in their Relation to Thomas More', in R. S. Sylvester (ed.), *St Thomas More: Action and Contemplation* (New Haven, Conn., 1972), 40. For the contemporary perception of the low status of the lesser clergy at the Inns of Court, see R. M. Fisher, 'The Reformation of Clergy at the Inns of Court, 1530–1580', *SCJ* 12 (1981), 82–3.   [103] *Kentish Visitations*, 85.

[104] Ibid. 98; P. Hughes, *The Reformation in England*: i. *The King's Proceedings* (1956), 104. The parishioners of Moore claimed to be unable to understand their curate. See *Visitation Articles*, ii. 53.   [105] GLRO, DL/C/206, 116ᵛ.

[106] R. M. Wunderli, *London Church Courts and Society on the Eve of the Reformation* (1981), 79.   [107] PRO, Req. 2, 10/251.

an 'Irish knave'.[108] In November 1548 Gilbert Myrows, parson of Somerton in Suffolk, claimed to have been insulted by a group of parishioners calling him 'thief', 'whoremonger', and 'Scot'.[109] Testators requesting masses for their souls sometimes specifically ruled out foreign priests as possible celebrants. John Darell of Little Chart in Kent asked for 'an honest English priest' to sing for his soul for five years in 1509, and similar stipulations are to be found in the wills of a number of his contemporaries, one Somerset man leaving £5 for masses for his soul 'provided always that the said priest be an Englishman'.[110] This kind of nationalistic attitude is seen at its clearest in the bequest of William Baily in 1515: 'to every English priest that cometh to my burying 8*d*.; to every French priest 6*d*.'[111] Such considerations as social status and na-tionality could perhaps cut across an integrated view of priesthood, making it difficult for us to identify a consistent or coherent set of lay attitudes towards priests. Yet to argue that the laity of early sixteenth-century England had no real sense of the identifying characteristics of the priest, and of his obligations to his office and to society, is ultimately unsustainable.

THE SEARCH FOR PRIESTLINESS

In their relations with priests laypeople must have had somehow to make sense of the constant opposition of image and reality, of the gap between the ideal of the priest as angelic bearer of a unique dignity, and their experience of the priest as fallible co-member of earthly society. It has been suggested that the church may have led laypeople to expect too much of the priesthood, but so far no evidence has been adduced to show that such expectations were actually generated, that lay men and women were able or prepared to compare the actual priests they encountered to some ideal standard, or that they actively expected a code of behaviour to be followed by priests recognizably distinct from that which applied to other Christians. In the section which follows it will be argued that though most laypeople may have had a shaky and incomplete grasp of the theology of orders, they had a firm sense at least of how a priest ought or

---

[108] PRO, STA. C. 2, 31/120.   [109] PRO, C. 1, 1309/73.
[110] PRO, PCC, Prob. 11, 24 Bennett; F. W. Weaver (ed.), *Somerset Medieval Wills 1501–1530*, SRS 19 (1903), 222. For further examples of the formula, see Marshall, 'Attitudes of the English People to Priests and Priesthood', 178.
[111] Weaver (ed.), *Somerset Medieval Wills 1501–1530*, 181.

ought not to behave, of what or who was or was not 'priestly'. It was with a sense of unease that Lord Lisle's man of business, John Husee, watched his master's stepson, James Basset, prepare for a career in the Church. He considered him 'much meeter to serve the temporal powers than the spiritual dignities'.[112] In other words, Basset was not priestly.

In what, then, did priestliness lie? In part it may have been an almost indefinable essence, a general demeanour whose presence contemporaries could detect and whose notable absence they could deplore. In the fifteenth century the East Anglian mystic, Margery Kempe, described a priest of her acquaintance as 'an amiable person, fair featured, well favoured in cheer and in countenance, sad in his language and dalliance, priestly in his gesture and vesture'.[113] More specifically, however, priestliness related to a conscientious performance of the duties to which the priest was bound. In 1527 John Cheyney of Sittingborne in Kent hoped that the executors of his will would find an honest priest to pray for his soul and 'to say divine service as appertaineth to a good priest'.[114] In 1540 Thomas Boswel of Derfield in South Yorkshire directed the priest celebrating for his soul 'to say mass three days in a week and ofter if he be priestly disposed'.[115] Priestliness also involved the avoidance of patterns of behaviour which contemporaries considered incompatible with the clerical vocation. Edmund Robyns of Appledore in Kent expressed what must have been a common aspiration in 1533 when he hoped that the priest celebrating for him would be 'of good behaviour as a priest ought to be'.[116] The pursuit of secular entertainments might be particularly frowned upon. It was reported of the Cornish priest, James Jencyll, that 'the said Sir James and his servants be men of great pleasure, more like temporal men than spiritual [they] do daily use hawking and hunting'.[117] Unsurprisingly, violent or uncharitable behaviour was regarded as exceptionally unsuitable for a priest. When one Kentish priest attacked another in 1511 he was described as having 'struck unpriestly with a naked sword'.[118] In 1513 an assault on one of his parishioners by Sir Thomas Flint, rector of Leigh in Somerset, was deemed by the victim as being against all clerical decency.[119] In the same year a dispute over tithes between Henry Rushton and Henry Lentham, vicar of Evenley in Northamptonshire, led

---

[112] St Clare Byrne (ed.), *Lisle Letters*, v. 231.

[113] M. Kempe, *The Book of Margery Kempe*, ed. S. B. Meech, EETS 212 (1940), 56.

[114] PRO, PCC, Prob. 11, 21 Porch.   [115] *Test. Ebor.* vi. 115.

[116] PRO, PCC, Prob. 11, 3 Hogen.   [117] PRO, STA. C. 2, 9/63.

[118] *Kentish Visitations*, 82.

[119] A. Watkin (ed.), *Dean Cosyn and Wells Cathedral Miscellanea*, SRS 56 (1941), 156.

to a violent exchange of blows, Rushton describing Lentham's behaviour as 'contrary to the good order of priesthood, more like a man raged and out of his mind than like a priest'.[120] Priests themselves, of course, recognized their obligation to abstain from such behaviour. In the early 1520s another dispute over tithes, this time between two Lincolnshire rectors, Anthony Benet and Robert Benson, resulted in an assault on the former by the latter, a circumstance for which Benet claimed he was completely unprepared 'because they were both priests and men of the Church'.[121] In 1523 when the London curate, Robert Shoter, struck a fellow priest, Peter Bowden, the latter declared that Shoter was 'more like a Bedlam man than like a curate to strike a priest in the church after this manner'.[122]

Priests did not need to be overtly physically aggressive to be regarded by their neighbours as acting out of character. The bitter quarrel between Elyn Hatche of Charing in Kent and her vicar, Henry Mastall, has already been referred to.[123] Hatche epitomized Mastall's actions by claiming that he 'doth wrongfully and unpriestly use him many and sundry ways', not only towards her, but also to 'divers other his poor parishioners, which dare not displease him nor complain against him though they have great cause'.[124] In 1526 a letter to Bishop Sherburne of Chichester complained of the behaviour of the curate of Cowfold, who refused to visit the sick and was apparently unable to get on with his parishioners. His disposition was said to be 'not priestly nor good in divers things'.[125] In 1533 Richard Alen, the parson of Clayhidon in Devon, was described as 'a tyrant not priestly'. The charges against him included overstocking of the common and making vexatious suits against the tenants of the manor. In his previous position as vicar of Colaton Raleigh he was said to have caused his parishioners to spend over £200 in defending themselves against suits he had forwarded against them.[126]

An 'unpriestly' priest was a walking anomaly, to be described as such was a serious imputation, expressive of a real sense of deeply felt grievance, not against priesthood as such, but against the failure of some priests to live up to the ideal they were supposed to exemplify. It is instructive that when in 1538 Bishop Longland of Lincoln sought for ways to attack the Pope, he chose to condemn him for his 'unpriestly

[120] PRO, STA. C. 2, 21/160.   [121] PRO, STA. C. 2, 4/202.
[122] GLRO, DL/C/207, fo. 212ᵛ.   [123] See above, 27.
[124] PRO, STA. C. 2, 25/333.
[125] S. J. Lander, 'The Diocese of Chichester 1508–1558', University of Cambridge Ph.D. thesis (1974), 234.   [126] PRO, STA. C. 2, 14/152.

presumption'.[127] Writing to Cromwell a year earlier, Latimer had passed on news of an 'unpriestly priest' whose 'damsel' was delivered of a child 'not without offence of many'.[128] Thus priestliness can be seen to embrace chastity, as well as diligence, an eirenical disposition, charity towards one's neighbours, and a healthy degree of other-worldliness. That this combination of virtues was regarded as desirable, if not essential, for an intending priest is confirmed by the evidence of ordinands' 'Letters Testimonial', an impressive set of which, from the reign of Mary, survive in the diocesan archives of York. These were certificates of good character to be presented to the bishop by a candidate for orders, and were generally signed by the incumbent of his home parish and a number of its leading laymen.[129] Sometimes these documents were witnessed by laymen alone,[130] and it is probably safe to suggest that they represent a fair summary of what respectable and conventional parish opinion considered to qualify a man for the priesthood, or at least, though the distinction is by no means a clear one, of what it believed the ecclesiastical authorities wanted to hear. A few of the letters draw attention to the learning of the bearer,[131] but in general the emphasis is on good character rather than scholarly aptitude. Most of the candidates were declared to be of 'honest conversation' and to possess a 'good name and fame'. Others were noted for their aversion to hawking, alehouses, adultery, or any other of the crimes, as one missive put it, 'whereby youth may be spotted and honesty defaced'.[132] The testimonial written for William Bache of Shropshire in 1554 is worth quoting as an illustration of a young man apparently considered a potential paragon of priestliness by his neighbours. Bache was said to be

of good and honest conversation and born in lawful matrimony, always applying learning and virtue, no hawker nor hunter nor commonly frequenting any common alehouse, nor using any evil and suspected places and company, nor no

---

[127] M. Bowker, *The Henrician Reformation: The Diocese of Lincoln under John Longland, 1521–1547* (Cambridge, 1981), 71.

[128] Latimer, *Sermons*, ii. 390–1. Lay reactions to this aspect of clerical misbehaviour will be discussed in the following chapter.

[129] I have found no reference to the existence of Letters Testimonial before 1553, and one is tempted to assume that they were an innovation of the Marian regime, perhaps designed to weed out candidates of questionable orthodoxy: a number of these documents make mention of their bearer's freedom from 'evil', 'heretical', or 'erroneous' opinions, or note his being a 'firm Catholic'. BIHR, Ord. 1554/1/7; 8; 11; 12; 1556/1/17; 25; 26; 29; 1557/1/33; 36; Adm. 1557/7; 30.

[130] BIHR, Ord. 1554/1/5; 28; 1557/1/33; 34; 36; Adm. 1557/2.

[131] BIHR, Ord. 1554/1/2; 5; 1556/1/25; 26; 27; 1557/1/33; 39.

[132] BIHR, Ord. 1555/1/16.

common carder nor dicer, nor busy player at any other unlawful and prohibited games, no brawler, chider, nor fighter, never contentious nor busy in erroneous questions and opinions, but ever of his nature gentle, courteous, and benign, in all his words, works, and deeds.[133]

A modern reader is struck by the absence in these documents of reference to the spiritual life of the candidates. Only one of the ordinands is specifically commended for 'godliness'.[134] Perhaps in a society where the basic tenets of Christianity were rarely if ever challenged, a necessary modicum of piety could be taken for granted, or perhaps a priest who managed to exhibit no trace of gross immorality, flagrant worldliness, or callous misanthropy, was usually regarded as acceptable by his lay neighbours.

The priestliness that laypeople hoped to encounter was in any case more easily comprehended in externals than in the inner motivations of the heart. Priests were expected not merely to behave differently or more punctiliously than lay folk, but to look distinctive. It was in how they dressed and presented themselves that priests could underline their distinctive status, and try to insulate themselves from the creeping secularity that surrounded them. Priests dressing in worldly fashion had represented a notable disciplinary problem in the Middle Ages, and a number of canons had been promulgated insisting that those in holy orders wear 'outward garments unlike to the garments of warriors or the lay'.[135] In 1533 an Act of Parliament sought to regulate the apparel that priests could wear, forbidding to the lower clergy various types of furs and silks, but the attire of some priests continued to be a problem.[136] In 1537 Bishop Rowland Lee of Coventry and Lichfield complained that 'certain priests in my diocese go in habit dissimulated more like the temporalty than of the clergy'. In 1542 Bonner of London noted the 'unseemly habit and apparel with unlawful tonsures' that some priests of his diocese affected, 'more like persons of the laity than of the clergy'. All priests were directed to dress and cut their hair that 'they may be known at all times from laypeople'.[137] The 'superfluous apparell' of some priests was a potent inspiration to anticlericals,[138] and a number of orthodox commentators insisted

---

[133] BIHR, Ord. 1554/1/5.   [134] BIHR, Ord. 1554/1/7.

[135] E. L. Cutts, *Parish Priests and their People in the Middle Ages in England* (1898), 164–82; *Lyndwood*, 48; R. S. Arrowsmith, *The Prelude to the Reformation* (1923), 63.

[136] 24 Henry VIII, *c*.13.

[137] *Visitation Articles*, 23, 86. See also D. M. Owen, 'Synods in the Diocese of Ely in the Latter Middle Ages and the Sixteenth Century', in G. J. Cuming (ed.), *SCH* 3 (1966), 220.

[138] J. Fyllol, *Agaynst the possessyons of the clergye* (1537), sig. B.i^v; E. Hall, *The Union of the two Noble and Illustre Famelies of Lancastre and Yorke*, ed. H. Ellis (1809), 593; F. J. Furnivall (ed.), *Ballads from Manuscripts* (1868), i. 161; Latimer, *Sermons*, ii. 82–3; Cigman (ed.), *Lollard Sermons*, 19.

on plainness and sombreness in dress. In *Dives and Pauper*, Pauper suggests that priests in their clothing 'should show sadness, honesty, and lowness, as nigh followers of Christ'.[139] The *Lyfe of Prestes* urged clerks to avoid 'manifold excess in garments' on the grounds that fine dress encourages pride, and might provoke the eyes of women. If priests wanted to be respected by the laity, 'the more simple, meek, and full of good example they ought to be in their apparel'. Priests who eschewed proper clerical dress 'dishonest their priesthood'.[140] Bishop Alcock of Lincoln remarked that 'if thou see a priest go like a lay man, with his tippet, slippers, and great sleeves, it is to presume that he repenteth him that ever he forsook the habit of a lay man and therefore he useth it'.[141] Such rebukes flowed readily from the pens of clerical moralists throughout this period. To Roger Edgeworth, the lamentable fact that many priests dressed in lay fashions suggested that 'we be ashamed of our order'.[142] As a consequence of such sensibilities, the ecclesiastical authorities were prepared to take action against priests who dressed or wore their hair in a secular fashion.[143]

It is perhaps not surprising if the same authorities who emphasized the unique and superior status of the priest also stressed the need for distinctive clerical clothing. But one recent writer, pointing out that 'exuberant gowns' were often left to priests by laypeople as gifts or mortuaries has suggested that the style of clerical dress may have been a matter of relative indifference to the laity.[144] While it is true that some testators did leave blue, violet, or scarlet gowns to priests, others made the effort to designate something more suitable. In 1527, for example, John Curtop, a clothier of Cranbrook in Kent, bequeathed to his clerical cousin, Richard Colyer, 'a convenient gown cloth of five yards'.[145] In 1529 Walter Frost of Westham left to his parish priest 'four broad yards of black cloth for a gown'.[146] Not surprisingly, black was considered the most suitable colour for any sartorial bequest to a priest, and some testators obviously took care in selecting an appropriate item of this shade. In 1536 George Maplisden of Marden in Kent bequeathed to his vicar 'my black gown that I wear in the Whitsun week'.[147] Where the colour of an item of

---

[139] *Dives and Pauper* (1534), 286ᵛ.

[140] Dionysius Carthusianus, *Lyfe of Prestes*, sigs. F.iᵛ, F.iiiʳ.

[141] Blench, *Preaching in England*, 239.   [142] R. Edgeworth, *Sermons* (1557), 94ᵛ.

[143] Harper-Bill (ed.), 'Register of John Morton', 195; Hale, *Precedents*, 131; *Lincoln Visitations*, ii. 2; M. Bowker (ed.), *An Episcopal Court Book for the Diocese of Lincoln, 1514–1520*, LRS 61 (1967), 4; BIHR, D/C AB 1, fo. 61ᵛ; GLRO, DL/C/330, fo. 196ᵛ.

[144] P. Heath, *The English Parish Clergy on the Eve of the Reformation* (1969), 109.

[145] PRO, PCC, Prob. 11, 26 Porch.   [146] Clay (ed.), *North Country Wills*, 124.

[147] PRO, PCC, Prob. 11, 5 Bucke.

clothing left to a cleric is specified in laypeople's wills, black occurs more than twice as often as all other shades combined. It is revealing that Christopher St German believed that private chaplains sometimes wore liveries 'not convenient for a priest to wear'.[148] Laypeople further down the social scale were not slow to register their disapproval when they felt that a priest had dressed in an unsuitable manner. In 1488 the men of Oakham in Leicestershire complained to Bishop Russell of Lincoln that their vicar was remiss in providing services and that he went 'to and fro [dressed] like a layman'.[149] In 1511 the charges against a Kentish priest included his going 'to Sutton and about in a canvas doublet and bow and arrows unpriestly'.[150] When Sir Godfrey Foliambe, knight, came to describe what he considered a wrongful and forced entry on to the estate of one of his wards in Leicestershire by the adherents of Simon Norwich, he took care to note that one of the party was a priest, dressed not in priestly garb, but rather 'arrayed like a temporal man'.[151] A similar observation was made in August 1523 when a dispute over parish boundaries led to a tense confrontation between Thomas Tyrrell, the rector of Gislingham in Suffolk, and Sir John Wiseman, knight, lay farmer of the parish of Thornham Magna. Both men and their servants arrived together in a field to collect the tithes they believed were due to them, and with Wiseman was his chaplain, Sir John Coverdale, dressed in a military tunic or jack, and armed with a pitchfork. Tyrrel took this as a golden opportunity to establish the moral superiority of his case, and led Coverdale to William Garsington, a royal servant who was present to keep the peace, saying, 'here is a priest in harness of Sir John Wyseman; I pray you bear witness of the same'. Garsington agreed that 'it was like no priest', and to milk the opportunity for all it was worth, Tyrrel went to fetch 'divers of his neighbours which came thither to see the demeanour there'.[152]

Contemporaries clearly had ideas about what constituted unacceptable wear for a priest, and what was normal and appropriate. In a case which came before a York diocesan court in 1540, a number of witnesses agreed that at the time of an alleged altercation the plaintiff was 'apparelled like a priest' and 'had on him a priest's raiment'.[153] Two cases from a Northamptonshire visitation made at the end of Henry VIII's reign similarly suggest that laypeople expected to be able to recognize instantly the difference between themselves and the clergy. It was complained of the

---

[148] St German, *Treatise concernynge the division betwene the spirytualtie and temporaltie*, 187.
[149] A. Hudson, *The Premature Reformation* (Oxford, 1988), 155 n.
[150] *Kentish Visitations*, 291.   [151] PRO, STA. C. 2, 15/139.
[152] PRO, STA. C. 2, 29/83.   [153] BIHR, CP. G. 273 1540.

curate of Sulgrave that he 'went to the market in Banbury in a layman's apparel, in a hat with a broach on it, to the evil example of many, and to the slander of all honest people'. At Norton Davy in July 1546 it was noted that the chantry priest, John Sheldon, 'sitteth in the choir without a surplice more like a serving man than a priest, to evil example of other'.[154] In addition to dressing correctly, the priest was supposed to keep his tonsured hair in good array. Here too, laypeople may have expected priests to maintain minimum and uniform standards. When the parson of Graffham in Sussex let his hair grow long so as to hide his tonsure in 1536, this action was said to have caused 'much murmuring among the people'.[155]

The concern for proper clerical dress and appearance seems to have been symptomatic of a wider sense that, despite the difficulties, priests should try to keep themselves aloof from secular affairs. Among the long catalogue of complaints levelled at Thomas Kyrkeby, priest of Halsall in Lancashire, in 1530 was the charge that he was 'a great intermeddler in temporal matters at Lancaster at the Assizes and in other courts and places otherwise than a priest ought to do, and contrary to his order'.[156] Whether such impulses always sprang solely from a feeling of high regard for the priesthood is perhaps open to question. In reporting to Wolsey his difficulty in collecting the Amicable Grant in 1525 Archbishop Warham admitted that 'some malicious persons say that it would be better for an old fool like him to take his beads in his hand, than to meddle in temporal business pertaining to war and general undoing of this country'.[157] The same attitude was exhibited at a more everyday level in Oxfordshire in the 1540s, when a Nuffield priest who involved himself in a quarrel between Thomas Spire and Agnes Browning over cattle was told by the latter that he was a 'pollshorn priest, and bid him meddle with that he had to do'.[158] Agnes Browning's scornful reference to the priest's shaven head reminds us that an unimpeachable clerical appearance was no guarantee of immunity from hostile comment.[159] Indeed, ironically, the

---

[154] A. G. Dickens, 'Early Protestantism and the Church in Northamptonshire', *North-amptonshire PP*, 8 (1983–4), 31–2. See also *Lincoln Visitations*, i. 78.

[155] *LP* x. 277.

[156] H. Fishwick (ed.), *Pleadings and Depositions in the Duchy Court of Lancaster, Time of Henry VII and Henry VIII*, Lancashire and Cheshire Record Society, 32 (1896), i. 200.

[157] A. Fletcher, *Tudor Rebellions*, 3rd edn. (1983), 14.

[158] OCRO, Oxf. Dioc. MSS d. 14, fo. 94ʳ.

[159] For other examples of hostile references to the tonsure, see GLRO, DL/C/206, fo. 60ᵛ; PRO, STA. C. 2, 10/153; J. G. Nichols (ed.), *Narratives of the Days of the Reformation*, CS 77 (1859), 37.

very distinctiveness of the clergy could be turned against them when quarrels erupted with their parishioners. When William Sevill, holy-water clerk of St Clement's, Eastcheap, fell out with Sir Thomas Warde in 1502, he urged him to 'go forth fool, and set a cock's comb on thy crown', words construed by the court as 'vile contempt of the priestly order'.[160] When defamatory words were offered to priests they almost invariably stressed the clerical status of the defamed party. 'False priest', 'knave priest', 'whoreson priest', 'whoremonger priest', were all common epithets, in each case the juxtaposition of adjective and noun serving to underline, whether consciously or unconsciously, the incompatibility be-tween the exercise of priesthood and the crime of which the cleric stood accused. The unique status to which priests laid claim was always a distinctly double-edged weapon.

CHALLENGES TO PRIESTLY STATUS

There were some, it appears, to whom the anointed status of the priest seemed to matter little. To assault a priest was a grave sin, represented as far worse than laying violent hands on a layman, yet violence offered to priests was in this period a relatively common phenomenon.[161] Even a straightforward appeal to one's priesthood could misfire, as was discov-ered by John Baker, rector of Bowers Gifford in Essex, when he became involved in a dispute with John Aleyn in 1513. The trouble began when Baker rebuked Aleyn's servant, John Gilbard, for sleeping through ves-pers. In response Gilbard showed the rector his backside, and Baker could not resist administering two or three blows with a stick, not maliciously, he claimed, but in the cause of correction. When Aleyn met up with Baker he rebuked him furiously for correcting 'every man's servant at thy pleasure like a proud whoreson priest', and threatened him with his sword. At this Baker 'appealed to his clerical tonsure and priesthood', but was none the less carried to the stocks on the orders of Aleyn, who was bailiff of Bowers, despite his pleading with his captors to 'beware and remember what you are doing, for I am a priest and your curate'.[162]

Although, as this case demonstrates, priests could not always rely on their office to shield them from lay opprobrium or retaliation, a theoreti-cal challenge to the sacramental status of priests was, before the 1520s,

---

[160] Hale, *Precedents*, 76.   [161] See below, 218–19.
[162] GLRO, DL/C/206, fos. 230ʳ–232ᵛ.

confined to the ranks of the Lollard heresy. Most Lollards seem to have
been satisfied with a robust anticlericalism, or antisacerdotalism, denying
the sacramental powers of priests, and sometimes deriding them as 'scribes
and pharisees'.[163] A few, however, went further and asserted that every
good Christian was a priest of God.[164] That Christ had instituted a
priesthood of all believers was later, of course, to be a central tenet of
Protestant belief. Among the heresies adjured by Roger Dichaunte, a
Newcastle merchant, in 1531 was that 'every Christian man is a priest and
hath power to consecrate the body of Our Lord, and to do all other things
which priests alone now use to do'.[165] This rejection of the Catholic view
of priesthood was rooted in an understanding of the all-sufficiency of
Christ's sacrifice. The notion that priests might somehow share in the
high priesthood of Christ was anathema. According to Nicholas Ridley,
Christ 'hath a priesthood that cannot pass to any other'.[166] To Protestants, the priest was essentially a preacher of God's word, and a minister
of His sacraments; they denied that priests had the power to offer Christ
in the sacrifice of the mass. Cranmer insisted that

Christ made no such difference between the priest and the layman, that the priest
should make oblation and sacrifice of Christ for the layman . . . the difference that
is between the priest and the layman in this matter is only in the ministration,
that the priest as a common minister of the Church, doth minister and distribute
the Lord's Supper unto other.[167]

Miles Coverdale agreed. Christ having been once offered up for us, 'I
cannot see what difference can be between priests and lay people, except
the governance of the Church and ministration of God's Word.'[168] Among
English Protestants there were inevitable differences of emphasis regarding the ministry, but all were in agreement that 'popish and outward
priesthood is crept into the Church of God, against the Word of God'.[169]
In particular, the idea that the reception of orders involved receiving a
distinctive sacramental character was firmly rejected. All Christians sharing a common priesthood, the ordained priest was simply a delegate of

---

[163] Wright (ed.), *Register of Thomas Langton*, 75, 79.

[164] Thomson, *Later Lollards*, 248.

[165] G. Hinde (ed.), *The Registers of Cuthbert Tunstal, Bishop of Durham 1530–1559 and James Pilkington, Bishop of Durham 1561–1576*, SS 161 (1952), 35.

[166] J. Ridley, *Works*, ed. H. Christmas, PS (1843), 208. See also J. Bradford, *Writings*, ed. A. Townsend, PS (1853), 312; Clark, *Eucharistic Sacrifice*, 155, 339; Messenger, *The Reformation, the Mass and the Priesthood*, i. 446.   [167] Ibid. 435.

[168] M. Coverdale, *Remains*, ed. G. Pearson, PS (1844), 471.

[169] R. Hutchinson, *The Image of God, or laie man's boke* (1560), 36ʳ.

the whole community, empowered to perform functions that all Christians were in fact competent to perform. At bottom there was to be no difference between layman and priest beyond that of function, and Henry Brinklow bewailed the tendency of his contemporaries to trust in the prayer of priests 'as though they were the peculiar people of God, and only beloved'.[170] Some Protestants jibed even at the word priest, Latimer maintaining that 'a minister is a more fit name for that office; for the name of a priest importeth a sacrifice'.[171] If there was to be no essential difference between priest and layman, then the traditional marks of external distinction were pointless and an insult to the laity. Hooper denied that priests 'must have necessarily that shaven crown and long gown . . . They be neither necessary nor commendable signs to know a priest by'.[172] To Protestants, the priest's shaven head was expressive of his pretended superiority, and hostility to the Catholic priesthood often focused on the tonsure, referred to variously as 'Balaam's mark' or 'the whore's mark of Babylon'.[173] In the reign of Edward, Protestant aversion to the tonsure received the backing of ecclesiastical authority, Archbishop Holgate of York ordering his cathedral clergy in 1552 'that no minister from henceforth . . . do shave his crown under pain of the censures of the Church'.[174] Some Protestant clergy went further in breaking with the past and began to cultivate beards, only to be ordered to shave them off again after Mary's accession.[175]

To English Protestants the traditions surrounding the Catholic ordination rite were not mere *adiaphora*, but positively unchristian. William Tyndale saw the shaving of the priest's crown as simply 'borrowed of the heathen priests', and the priest's anointing as 'but a ceremony borrowed of the Jews'.[176] Moreover, he poured score on the inability of Catholic authorities to decide exactly what comprised the sacramental matter of holy orders: 'one singular doubt they have: what maketh the priest? The anointing, or putting on of the hands, or what other ceremony, or what words? About which they brawl and scold, one ready to tear out another's

---

[170] H. Brinklow, *Lamentacyon of a Christen Agaynst the Cyte of London*, ed. J. M. Cowper, EETS es 22 (1874), 88.

[171] Latimer, *Sermons*, ii. 264. See also A. G. Dickens (ed.), *Tudor Treatises*, YAS 125 (1959), 47; P. E. Hughes, *The Theology of the English Reformers* (1965), 167–8.

[172] J. Hooper, *Early Writings*, ed. S. Carr, PS (1843), 245.

[173] *LP* xviii (2). 546, p. 315; Wilkins, *Concilia*, iii. 805; Strype, *Ecclesiastical Memorials*, i (2). 262. [174] BIHR, Reg. 27, fo. 59ʳ.

[175] J. F. Williams, 'The Married Clergy of the Marian Period', *Norfolk Archaeology*, 32 (1961), 93; Hazlitt (ed.), *Old English Plays*, iii. 10.

[176] Tyndale, *Answer to More*, 20.

throat. One saith this, and another that; but they cannot agree.'[177] Some of the Protestant objections to the traditional form of making priests were incorporated into the ordinals of 1550 and 1552, though the framers of the new rites were careful to preserve something of the old ordination ceremony as a sop to conservative consciences. Although the 1550 ordinal retained the tradition of the instruments, the chalice and bread and a Bible being presented to the candidate, and still employed the form 'receive the holy ghost' and the imposition of hands, a number of important changes were made. All references to the priest's power to offer the body of Christ in the mass were dropped, as was the analogy between the priesthoods of the Old and New Testaments. The investiture in stole and chasuble, and the blessing and anointing of the priest's hands were also omitted, and instead of being granted 'power' to celebrate mass for living and dead, the candidate was provided with 'authority to preach the word of God, and to minister the holy sacraments in this congregation'. In 1552 a further change was made when the candidate was no longer presented with the chalice and bread, and the Bible became the only instrument.[178] The Edwardian ordinals encapsulated the new official view of ministry. A priest was to be first of all a preacher of God's word to the congregation, a minister rather than a sacrificing priest.

To some, this mutation must have seemed liberating; no longer must salvation be seen as contingent upon clerical caprice. A Wakefield man articulated the views of a growing minority in 1548 when he insisted that 'there is but . . . one mediator betwixt man and God, which is Jesus Christ, so that I accept none in heaven, neither in earth, to be my mediator betwixt God and me, but he only'.[179] Yet for others it may have been difficult to accept or comprehend the shift of emphasis, and there are clear indications that laymen may have been more reluctant to offer themselves for ordination under the new rite.[180]

Naturally, Protestant writers hoped that there would be no diminution in the respect laypeople should feel for the ministers of Word and sacraments. Thomas Becon was as convinced as any Catholic encomiast of

---

[177] W. Tyndale, *Doctrinal Treatises*, ed. H. Walter, PS (1848), 258. It was something of an open question in medieval theology whether the 'tradition of the instruments' or the imposition of hands represented the crucial moment of ordination: Nichols, *Holy Order*, 82; J. H. Crehan, 'Medieval Ordinations', in C. Jones, G. Wainwright, and E. Yarnold (eds.), *The Study of Liturgy* (1978), 330–1.

[178] Clark, *Eucharistic Sacrifice*, 191 ff.; Messenger, *The Reformation, the Mass and the Priesthood*, i. 446 ff.

[179] E. W. Crossley (ed.), *Halifax Wills 1545–1559* (Leeds, n.d.), 39.

[180] See below, 229–30.

priesthood that the Gospel metaphors 'light of the world' and 'salt of the earth' applied wholly to the ministry. 'Who', he asked rhetorically, 'hearing the ministers of God's Word to be called with such honourable names is not straightways moved to give honour and reverence unto them?'[181] Yet, as will be argued more fully in a later chapter, by the 1550s clerical claims to honour and reverence may have been ringing increasingly hollow in the ears of the English people.[182] It is important not to slip into facile optimism about lay–clerical relations in the pre-Reformation Church. It has been the contention here that the attitude of many laypeople towards priests and the priesthood may always have been something of an ambivalent one, the product of a structurally complex relationship.[183] Priests seldom lived up to the standard set for them by educated opinion, and some laypeople may sometimes have become cynical or resentful as a consequence. Yet the fact that priests were often too worldly in their outlook and behaviour almost certainly did not mean that the laity despaired of the priesthood or became irredeemably anticlerical. The view that priests were 'anointed people', that they should dress and behave in a distinct and more exacting way, was deeply rooted in the consciousness and aspirations of the English laity. Nowhere is this seen more clearly than in their attitudes to the celibacy of the priesthood, and it is to that topic that we now turn.

[181] T. Becon, *Catechism*, ed. J. Ayre, PS (1844), 91–2; *Prayers and Other Pieces*, ed. J. Ayre, PS (1844), 290. See also J. Chandos, *In God's Name: Examples of Preaching in England from the Act of Supremacy to the Act of Uniformity, 1534–1662* (1971), 29.

[182] See below, 226–32.

[183] Similar conclusions have been arrived at by R. N. Swanson, who epitomizes the paradox of the priesthood's economic dependence on the laity, and the latter's spiritual dependence upon priests: 'the host was dependent on the parasite', 'Problems of the Priesthood in Pre-Reformation England', EHR 417 (1990), 861.

5

The Priest as Celibate

THE CELIBATE IDEAL AND THE 'LEWD PRIEST'

More perhaps than anything else, it was the call to celibacy which marked out the parish priest from the laymen among whom he lived, which defined and delimited his unique and superior status. Serious episcopal efforts to achieve a completely unmarried clergy dated back only to the Gregorian Reform of the twelfth century, but the ideal of a celibate ministry was as old as Christianity itself, and had found forceful advocates among many of the church fathers.[1] In early sixteenth-century England the priesthood's renunciation of sex and marriage was held to constitute both pledge and proof of its nearer approximation to the will and mind of God, for some commentators an essentially Neoplatonic idea. The *Lyfe of Prestes* reported with approval the opinion of the pseudo-Dionysius that 'no man ought to presume to be a leader in any divine office or service, but such as be most like or very nigh fashioned unto God'; since the lowest representative of the higher order ought to correspond to the highest of the lower hierarchies, epitomized in this case by the company of angels and the priesthood respectively, 'priests therefore and clerks are bound to live purely and chastely like angels'.[2] There were other reasons cited by this author why priests should be chaste: their vow at ordination, the provisions adumbrated in the Mosaic Law; but there is no doubting that to many contemporary theorists of priesthood the paramount argument for priestly celibacy was that it demonstrated more clearly than almost anything else the unique and superior status which belonged naturally to the consecrated person of the priest. Comparing the sacraments of orders and matrimony, the canon law of the English church suggested that the former agreed with the perfect, the latter only with the imperfect.[3] 'Men of Holy Church' declared the author of *Dives and Pauper*, 'may better withstand the fleshly temptation

---

[1] H. C. Lea, *History of Sacerdotal Celibacy in the Christian Church*, 3rd edn. (1907); G. Sloyan, 'Biblical and Patristic Motives for Celibacy of Church Ministers', *Concilium*, 8 (1972).
[2] Dionysius Carthusianus, *Lyfe of Prestes*, sigs. H.iii ᵛ, G.iii ʳ.   [3] *Lyndwood*, 15.

than wedded men, for they ought to pass the people in cunning and virtue'.[4]

Such attitudes were rooted in a wider exaltation of the merits of virginity, which was deeply entrenched in the religious culture of late medieval England. Chaste women saints were held up as exemplars in hagiographies and sermons, and devotional writers might even suggest that 'to live chastely in this mortal body is the life of an angel: that is to say, it is more to live chastely in this wretched world than to raise one from death to life'.[5] In the Minster of Ripon in Yorkshire there was even supposed to be a narrow passage in the crypt discriminating enough to admit only the chaste.[6] This impulse to exalt chastity was not limited to the exponents of the most populist devotion: Thomas More's Utopians possessed a profound reverence for consecrated virginity, and Richard Whitford was eager to stress the prelapsarian origins of the celibate state.[7] The contemporary clerical attitude found no more emphatic expression than in Bishop John Fisher's contention that while marriage results in a thirtyfold increase of grace, and widowhood in a sixtyfold, virginity increases grace one hundredfold.[8] Naturally enough, the obverse of this preoccupation with virginity was a fear of and hostility towards sexual licence, and preachers like Fisher and Bishop Longland warned their audiences of the traps hidden by the Devil in 'the unlawful pleasures of the body'.[9] While the inherent sinfulness of the sexual act could to a greater or lesser extent be obviated by the sacrament of marriage, this was viewed as a very definite second-best. Clerical moralists remained keenly alive to the possibilities of sin even between married couples, and wives and husbands were expected to abstain from intercourse at certain holy times of the year.[10]

These, of course, were the normative prescriptions of men who were themselves celibates, but it would be perverse to suppose that such

---

[4] *Dives and Pauper* (1534), 225ʳ.

[5] *The assaute and co[n]quest of heven* (1529), sig. B.iʳ; R. Marius, *Thomas More* (1985), 34–7; P. Tudor, 'Changing Private Belief and Practice in England: Devotional Literature, *c.*1475–1550', University of Oxford D.Phil. thesis (1984), 139–41.

[6] A. G. Dickens, *Lollards and Protestants in the Diocese of York* (1959), 125 n.

[7] T. More, *Utopia*, eds. E. Surtz, S.J. and J. H. Hexter, *CW* 4 (1963), 227; R. Whitford, *The Pype or Tonne of the Lyfe of Perfection* (1532), 27ᵛ.

[8] E. Surtz, *The Works and Days of John Fisher* (Cambridge, Mass., 1967), 334.

[9] J. W. Blench, *Preaching in England in the Late Fifteenth and Sixteenth Centuries* (Oxford, 1964), 233, 242.

[10] W. Harington, *The Comendacions of Matrymony* (1528), sig. D.ivʳ; J. Bossy, *Christianity in the West, 1400–1700* (Oxford, 1985), 50; T. N. Tentler, *Sin and Confession on the Eve of the Reformation* (Princeton, NJ, 1977), xix, 165–6, 188–9, 214.

assumptions could not have taken root also among the laypeople who were their intended audience. After all, the many thousands of secular priests and religious in pre-Reformation England had once been laymen themselves, and it seems likely that the celibate priest embodied widely held ideals, perhaps even satisfied vicariously aspirations towards sanctity which most people were unable to achieve in their own lives.[11] Thomas More turned away from a strong sense of vocation to the priesthood, so Erasmus informed Ulrich von Hutten, because 'he could not shake off the desire to get married. And so he chose to be a god-fearing husband rather than an immoral priest'.[12] More was not unique in his scrupulosity: thirty years earlier Margaret Paston had warned her son Walter to take his time before proceeding to holy orders, declaring 'I will love him better to be a good secular man than to be a lewd priest.'[13] Years later, in 1538, the Bishop of Salisbury, Nicholas Shaxton, was to remark disdainfully of a canon who had been degraded from his priesthood for marrying, 'he is now, at least, an honest layman'.[14] Such remarks pose for us a type of question already familiar: what if priests failed to conform to the pristine standard of celibate excellence? What, in popular opinion, was the status of a 'lewd priest'?

Attempts to ascertain the actual extent of unchastity among the pre-Reformation clergy can never be more than provisional. The archidiaconal or episcopal visitation provides perhaps the safest context within which some attempt at quantification can be made, as it was here that lay opinion in the parish, at any rate respectable opinion, had the opportunity to voice its complaints freely. Of course, if laypeople commonly knew of, yet failed to report, the sexual misdemeanours of their pastors, figures derived from visitation returns are worthless, but as we shall see, there are good reasons for supposing this not generally to have been the case. A number of surviving records of visitation touch upon the question of clerical morality, and what these demonstrate raises important questions. In 1499 a visitation of 478 Suffolk parishes produced only five allegations of priestly immorality, while from more than 260 Kent parishes, visited by Archbishop Warham in the autumn of 1511, there were only nine

---

[11] The anthropologist M. Douglas gives examples of this kind of 'vicarious satisfaction' among primitive peoples in *Purity and Danger: An Analysis of the Concepts of Pollution and Taboo*, paperback edn. (1984), 162–3.

[12] Erasmus, *Collected Works*, tr. R. A. Mynors, ed. B. G. Bietenholz (Toronto, 1987), vii. 21.

[13] N. Davis (ed.), *Paston Letters and Papers of the Fifteenth Century* (Oxford, 1971), i. 370.

[14] *LP* xiii (1). 571.

accusations.[15] A visitation of the 230-odd parishes of the archdeaconry of Winchester in 1527–8 led to proceedings against eleven clerics; ten years later the archdeaconry of Norwich produced eight suspect priests from 200 parishes.[16] The figures from the 1,006 parishes visited by the Bishop of Lincoln and his deputies in 1514–21 are more problematic, owing to difficulties in ascertaining what the visitors meant by recording that a priest had a 'suspect' woman in his house.[17] In any case, the numbers involved are once again comparatively small, a minimum of 25 and a maximum of 102 incumbents may have been suspected of misconduct by their parishioners.[18] These examples suggest that the number of parishes in which at any one time a priest was suspected of unchastity was probably something under 5 per cent of the total.[19] It was certainly a problem which had to be addressed, but rampant immorality was hardly the characteristic hallmark of the pre-Reformation priesthood.

The relative paucity of cases of proven or suspected immorality among the parish clergy leads one to wonder why it was that this issue seems to have exercised such a strong hold on the imaginations of early Tudor English men and women. The probably very limited extent of clerical unchastity needs somehow to be reconciled with an apparently widespread belief in its prevalence, or at least in the omnipresent nature of the threat. Widespread concern about the incontinent priest may have had a somewhat inadequate empirical base, but its intensity transcended the statistical significance of the problem. Certainly, it was to claims of rampant immorality that Protestant propagandists instinctively turned in their efforts to blacken and defame the Catholic priesthood. It was claimed by George Joye that 'all the world speaks evil and shame of them and everyman abhors them for their pride and unclean living'.[20] John Bale, who

---

[15] C. Harper-Bill, 'A Late Medieval Visitation: The Diocese of Norwich in 1499', *Proceedings of the Suffolk Institute of Archaeology and History*, 34 (1977), 45; *Kentish Visitations*, *passim*.

[16] R. Houlbrooke, *Church Courts and the People during the English Reformation* (Oxford, 1979), 178–9.

[17] M. Bowker, *Secular Clergy in the Diocese of Lincoln*, 1485–1520 (Cambridge, 1968), 117–18. '*Mulier suspecte*' may simply have been applied to any young woman who was not a close relative. [18] Ibid. 116.

[19] A somewhat higher figure of 15% has been postulated for the archdeaconry of Chichester in this period: S. Lander, 'Church Courts and the Reformation in the Diocese of Chichester, 1500–58', in R. O'Day and F. Heal (eds.), *Continuity and Change: Personnel and Administration of the Church in England, 1500–1642* (Leicester, 1976), 218.

[20] F. J. Furnivall (ed.), *Ballads from Manuscripts* (1868), i. 75. See also *ibid.* 95; J. Barlow, *Burial of the Mass*, in E. Arber (ed.), *English Reprints* (1871), 31, 33, 72, 76, 95–6, 117; H. Brinklow, *The Complaynt of Roderyck Mors*, 46, 63, and *Lamentacyon of a Christen*, ed. J. M.

found his true *métier* in the genre, argued that even the chastest among
priests were 'lecherous as goats' and that it required the services of a
'well-papped pigeon of Paul's' (a London prostitute) to 'cool the conta-
gious heats of a coltish confessor'.[21] The author, possibly Cranmer, of *A
Confutation of Unwritten Verities* claimed that not one in three priests in
England was truly chaste, an estimate shared by Robert Barnes.[22] Such
charges, along with the outrageous claim of Simon Fish that priests had
corrupted 100,000 women in England, were the product of fantasy not of
research.[23] Yet such suggestions would have been worthless as propaganda
had they borne no affinity to popular experience or prejudice.

To Thomas More, it was a recurrent source of concern that laypeople
were often prepared to believe the worst of the clergy in this regard. The
Messenger in More's *Dialogue Concerning Heresies* is frequently ready with
a 'merry tale' to satirize the morals of the clergy, suggesting, for example,
that even when priests sued successfully for defamation in response to
sexual slander, they were not invariably innocent.[24] In exasperation, More
eventually castigates the apparent eagerness of his contemporaries to tar
all priests with the same brush:

> If a lewd priest do a lewd deed, then we say 'Lo, see what example the clergy
> giveth us!', as though that priest were the clergy . . . Let a good man preach, a
> short tale shall serve us thereof, and we shall neither much regard his exhortation
> nor his good example. But let a lewd friar be taken with a wench, we will jest and
> rail upon the whole order all the year after . . .

This reproach merely elicits from the Messenger a rehearsal of the contemporary witticism 'that if a woman be fair then is she young, and if a
priest be good then he is old'.[25] In the *Supplication of Souls*, More remarked that accusations of rape against the clergy, though frequently
unfounded, were none the less commonplace in England: 'You see not
very many sessions pass, but in one shire or other this pageant is played.'[26]
The observation had a polemical purpose, in so far as More's point was
to insist that laypeople could safely bring charges against the clergy

---

Cowper, EETS es 22 (1874), 110–11, 112; L. Shepherd, *A Pore Helpe*, in W. C. Hazlitt
(ed.), *Remains of the Popular Poetry of England* (1864), i. 256; J. N. King, *English Reformation
Literature* (Princeton, NJ, 1982), 269; J. Bale, *The Acts of Englysh Votaryes* (1560).

[21] J. Bale, *The Vocacyon of Johan Bale to the bishoprick of Ossorie in Irelande* (1553),
43ʳ⁻ᵛ.

[22] T. Cranmer, *Miscellaneous Writings and Letters*, ed. J. E. Cox, PS (1846), 37–8; W. A.
Clebsch, *England's Earliest Protestants, 1520–1535* (New Haven, Conn., 1964), 73.

[23] S. Fish, *A Supplicacyon for the Beggars*, ed. F. J. Furnivall, EETS 13 (1871), 6.

[24] More, *Dialogue*, 69.   [25] Ibid. 296–7.

[26] T. More, *Supplication of Souls*, ed. F. Manley *et al.*, CW 7 (1990), 131.

without incurring suspicion of heresy, but the passage does reveal its author's sensitivity over the issue.

Despite his tendency to generalize, More's perceptions were probably coloured by his experience of London, where the high concentration of unbeneficed clergy, and the greater opportunities for misbehaviour perhaps made the disciplinary problem more acute than elsewhere.[27] Yet the cynical attitude to the chastity professed by the clergy, exemplified by More's Messenger, may have been a more widespread phenomenon. In 1534, for example, a woman in Brentford, Middlesex, said of her neighbour: 'Why and is that young fellow Lydgold so foolish [as] to let a priest a house so nigh him, he having so young a wife?'[28] For some the concupiscence of priests was practically legendary, and the layman who alleged that there were six Gods, one of which being 'a priest's concubine being in his chamber twelve months and more', was as probably indulging in gnomic wit, as the radical gnosticism his interrogators suspected him of.[29] Equally poignant were the remarks attributed to Edmund Ecleston of Leeds in the reign of Edward VI. When news circulated in the parish that Janet Cowper had been seen going to York in the company of a priest, Ecleston clearly enjoyed speculating publicly as to which of the local clergy was implicated in this unpriestly behaviour. Sir Thomas Jeffrason was a possibility; he would not, remarked Ecleston 'jape the goodman if the wife be at home'. Sir Christopher Bradley could 'draw women well'; Sir John Matthew was 'the greatest whoremaster in a country'; and Sir Robert Brasbrigge was 'such a fellow that will be creeping into every hole'. In short, 'we have such a sort of naughty priests as be not in a shire'.[30] Ecleston's acid tongue was probably not representative of opinion in Leeds as a whole, and some of his neighbours were quick to reproach him 'that he did evil to slander these priest men'. None the less, the incident demonstrates the keen interest which could be taken in the deportment of the local clergy, as well as the potential of gossip as a medium helping to shape popular perceptions.[31]

Ecleston was not alone in spreading stories about the lewd behaviour of the clergy. When priests sued laypeople for defamation in the church courts it was almost invariably in response to sexual slander, and terms

---

[27] R. M. Wunderli, *London Church Courts and Society on the Eve of the Reformation* (1981), 89. [28] PRO, Req. 2, 11/114.
[29] Guildhall Library, MS 9531/9, fo. 26ᵛ. [30] BIHR, CP 423 1550.
[31] R. Whiting, *The Blind Devotion of the People* (Cambridge, 1989), 129, cites a similar case of a group of Exeter laymen in 1541 who turned to 'jesting upon priests', in particular their sexual delinquency.

such as 'whoremaster', 'whoremonger', and 'bawdy' priest seem to have slipped easily from laypeople's mouths.[32] Conversely it was the jibe 'priest's whore' which most often impelled laywomen to resort to the courts.[33] When in 1522 one London woman accused another of being 'bolder than a priest's whore', the charge had already an almost proverbial ring to it, and in fact the expression 'as tender as a parson's leman' was included in John Heywood's proverb collection of 1546.[34] Yet such name-calling commonly conveyed bitterness and menace as readily as levity. In April 1529 the parish priest of St Michael, Queenhithe, laid violent hands upon his own mother and rebuked her with these words: 'Priest's whore! A priest hath kept thee all thy life. I shall write and set up bills in every open place in London that every man shall know thee for a priest's whore.'[35] The moral errancy of the clergy, then as now, may have served some with an occasion for salacious humour, but underlying the mirth may have been a genuine apprehension about the contingency of clerical celibacy, a potent resentment of the unchaste priest.

To Tudor minds, sexual licence of any sort represented disorder: fornication was not merely a sin, but a crime cognizable in the church courts. The disorder was compounded when the sinner was a priest, a man vowed to perpetual chastity.[36] Behind the celibate priest some contemporaries could not fail to glimpse the spectre of the cuckold, a figure guaranteed to outrage the proprietorial instincts of early Tudor husbands; the extent to which the confession of women could promote such fears has been referred to already.[37] In the interlude *Hickscorner*, Freewill

[32] I have attempted to compile a list from records of ecclesiastical and secular courts of insulting epithets offered to priests in this period; it comprises around a dozen main designations, used on 110 occasions, and excludes derogatory language from an overtly heretical context. The ranking order is: 'whoremaster'/'whoremonger' and variants (25); 'knave' (18); 'false' (16); 'whoreson' (12); 'naughty' (9); 'bawdy' (8); 'drunken' (4); 'foolish' (3); 'Irish'/'Scottish' (3); 'lecherous' (2); 'lewd' (2); 'poll-shorn' (2); others (6). The statistic is, of course, entirely artificial, but it is none the less interesting to note that (if one allows the slighty ambiguous 'naughty'), 42% of the total 'volume' of recorded 'anticlerical' abuse carried some implication of sexual misconduct.

[33] Houlbrooke, *Church Courts and the People*, 81; GLRO, DL/C/206, fo. 485ʳ; DL/C/207, fo. 201ᵛ; DL/C/ 208, fos. 16ᵛ, 83ʳ, 161ʳ; R. H. Helmholz (ed.), *Select Cases on Defamation to 1600*, Selden Society, 101 (1985), 24; Whiting, *Blind Devotion of the People*, 128–9; W. M. Palmer (ed.), 'Fifteenth-Century Visitation Records of the Deanery of Wisbech', *CAS* 39 (1940), 73.

[34] GLRO, DL/C/207, fo. 150ᵛ; M. P. Tilley, *Dictionary of Proverbs in England in the Sixteenth and Seventeenth Centuries* (Ann Arbor, Mich., 1950), 523.

[35] GLRO, DL/C/330, fo. 172ʳ.

[36] In fact, only members of religious orders took an explicit vow of chastity, but contemporaries clearly saw a similar votive commitment as implicit in the consecration of a secular priest.

[37] See above, 23–5.

taunts Imagination with comments about 'that cuckold thy father . . . the last night I saw Sir John and she [his mother] tumbled on the floor'.[38] In one of John Rastell's 'Merry Tales' it is significantly the priest who gains the upper hand when a stranger hails him familiarly as 'Sir John', 'because every foolish priest most commonly is called Sir John'. The layman is greeted in turn as 'Master Rafe', the usual name for 'every proud cocold'.[39]

The incontinent priest was a threat, the control and punishment of which could not safely be left to the ecclesiastical authorities. In London the mayor and aldermen had since the late fourteenth century assumed the right to punish immoral priests, and the punishments meted out by the city courts were invariably stricter than those imposed by the Church.[40] Both in London and elsewhere it is remarkable how unchaste priests could become the targets of aggressive communal lay action. In London in 1529 a priest was caught with a woman in his chamber at 5 a.m. by an alderman's deputy, and the parish constable 'with a great multitude'.[41] In the early 1520s the mayor and parishioners of Arundel waged a relentless campaign in the courts against their vicar, Thomas Combes, on account of his relationship with Elizabeth Huchyns. In the course of this Combes was arrested by the constable and sergeants after being found alone with her at night.[42] At Warthill in Yorkshire in 1528 the vicar, William Marton, was similarly taken unawares with Alison Cobbe by a group headed by the village constable. This party broke into the vicarage at 11 p.m. as Marton and his mistress attempted unsuccessfully to flee and were reduced to begging for their clothes 'in the honour of womanhood'. With commendable thoroughness the intruders 'put their hands in the bed and found both sides of the bed warm', proof positive of libidinous behaviour.[43] In identical fashion in 1545 a woman was found in the chamber of the vicar of Kelvedon, Essex, at 2 a.m. by 'the watchman, constable, and other honest men'.[44] The following year James Baron, the rector of Pilton in Northamptonshire was arrested naked by the churchwardens and others in the chamber of Robert Thurlbie, in the company of Thurlbie's wife.[45] None of these could have been merely chance encounters.

---

[38] W. C. Hazlitt (ed.), *A Select Collection of Old English Plays*, 4th edn. (1874), i. 166–7.
[39] H. Oesterly (ed.), *Shakespeare's Jest Book* (1866), 2–3.
[40] Wunderli, *London Church Courts*, 88–91.
[41] GLRO, DL/C/330, fo. 179ᵛ. See also ibid., fo. 188ᵛ.
[42] Lander, 'Diocese of Chichester, 1508–1558', 228–9.
[43] BIHR, D/C CP 1528/5.
[44] J. E. Oxley, *The Reformation in Essex* (Manchester, 1965), 146.
[45] A. G. Dickens, 'Early Protestantism and the Church in Northamptonshire', *Northamptonshire PP*, 8 (1983–4), 32.

Clearly, some local communities entertained deep suspicions of their pastors, and were prepared to use all the powers at their disposal to bring them to account.

ATTITUDES TO CONCUBINAGE

If the root cause of hostility to unchaste priests was concern for the safety of wives and daughters, the suspicion that priests were, as Richard Morison put it, 'sowing seed in other men's furrows', then one might expect laypeople to have distinguished between merely promiscuous behaviour on the part of clerics, and the monogamous, quasi-marital relationships of concubinary priests and their consorts.[46] These, as a far lesser threat to social cohesion, may have been viewed in a more tolerant light, particularly if the irregular fornicators were guilty of other forms of socially disruptive behaviour as well. In 1511, for example, a priest of Maidstone in Kent was reported to be prowling around at night armed with bow and arrows and a knife. His peculiar habit of exercising his dogs at midnight had resulted in unfortunate injury to a local pauper, and his reputation as a 'common fornicator' was such that women would go out of their way to avoid him in the street.[47] An otherwise unexceptionable priest who lived peacefully with his housekeeper could surely not have aroused comparable resentment, or could he?

For late medieval and early modern continental Europe, several historians have argued a *de facto* toleration of concubinage, while of late medieval Wales Glanmor Williams has written 'lay opinion as a whole accepted clerical "marriages" without demur'.[48] Some writers have similarly characterized the situation in England. Henry Maynard Smith thought that 'public opinion was on the whole tolerant' of concubinage, while more recently and more cautiously, Peter Heath has suggested that monogamous relationships caused much less scandal and were less injurious to

---

[46] D. S. Berkowitz (ed.), *Humanist Scholarship and Public Order: Two Tracts against the Pilgrimage of Grace by Sir Richard Morison* (Washington, DC, 1984), 94.

[47] *Kentish Visitations*, 291.

[48] O. Chadwick, *The Reformation* (Harmondsworth, 1972), 409; J. H. Elliot, *Imperial Spain, 1469–1716* (Harmondsworth, 1970), 103; J. Delumeau, *Catholicism between Luther and Voltaire*, tr. J. Moiser (1977), 155; L. G. Duggan, 'The Unresponsiveness of the Late Medieval Church: a Reconsideration', *SCJ* 9 (1978), 20–1; E. Cameron, *The European Reformation* (Oxford, 1991), 36; Bossy, *Christianity in the West*, 65–6 (with significant reservations about parts of northern Europe, which support the argument presented here); G. Williams, *The Welsh Church from Conquest to Reformation* (1962), 342.

lay–clerical relationships than irregular incontinency.[49] In his study of Tudor Lancashire, Christopher Haigh describes the 'common-law wives' of priests as 'perhaps an accepted part of the parochial scene'.[50] Certainly there is evidence which appears to support these assertions. In 1535 it was reported of the vicar of Budworth in Cheshire that he kept a woman in his house and had several children by her; the vicar of Runcorn was said to have had ten or twelve children by Agnes Habram.[51] Richard Bennett, the vicar of St Neots in Cornwall, seems to have kept Jane Erle as his concubine for over ten years and to have had several children by her, before confessing to this at a general session at Bodmin in 1544.[52] In 1539, John Palmes, the rector of Bentworth in Hampshire, complaining to Cromwell of harassment by Bishop Gardiner's officials on account of his marriage, pointed out that 'the parson of Burghfield, priest in holy orders, has kept a concubine these twenty years openly . . . and no man sayeth black is his eye'.[53] Palmes, of course, had a pressing personal grievance, and a reason to appeal to Cromwell's reforming sympathies, while the other cases cited did eventually come to light, presumably through lay denunciation. As further evidence is examined, the case for lay toleration of concubinage becomes harder to sustain.

In England the ecclesiastical atmosphere was notably less conducive to widespread concubinage than it was in parts of the Continent. With the notable exception of Wolsey, the English bench of bishops in the early sixteenth century consisted of men who respected their own chastity, and it was Bishop Fox's proud boast that he had been lenient with his clergy 'except it were for manifest fornication or advowtery'.[54] Unlike some of their Continental counterparts, the English bishops did not derive large sums from concubinage fines, and fees for the legitimization of priests' children.[55] Thomas More claimed that the 'honest living' of the English clergy could match any in Europe, and even Tyndale conceded obliquely that concubinage was less evident in England than in Germany, Scotland, France, or Spain. He went on, significantly, to characterize the usual response of the laity to this abuse as to 'go to law with them, to put away their whores'.[56]

---

[49] H. M. Smith, *Pre-Reformation England* (1938), 48; P. Heath, *English Parish Clergy on the Eve of the Reformation* (1969), 106.

[50] C. Haigh, *Reformation and Resistance in Tudor Lancashire* (Cambridge, 1975), 50.

[51] *LP* viii. 496.   [52] PRO, C. 1, 1201/15.

[53] *LP* xiv (1). 120, 206; G. R. Elton, *Policy and Police* (Cambridge, 1972), 42–3.

[54] R. Fox, *Letters of Richard Fox, 1486–1527*, ed. P. S. and H. M. Allen (Oxford, 1929), 151.

[55] O. Vasella, *Reform und Reformation in der Schweiz* (Münster, 1965), 28–32.

[56] More, *Dialogue*, 295; W. Tyndale, *Doctrinal Treatises*, ed. H. Walter, PS (1848), 41.

Tyndale's intuition is confirmed by the reaction of several parishes where there seems to have been no objection to the priest other than his living with a woman. At Patrixbourne in Kent, for example, the sole *compertum* of the parish spokesmen at the visitation of 1511 was that 'the vicar of the said church keepeth Alice Claryngbole and doeth advowtery, the which is openly known'.[57] At nearby Challock it was reported that 'Sir Richard Garford keepeth a woman in boldly that all the parish will report.'[58] Such phrases suggest a solid front of resentment. The visitations of Bishop Atwater of Lincoln in 1518–19 furnish further examples of parishes eager to co-operate with the ecclesiastical authorities in eliminating concubinage. At Hareby in Lincolnshire the visitors were informed that all was well in the parish, except that the rector had established a woman in a little house just north of the village and was keeping her there despite the frequent injunctions of the Archdeacon and the Commissary.[59] At Hallington it was reported that 'the vicar keeps in his house a widow . . . which scandalizes all the inhabitants there'.[60] At Bringhurst in Leicestershire the vicar was reported to have had two children by his servant, 'to his great shame'. The parishioners were to be rewarded with the spectacle of their vicar performing public penance in the parish church, and his suspension from the performance of divine service within the diocese.[61]

During a visitation the initiative lay in a sense with the ecclesiastical authorities, but these are not the only contexts in which such complaints are to be heard. In around 1540 the parson of Shawell in Leicestershire was described by a parishioner on account of his keeping a concubine as 'a man of evil disposition, and living incontinently in the sin of advowtery, not regarding the dread of God . . . [an] evil example of all good Christian people'.[62] The vicar of Barnby Moor in Nottinghamshire was prosecuted in 1547 at the instigation of a watchful parishioner who clearly resented his failure to reform his behaviour in the wake of a visitation: 'the said vicar hath daily and weekly since the said visitation resorted unto the house and company of . . . Alison Bucke very suspiciously, and suffered the same Alison Bucke to report unto his chamber'.[63] When in 1543 the rumour spread that Sir Richard Borowe, the vicar of Ardleigh in Essex,

[57] *Kentish Visitations*, 185.   [58] Ibid. 174.

[59] *Lincoln Visitations*, i. 77. See also C. Harper-Bill (ed.), 'An Edition of the Register of John Morton, Archbishop of Canterbury, 1486–1500', University of London Ph.D. thesis (1977), 588.   [60] *Lincoln Visitations*, i. 75.

[61] *Lincoln Visitations*, i. 26; M. Bowker (ed.), *An Episcopal Court Book for the Diocese of Lincoln, 1514–1520*, LRS 61 (1967), 64.   [62] PRO, STA. C. 2, 17/88.

[63] BIHR, D/C CP 1547/3.

was keeping an unknown woman in his house, the parishioners were said to be 'much offended thereat' and the story had caused 'much trouble in the parish of disquietness; for it is thought by us that he keepeth her contrary to God's laws, and we are sure contrary to the King's injunctions'.[64] By this date the King's injunctions comprehended the savagery of the Act of Six Articles, which declared concubinage to be a felony, punishable by death in the second instance.[65] In the year the Six Articles were implemented, Cromwell's agent in Nottinghamshire, John Marshall, reported that for fear of the laity, priests now 'flee much the occasions of carnal sin'.[66] If concubinary priests were so heartily resented, one can imagine the attitude taken towards their partners. In the mid-1530s, a young woman who had been for a time a priest's concubine in Jersey, took secret passage to England after he had turned her out of his house, since she 'for shame durst not come home again amongst her friends, nor be seen in the country'.[67] Undoubtedly, personal rivalries and resentments played their part in bringing to light the irregular sexual relationships of priests, and some liaisons and partnerships may remain to this day unreported. None the less, there is little contemporary evidence that clerical concubinage served other than to focus attention on the fallibility of priests, and to undermine their moral authority within the parish.

SOCIAL REPERCUSSIONS OF UNCHASTITY

The imputation of sexual irregularity of any sort was for the clergy a very great stigma, and priests under suspicion were naturally eager to clear their names. Some, as we have seen, attempted to do so by suing their defamers, others made fulsome protestations of their innocence. A London rector accused of rape in 1501 or 1502 claimed that 'it is known he ever hath continued of good name and fame [all the] days of his life'.[68] When in about 1540 Thomas Pykyll, the parish priest of St Giles-without-Cripplegate, was imprisoned on account of his supposedly suspicious behaviour with Agnes Clerke, he argued that the accusation was false, that he had been 'continually of good name, fame, and conversation from the time of his nativity hitherto', and that in the three years he had been

---

[64] Hale, *Precedents*, 126–7.
[65] Lea, *History of Sacerdotal Celibacy*, ii. 112. An act of 1540, however, moderated this, substituting confiscation of all property and revenue for capital punishment.
[66] Elton, *Policy and Police*, 329–30.   [67] PRO, C. 1, 867/72.
[68] PRO, C. 1, 240/26.

parish priest he had been 'reputed and taken amongst all the parishioners of the said parish of good and honest conversation and of chaste and continent living and behaviour'.[69] In both these cases the good opinion of the parish was presented as the decisive factor. It is notable that when in 1530 Sir James Marshall, a chantry priest of Harlow, was hauled before the church court this was on account of 'a rumour and a slanderous noise by the parish' of his 'suspicious conversation' with Alice Shakyll.[70] Conversely, a priest who provided shelter for an old family friend on the pretext that she was his sister, was dismissed with a light penance in July 1533 because this had taken place 'without becoming the subject of evil rumour'.[71] During their visitation of 1520, the Bishop of Lincoln's officials reported the presence of a girl in the house of the vicar of Taynton in Oxfordshire, but noted that she was a relative and 'said to be honest'.[72] All the evidence suggests that parishioners took a keen interest in what was going on at the vicarage or rectory: at Thornton in Buckinghamshire opinion was divided in 1518 as to the honesty of the rector's housekeeper.[73] When the church courts took action against incontinent priests in this period, the basis of the accusation was usually described as '*fama publica*', and for such clerics open discussion and condemnation of their behaviour among the laity may have been the norm.[74] Robert Buckburge of Billingborough in Lincolnshire seems to have been exceptional in his delicacy when he 'charitably and very secretly advertised and exhorted' the vicar, William Tyngle, to 'leave his incontinent living'.[75] If his reputation were bad enough a priest's relations with his parish could become intolerable. One 'whoremaster priest' was reported to have fled the parish of Wharram Percy in 1545 after impregnating a woman.[76] In about 1530, it was reported of Simon Taillour, the vicar of Haverhill in Suffolk, that 'for his incontinence of his vicious living he was driven from Fulbourn in the county of Cambridge into Sampford in Essex, and from there to Lyttyng Wrottyng [?] in Suffolk, as all the country will testify'.[77]

A reputation for incontinence could thus do much to undermine the credibility of a priest as a Christian exemplar, and laypeople who quarrelled with priests were often quick to allege the notorious immorality of their adversary as further proof of the rightness of their cause. In 1539

---

[69] PRO, C. 1, 1044/69.   [70] GLRO, DL/C/330, fo. 199[r].   [71] Ibid. 230[r].
[72] *Lincoln Visitations*, i. 134.   [73] Ibid. 46.
[74] J. Raine (ed.), *The Injunctions and other Ecclesiastical Proceedings of Richard Barnes, Bishop of Durham, 1576–1587*, SS 22 (1850), App. I, p. xxiv; GLRO, DL/C/330, fos. 174[r], 179[v], 190[r], 199[r].   [75] PRO, C. 1, 1108/51.
[76] BIHR, CP G 338 1545.   [77] PRO, STA. C. 2, 31/61.

when Sir William Paston was disputing rights to a wreck with Sir John Clere, he claimed that one of the latter's clerical supporters, Robert Payntour, was a man 'whose lewd demeanour, unthrifty disposition, and naughty living, is well and manifestly known through all the whole said county of Norfolk'.[78] By promoting such reports a priest's enemy might justifiably hope to do irreparable damage to his standing with his flock: in 1547 the known 'incontinency and unclean living' of Ralph Wyllet, vicar of Shipton-under-Wychwood in Oxfordshire, was said to be an occasion of 'great loathsomeness of all his parishioners, in so much that scarce any one of them could abide his company'.[79]

Not surprisingly, some priests went to great length to keep such activity secret, discovery implying a possible appearance in court as well as the wrath of their parishioners.[80] In Edward VI's reign, the rector of Easton Grey in Wiltshire resorted to kidnapping the twenty-year-old daughter of a parishioner because he feared he had got her with child.[81] Especially interesting in this context are the cases in which priests claim to have been falsely accused, or to have been tricked into a compromising situation, either to undermine their reputation or to extort money from them. Of course, it is valid to suspect that such stories were inventions, dreamt up to evade the consequences of discovery, but in a number of instances there seems a strong possibility that the priests concerned were indeed 'set up'. In around 1480, a London cleric, William Pierson, claimed that a certain Agnes Coll had come to visit him under false pretences, bringing with her a group of 'evil disposed persons' whom she instructed to wait outside till she was inside the house. They then entered, calling out 'Thou false priest! What doest thou with that woman?', and demanded payment, or they would have him to prison 'and utterly shame him'.[82] Pierson seems successfully to have called their bluff, but not all clerics had the same presence of mind. When Sir John Palsgrave took lodgings with Thomas Lydgolde, a butcher of Brentford, Middlesex, he recognized that his presence in the house might give rise to malicious gossip, and so told Lydgolde that if he wished it, he would be careful to avoid the

[78] PRO, STA. C. 2, 29/121.   [79] PRO, Req. 2, 18/42.

[80] Houlbrooke, *Church Courts and the People*, 180, interestingly regards court proceedings against incontinent priests as fairly ineffectual, and ascribes the apparent rarity of cases 'more to the clergy's sense of responsibility or at least knowledge that inchastity would destroy the respect of their flocks, than to fear of the sanctions at the disposal of the church courts'.   [81] PRO, STA. C. 3, 6/68.

[82] C. T. Martin (ed.), 'Clerical Life in the Fifteenth Century', *Archaeologia*, 60 (1907), 358–9. See also, R. L. Storey, 'A Fifteenth-Century Vicar of Laxton', *Transactions of the Thoroton Society of Nottinghamshire*, 88 (1984), 40.

company of his young wife, Katherine. The conversation seems to have put an idea in Lydgolde's head, for when Palsgrave came to view his room in the butcher's house, Lydgolde pretended he had to go out to see to his cattle, and Katherine alone took Palsgrave up to the chamber, where two accomplices were lying in wait. These at once jumped out, saying 'Thou whoreson priest! What makest thou here alone in a chamber with a man's wife?' Thinking to make a joke of it, Palsgrave held up his breviary saying, 'thou mayest see what I do', but was none the less induced at knife-point to part with his purse. The story sounds rather contrived, but Thomas and Katherine Lydgolde subsequently confessed to the deception.[83]

Another priest who claimed to have been maliciously blackmailed was Robert Rycket, parish priest of Lanteglos, Cornwall. Rycket recounted how he had been tricked into coming late at night to the house of John Trevyhan, a physician of St Teath, on the pretence that his arbitration was needed to determine what fee his kinsman, a patient of Trevyhan's, should pay for the healing of his hand. On arrival at the house Rycket found no one at home but Trevyhan's concubine, Jane, who informed him that her master had gone away for three or four days, but that 'if he would tarry there all night he should have such entertainment and cheer as she was able to make him', an offer which Rycket assures us he 'utterly refused and abhorred'. The priest was on the point of leaving when Trevyhan and an armed accomplice arrived, beat him, and demanded twenty nobles, a sum Rycket agreed to pay only after being tied to a house, and led through the countryside in fear of imminent murder. Rycket concluded that Trevyhan's actions were intended to bring him 'into the infamy and obloquy of all honest persons'.[84]

Such accounts may represent garbled versions of the truth, designed to cover an indiscretion, but since the priests involved instigated action in the courts, it would seem likely that the substance was as they described it. In any case, they testify to the lengths to which priests would go to be thought innocent of all sexual misdemeanour. It was precisely because priests were so vulnerable on this issue that discontented laypeople were so ready to allege immorality, and accusations were usually vehemently denied, and sometimes shown to be false.[85] In some of these cases an ulterior motive can be discerned. In 1526, for example, the enemies of John

---

[83] PRO, Req. 2, 11/115.   [84] PRO, STA. C. 3, 1/90.

[85] Lander, 'Diocese of Chichester', 74; J. A. F. Thomson, 'Clergy and Laity in London, 1376–1531', University of Oxford D.Phil. thesis (1960), 269–71; Whiting, *Blind Devotion of the People*, 131; GLRO, DL/C/330, fo. 246ʳ.

Roo, curate of St Christopher-next-the-Stocks, London, were said to have bribed 'a single woman of lewd disposition' to claim that she had borne his child, and thereby to have sought to effect his removal from the cure.[86] There seems to have been a similar plot to deprive a London chantry priest by bribing a woman to accuse him at St Stephen's, Colman Street, in 1529.[87] An attempt in the mid-1540s to indict a Cornish priest for incontinence, alleging the 'common fame and report in the parish', failed both before the Justices of the Peace and in the Archdeacon's court.[88] As Thomas More had observed, an accusation of incontinence was not proof of guilt, yet there were enough proven cases to make such accusations plausible and therefore damaging. An adulterous or fornicating priest could readily become a local *cause célèbre*. It was said of the relationship between Thomas Cornwallis, rector of Franston in Suffolk, and the wife of Robert Crane that 'these most abominable crimes be openly noised throughout all the country'.[89]

Of course, there was a leavening of disreputable priests who do not seem to have cared what their parishioners thought. The rector of Denton in Kent was said in 1511 to resort suspiciously to the wife of John Cosyn, and was in the habit of declaring openly that 'he shall never have penny, but she shall have part'.[90] The rector of Chillington in Bedfordshire was reported in 1535 to keep in his house 'a light woman with whom he hath carnal cognition', and in his rages he would push her out into the street, shouting 'Avaunt thou, strong whore!', 'nothing ashamed of his ill demeanour'.[91] In 1540 the rector of Black Bourton in Oxfordshire was accused of boasting publicly about his adultery, 'even before honest neighbours'.[92]

Even among this selection of unruly clerics, the conduct of Henry Tailor, chantry priest of Aberford in Yorkshire, seems to have been extreme. In 1522 Tailor was accused of having conceived three children by Margaret Fieldhouse, and of persuading her to have them aborted 'with drinks and other crafts'. He was supposed to have said in front of the rector and other witnesses that 'he would keep a whore, letting for no man', which his listeners thought, with considerable understatement, 'no goodly words for a priest to speak'. He slandered the women of the parish

[86] *LP* iv (2). 2754.   [87] GLRO, DL/C/330, fo. 188ᵛ.
[88] PRO, STA. C. 2, 31/178. See also PRO, C. 1, 965/25.
[89] PRO, STA. C. 2, 24/20.   [90] *Kentish Visitations*, 140.
[91] PRO, STA. C. 2, 26/15.
[92] H. Salter (ed.), 'A Visitation of Oxfordshire in 1540', *Oxfordshire Archaeological Society Reports*, 75 (1930), 299.

as whores, and elaborated in a way, our witness reports, 'the which I am ashamed to speak of'. Tailor's response to reproaches about his conduct was that 'he would ding the devil of his breek forth at a whore's arse, letting for no man, and then might he serve God the better all the week after'. It is fair to note that Tailor was suing for defamation, but the readiness of the defendant to repeat the charges, and to cite witnesses who could testify to their reliability, suggests that his behaviour had caused intolerable offence.[93] Tailor's apparent disregard for the good opinion of his neighbours was matched by a London priest, Robert Shoter, who in 1523 went so far as to pronounce sentence of excommunication on those of his parishioners who had given evidence against his concubine to the wardmote enquest.[94]

Predictably, it was priests such as these who aroused the greatest antipathy, and Shoter's enormities seem to have induced a number of his parishioners to withhold their tithes.[95] The notion that tithes were not required to be paid to a lecherous priest had some standing in canon law, but the issue was naturally a sensitive one, and the fact that in England the concept had become closely associated with the Donatist attitude of the Lollards had discredited it with the ecclesiastical establishment.[96] The evidence does not suggest that tithe-payers frequently invoked this ultimate sanction on overtly moral grounds; had they done so, their pastors might easily have recovered the deficit at law. Yet that lay men and women were reluctant to contribute to the support of a known evil-liver may hardly be doubted. In 1524 a York chaplain is found suing a layman for spreading a scurrilous rumour: the priest had been surprised with a woman within the minster precincts 'so hastily that he had no leisure to tie up his cod-piece'. The cleric had good reason for wishing to clear his name, as a witness confirmed that as the story spread, many parishioners who 'were disposed to give him any devotions [i.e. offerings] afore . . . intend now to give him no more, except he could clear himself of this crime'.[97]

If some incontinent priests behaved notoriously, other concubinaries presumably tried hard to avoid confrontation, and to carry out their

[93] BIHR, CP G 166 1522.

[94] S. Brigden, 'Tithe Controversy in Reformation London', *JEH* 33 (1982), 290.

[95] Ibid.

[96] *Dives and Pauper*, 258ᵛ–259ʳ; K. B. McFarlane, *Wycliffe and English Nonconformity* (Harmondsworth, 1972), 110; Brigden, 'Tithe Controversy in Reformation London', 291–2; R. N. Swanson, 'Problems of the Priesthood in Pre-Reformation England', *EHR* 417 (1990), 850; A. T. Bannister (ed.), *Registrum Thome Spofford, Episcopi Herefordensis, 1422–1448*, CYS 23 (1914), 154.				[97] BIHR, D/C CP 1524/13.

pastoral duties conscientiously. Of these Margaret Bowker has written: 'the dichotomy between the morality of a priest and his ability to perform the duties of his office, taken with the very extent of moral offences, must have continually raised the question of whether celibacy was absolutely necessary to the priesthood'.[98] This, however, may be to beg the question somewhat. Although a serious disciplinary problem, clerical unchastity does not seem to have been prevalent, and it was precisely because celibacy *was* seen as absolutely necessary to the priesthood that an unchaste priest by definition was failing in the duties of his office, not least in his duty to be a mirror to the laity, a light shining in the darkness. To the (no doubt clerical) author of *Dives and Pauper*, unchastity in a priest was a form of sacrilege, a misuse of something consecrated to God.[99] Yet there were laypeople too who were capable of rationalizing the outrage they so evidently felt. At the start of Edward VI's reign, a priest in Chester was reported to have had a child by a single woman, 'neglecting his duty, profession, office of priesthood and vocation'.[100] In around 1540, Nicholas Stubys claimed that a priest had committed adultery with his wife 'nothing prepending nor weighing his vow of chastity made to God, nor the danger of the infringing and breaking of the King's Highness most gracious laws, no nor his own honesty'.[101] A priest who entered into a sexual relationship could rely neither on the ignorance nor the indifference of his parishioners to shield him from the consequences.

SEX, SANCTITY, AND SACRAMENTS

It seems unlikely that the firmly entrenched hostility of the laity to the moral lapses of their pastors had causes no deeper than a sense of broken trust, or even of the besmirching of a holy and consecrated thing. In an earlier chapter we considered the extent to which the inward state of the celebrant of the mass may have excited anxieties among some laypeople as to the sanctity or even validity of the action he was undertaking. This problem was at its most acute when the celebrant was known or suspected to be 'in unclean life'. The notion that priests in a state of mortal sin through sexual lapse might handle and consume the body of Christ was one which disgusted contemporaries, and by 1500 a long tradition of homilectic denunciation had inveighed against such priests. Even married

---

[98] Bowker, *Secular Clergy in the Diocese of Lincoln*, 121.
[99] *Dives and Pauper*, 226^r. See also Dionysius Carthusianus, *Lyfe of Prestes*, sig. G.ii^v.
[100] PRO, C. 1, 1275/52.   [101] PRO, C. 1, 1069/63.

laypeople were expected to abstain from sex for three days before receiving the sacrament; how much more did this need for purity apply to the priests who were actually to consecrate it. William de Rymyngton, a fourteenth-century chancellor of Oxford University, imagined a layman rebuking a wayward priest: 'You are far more bound to observe the stainlessness of chastity than I am, many times over, you who daily consecrate and consume the body and blood of Jesus Christ.'[102] It was in the juxtaposition of the most awesomely sacred with the most repellantly profane that preachers found the inspiration for their most forceful indignation, and a number of late medieval preachers laid before their listeners the horrendous image of a priest going from handling the flesh of a prostitute to handling the flesh of Christ.[103]

These concerns are equally evident in the homilectic and devotional writings on offer in the sixteenth century. John Colet's statutes for the cathedral church of St Paul's maintained that even the vergers should be single men, and not widowers, 'for it is fitting that those who approach so near to the altar of God, and are present at such great mysteries, should be wholly chaste and undefiled'.[104] The *Lyfe of Prestes* remarked how scandalous it was that sacraments of the Church should be ministered by priests tainted with 'that most foul, filthy, and abominable sin of the flesh and beastly concupiscence; yea and to presume to serve, and to receive so deep a fountain of purity and cleanness with so foul and corrupt a mouth'.[105] *Dives and Pauper* recommended harsh punishments for priests who 'presume to touch God's body, or to minister at God's altar, when they have commoned with other men's wives, or with their concubines'.[106] In similar fashion, the *Orchard of Syon* saw the apotheosis of priestly wickedness in the actions of those 'with a defouled soul and of corrupt body that hath lain all night in deadly sin ... [then] go and say mass'.[107] According to the *Doctrinal of Sapyence*, lecherous priests who received the sacrament were as 'culpable of the body of Our Lord Jesus Christ ... as if he had slain him'. The barking of dogs and the grunting of swine was more pleasing to God than 'the song of such priests that be so much lecherous'.[108] It was significantly to this theme that the Protestant satirist, John Ramsey, turned in 1548, in his *Plaister for a galled horse*, in what looks

[102] G. R. Owst, *Literature and Pulpit in Medieval England*, 2nd edn. (Cambridge, 1961), 273.
[103] Ibid. 244, 247, 267; G. R. Owst, *Preaching in Medieval England* (Cambridge, 1926), 250. [104] J. H. Lupton, *Life of John Colet*, 2nd edn. (1909), 135.
[105] Dionysius Carthusianus, *Lyfe of Prestes*, sig. C.v^v. [106] *Dives and Pauper*, 224^r.
[107] Catherine of Siena, *Orchard of Syon*, sig. F.iv^v.
[108] G. de Roye, *The Doctrinal of Sapyence* (1489), sigs. H.vii^v, I.ii^{r–v}.

like a clear attempt to play on long-standing Catholic anxieties: when the priest performed the *lavabo*, the ritual washing which preceded the consecration, this was because 'he hath handled some whore's tail'.[109]

As its rehearsal at this level indicates, the topic of the sacramental acts of unchaste priests was no remote or abstruse concern of theologians. Indeed, it could not have been when in a significant minority of parishes masses said by such priests would have been the norm. Although various authorities advised laypeople to absent themselves from the masses of lecherous priests, we have no evidence that this ever happened on a significant scale.[110] It would be unwise to deduce from this, however, that the morality of the celebrant was a matter of indifference to mass-goers. As we have seen, parishioners were not loath to complain of incontinent priests to the authorities, and studies of fifteenth-century Norwich and early sixteenth-century Leicester archdeaconry have concluded that the laity were more likely to report clerics for sexual sins than for other failings.[111] It is notable too that suspension from saying mass was very often the Church's disciplinary response to the problem.[112] In 1532 in the London parish of St Andrew, Eastcheap, the putative adulterer, Sir Thomas Kyrkham, was called a 'bawdy priest', and told that 'it were more fitter for thee to sing mass underneath a hedge than in a church'.[113] Here was an earthy and idiosyncratic expression of a perhaps more widespread sentiment. In 1531 when Catherine Toller described her abduction and rape by Henry Browne, the vicar of Harlow, she took care to report that Browne had risen early from the bed, saying that 'he wanted to celebrate mass'.[114] Popular insistence on the need for sexual purity in the celebrants of masses may even have extended to some of those who were self-consciously nonconformist in matters of faith. In 1491, for example, a Lollard suspect who conceded that priests should have wives, was also of the opinion that they should celebrate mass only at times when they were not sleeping with them.[115]

In a previous chapter it was shown how bequests for masses in

---

[109] J. Ramsey, *A Plaister for a galled horse* (1548), unpaginated.

[110] More, *Dialogue*, 300; *Dives and Pauper*, 224ᵛ; A. Hudson, *The Premature Reformation* (Oxford, 1988), 215; J. Herolt, *Sermones Discipuli* (1510), 153ʳ.

[111] N. P. Tanner, *The Church in Late Medieval Norwich, 1370–1532* (Toronto, 1984), 53–4; J. F. Fuggles, 'The Parish Clergy in the Archdeaconry of Leicester, 1520–1540', *Leicestershire Archaeological and Historical Society Transactions*, 46 (1970–1), 37–8.

[112] Harper-Bill (ed.), 'Register of John Morton', 588, 687–90, 692–3; Wilkins, *Concilia*, iii. 364; S. Brown, *The Medieval Courts of the York Minster Peculiar* (York, 1984), 27.

[113] GLRO, DL/C/208, fo. 161ʳ.   [114] GLRO, DL/C/330, fos. 204ᵛ–205ʳ.

[115] Hudson, *Premature Reformation*, 469.

laypeople's wills very often reflected the widespread conviction that celebrants of the mass should if possible be men of the highest calibre. In addition, the terms of chantry foundations commonly included a clause that the chantry priest was to be deprived if his behaviour proved unsatisfactory, and fornication was usually listed among the offences which would bring about deprivation.[116] In London in 1521, the churchwardens of St Christopher-in-the-Stocks took action to dismiss the chantry priest, William Wyche, on the grounds that he was 'accused of incontinence with a certain woman, called Person's wife . . . by the greater part of the said parish, and by all the churchwardens'.[117] Testators often sought to avoid such an outcome by nominating an 'honest priest' to sing for their souls, and it has been suggested above that this disarmingly vague expression was to a great extent shorthand for a priest known to be continent. A brief rehearsal of some sixteenth-century sources should help to establish that this was the intention foremost in contemporaries' minds. One can cite Miles Coverdale, for example, translating a passage in the second book of Esdras 'like as an whore envieth an honest woman', or in the context of the ban on clerical marriage, 'if he against all honesty take a harlot . . .'.[118] In recounting the religious changes of the 1540s, the conservative Yorkshire curate, Robert Parkyn, used the appellation 'honest priests' in clear contradistinction to those 'so blinded with carnal concupiscence' that they had affirmed and practised clerical marriage.[119] Note also the priest who in 1540 was reported to have committed adultery in derogation of 'his own honesty'.[120]

Some of the other qualifications stipulated by testators seem also to presuppose the chastity of the designated priest. Eighteen wills in the sample specified a priest 'of good conversation', and a further eight stipulated that he be 'of good name and fame'. It is relevant here that when in about 1540 the vicar of Tarrington in Herefordshire was indicted for incontinent living, he was described as 'a man of evil name and fame, and of ungodly conversation'.[121] As we saw above, when the parish priest of St Giles-without-Cripplegate was accused of incontinence, he asserted his being 'continually of good name, fame, and conversation'.[122] Twenty-one

[116] K. L. Wood-Legh, *Perpetual Chantries in Britain* (Cambridge, 1965), 17, 85–9, 170–1, 255; G. H. Cook, *Medieval Chantries and Chantry Chapels* (1963), 16; C. Platt, *The English Medieval Town* (1976), 169.   [117] GLRO, DL/C/207, fo. 50ᵛ.

[118] W. W. Skeat and A. L. Mayhew (eds.), *A Glossary of Tudor and Stuart Words* (Oxford, 1914), 198; M. Coverdale, *Remains*, ed. G. Pearson, 484.

[119] A. G. Dickens (ed.), 'Robert Parkyn's Narrative of the Reformation', in A. G. Dickens, *Reformation Studies*, 2nd edn (1982), 297.   [120] PRO, C. 1, 1069/63.

[121] PRO, C. 1, 1093/1.   [122] PRO, C. 1, 1044/69.

testators wished their priest to be 'well disposed'—unlike the vicar of Billingborough in Lincolnshire, a man of 'incontinent living' who was keeping the company of an 'evil disposed woman'.[123]

Laypeople were concerned about clerical celibacy because at root it was an issue which touched their very salvation. In spite of the orthodox teaching that the sacraments were unaffected by the wickedness of the minister, the virulence of some lay attacks on incontinent priests leads one to suspect that, perhaps unconsciously, clerical unchastity was regarded in quasi-Judaic terms as a ritual pollutant, an objective threat to the efficacy of priestly functions. This outlook was mocked by the anticlerical poem, *The Image of Ypocresye*, which suggested that people believed souls could not be released from purgatory

> Till mass of Scala Celi,
> At Bath or at Ely,
> Be by a friar said,
> That is a virgin maid.[124]

But to those for whom the mass represented an effusion of divine grace, and a personal encounter with the crucified and risen Christ, the anxiety was a very real one. Psychologically, it was easy for Tyndale to ridicule More's concern that priests should live chaste for reverence of the sacraments, and to insist that 'the hands defile not the man . . . and much less can they defile Christ', since he did not believe Christ's natural body to be present.[125] Most English men and women probably did, however, continue to hope for a physically real presence in the eucharist, and for the circumstances which would, beyond doubt, guarantee that presence. It is in the context of this mental climate that we must proceed to discuss the contemporary controversy over the issue of priests' marriages.

MARRIED PRIESTS: FOR AND AGAINST

Protestant writers based the case for clerical marriage firmly on the argument that universal priestly celibacy could never be other than a delusion and a deceit. The celibacy of the Catholic priesthood was simply 'unchaste chastity', mere 'pretence of chaste continence'.[126] Protestant emphasis on

---

[123] PRO, C. 1, 1108/51.   [124] Furnivall (ed.), *Ballads from Manuscripts*, i. 261.
[125] W. Tyndale, *An Answer to Sir Thomas More's Dialogue*, ed. H. Walter, PS (1850), 162–3.
[126] Ibid. 158; J. Bale (?), *An answere to a papystycall exhortacyon*, in H. Huth and W. C. Hazlitt (eds.), *Fugitive Tracts* (1875), unpaginated.

the enormity of the Fall, and an unwillingness to allow fallen man any participatory role in the process of redemption, informed an outlook which regarded celibacy as psychologically impossible for all except a small minority. In recognition of this, God had ordained marriage as a remedy for fornication, a remedy revealed in scripture.[127] Thus a concomitant of the Protestant revolt against papal authority and Catholic doctrine was the appearance, both in England and on the Continent, of a number of works asserting the right of all persons to marry, and denouncing votive chastity as presumptuous and displeasing to God.[128] In his *Actes of Englysh Votaryes* John Bale even set out to show how the whole history of the unreformed Church in England could be explained in terms of the sexual corruption consequent upon enforced clerical celibacy.[129] In general, the literary debate over the lawfulness of clerical marriage focused on scripture and the practice of the early Church, as well as on the extent to which the advocacy of celibacy, or its denial, could be associated with the teaching of heretics through the ages.[130] Yet there is a sense in which the Reformation arguments were less about detailed scriptural exegesis than they were a reflection of profoundly divergent views as to the post-lapsarian potential of mankind. It is a striking feature of the early Protestant apologetics that the emphasis tended to be on the avoidance and containment of illicit sexuality rather than on the advantages of the married state. Ironically perhaps, Tyndale and Barnes, who both wrote extensively on the utility of marriage as a means of avoiding temptation, remained single men; the outlook is perhaps better exemplified by the apologia of the Henrician martyr, Thomas Bennet: 'because I would not be a whoremonger, or an unclean person, therefore I married a wife'.[131]

To their Catholic opponents the Protestants' insistence that marriage of the clergy was a lawful ordinance of God signified nothing but the purest hypocrisy, and Thomas More regarded as 'plain false' the notion that only very few men could live chastely.[132] The Marian chancellor of Winchester, Thomas Martin, began his broadside against clerical marriage in 1554 with the contention that 'heresy and lechery be commonly joined

---

[127] See e.g. P. Melanchthon, *A godly defense . . . defending the mariage of preists*, tr. G. Joye (Antwerp, 1541).

[128] S. Ozment, 'Marriage and the Ministry in the Protestant Churches', *Concilium*, 8 (1972); J. K. Yost, 'The Reformation Defence of Clerical Marriage', *Church History* (1981).

[129] Bale, *Actes of English Votaryes*, facs. edn. (Amsterdam, 1979); L. P. Fairfield, *John Bale: Mythmaker for the English Reformation* (West Lafayette, Ind., 1976), 54.

[130] T. Martin, *A Treatise declaring and plainly provyng, that the pretensed marriage of priestes . . . is no marriage* (1554); J. Ponet, *A defence for mariage of priests* (1556).

[131] Foxe, *Acts and Monuments*, v. 19.   [132] More, *Dialogue*, 308.

together, and that they two be the only causes of priests' pretended matrimony'. The advocates of clerical marriage, while pretending to accomplish the will of Christ, in reality sought only 'the satisfaction of their own carnal lusts and amorous fancies'.[133] It was practically axiomatic that this lay at the very root of the revolt against the Church. To Catholic writers, Luther was quintessentially the 'lewd friar': his marriage in 1525 to the former nun, Katharina von Bora, provoked a torrent of invective, and Thomas More does not appear at his best in repeated references to Luther's 'harlot, whom he abuseth in continual incest and sacrilege under the name of a wife'.[134] Even More's fellow martyr, the saintly John Fisher, was not above indulging in some personal abuse, remarking sarcastically that the birth of a child within six weeks of the marriage 'must be a great miracle'.[135] To loyal Catholics, priests' marriages were ever 'pretensed marriages'; in confronting the spectre of the married priest the Church's perpetual struggle against fleshly corruption had merely entered a new and more crucial phase. The Protestant insistence that clerical marriage was essential to contain immorality, both among the clergy and the community more widely, was inherently ridiculous: 'how can there by the marriage of priests . . . be fewer whores and bawds, when by the very marriage itself being as it were incestuous and abominable, all were stark harlots that married them, and all stark bawds that should help to bring them together?'[136] It was attitudes like this which were to underlie the deprivation of married priests under Mary, and which help to explain its thoroughness and severity.

LAY REACTIONS TO CLERICAL MARRIAGE

Of all the major theological debates of the Reformation, that concerning the lawfulness or otherwise of priests' marriages may have touched the

---

[133] Martin, *Pretensed marriage of priestes*, sig. A.i^r. It was believed by John Ponet that 'Thomas Martin' was a pseudonym of Stephen Gardiner, and it is possible that Gardiner played some part in the composition of his chancellor's work: J. A. Muller, *Stephen Gardiner and the Tudor Reaction* (1926), 317.

[134] More, *Dialogue*, 165. The recent biography of More by Richard Marius has suggested that this issue was an obsession of More's, stemming from his own thwarted desire to serve God as a celibate priest: R. Marius, *Thomas More* (1985), 308 and *passim*. It is fair to point out, however, that virulent abuse of married priests was commonplace among English Catholic writers and preachers. In addition to the examples cited in this chapter, see J. Wilson, 'The Sermons of Roger Edgeworth: Reformation Preaching in Bristol', in D. Williams (ed.), *Early Tudor England: Proceedings of the 1987 Harlaxton Symposium* (Woodbridge, 1989), 238.   [135] Surtz, *Works and Days of John Fisher*, 335.

[136] More, *Supplication of Souls*, 156–7.

religious life of the ordinary layperson as closely as any, and it is probably
no coincidence that practically all the books composed on this subject
appeared in the vernacular.[137] To a partisan like Robert Barnes, the arguments in favour of clerical marriage were 'so plain that I marvel how any
man should doubt in it', yet after the accession of Edward VI it took two
years for Parliament to sanction the practice, and the act of February 1549
which permitted priests to marry was firm in its insistence that 'it were
. . . better for the estimation of priests and other ministers in the Church
of God to live chaste, sole, and separate from the company of women and
the bond of marriage'.[138] This was hardly a positive endorsement, and it
reflects the extent to which the issue was a divisive one among the élite.
As with many of the topics discussed in this book, 'popular' attitudes are
impossible to quantify, yet there is evidence from a variety of sources that
many ordinary laypeople may have found the idea of priests contracting
marriages both bewildering and offensive, essentially no different from
the practice of concubinage, which as we have noted, could do so much
to activate lay anxiety and disapproval.

The numbers of priests deprived of their benefices in Mary's reign
gives an indication of the extent to which the English clergy responded to
the relaxation of the law against clerical marriage and took wives in the
period 1549–53. In the north, predictably, the percentage was relatively
low, about one in ten of the incumbents in the diocese of York married,
and in the highly conservative city of York only four priests are known to
have married in Edward's reign.[139] In Lancashire fewer than one in twenty
priests married. Further south priests seem to have been less loath to take
advantage of this new latitude: in London nearly one-third of the parish
clergy married, and a quarter did so in Essex, Suffolk, and Norfolk.[140] At
any event, in both north and south, the number of legally married priests
was almost certainly much greater than the number of those known or
suspected to have been unchaste before 1549. If popular attitudes had not
changed sufficiently to allow the possibility of a priest living with a

---

[137] Yost, 'Reformation Defence of Clerical Marriage', 154.

[138] Ibid.; 2 & 3 Edward VI, c. 21.

[139] D. M. Palliser, 'Popular Reactions to the Reformation during the Years of Uncer-
tainty, 1530–1570', in F. Heal and R. O'Day (eds.), *Church and Society in England: Henry
VIII to James I* (1977), 42; C. Cross, 'Priests into Ministers', in P. N. Brookes (ed.),
Reformation Principle and Practice (1980), 216.

[140] Palliser, 'Popular Reactions to the Reformation', 42. In most cases one can only
speculate as to how many of the unbeneficed clergy married, though given their often
insecure circumstances, it may have been fewer than among the beneficed: R. M. Spielmann,
'The Beginning of Clerical Marriage in the English Reformation: The Reigns of Edward
and Mary', *Anglican and Episcopal History*, 56 (1987), 258.

woman, then the relationship between priest and parishioners may in some parts have been coming under increasing strain.

Thirty years ago, Professor Dickens recorded his belief that clerical marriage and celibacy were not 'matters for discussion primarily along doctrinal lines', that the issue was not in essence a theological one.[141] Yet it is hard to resist the conclusion that priests who married must have felt they were making some kind of statement, if only a negative one against the weight and authority of Catholic tradition. The correlation between the incidence of clerical marriage and the generally attested receptivity of areas to the Reformation is also clearly marked. In the case of priests marrying illegally before 1549, it seems safe to assume Protestant motivation or inclinations. Priests had begun marrying in noticeable numbers in the 1530s: Foxe cites a case of a Hertfordshire rector marrying his curate to a maidservant in 1530, and the London chronicler, Wriothesley, noted that marriage was spreading among the clergy of Suffolk.[142] By 1538 the practice had become sufficiently widespread for a royal proclamation to fulminate against those 'light persons' who had proceeded to marry 'without a common consent of his highness and his realm'.[143] Within a year the Act of Six Articles was to make married clerics culpable of a serious criminal offence, a reflection probably both of Henry VIII's personal animus against priestly marriage, and of nervous official reaction against the advanced ideas such priests might safely be assumed to hold.[144] Robert Parkyn noted that even before the promulgation of the 1549 Prayer Book, married priests omitted the elevation of the host at mass, and it may be that in some cases theological radicalism compounded the scandal given to their parishioners by their marriages.[145]

It remains to be proved, of course, that parishioners were scandalized. Between 1549 and 1553 hostility to clerical marriage could not be voiced publicly without fear of judicial proceedings, but in the latter part of Henry VIII's reign many did not hesitate to make their feelings known. When the vicar of Mendlesham in Suffolk married in 1537, and brought his wife and children to the vicarage, it was said that 'this act by him done is in this country a monster, and many do grudge at it'. His action was

---

[141] Dickens, *Lollards and Protestants*, 188.

[142] Foxe, *Acts and Monuments*, v. 35; C. Wriothesley, *A Chronicle of England during the Reigns of the Tudors*, ed. W. D. Hamilton, CS NS 11 (1875), i. 83; *LP* ix. 661. A priest who admitted to having married claimed before the Mayor of Rye in 1537 that 'he knew a hundred priests married': *LP* xii (2). 450.

[143] P. L. Hughes and J. F. Larkin (eds.), *Tudor Royal Proclamations* (New Haven, Conn., 1964), i. 274.   [144] J. J. Scarisbrick, *Henry VIII* (1968), 418–19.

[145] Dickens, 'Robert Parkyn's Narrative of the Reformation', 297.

reportedly 'abominable in the judgement of the lay people'.[146] Another priest who married prematurely in 1539, having, so he said, 'conceived untruly God's Word' soon found out 'by the noise of the people' that he had made a mistake, and wrote to Cromwell suing for the King's pardon.[147] It is significant that Cromwell's agent, Christopher Mont, believed that the inspiration for the prohibition of clerical marriage in the Six Articles had been 'for the credit of priests with the common people, who are yet weak in the knowledge of the Word'.[148] A ballad circulating in London in the 1540s proposed various scenarios of the world turned upside down:

> When wrens wear woodknives, cranes for to kill
> And sparrows build churches upon a green hill . . .
> And cats unto mice do swear obedience . . .

each stanza ending resoundingly: 'then put in priest's wives your trust and confidence'.[149] The Act of Parliament of 1549 which allowed priests to marry seems initially to have made little impact on popular attitudes, perhaps not surprisingly, since, as we have seen, it still presented celibacy as the ideal. In the same year a demand for the restoration of compulsory sacerdotal celibacy was implicit in the call of the South-Western rebels for the reinstatement of the Six Articles, and in one of the versions of the rebels' articles the demand was made explicit.[150]

Such feelings were not confined to the 'dark corners of the land'. The visitation articles of Archbishop Cranmer for his diocese of Canterbury demanded to know whether there were any in the diocese who condemned married priests 'and for that they be married will not receive the communion or other sacraments at their hands'.[151] Leading Protestants remained acutely aware of the people's unsoundness on this issue. On the eve of Edward's accession, John Hooper observed that 'the most shameful celibacy of the clergy' was 'never before held by the people in greater esteem than at the present moment'.[152] As Bishop of Gloucester, Hooper

---

[146] T. Wright (ed.), *Three Chapters of Letters Relating to the Suppression of the Monasteries*, CS 26 (1843), 160; *LP* xii (2). 81. It is fair to suggest here that opinion in the parish was probably not uniformly hostile, since Mendlesham was notorious as a centre of religious radicalism: D. MacCulloch, *Suffolk and the Tudors* (Oxford, 1986), 178.

[147] Wright (ed.), *Letters Relating to the Suppression of the Monasteries*, 160–1; *LP* xiv (1). 1125. [148] *LP* xiv (1). 844.

[149] Furnivall (ed.), *Ballads from Manuscripts*, i. 313–15; *LP* xiv (2). App. 48, p. 370. An earlier version of the piece employed the more overtly misogynistic refrain, 'then put in a woman your trust and confidence': R. Dyboski (ed.), *Songs, Carols and other Miscellaneous Poems from the Balliol MS 354: Richard Hill's Commonplace-Book*, EETS ES 101 (1908), 114.

[150] Lea, *History of Sacerdotal Celibacy*, ii. 120. [151] *Visitation Articles*, ii. 189.

[152] H. Robinson (ed.), *Original Letters Relative to the English Reformation*, PS (1846), i. 36.

was to manifest a near obsession with the tendency of his flock towards Catholic recidivism which perhaps led him into rhetorical exaggeration, but he was not alone in noting the regrettable lack of enthusiasm for clerical marriage. In a sermon of 1550, Latimer sought to inspire his godly listeners by suggesting that Christ would give wisdom to his followers which their adversaries would not be able to overcome: 'They may rail upon it, as in many places lewd fellows do against priests' marriages; "that dame, his wife, his whore &c", but they cannot deny it by any scripture.'[153] Latimer must have felt deeply about the popular rejection of a married ministry, as he returned to the topic in a sermon of 1552, here using it to illustrate the truth that an honest deed must never be left undone, simply because some people will be offended by it:

As for an example, here is a priest which perceiveth by himself that he hath not the gift of chastity, and therefore would fain marry; but he is afraid that some of his parishioners should be offended with his marriage. Now, shall he leave his marriage because some will be offended with him? No, that he shall not: let the priest instruct his parishioners, tell them out of the Word of God, that it is as lawful for him to marry as well as for another man. After that he hath taught them, if they will not believe him, or refuse his doctrine, let him marry and care not for their offence.[154]

A somewhat defeatist tone is discernible here, but most Protestants refused to accept that lay sensibilities on this matter were immutable, and continued the campaign of persuasion, often harping on the connection between clerical celibacy and 'whoredom'. In his *Answer to the Commoners of Devonshire and Cornwall*, Philip Nichols was at pains to stress that it was not 'the best priests or most chaste livers that most cry out against the marriage of priests', but the lascivious ones who did not want to be tied down to one wife.[155] The putative link between celibacy and promiscuity was also drawn in a passage incorporated into Tyndale's prologue to the Book of Numbers in the Mathew–Becke Bibles of 1549 and 1551, and the Mathew Bible of 1551.[156] Yet despite this, popular hostility to clerical marriage remained a disciplinary preoccupation of the Edwardian authorities. Hooper's interrogatories for the dioceses of Gloucester and Worcester in 1551–2 complained of those 'that raileth, speaketh uncharitably, or calleth any minister's wife whore, and abhor their companies' and noted that some midwives refused to attend them in

---

[153] Latimer, *Sermons*, i. 293.   [154] Ibid. ii. 77–8.
[155] N. Pocock (ed.), *Troubles Connected with the Prayer Book of 1549*, CS NS 37 (1884), 152.   [156] Tudor, 'Changing Private Belief and Practice in England', 213.

childbirth.[157] In 1552 a second Act of Parliament sought to correct the grudging tone of the 1549 Act which had seemed to depict clerical marriage as a necessary evil 'so that thereby the lawful matrimony of priests in the opinion of many, and the children procreated and born of such lawful matrimony, rather be of a great number of the king's subjects accounted as bastards than lawfully born'. As a consequence of such 'uncomely railings of matrimony and slanderous reproaches of the clergy', the Word of God was not being heard reverently, or the King proceedings received with due obedience.[158]

Recorded instances of reactions to individual married priests and their wives are few, but sufficient to sustain the impression of solid hostility conveyed by the foregoing generalizations. In Oxford, Peter Martyr's wife was abused by the populace, and their house was pelted with stones.[159] Thomas Hancock, the radical minister of Poole in Dorset, provoked a similarly robust response in 1547 when he refused his parishioners' request for intercessory prayer on All Souls' day: 'Then did they all . . . with one mouth call me "knave", and my wife "strumpet".'[160] In Cambridgeshire in 1549, the curate of Newton found his banns challenged by a parishioner on account of his priesthood when they were read in the church.[161] The divisive potential of a married priest, especially in notoriously conservative areas, is well illustrated by the difficulties experienced by George Grayme after his marriage to Anne James, the widow of a Carlisle merchant. Grayme claimed that his attempts to recover debts due to his wife's late husband had been frustrated by the mayor and bailiffs of Carlisle, and the steward of the Sheriff of Cumberland, for no other reason than that he 'before his said marriage had received the order of priesthood'. Nor would the mayor and burgesses allow Anne to trade from her shop in the city, unless it could be proved to them 'by good certificate and authority that priests may marry by God's laws'.[162] The antagonism to Grayme in Carlisle seems to have been orchestrated by Alexander Stagg, curate of the cathedral church, described by Grayme as a 'seditious person, bearing inward grudge against your majesty's most godly proceedings'. Stagg had been openly declaring his opinion that 'the marriages of priests is damnable and contrary to God's law', and on

---

[157] *Visitation Articles*, ii. 292–3.   [158] 5 & 6 Edward VI, c. 12.

[159] J. Loach, 'Reformation Controversies', in J. McConica (ed.), *The History of the University of Oxford* (Oxford, 1986), iii. 374.

[160] J. G. Nichols (ed.), *Narratives of the Days of the Reformation*, CS 77 (1859), 78.

[161] E. J. Carlson, 'Clerical Marriage and the English Reformation', *JBS* 31 (1992), 7.

[162] PRO, STA. C. 2, 16/216.

several occasions had tried to persuade Anne to separate from her husband. Grayme clearly identified his own difficulties with the cause of reformation in the north; if justice was denied him 'it shall be a great hindrance against your majesty's most godly proceedings in those parts'.[163]

Stagg was not the only northern cleric encouraging disaffection with official policy on this subject. In 1552 a Yorkshire priest, William Brogden, was accused by Archbishop Holgate of announcing publicly that 'he had not read in any ancient doctor of the Church that it was lawful for priests to marry'.[164] Even among Holgate's own cathedral clergy there were those, or so it was later claimed, who insisted that 'it were better for priests not to marry than to marry'.[165] Instances of disapproval of clerical marriage have also been discovered in neighbouring Cheshire. In early 1549 a married priest of Warrington had to sue a local woman for slander, and in the summer of that year a prebendary of Chester testified that his intended spouse had insisted on delaying their union 'until there were some other priests married'. The marriage, in fact, never took place.[166]

If hostility to the concept of clerical marriage was as widespread as has been suggested here, then there could have been little inducement for respectable women to have sought priests as partners, and it is conceivable that clergy wives may very often have been drawn from sections of society to which such opprobrium mattered relatively little. The indefatigable Marian propagandist, Miles Huggarde, claimed that priests who married 'cared not upon whom they had bestowed themselves' and that 'the women of these married priests were such for the most part that either were kept of other before, or else as common as the cartway'.[167] Thomas Martin suggested that some priests married widows, some other men's wives, some their own concubines, and some 'common strumpets' to the peril of their souls and 'the notable contempt of the ministry'.[168] Huggarde and Martin were, of course, concerned to make cheap propagandist points; some of the wives of Edwardian priests were undoubtedly courageous women who shared the reforming vision of their husbands. Yet by no means all married clerics were convinced Protestants, and if priests in fact did commonly marry their concubines or women who were

---

[163] PRO, STA. C. 3, 5/48.   [164] BIHR, CP G 431.

[165] Dickens, 'Two Marian Petitions', in *Reformation Studies*, 89. Holgate's own marital difficulties have been described by Professor Dickens, ibid. 344–6.

[166] Haigh, *Reformation and Resistance in Tudor Lancashire*, 182.

[167] M. Huggarde, *The displaying of the Protestants* (1556), 73ᵛ–74ʳ.

[168] Martin, *Pretensed marriage of priestes*, sig. D.iᵛ.

in some other way social outsiders, laypeople could hardly be blamed for continuing to think of them as 'priests' whores'.

The issue, of course, had a pastoral as well as a dogmatic and moral dimension. If parishioners had reason to fear that clerical marriage might lead to neglect of the cure (as Martin argued it would), this could provide another reason for the laity to feel uneasy. In a letter to William Cecil, the Duke of Northumberland, who paraded himself as a champion of advanced Protestantism, was prepared to sneer at the married clergy in this regard: 'These men, for the most part, that the King's Majesty hath of late preferred be so sotted of their wives and children that they forget both their poor neighbours and all other things which to their calling appertaineth.'[169] Whether this sketch accurately captures popular experience of a married ministry is difficult to judge. In some cases the acquisition of a wife and children might have relieved the incumbent of burdensome and distracting domestic and agricultural responsibilities; on the other hand, the added incentive for financial security that a family inevitably brought may have made married priests more determined to defend their pecuniary rights, and perhaps partially accounts for the growing volume of tithe disputes in the 1540s and 50s.

The case for social ostracism and antagonism towards priests' wives can perhaps be overstated: in 1553, for example, the churchwardens of Ashburton in Devon were apparently happy to pay '2s. to Sir Nicholas's wife for washing vestments', a minor parochial duty which elsewhere was often performed by the sexton's wife.[170] While it is true that discord is notably more successful than concord at imprinting itself upon the historical record, the apparent paucity of such neutral or positive references to clergy wives ought to give one pause for thought. An examination of over 400 wills from the Edwardian period has failed to produce a single instance of a bequest to anyone clearly identifiable as a priest's wife. It seems an unavoidable conclusion that the Marian deprivations, which in some cases involved public penance and abjuration before the assembled parish, must have enjoyed a good deal of popular support, an assertion supported by the testimony of Robert Parkyn who reported that the common people had disliked married priests and rejoiced to see them forcibly parted from their 'concubines and harlots'.[171] In Elizabeth's reign hostility towards clerical marriage seems to have remained a relatively

---

[169] T. M. Parker, *The English Reformation to 1558* (Oxford, 1950), 138.

[170] A. Hanham (ed.), *Churchwardens' Accounts of Ashburton, 1479–1580*, Devon and Cornwall Record Society, NS 15 (1970), 128.

[171] Dickens, 'Robert Parkyn's Narrative of the Reformation', 308, 311.

common phenomenon. In the 1560s, even the 1580s, some people would call the minister's wife 'priest's whore' just as they had clerical concubines in the 1520s.[172]

In the short term at least, the implications for lay–clerical relations of the sanctioning of clerical marriage were probably far from happy. Thomas Martin may not have been exaggerating too wildly when he wrote: 'what discord and envy hath of late grown between the common multitude and the clergy since marriage of priests hath been practised.'[173] If this was so it was because enjoyment of the married state was judged to be incompatible with the proper fulfilment of the office of priesthood: orders and matrimony were alternative not complementary sacraments. As we have seen, the expectation of the laity was not merely that priests would stay single, but that they would remain completely chaste in their personal lives. If there were deep psychological motives for this attitude, these are probably beyond the competence of the historian to ascertain.[174] What one can say is that there seems to have been a widespread perception that the man who celebrated the mass and administered the other sacraments ought to have been able to transcend the sexual and emotional needs of other men, ought to have been different. The late medieval Church had demanded that priests be accorded a respect and status commensurate with their unique soteriological power, and the laity demanded in return a public token of sanctity as pledge and proof of that power. The Edwardian and Elizabethan authorities hoped to remodel the equation on a new theological basis, but for as long as laypeople, or a substantial number of them, rejected clerical marriage, the idea of a priesthood of all believers could make only slow and uncertain progress.

[172] Examples of continuing hostility to clerical marriage in Elizabeth's reign are given in Lea, *Sacerdotal Celibacy*, ii. 148; Chadwick, *The Reformation*, 411–12; Dickens, *Lollards and Protestants*, 187; P. Tyler, 'The Status of the Elizabethan Parochial Clergy', in G. J. Cuming (ed.), *SCH* 4 (Leiden, 1967), 87; Cross, 'Priests into Ministers', 218; C. Haigh, 'The Church of England, the Catholics and the People', in C. Haigh (ed.), *The Reign of Elizabeth I* (1984), 216; Collinson, *Birthpangs of Protestant England*, 67–8; A. L. Rowse, *Tudor Cornwall*, 2nd edn. (1969), 311. The conclusion of E. J. Carlson, 'Clerical Marriage and the English Reformation', *JBS* 31 (1992), 26–8, that popular resentment against priests marrying virtually evaporated in the 1560s, seems rather premature on the basis of the available evidence.   [173] Martin, *Pretensed marriage of priestes*, sig. Ll.iii^r.
[174] The issue has been addressed in a contemporary context by J. E. Dittes, 'The Symbolic Value of Celibacy for the Catholic Faithful', *Concilium*, 8 (1972).

6

The Priest as Pastor

THE CURE OF SOULS

When early Tudor Englishmen and women thought about priests and priesthood, they probably thought first of their curate, the rector, vicar, or assistant who had the cure of their souls, and the reciprocity of their relationship with him was a fundamental determinant of the attitudes this book is attempting to discern.[1] The alleged failings of the late medieval Church in the provision of pastoral care is a familiar theme to students of the English Reformation, as is the contention that the later sixteenth century witnessed a far-reaching reappraisal of the pastoral responsibilities of the ordained ministry.[2] According to Rosemary O'Day, the role of the priest in the pre-Reformation Church was 'not defined in terms of his relationship with his flock but in terms of his relationship with God. It was entirely conceivable that a priest should have no flock, whereas it was inconceivable that he should have no mass.'[3]

It is, of course, true that there were many priests who as diocesan or royal administrators, private chaplains, or enclosed religious, had no formal cure of souls, yet it may be unwise to posit too sharp a distinction between the sacerdotal/sacramental and pastoral actions of the priest, and thus risk falling into an unconsciously Protestant teleology of clerical function. For most priests, hearing confessions and saying mass were quintessentially pastoral acts, and it is worth bearing in mind that even a priest without cure saying a solitary mass was, by his own understanding, not only offering sacrifice but performing a powerful invocation on behalf of all Christian men and women. On the theoretical level, the Lutheran and Reformed theologies of ministry, predicated upon the 'call' to minister to a particular community, do seem intrinsically more pastoral in

---

[1] Throughout this chapter 'curate' is taken to mean any priest with the cure of souls.

[2] P. Collinson, *The Religion of Protestants: The Church in English Society 1559–1625* (Oxford, 1982), ch. 3; R. O'Day, *The English Clergy: The Emergence and Consolidation of a Profession 1558–1642* (Leicester, 1979), ch. 16.

[3] R. O'Day, 'The Anatomy of a Profession: The Clergy of the Church of England', in W. Prest (ed.), *The Professions in Early Modern England* (Beckenham, 1987), 32.

emphasis than the Catholic doctrine of sacramental order, but in practice the pre-Reformation Church laid very great stress on the diligent serving of the cure of souls. In the traditional imagery, the priest was the shepherd, the people his flock, a distinction which could only acquire greater clarity from the polemical rejection of the Lutheran concept of the common priesthood of Christians. In his last manuscript work in vindication of the rights of the clergy, John Fisher insisted that Christ's charge to Peter to 'feed my sheep' was 'not only said unto Peter for himself, but for all other that after him was deputed unto that office'.[4] Earlier he had asked rhetorically, 'who is so dull as not to know the difference between the vineyard and its cultivator, the flock and the shepherd, in a word, between those who are ruled and their ruler?'[5] The metaphor of shepherd and flock expressed well the laity's complete dependence on the sacramental ministry of priests, but in so far as it seemed to ascribe to the laity the simple docility of sheep, it was misleading. The flock was not always uncritical or undemanding in its attitude towards its pastor, and the sheep may well have had their own ideas as to what constituted an adequate standard of care.

The duties of the curate *vis-à-vis* his parishioners were various, and well known to each member of his flock. To a reformer like Robert Crowley, most of these tasks were at best irrelevant and at worst damnable, but his diatribe may stand as a reasonable summary of the duties of the pre-Reformation priest: 'What call they serving of a cure? For sooth, to say mass, matins and evensong on the holy day, to make holy water and holy bread, to conjure the fount and volow [baptize] the child, to shrive, housel, and anoint the sick, to say dirige and mass, and bury the dead.'[6] Essentially, the priest was required both to administer the important rites of passage which punctuated the layperson's life—baptism, marriage, anointing in preparation for death—and to provide for them ongoing spiritual succour in the form of (probably annual) absolution and communion, and the recurrent round of divine service. It was hoped also, as we have seen, that the priest would periodically preach to the people, or at least attempt to impart a modicum of religious knowledge. In addition a curate was expected to visit his sick parishioners, and to provide hospitality and relief for the needy.

---

[4] PRO, SP 6/11, fo. 221^v.
[5] J. Fisher, *The Defence of the Priesthood*, tr. P. E. Hallett (1935), 114.
[6] R. Crowley, *The Confutation of xiii articles wherunto N. Shaxton subscribed* (1548), sig. G.iv^r. Crowley went on to complain that 'as for preaching, [it] shall be nothing of the curate's charge'.

How assiduous priests were in performing these duties, and how assiduous laypeople hoped or expected them to be, are questions which will
allow of no definitive answers. The main type of source for these purposes, the visitation record, provides evidence of what parishioners, or at
least the more substantial among them, felt to be amiss in the cure of
souls, but the ideal of the pastor which emerges is inevitably to some
degree that of a man who merely obeyed the rules, perhaps merely went
through the motions. Whether laypeople expected more than the simple
fulfilment of stipulated duties is difficult to ascertain; it is only occasionally
that we can catch a glimpse of more positive lay aspirations. Silence in a
visitation record is not necessarily proof that the rector, vicar, curate, or
parish priest was performing his duties to the letter, merely that the
parish was satisfied enough not to complain. Certainly, some visitations
have little to report in the way of pastoral failings. In the diocese of
Chichester only three curates were presented for neglect of the cure of
souls in the surviving returns for visitations of 1521 and 1530.[7] Visitations
of the archdeaconry of Leicester in 1522–3 and 1526 produced no more
than two complaints of irregularity in the times of services.[8] Similarly,
episcopal visitations of the huge diocese of Lincoln over the period 1500–
21 revealed relatively few cases of pastoral inadequacy.[9] Proportionately
rather more complaints were made during Archbishop Warham's visitation of Canterbury in 1511, but overall the safest assumption would
appear to be that in the great majority of parishes the cure was served
properly, and one recent historian has rightly remarked that 'concentration
on normality rather than on isolated eye-catching abuses transforms our
view of the parish clergy'.[10] None the less, it is worth examining the
'abuses' that were recorded as these can help to establish the standard of
service that laypeople considered normative. It is fairly clear that when
parishioners complained to the visitors about the behaviour of their
curate, they did so not because they disliked priests, but because an individual cleric had in some way disappointed their expectation, had failed
to correspond to the model of the pastor which they held in their minds.

[7] S. Lander, 'Church Courts and the Reformation in the Diocese of Chichester, 1500–
1558', in R. O'Day and F. Heal (eds.), *Continuity and Change: Personnel and Administration
of the Church in England, 1500–1642* (Leicester, 1976), 230.
   [8] Fuggles, 'The Parish Clergy in the Archdeaconry of Leicester, 1520–1540', Leicestershire Archaeological and Historical Society Transactions, 46 (1970–1), 37.
   [9] M. Bowker, *The Secular Clergy in the Diocese of Lincoln, 1485–1520* (Cambridge, 1968),
114.
   [10] *Kentish Visitations, passim*; C. Harper-Bill, 'Dean Colet's Convocation Sermon and the
Pre-Reformation Church in England', *History*, 73 (1988), 205.

RESIDENCE AND NON-RESIDENCE

To be an effective pastor a priest had naturally to reside amongst his people. For a variety of reasons, a considerable number of rectors and vicars did not do so, but spent most of their time absent from their benefices. Some absentees were students at the universities, others were royal or diocesan officials for whom a benefice stood in lieu of a salary. Non-residence for these reasons was perhaps defensible, since it could be argued that the Church or the state as a whole benefited from the system, but other absentees were simply pluralists, those who held more than one benefice with cure of souls, a practice officially forbidden and condemned by the moralists, but for which licences were relatively freely obtainable.[11] At his institution, a vicar was required to swear to keep residence and to minister personally, but a considerable number, perhaps a quarter of the total, did neither.[12] It is difficult to say for certain just how ordinary laypeople may have viewed pluralism and non-residence. Christopher St German claimed that the proliferation of licences and dispensations for non-residence had been to the 'great grudge, and murmur, and evil example of all the people', and it has been suggested that parishioners may sometimes have resented paying tithes to absentee incumbents.[13] Notorious pluralists were perhaps sometimes disliked for their affluence and power. In 1532, for example, a complaint against the pluralist cleric, John Hogg, in Shropshire listed with disapproval his 'great possessions and profits'.[14] In some parishes it is clear that the non-residence of the incumbent was deeply resented, and could be characterized in terms more suggestive of a failure of charity, than of mere canonical irregularity. The lack of a priest induced the parishioners of Masham in Yorkshire to complain to the visitor in 1510 that 'they had great wrong'; those at Waghen declared that 'we think that Mr Vicar abides not among us, as a

[11] J. H. Lupton, *Life of John Colet* (1909), 300; Dionysius Carthusianus, *The Lyfe of Prestes* (*c*.1533), sig. k.ii^v.

[12] M. Bowker, 'Non-Residence in the Lincoln Diocese in the Early Sixteenth Century', *JEH* 15 (1964); *Secular Clergy in the Diocese of Lincoln*, 75; *The Henrician Reformation: The Diocese of Lincoln under John Longland, 1521–1547* (Cambridge, 1981), 43; P. Heath, *The English Parish Clergy on the Eve of the Reformation* (1969), 56; F. Heal, 'Parish Clergy and the Reformation in the Diocese of Ely', *CAS* 66 (1977), 114; S. Brigden, *London and the Reformation* (Oxford, 1989), 57.

[13] C. St German, *A treatise concernynge the division between the spirytualtie and temporaltie*, *CW* 9 (1979), 204; R. Houlbrooke, *Church Courts and the People during the English Reformation* (Oxford, 1979), 184; C. Harper-Bill, 'A Late Medieval Visitation: The Diocese of Norwich in 1499', *Proceedings of the Suffolk Institute of Archaeology and History*, 34 (1977), 41.   [14] PRO, STA. C. 2, 2/54.

curate ought to do, for if he would, we would be content therewith . . .
[if] he would do his duty which belongs to his charge and abide with
us'.[15] At Pluckley in Kent in 1511 it was reported that 'the parson is not
resident as he should be', and at Newchurch, 'the vicar is not personally
resident as he is bound'. At Ivychurch the parish noted ruefully that 'the
parson is an outlandish man and he never came among us since his
induction'.[16]

Some laypeople evidently felt that a non-resident incumbent was failing in the exercise of his priestly duties, yet others may have been less
concerned with the question of non-residence as such, and were perhaps
satisfied so long as the absentee provided an adequate deputy to serve the
cure. This attitude was clearly exhibited in a petition sent in 1543 to
William Plumpton, patron of the parish of Sacombe in Hertfordshire,
informing him of the death of the present incumbent, and expressing the
hope that 'he that shall succeed him, be of no worse sort than he hath
been'. The former rector had been an absentee, and the letter requested
that if his successor 'be minded to be resident and abide upon the same
parsonage', Plumpton would urge him to retain as his deputy Sir
Christopher Bird, 'who honestly did keep the cure under the foresaid late
parson, and the maintainment of God's service'.[17] To the parishioners of
Sacombe it mattered little whether their rector was resident or not, so
long as there was an honest priest like Sir Christopher to serve the cure.
In 1542 the parishioners of Pattiswick in Essex complained that their
rector, Sir William Harbotell, did not personally serve the cure 'as it
ought to be; nevertheless he hath such a priest as is good and sufficient,
to discharge him in his cure, and the parishioners well content with'.[18] A
salaried curate could be as effective a pastor as a beneficed rector, and
Mrs Bowker has shown that unsupervised curates were not in general
more likely to misbehave than other priests.[19]

Yet not all parishes were as fortunate as Sacombe or Pattiswick. Where
non-residence led to neglect of the cure, due to the absence or inadequacy
of a deputy, it must have seemed an indefensible abuse. At Kingsdown in
Kent in 1511 the absence of the parson meant that there was service 'but
once in a fortnight'. At Dymchurch the cure was 'often times unserved'.
At Harbledown the parsonage was said to be in decay, 'and the cure there

[15] J. Raine (ed.), *The Fabric Rolls of York Minster*, SS 35 (1858), 263, 265.

[16] *Kentish Visitations*, 201, 146, 148.

[17] T. Stapleton (ed.), *Plumpton Correspondence*, CS 4 (1839), 244.

[18] Hale, *Precedents*, 119.

[19] Bowker, *Secular Clergy in the Diocese of Lincoln*, 109.

is not duly served by a priest sufficient'. At Selling there had been no curate for nineteen weeks, and at Reculver 'the chantry priest and his clerk will not come in to sing divine service as it hath been used afore time because the vicar and his parish priest be not resident there'.[20] At Ellesborough in Buckinghamshire in 1519 it was complained that the rector neither served the cure himself 'nor by any honest curate'.[21] Not all absentees were so careless of their responsibilities; most did provide an adequate curate, and some even made the effort to visit their parishes at Easter to minister the sacraments in person to their parishioners, though one suspects that supervision of the collection of tithes may have been a central factor in a decision to visit the cure at this time.[22] In the Norwich visitation of 1499, from forty-eight parishes where the incumbent was non-resident there were complaints of neglect from only two.[23] Nevertheless, in parishes where neglect did occur, laypeople would not have hesitated to put the blame on non-resident priests. The worst type of absenteeism was that put to the charge of the royal chaplain Geoffrey Wren, parson of Sezincote in Gloucestershire, that 'there is not any priest there neither the said Geoffrey nor any curate for him to do matins, mass, nor evensong, nor to minister the sacraments, nor to inform or instruct the parishioners there as ought to be by the law of God'.[24] Priests who displayed contempt for the cure of souls by failing to provide a deputy during their absence were certain to be deeply unpopular. One such was the litigious curate of St Botolph, Aldersgate, Robert Shoter, who reacted angrily when told by a fellow-priest, Peter Bowden, that 'the clerk or the sexton should know where to find you when you be out of the way, or else to speak to . . . [another priest] or to me to keep your cure in your absence'. Shoter's response was to call Bowden a 'whoreson Irish knave' and to suggest that he was trying to take his curacy away from him.[25] Priests like Shoter regarded their benefice as a privilege, untramelled by responsibilities, an attitude the laity was not prepared to tolerate.

THE PROVISION OF SACRAMENTS

The principal test of whether the cure was served as it ought to be was whether divine service was said properly and regularly. Late medieval

---

[20] *Kentish Visitations*, 250, 155, 66, 165, 88.   [21] *Lincoln Visitations*, i. 40.
[22] PRO, C. 1, 363/39; C. 1, 827/1.
[23] J. R. Lander, *Government and Community, England, 1450–1509* (Cambridge, Mass., 1980), 135.   [24] PRO, STA. C. 2, 35/68.
[25] GLRO, DL/C/207, fo. 211ʳ.

theology asserted that the first and most fundamental duty of the priest was to say mass, and popular sentiment almost certainly agreed. Unsurprisingly, a particular source of irritation were those priests who were remiss in celebrating mass, or who celebrated at irregular times. At Ospringe in Kent in 1511, the parish complained that 'the vicar singeth not the service at due hours, nor keepeth none order. But now he singeth at one hour, now at another, at his own pleasure.'[26] The mass may have been a sacerdotal sacrifice, realized by the celebrant's partaking in the high priesthood of Christ, but to the faithful of late medieval England it was also an important expression of communal spirituality that could not be wholly subject to the whim of a priest. Similar complaints recur throughout the visitation material. The curate of Hawrigge in Buckinghamshire began mass too early on feast-days, as did the London chantry priest, William Barton, and the parson of Little Tey in Essex.[27] Another Essex curate was reported in 1542 for beginning the service before the congregation assembled, a practice which the aggrieved parishioners described as 'contrary to the usage of other curates'.[28] Lay insistence on the proper provision of masses was the inevitable consequence of the devotional habits which were discussed in Chapter 2. By the late fifteenth century there was an expectation in many parishes that a daily mass should be available, and the failure of a North Yorkshire curate to celebrate mass in the parish church, on the three days of the week when he was responsible for an outlying chapel, was said in 1472 to be 'to the great peril of the parishioners there'.[29] Where the cause of such neglect was clerical indolence or avarice rather than overwork, parochial discontent might be correspondingly greater. At St Mary's in Dover there were no masses on Wednesdays and Fridays 'if there be any mind [a memorial service] within the town where our curate may get a groat'.[30] At Sturry there was 'sung but once or twice mass in the week at most'. When the parishioners asked the vicar to celebrate more often, he answered 'would ye have me sing mass whan I am not disposed?' Such an answer was no more likely to impress than the posture struck by the incumbent of Wooton, a priest equally remiss in the provision of divine service: he 'beareth himself bold upon my Lord's grace, saying that he is in such

[26] *Kentish Visitations*, 226.

[27] *Lincoln Visitations*, i. 44; PRO, STA. C. 2, 3/200; Hale, *Precedents*, 123.

[28] Ibid. 119. See also *Lincoln Visitations*, i. 49, 53, 59, 61, 67, 88, 119, 125, 128, 130, 132, 134; ii. 13; BIHR, D/C CP 1547/3; D/C AB 1, fo. 228ᵛ.

[29] G. H. Cook, *The English Medieval Parish Church* (1954), 35; Lander, *Government and Community*, 116.   [30] *Kentish Visitations*, 132.

favour with your noble grace [Archbishop Warham] and his officers that he may do what it pleaseth him'.[31] The parishioners of Sturry and Wooton were apparently more restrained than those of East Chinnock in Somerset, who in 1498 assaulted their vicar because he had gone to celebrate in East Coker, and had left them without mass for a day.[32]

While the mass should have been celebrated regularly and at specific times, there were other sacraments which priests should have been ready to minister at all times, sacraments upon which, so it was believed, the very salvation of souls might depend. A child who died unbaptized would never be admitted to heaven, and not all medieval theologians were compassionate, or inconsistent, enough to substitute an Elysian limbo for the eternal torments of the damned.[33] A man or woman who died unconfessed might be consigned to years of needless expiation in purgatory.[34] Small wonder, then, if orthodox laypeople were to insist that everyone 'must needs have a priest at his coming into the world, and a priest at his departing', or to ask themselves 'what were a man at his first beginning and his latter ending without the help of a priest?'[35] If laypeople monitored the performance of priests in these areas, they did so not out of a disinterested concern for clerical discipline, but because these were matters that touched their eternal destiny.

Complaints that priests had failed to minister the sacrament of baptism seem to have been relatively few in this period, perhaps because of the assiduity of priests in ensuring that this most basic of Christian rites was carried out properly, or perhaps because it was accepted that in an emergency laymen, even laywomen, could baptize, and priests were instructed to ensure that their congregations knew the correct form.[36] Nevertheless, the prompt and valid baptism of infants was clearly a preoccupation of many laypeople on the eve of the Reformation, and some parishes showed considerable concern over the state of the font.[37] The South-Western rebels were insistent that baptisms be celebrated on weekdays as well as Sundays, and in 1540 an Oxford priest was reported to the authorities for failing to teach midwives how to

---

[31] Ibid. 62, 140.

[32] A. Watkin (ed.), *Dean Cosyn and Wells Cathedral Miscellanea*, SRS 56 (1941), 155–6.

[33] K. Thomas, *Religion and the Decline of Magic* (1978), 40.

[34] See above, 16n.

[35] PRO, STA. C. 2, 2/267; D. P. Wright (ed.), *The Register of Thomas Langton, Bishop of Salisbury, 1485–1493*, CYS 74 (1985), 70.

[36] W. Harington, *The Comendacions of Matrymony* (1528), sig. E.i[v]; *Visitation Articles*, ii. 49–50.

[37] *Lincoln Visitations*, i. 122, 126, 128, 129, 134, 138; Heath, *English Parish Clergy*, 63.

baptize.[38] Tyndale has bequeathed to us a valuable vignette of the contemporary ceremony which, allowing for caricature and the prejudices of the author, is suggestive of the seriousness with which the laity looked to the proper administration of the rite:

> If ought be left out, or if the child be not altogether dipped in the water, or if, because the child is sick, the priest dare not plunge him into the water, but pour water on his head, how tremble they! How quake they! 'How say ye, Sir John (say they), is this child christened enough? Hath it his full christendom?'[39]

A priest who had satisfied the parents and godparents that the sacrament was indeed validly performed might be regarded as 'as fair a volower as ever a priest within this twenty miles'.[40] John Bossy has suggested that in parts of Northern Europe priestly involvement in baptism was popularly regarded as essential because the rite partook of the character of an exorcism.[41] Whether this holds good for sixteenth-century England is difficult to judge, but the complaint of a Devon parish in the 1530s is revealing: through the negligence of the rector a child had died 'unchristened except that the midwife did to it'.[42] If there was uncertainty as to the status of lay baptism, then dependence on the clergy was reinforced, and the resentment that sprang from lack of dependability was heightened.

The same tensions pervaded the rites surrounding death. It was held to be axiomatic that a priest should be prepared at all times to minister the sacraments of unction, confession, and communion to the dying 'at all times of the day and night as necessity shall require'.[43] Doubtless, most priests were conscientious in this regard, like the vicar of Rosthone in Cheshire who in 1529 was tricked out of possession of his church when he was summoned to 'visit a man that was not [really] sick'.[44] But there were others, like the curate of Loughborough, who refused to leave his fishing and fowling in order to visit the sick, and who tried to pass the

---

[38] A. Fletcher, *Tudor Rebellions* (1983), 115; H. Salter (ed.), 'A Visitation of Oxfordshire in 1540', *Oxford Archaeological Society Reports*, 75 (1930), 300.

[39] W. Tyndale, *Doctrinal Treatises*, ed. H. Walter, PS (1848), 276.

[40] Ibid.: 'Baptism is called volowing in many parts of England because the priest sayeth "volo, say ye".'

[41] J. Bossy, *Christianity in the West, 1400–1700* (Oxford, 1985), 14.

[42] PRO, SP 1, 100/107[r].

[43] M. Bowker, *The Henrician Reformation* (Cambridge, 1981), 46 (a sermon of Bishop John Longland).

[44] R. Stewart-Brown (ed.), *Lancashire and Cheshire Cases in the Court of Star Chamber*, Lancashire and Cheshire Record Society, 71 (1916), 110.

responsibility on to the other chaplains of the parish.[45] If parishioners were to die without having received the sacraments of the Church such priests were clearly culpable. According to *Dives and Pauper*, priests 'that denieth the sacrament of penance to man or woman in his last end' were 'manslayers ghostly'.[46] They could expect little sympathy from their anxious congregations. In 1511 the parishioners of St Margaret-at-Cliffe in Kent complained that 'through the absence and negligence of the curate a woman died without shrift or housel', a baleful indictment which punctuates the documents of the period with the regularity of a tolling bell.[47] It was the fear of sudden death that made laypeople feel uneasy unless they had a priest constantly on hand. A Bedfordshire Protestant of Henry VIII's reign was caustic in his description of his contemporaries, rushing from the bed of a dying man and crying to the priest, 'come, come, he will be gone', but there was no doubting the genuineness of their anxiety.[48] A decade earlier, a Yorkshire heretic had declared that he would not seek the help of a priest even 'if I were at the point and article of death'.[49] The statement was intentionally provocative, since for most English men and women the presence of a priest was more essential at the end of their adult lives than at any point during them. In 1528 Edward Beresford of Winksworth in Derbyshire recorded in his will his heartfelt hope that it would not 'please God to call me to His mercy before the said vicar come'.[50] Ten years later, a Newcastle merchant struck with 'the visitation of Almighty God' threw himself entirely upon God's mercy, since 'I . . . cannot have a priest as I would'.[51]

Given these attitudes, the concern of the parishioners of Eversholt in Bedfordshire seems very understandable: they admitted that the rector served the cure well, but were anxious on account of the fact that he did not sleep within the parish, and petitioned that he might be compelled to

---

[45] *Lincoln Visitations*, i. 30. See also ibid. 50, 132, 138, 139.

[46] *Dives and Pauper* (1534), 177^{r-v}.

[47] *Kentish Visitations*, 115, 64–5, 119; *Lincoln Visitations*, ii. 13, 50; J. T. Fowler (ed.), *Acts of the Chapter of the Collegiate Church of SS Peter and Wilfrid, Ripon 1452–1506*, SS 64 (1875), 22; A. P. Moore (ed.), 'Proceedings of the Ecclesiastical Courts in the Archdeaconry of Leicester, 1516–1535', *Associated Architectural Societies Reports and Papers*, 28 (1905), 196, 660; Hale, *Precedents*, 114, 123; A. G. Dickens, 'Early Protestantism and the Church in Northamptonshire', *Northamptonshire PP*, 8 (1983–4), 31; PRO, SP 1, 100/107^r; STA. C. 2, 31/120.

[48] J. Fines, *A Biographical Register of Early English Protestants . . . 1525–1558* (1981), s.v. Carter, John; Bowker, *Henrician Reformation*, 168–9.   [49] BIHR, Reg. 27, fo. 132^r.

[50] *Test. Ebor.* v. 250.

[51] J. W. Clay (ed.), *North Country Wills*, SS 116 (1908), 43.

do so.[52] This insistence that priests should be available day and night to minister the sacraments probably explains the hostility which was sometimes shown to the idea of regular clergy, monks, canons, and friars serving parochial cures.[53] These would generally return at night to their community, leaving the parish without sacramental protection. At Thanington in Kent in 1511 it was complained that 'there is no secular priest in the parish church . . . but the prior of St Gregory's causeth one of his canons to serve it on day time, and at nights is at his place and when they have need of a priest they go to seek them a priest, whereby many have died without shrift or housel'.[54] Another Kent parish served by the priory aired the identical complaint: the canon left the parish at night 'and when we should have him, [as] oftentimes is required in the night season, we cannot have him'.[55] The Devon parish of Wembury, served by the Augustinian priory of Plympton, was in no better case: the priory was eight miles distant, mass was said irregularly, and at least seven parishioners had died 'without shrift and housel, or any sacrament ministered to them'.[56]

If through negligence, non-residence, or appropriation to a religious house, the standard of pastoral care in a parish was unbearably low, the logic of the situation was compellingly obvious: parishes hired their own priests, either on an *ad hoc* basis, or on a permanent footing. The parishioners of Wembury took the latter course and a number of Kent parishes were found to have done the former in 1511.[57] When Thomas Sprent, vicar of Pawlett in Somerset, was absent from his parish in 1540, it was claimed that the parishioners were 'fain to hire a priest at their [own] costs and charges'.[58] Whether such developments really represent, as Peter Heath has cautiously suggested, the laity 'assuming responsibility for their own salvation, albeit within the framework of the Church' is perhaps open to question.[59] They certainly illustrate the deep hold that the Church's

[52] *Lincoln Visitations*, i. 108. See also ibid. 52, 63, 73, 96, 119, 121, 137.

[53] *Kentish Visitations*, 95, 124, 126, 158, 184; *Lincoln Visitations*, i. 132, 134; PRO, STA. C. 2, 18/290; *LP* xiii (1). 1150; Lander, 'Church Courts and the Reformation in the Diocese of Chichester', in O'Day and Heal (eds.), *Continuity and Change*, 224; D. M. Owen, *Church and Society in Medieval Lincolnshire* (Lincoln, 1971), 135. The ecclesiastical authorities were also keen to discourage the practice: *Visitation Articles*, ii. 21; S. J. Lander, 'Diocese of Chichester, 1508–1558', Ph.D. thesis (Cambridge, 1974), 173; Heal, 'Parish Clergy and the Reformation in the Diocese of Ely', 148.   [54] *Kentish Visitations*, 64–5.

[55] Ibid. 70.   [56] PRO, SP 1, 100/107ʳ.

[57] Ibid. 109ʳ; *Kentish Visitations*, 98, 129, 173.

[58] PRO, STA. C. 2, 31/120. For further examples of parishes hiring priests to compensate for inadequate pastoral care, see Raine (ed.), *Fabric Rolls of York Minster*, 254; C. Cross, *Church and People 1450–1660* (1976), 44; Heath, *English Parish Clergy*, 64–8.

[59] Heath, ibid. 68.

sacramental system exercised over the lives of ordinary English men and women well into the sixteenth century. None the less, the fact that the Church made the reception of sacraments an effective condition of salvation, yet could not through its parochial agents always guarantee their availability, was a situation which perhaps could not fail to have theological implications. The parishioners of Denton in Kent confessed in 1511 that they 'cannot tell whither to resort' when their rector was missing from the parish.[60] Thirty years later the people of Black Notley in Essex were similarly perplexed: 'we know not where to seek the priest when need is, in time of God's visitation'.[61] In most places it seems likely that the cure was adequately served, but where it was not, the thought may have occurred to some disgruntled laypeople that a sacramental ministry which failed to minister sacraments was in many ways worse than useless.

THE DENIAL OF SACRAMENTS

Priests who were remiss in saying services, or, whether through absence or indolence, negligent in ministering the essential sacraments to their congregations, attracted understandable obloquy. But there were also instances in which priests consciously and deliberately refused to minister sacraments and sacramentals to laypeople, or to carry out some specified pastoral duty. Most commonly this involved a refusal to allow someone to 'take his rights', that is, to take communion, at Easter. Since most laypeople received the sacrament only annually, exclusion must have been deeply felt, and could lead to potent resentment against the priest. In some cases priests had good reasons for denying laypeople the sacrament. They were supposed, for example, to bar those who were excommunicate, or who were unconfessed and knew themselves to be in a state of sin. No one was to be admitted to receive the sacrament if he had a stomach upset, and was likely to vomit. The sacrament was also to be withheld from those who were 'out of charity' with their neighbours, who had quarrelled and refused to be reconciled.[62] In 1524 the vicar of Wakefield, Dr Knolles, a priest who seems to have shared the concern for his flock of his fictional successor, used the threat of withdrawing the sacrament in an attempt to reconcile the estranged James and Isabell Roke. James was urged

divers times and many, and specially of divers Good Fridays, for the love of Christ to have taken the said Isabell lovingly and [Knolles] put him in fear as

[60] *Kentish Visitations*, 140.   [61] Hale, *Precedents*, 126.
[62] Balliol College MS 354, fo. 180[r].

much as he could conveniently that he should not have the sacrament ministered
to him at Easter, except he would live after the laws of God, and take his wife to
him.[63]

By contemporary standards, the vicar's conduct here seems beyond reproach. More difficult was the position the vicar of Twickenham, Thomas
Stanard, found himself in at Easter that same year in attempting to
compose the quarrel of Roger Colyns and Gerard Stoker. The latter
proved unrepentant, declaring 'I shall never be in charity with him . . . as
long as I have these two eyes to see.' In the circumstances, Stanard had
no option but to refuse Stoker his 'rights'. Unperturbed, Stoker told the
vicar not to trouble himself 'for and you will give me my rights not,
another shall', and he proceeded to air his grievance at the house of
Trinitarian friars at Hounslow. The sequel was a rather frosty exchange
between Stanard and Friar Richard Richardson, the vicar claiming, rea-
sonably enough, that Stoker could 'have had his rights if he would', the
friar countering that it was not right to 'compel any man to take a man by
the hand or eat and drink with him, but if he will', and that the friars
were prepared to admit him to communion.[64] The case shows a priest
attempting to behave with rectitude, and using the sacrament as a means
of restoring, at least on a formal level, social harmony within the parish.
It also illustrates the limited moral authority of the incumbent in places
where the mendicants were able to offer an alternative ministry.

Very different were those priests who denied communion because they
themselves had quarrelled with parishioners and were unwilling to be
reconciled, or because parishioners had been remiss in paying tithes or
dues. In 1530, for example, Nicholas Tyting of Little Plumstead in Norfolk
was reduced to tears because 'the parson and he could not agree'. A
neighbour remonstrated with the rector, 'it is pity that he should go his
way without his rights', but the priest was intransigent.[65] In around 1540,
a group of poor cottagers of Tarrington in Herefordshire claimed that
because they had refused to depose on behalf of their vicar in a recent
lawsuit, he had refused to minister the sacrament to them at Easter.[66]
Equally reprehensible was the London curate who refused sacraments to
the sick unless he was paid in advance for his trouble.[67] Such behaviour
was strongly condemned by the moralists. *Dives and Pauper* remarked that
'if the curate will not bury the dead body nor suffer it to be buried, but

---

[63] J. Lister (ed.), *Yorkshire Star Chamber Proceedings*, YAS 70 (1927), iv. 40.
[64] GLRO, DL/C/207, fos. 284ʳ–287ᵛ.   [65] NCCD, no. 428.
[66] PRO, C. 1, 1093/11. See also C. 1, 1068/80.   [67] Hale, *Precedents*, 62.

in covenant that he shall have his bed, or his best cloth, or some other thing, he doth simony, although it be custom to pay that he asketh'.[68] The line between lawful recompense for labour and outright simony was inevitably a somewhat delicate one; the correct etiquette was for priests to carry out their duties first, then request the customary payment. Nevertheless, there clearly were priests who regarded the performance of their pastoral duties as a *quid pro quo* for financial satisfaction.[69] This type of behaviour prompted some citizens of London to complain in 1514 against the exorbitant fees that were being demanded for marriages, burials, and communion at Easter, and a parliamentary petition of the following year complained of parish priests refusing to bury corpses unless a mortuary were paid, and hoped that every priest would be put under financial penalties to 'administer the sacraments of holy church, when required, to every sick person in his parish'.[70] That a priest might refuse, or only conditionally perform these basic duties was, as we have seen, a cause of real and pressing concern. For most purposes, however, grasping priests probably found the withdrawal of Easter communion the most effective of the sanctions at their disposal. At Bridge in Kent in 1511 it was claimed that the vicar 'will give no rights to them that will not content his mind and when they do not agree with him after his pleasure'. In other words he had been refusing the sacrament on account of unpaid debts.[71] A similarly venal priest was Robert Shoter, curate of St Botolph Aldersgate in London, who in 1523 was in trouble with the authorities for refusing communion to those who would not pay what they owed.[72] In the 1530s a number of priests were reported for withholding the sacrament from those who would not pay the now illegal 'Peter's Pence'.[73] For sheer pathos it is difficult to match the complaint made against their curate by the churchwardens of Elsenham in Essex in 1540: 'On Easter day last past, a poor woman, called one Craknell kneeled down at God's board, to have received the sacrament and he passed by, and said that she owed him a groat, and until she had promised the payment of it, he would [not] minister.'[74] In cases like this, when priests were seen to exploit their

---

[68] *Dives and Pauper*, 262[r–v]. See also *Lyndwood*, 119.

[69] *Lincoln Visitations*, i. 61, 138; PRO, SP 1, 100/fo. 106[v]; C. 1, 900/34; Hale, *Precedents*, 64, 75.

[70] *LP* i. 3602; ii (1). 1315. The timing of this petition may have owed much to the recent death of Richard Hunne in the Bishop of London's prison.

[71] *Kentish Visitations*, 184.

[72] S. Brigden, 'Tithe Controversy in Reformation London', *JEH* 33 (1982), 290; 'Religion and Social Obligation in Early Sixteenth-Century London', *PP* 103 (1984), 80.

[73] PRO, C. 1, 827/1; STA. C. 2, 12/196.   [74] Hale, *Precedents*, 112.

privileged position as ministers of the sacraments for their own pecuniary gain, the reciprocity that was supposed to inform and meliorate the division between clergy and laity could come under intolerable strain. As with other forms of clerical misdemeanour, we have no way of knowing for certain how prevalent such practices were. Yet the grievance felt by laypeople who had been treated in this way was potent enough to be trumpeted in the 1530s by the political enemies of the Church's ascendancy. In 1531 a draft parliamentary bill drawn up by Christopher St German roundly attacked the pastoral failings of the parish clergy and insisted that 'no curate shall hereafter prohibit any of his parishioners of their houseling for no debt, duty, spiritual nor temporal'.[75] The following year, the Commons' *Supplication against the Ordinaries*, which was probably drafted by Thomas Cromwell in the interests of the Crown, complained that the prelates

daily do permit and suffer the parsons, vicars, curates, parish priests, and other spiritual persons having cure of souls within this your realm ministering, to exact and take of your humble and obedient subjects divers sums of money for the sacraments and sacramentals of Holy Church, sometimes denying the same without they be first paid the said sums of money.[76]

Priests who used the sacraments to blackmail their parishioners made a mockery of their claim to be pastors feeding spiritually the flock entrusted to their care. They were a minority, but visible enough to attract censure to the clergy as a whole.

HOSPITALITY AND CHARITY

Priests' responsibilities towards their flocks did not start and end with spiritual nourishment. Incumbents were supposed to provide, either themselves or by their farmers or deputies, 'hospitality' in their parishes,

---

[75] J. A. Guy, *Christopher St German on Chancery and Statute*, Selden Society, suppl. ser. (1985), 130.

[76] H. Gee and W. J. Hardy (eds.), *Documents Illustrative of English Church History* (1896), 148–9. For the genesis of the document see G. R. Elton, 'The Commons Supplication of 1532: Parliamentary manœuvres in the reign of Henry VIII', *EHR* 66 (1951); *Reform and Reformation: England 1509–1588* (1977), 150–6; J. P. Cooper, 'The Supplication against the Ordinaries Reconsidered', *EHR* 72 (1957); M. Kelly, 'The Submission of the Clergy', *TRHS*, 5th ser. 15 (1965); J. J. Scarisbrick, *Henry VIII* (1968), 297–300; S. E. Lehmberg, *The Reformation Parliament, 1529–1536* (Cambridge, 1970), 138–42; J. Guy, *The Public Career of Sir Thomas More* (New Haven, Conn., 1980), 186–90.

relieving the poor and providing help to strangers and wayfarers.[77] Traditionally, priests were supposed to devote about a third or a quarter of
their income to the relief of the poor, though some commentators were
more exacting in their requirements, the *Lyfe of Prestes* quoting with
approval St Bernard's dictum that 'the ecclesiastical goods be the patri-
mony and heritage of the poor people. And whatsoever the ministers of
the Church do take besides their simple and necessary food and apparel,
it is violently stolen from the poor people as cruel sacrilege'.[78] This was
a counsel of perfection that few priests could be expected to embrace, but
many did claim to take their duty of hospitality seriously. In 1525 the
clergy of Kent claimed that if they were forced to pay the sums demanded
of them for the 'Amicable Grant' it would mean the end of all hospitality.[79]
When a Sussex priest was indicted on an action of trespass for taking
some timber he believed to be his by right, he described his predicament
as being 'to the great let and impediment of hospitality to be kept in the
parish'.[80] In 1551 when Richard Halsall, the eponymous rector of Halsall
in Lancashire, claimed that lands were being wrongfully withheld from
him it was 'to the great decay of the poor hospitality and house-keeping
of your said orator'.[81] A priest giving himself a character reference in 1514
described how he had continually 'kept residence and hospitality in his
benefice'.[82] The fact that clerical inventories frequently describe large
amounts of bedding suggests that the duty was being undertaken.[83] If this
was so, it was probably no less than their parishioners expected. The
charge that priests were neglecting hospitality was by no means the most
common cause of dissatisfaction with the clergy, but it occurs frequently
enough to suggest that it was a matter of some importance to the laity.[84]
In 1535 a parishioner of Ash in Kent complained that the canons of
Wingham, to whom the benefice belonged, were denying the vicar the

---

[77] F. A. Gasquet, *Parish Life in Medieval England* (1906), 18; F. Heal, *Hospitality in Early Modern England* (Oxford, 1990), ch. 6.

[78] F. Heal, 'Economic Problems of the Clergy', in F. Heal and R. O'Day (eds.), *Church and Society in England, Henry VIII to James I* (1977), 100; P. Heath (ed.), *Medieval Clerical Accounts* (York, 1964), 14; *Dives and Pauper*, 258ʳ; *Lyfe of Prestes*, sig. F.iiiᵛ.

[79] G. W. Bernard, *War, Taxation and Rebellion in early Tudor England* (1986), 102.

[80] PRO, C. 1, 346/77.

[81] H. Fishwick (ed.), *Pleadings and Depositions in the Duchy Court of Lancaster*, Lancashire and Cheshire Record Society, 40 (1899), 127.

[82] W. Brown (ed.), *Yorkshire Star Chamber Proceedings*, YAS 41 (1909), i. 167.

[83] Heath, *Clerical Accounts*, 14.

[84] *Lincoln Visitations*, i. 62, 63, 131, 132, 133, 134; Moore, 'Proceedings of the Ecclesiastical Courts in the Archdeaconry of Leicester', 128; Dickens, 'Early Protestantism and the
Church in Northamptonshire', 32; Harper-Bill (ed.), 'Register of John Morton', 765; *Kentish Visitations*, 119; Salter, 'Visitation of Oxfordshire in 1540', 299, 300, 302.

tithes of wool and lambs he needed to maintain hospitality in the parish.[85] The following year, during the Pilgrimage of Grace, the commons of Westmorland petitioned Lord Darcy against the men holding benefices in the area. They hoped that 'they may put in their room others that would be glad to keep hospitality'.[86] Among the charges levelled at the vicar of Halifax in 1534 was that 'because the poor people knoweth him to be no alms man they never resort to his house'.[87] Hospitality was probably not purely a matter of almsgiving; in her recent study of early modern hospitality in England, Felicity Heal has suggested that complaints against the clergy reflect the expectation 'that a cleric would be an active participant in the social life of his community, offering on occasions a focus for general good neighbourliness and fellowship'.[88] A priest was expected to be liberal and open-handed, and episcopal visitation articles continued to insist on the duty of hospitality throughout this period.[89]

Parish clergy had another rather more intangible duty, that of promoting peace and concord in their parishes, of preventing the spread of rancour and ill will. This obligation was laid out in canon law, and reiterated in the injunctions of bishops.[90] Archbishop Lee of York required in 1538 that curates 'must always employ themselves to maintain charity and peace in Our Lord Jesu among their parishioners, and to avoid all rancour and dissension among them', a precept that was repeated by Bonner of London in 1542. It was greatly to be hoped that priests would never be, as Ridley put it, 'sowers of discord rather than charity among their parishioners'.[91] Yet given the vagaries of human nature, and the petty rancour which small communities can all too easily engender, there were inevitably some such. In 1511 the parishioners of Littlebourne in Kent passed the revealing comment on their pastor that 'the vicar sometimes is malicious and looketh on his neighbours with a grim and sour countenance, whereas they think him, God knoweth, no hurt'.[92] The vicar of Broadwell in Oxfordshire was reported in 1519 not to bear himself well towards his parishioners, while the parson of Down St Mary in Devon was said to have 'sown infamy grudge and displeasure' among his flock.[93] A Kentish chantry priest at Reculver was seen to 'sow discord between the vicar and his parishioners' in 1511; the rector of

---

[85] M. L. Zell, 'The Personnel of the Clergy in Kent in the Reformation Period', *EHR* 89 (1974), 521.   [86] *LP* xi. 1080.
[87] PRO, C. 1, 827/1.   [88] Heal, *Hospitality in Early Modern England*, 254.
[89] *Visitation Articles*, ii. 10, 106, 121, 180, 305.   [90] *Lyndwood*, 28.
[91] *Visitation Articles*, ii. 51, 85, 231.   [92] *Kentish Visitations*, 180.
[93] *Lincoln Visitations*, i. 134; PRO, C. 1, 900/34.

Charlton was 'full of malice and ready to fight' when his parishioners wished to discuss with him the upkeep of lights in the church.[94]

Quarrels between priests and their parishioners all too frequently ended up in the courts, particularly where tithes and dues were concerned. Clerical moralists like Melton and Colet hoped that priests would not be quarrelsome and would refrain from vexatious litigation.[95] It was perhaps unrealistic to expect incumbents never to resort to law to protect their financial rights, and it would be unduly pessimistic to suppose that every tithe dispute permanently poisoned relations within a parish. None the less, it ill befitted a pastor to be constantly taking members of his flock to court, and the behaviour of some priests was notorious, even by the standards of a litigious age. The aged vicar of Townstal in Devon, Simon Rede, was described as 'a man of most trouble and unquietness' who 'hath scantly consumed one year in quietness, but in continual suit with some one man or other'.[96] Henry Tankard, the rector of Barfreston in Kent, was said by his parishioners to be 'very malicious among us', and to have made unaccustomed and exorbitant demands for tithe which he would not settle peacefully 'but of malice purchased a citation against five of us and would not release us until we agreed with him'.[97] The vicar of Denton in Oxfordshire was regarded as 'a common maintainer and broker of quarrels'; the rector of Cotton in Suffolk as 'none charitable man' for his tenacity in pursuing tithe claims through the courts.[98] The lay ideal was of a priest who would endeavour to the utmost to deal charitably with his parishioners, who resembled Chaucer's poor parson in his reluctance to 'curse for his tithes'.[99] The ideal was not unattainable, but the overt careerism of some incumbents, and the welter of fiscal obligations which underpinned the social organization of the parish, made it all too often fleeting and intangible.

THE MODEL PASTOR

In many ways the priest's role in the cure of souls changed little during this period. In 1560 as in 1500 priests were expected to baptize, marry, and bury their parishioners, to visit the sick and offer hospitality to the

[94] *Kentish Visitations*, 78, 119.
[95] W. Melton, *Sermo exhortatorius cancellarii Eboracensis* (*c.*1510), sig. A.iv[r]; Lupton, *Life of Colet*, 73–4.   [96] PRO, STA. C. 3, 3/81.
[97] *Kentish Visitations*, 47.   [98] PRO, C. 1, 746/36; STA. C. 2, 29/78.
[99] G. Chaucer, *The Canterbury Tales*, ed. N. F. Blake (1980), 51.

poor, to minister to their congregation the sacrament of holy communion. But within the apparent continuity a number of shifts of emphasis had occurred. The authorities had come to place a much greater stress on the role of preaching in the cure of souls, a change for which not all laypeople may have been prepared. Conversely, under Edward the role of sacraments and sacramentals was downgraded. Admittedly, laypeople were now urged to receive the sacrament of the eucharist more frequently, though the precise nature of what they were receiving remained somewhat vague. In general, however, it is fair to suggest that laypeople were less dependent on the ministrations of a priest than hitherto. Lay men and women who had knelt before a priest to receive the imposition of ashes on Ash Wednesday, or had knelt and kissed the priest's hand at the reception of holy bread each Sunday after mass, were from 1548 no longer required, or able, to do so.[100] Priests might still be encouraged to visit the sick, but this was no longer a pressing soteriological necessity. Final confession, previously imperative, was in Edward's reign no more than a luxury permitted to those whose conscience demanded it, and an increasing number of English men and women were coming to place their trust 'in the merits of Christ's passion alone'.[101] Extreme unction, the anointing with oil, was no longer a sacrament, and had become similarly optional 'if the sick person desire to be anointed'. Bishop Hooper was insistent that the curates of his diocese should not 'give any reverence to the oil, or else persuade or teach any man to put any trust in the oil, or use it as they did before time under the pope'.[102] It is probable that the practice, like deathbed confession, suffered a significant decline during Edward's reign. The reduced demand for these rites seems the likeliest explanation for the decline in the number of testators wishing clerics to be present and witness their wills.[103] Taken all in all, however, the element of continuity is probably more important than the element of change so far as the pastoral role of the priest is concerned. Lay congregations continued to expect diligence, continence, and sobriety in their pastors, as well as a calm and eirenical disposition, and the evidence of episcopal visitations in Elizabeth's reign shows, unsurprisingly, that absenteeism, incontinence, and irregularity of services continued to excite disquiet.[104]

[100] *Visitation Articles*, ii. 184–5.
[101] This or a similar formula was beginning to appear more frequently in will preambles in the 1550s.   [102] *Visitation Articles*, ii. 195, 303–4.
[103] This fell from over 70% in the Henrician period to around half in the reign of Edward.
[104] See e.g. C. J. Kitching (ed.), *The Royal Visitation of 1559*, SS 187 (1975); J. S. Purvis (ed.), *Tudor Parish Documents of the Diocese of York* (Cambridge, 1948), 15–34.

It would be wrong, however, to close this chapter suggesting that the attitude of laypeople towards their pastors never veered from the twin poles of defeated expectation and bare satisfaction. The early sixteenth-century English parish clergy may not have produced any saints, but some among them seem to have been effective and caring pastors who elicited respect and affection from their flock. Occasionally, the clerical beneficiary of a bequest is described as 'curate of my soul', an expression which goes beyond the conventional or formulaic.[105] Sometimes good pastoral care was explicitly rewarded. In 1513 Richard Aylond of Tenterden in Kent left 10s. to Sir William, the parish priest, in recompense 'for his labour'.[106] In 1540 William Warner, an alderman of Rochester, left the same sum to 'the vicar of St Nicholas, my curate, for his labour and pain taking divers ways with me whilst I was sick'.[107] Similar bequests were made by the Londoner, Robert Roff, and the Yorkshireman, Thomas Wastyll, in 1543.[108] It was even said of one Oxfordshire vicar in 1520 that he was accustomed to visit the sick in other parishes as if they were his own parishioners.[109] It is significant that the main clerical beneficiaries of lay wills tended to be the unbeneficed and resident curates, the men who actually lived and worked in the parishes, rather than the incumbents.[110] The recorded payment of 8d. by the churchwardens of Ludlow in 1547 to a priest for 'taking pain for us this year' shows that good service did not always pass unrecognized.[111] A dutiful curate, and there is no reason to believe that the majority were not dutiful, might have been held in considerable regard by his parishioners, or at least have elicited the kind of laconic approbation manifested by one Yorkshire parish in 1510: 'And for the parish priest and clerk, we find with them no fault, so they do their service at due times.'[112]

---

[105] *Test. Ebor.* v. 175; I. Darlington (ed.), *London Consistory Court Wills, 1492–1547*, LoRS 3 (1967), 69; F. W. Weaver, ed., *Somerset Medieval Wills, 1501–1530*, SRS 19 (1903), 11.

[106] PRO, PCC, Prob. 11, 8 Holder.   [107] PRO, PCC, Prob. 11, 31 Alenger.

[108] Darlington (ed.), *London Consistory Court Wills*, 121; G. D. Lumb (ed.), *Testamenta Leodiensia*, Thoresby Society, 19 (1911–13), 96.

[109] *Lincoln Visitations*, i. 103. The motive here may, of course, have been a disreputable one, such as to solicit bequests, but there is no suggestion of this in the source, which reflects rather the proprietorial attitude of his own parishioners.

[110] L. M. Stevens Benham, 'The Durham Clergy, 1494–1540: A Study of Continuity and Mediocrity among the Unbeneficed', in D. Marcombe (ed.), *The Last Principality: Politics, Religion and Society in the Bishopric of Durham, 1494–1660* (Nottingham, 1987), 28; D. Jones, *The Church in Chester 1300–1540*, ChS (1957), 35.

[111] T. Wright (ed.), *Churchwardens' Accounts of the Town of Ludlow in Shropshire from 1540 to the End of the Reign of Queen Elizabeth*, CS 102 (1869), 31.

[112] Raine (ed.), *Fabric Rolls of York Minster*, 266.

7

The Priest as Neighbour

FAMILY AND BELONGING

Lay attitudes towards priests were not formed in a vacuum, nor for the most part in the rarified atmosphere of theological speculation. In each of England's 9,000 or so parishes, priests and laity lived and worked in close proximity. Priests could be neighbours, kinsmen, employers, or servants as well as spiritual pastors, and the manner of their participation in the life of the community qualified and informed the attitude taken to them by their parishioners. The priest was, in theory, a man set apart, a member of a distinct and superior order in society, yet in practice, the priests who actually served the parishes were enmeshed in a complex nexus of social relations.

During his earthly ministry Christ transferred the description 'mother and brothers' to His followers, but the early sixteenth-century parish clergy seem to have been as subject to the natural ties of kindred and affinity as any of their contemporaries. Clerical wills suggest that many remained in close touch with their families; priests were more likely to bequeath their goods to lay relatives than to fellow clerics, and many did not hesitate to involve themselves in the secular disputes of their kinsmen.[1] Two priests who took part in a violent dispute over pasture rights between the Herefordshire farmers Richard Browne and Richard Smith were described by the former as 'kin and allies to the said Richard Smith and his wife'.[2] It was not uncommon in this period to find the relatives of priests, particularly widowed mothers, residing with them in the rectory or vicarage.[3] In 1533 the rector of Layer Breton in Essex brought his mother down from her home in Nottinghamshire so that 'she might be aided comfortably and secured in her great age'.[4] Of course, proximity to

---

[1] PRO, STA. C. 2, 31/155; STA. C. 2, 33/1; STA. C. 2, 29/149; Req. 2, 10/251; W. Brown (ed.), *Yorkshire Star Chamber Proceedings*, YAS 41 (1909), 31.

[2] PRO, STA. C. 2, 30/114.

[3] *Lincoln Visitations*, i. 46, 68, 72, 73, 74, 76, 79, 80, 82, 85, 86, 126, 138.

[4] PRO, STA. C. 2, 16/37.

one's relatives was not always an entirely unmixed blessing. A late fifteenth-century vicar of Wadhurst in Sussex must have regretted persuading the churchwardens to accept his cousin as parish clerk when the latter embezzled some of the parish's books and vestments.[5] In 1537 a quarrel between Sir John Aleyn and his brother Richard over the ownership of certain lands in North Kilworth in Leicestershire led to an unseemly brawl between them in a tavern.[6] For most priests, however, the sense of family remained strong and there were some incumbents who owed their benefices to the fact that they had been appointed by lay relatives; these had sometimes bought the right of 'next presentation' specifically for this purpose.[7] Family ties reflected and reinforced the inveterate localism of the parish clergy. Some priests, particularly the unbeneficed, may have had to move parishes relatively frequently in search of an adequate stipend, but such mobility was usually within the confines of the diocese, and many pre-Reformation priests were overtly local figures, serving in the areas where they had grown up.[8] Prophets may sometimes be despised in their own country, but the parish clergy of this period seem to have felt more comfortable there. In around 1520 the new vicar of Oswestry in Shropshire was reportedly uneasy at his having 'small or in manner none acquaintance in the said parish'.[9] A priest who found himself in trouble in London in 1526 claimed that he would be unable to get a fair trial, as he was 'but a stranger within the said city'.[10] An even keener sense of persecution pervades the complaint of George Wellflett, rector of Chipping in Lancashire, in 1545. Wellflett insisted that a group of laymen 'being heads of the parish, secretly counsel the rest of the parishioners . . .

[5] C. T. Martin (ed.), 'Clerical Life in the Fifteenth Century as Illustrated by Proceedings of the Court of Chancery', *Archaeologia*, 60 (1907), 367.

[6] PRO, STA. C. 2, 1/82–3, 90–1.

[7] Barratt, 'The Condition of the Parish Clergy between the Reformation and 1660, with Special Reference to the Dioceses of Oxford, Worcester and Gloucester', University of Oxford D.Phil. thesis (1949), 375, 387; C. Haigh, *Reformation and Resistance in Tudor Lancashire* (Cambridge, 1975), 25.

[8] M. L. Zell, 'The Personnel of the Clergy in Kent in the Reformation Period', *EHR* 89 (1974), 519; 'Economic Problems of the Parochial Clergy in the Sixteenth Century', in R. O'Day and F. Heal (eds.), *Princes and Paupers in the English Church, 1500–1800* (Leicester, 1981), 24–5; D. Jones, *The Church in Chester*, 26; Haigh, *Reformation and Resistance in Tudor Lancashire, 1300–1540* (1975), 40, 84; D. M. Owen, *Church and Society in Medieval Lincolnshire* (Lincoln, 1971), 132; J. J. Scarisbrick, *The Reformation and the English People* (Oxford, 1984), 44; L. M. Stevens Benham, 'The Durham Clergy, 1494–1540', in D. Marcombe (ed.), *The Last Principality* (Nottingham, 1987); 56; A. Garrity, 'The Parish Clergy in the Deanery of Holderness, 1475–1550', University of York MA thesis (1981), 26–8.　　　　　　　　　　　　　　　　　　　　　[9] PRO, STA. C. 2, 24/359.

[10] PRO, C. 1, 469/54.

to stay their tithe corn and all their dues to the church, intending by such means to drive [me], being a stranger, out of [the] said parish'.[11]

Suspicion of outsiders was a characteristic feature of English society in this as in most periods, and the clergy were clearly not exempted from it on account of their office alone. Yet the question of how the customary deep-rootedness of the parish clergy within a particular locality may have shaped lay perceptions of their order is by no means a straightforward one. On the one hand, parishioners may have found little to object to when their curate shared with them a common mental outlook and breadth of acquaintance and interest. Yet a priest in this position was more readily drawn into local disputes, and the suspicion remains that if the parish was all too familiar with the history, habits, and heritage of its pastor, then the high clerical image of priesthood must sometimes have seemed remote or unreal. This difficulty could only have been accentuated by the great gradation of types to be found among the parish clergy, and the position that a status-conscious society accorded to each.

SOCIAL STANDING

The principle and practice of hierarchy permeated the pre-Reformation English Church. A great gulf separated the beneficed from the unbeneficed, and within each group wide variations of wealth and opportunity were evident. Leaving aside the really wealthy incumbents, who were all too often absentees, most rectors and vicars seem to have enjoyed an income which put them, in material terms, on a par with prosperous yeoman farmers.[12] Most of the stipendiary curates, by contrast, earned little more than an agricultural wage labourer. Their income had been fixed by statute in 1414 at £5 6s. 8d. per annum, and in the early sixteenth century few were receiving more than this.[13] The opportunity to inherit valuable goods, or to acquire small amounts of land, probably saved most priests from outright poverty, but outside the ranks of the beneficed few could be described as affluent, and their social status may have been consequently low.[14] One curate in Henrician Ipswich was known locally as 'Little Sir

---

[11] H. Fishwick (ed.), *Pleadings and Depositions in the Duchy Court of Lancaster*, Lancashire and Cheshire Record Society, 35 (1897), 211.

[12] F. W. Brooks, 'The Social Position of the Parson in the Sixteenth Century', *Journal of the British Archaeological Association*, 3rd ser., 10 (1945–7), 25–37; J. C. Cornwall, *Wealth and Society in Early Sixteenth-Century England* (1988), 92.

[13] Cornwall, ibid. 92–3, 133; Zell, 'Economic Problems of the Parochial Clergy', 26.

[14] J. Pound, 'Clerical Poverty in Early Sixteenth-Century England: Some East Anglian Evidence', *JEH* 37 (1986), 389–93; Cornwall, *Wealth and Society*, 92.

John', while a Shropshire chaplain was simply 'Black Sir John'.[15] Such sobriquets may well indicate affection rather than contempt, but a priest so-called could hardly have been regarded by many as a figure to be feared and revered.

The social standing of secular priests was in all probability dictated not merely by the amount of income they received, but by where that income came from. Rectors and vicars were supported in the main by the tithes paid, more or less grudgingly, by their parishioners, and if necessary they could enforce this right at law. The acquisition of a desirable benefice might require the backing of a lay patron, but once installed, a beneficed priest possessed effective financial independence. Among those who did not enjoy this enviable position, many were directly dependent on lay patronage, and could be hired and fired almost at will. This could not fail to introduce a discordant note into the oft-repeated injunction to the laity, to reverence the priest for his office's sake. The paradox is most evident in the case of private chaplains, references to which are frequent in the documentation of the period.[16] To Thomas More, the proliferation of private chaplains was to the great dishonour of priesthood: 'every mean man must have a priest in his house to wait upon his wife, which no man almost lacketh now, to the contempt of priesthood in as vile office as his horse keeper.'[17] More perhaps exaggerated the number of private chaplains, but he was right about their lowly social status. In 1549 Thomas Dutton of Thormanton in Gloucestershire complained that his house had been set on fire at the orders of Thomas Parker by 'Sir William his chaplain and other his household servants'.[18] In 1542, the will of Christopher Pykering of Cleasby in North Yorkshire included a bequest to 'Sir James Edwarde, my servant', and among the eleven priests working in the household of the Percy Earl of Northumberland in the early sixteenth century was 'a chaplain for my Lord's eldest son, to wait upon him daily'.[19] The character in Stendhal's *Scarlet and Black* who regarded priests as 'a species of upper manservant necessary to her salvation' was not so far removed from the mentality of some of the laity of Henrician England. Unusually, Christopher St German agreed with More on this point, arguing that the prevalence of private chaplains did little good for

---

[15] D. MacCulloch, *Suffolk and the Tudors* (Oxford, 1986), 175; PRO, STA. C. 2, 5/130.
[16] See e.g. PRO, STA. C. 2, 28/105; STA. C. 2, 31/60; STA. C. 2, 31/120; STA. C. 2, 9/137; Req. 2, 3/293; Req. 2, 6/101.   [17] More, *Dialogue*, 301.
[18] PRO, STA. C. 3, 5/16.
[19] J. Raine (ed.), *Wills and Inventories from the Registry of the Archdeaconry of Richmond*, SS 26 (1835), 35; E. L. Cutts, *Scenes and Characters of the Middle Ages*, 6th edn. (1926), 208.

the estimation of priesthood since their masters would command them 'to go on hunting, hawking, and such other vain disports. And some would let them lie among other lay servants, where they could neither use prayer nor contemplation.'[20]

Domestic chaplains were only one among a variety of types of priest directly dependent upon the patronage of the laity. Chantry priests and temporary stipendiaries were appointed by executors to sing for the souls of the departed, and could usually be removed for misconduct. The almost ubiquitous lay fraternities of pre-Reformation England often employed their own chaplains, and these depended upon the goodwill of the fraternity's members to retain their posts.[21] Moreover, in many places curates and parish chaplains were paid not by the incumbent, but retained directly by the parish.[22] In the London parish of St Mary at Hill, a priest performed his duties 'by the commandment of the parish'.[23] Even where the stipend of the curate was paid by the incumbent, the churchwardens would sometimes pay him for extra services, and it was not uncommon for parishes to hire priests on an *ad hoc* basis to help out at busy times of the year, such as Christmas, Easter, and the feast of Corpus Christi.[24] In

---

[20] C. St German, *A Treatise concernynge the division betwene the spiritualtie and temporaltie*, in *CW* 9 (1979), 187.

[21] Scarisbrick, *Reformation and the English People*, 22; C. M. Barron, 'The Parish Fraternities of Medieval London', in C. M. Barron and C. Harper-Bill (eds.), *The Church in Pre-Reformation Society* (Woodbridge, 1985), 33–4; H. F. Westlake, *The Parish Gilds of Medieval England* (1919), 44–5.

[22] W. T. Mellows (ed.), *Peterborough Local Administration: Parochial Government before the Reformation*, Northamptonshire Record Society, 9 (1937), 183; H. F. Swayne (ed.), *Churchwardens' Accounts of S. Edmund and S. Thomas Sarum, 1443–1702*, Wiltshire Record Society (1896), 277; 'Churchwardens' Accounts of the Parish of St Margaret Pattens, London', *The Sacristy*, 1 (1871), 261; J. Amphlett (ed.), *The Churchwardens' Accounts of St Michael's in Bedwardine, Worcester, 1539–1603*, Worcestershire Historical Society (1896), 31; A. S. Gatty (ed.), 'Churchwardens' Accounts, 1520–1546', in *Registers of Ecclesfield Parish Church, Yorkshire* (1878), 154; C. Kerry, *A History of the Municipal Church of St Lawrence, Reading* (Reading, 1883), 223; T. North (ed.), *The Accounts of the Churchwardens of St Martin's, Leicester, 1489–1844* (Leicester, 1884), 59; W. Holland and J. J. Raven (eds.), *Cratfield Parish Papers* (1895), 51; H. B. Walters (ed.), 'The Churchwardens' Accounts of the Parish of Worfield, 1500–1572', *Shropshire Archaeological and Natural History Society*, 9 (1909), 115; J. E. Foster (ed.), *Churchwardens' Accounts of St Mary the Great, Cambridge, 1504–1635*, CAS 35 (1905), 125–6; E. Hobhouse (ed.), *Churchwardens' Accounts of Croscombe, Pilton, Yatton, Tintinhull, Morebath, and St Michael's, Bath, 1349–1560*, SRS 4 (1890), 130; D. MacCulloch and J. Blatchly, 'Pastoral Provision in the Parishes of Tudor Ipswich', *SCJ* 22 (1991), 458.

[23] H. Littlehales (ed.), *The Medieval Records of a London City Church (St Mary at Hill), 1420–1559*, EETS 125 (1904), 347.

[24] A. Hanham (ed.), *Churchwardens' Accounts of Ashburton, 1479–1580*, Devon and Cornwall Record Society, NS 15 (1970), xvi; J. Maclean, 'Notes on the Accounts of the Procurators, or Churchwardens, of the Parish of St Ewen's, Bristol', *Transactions of the Bristol and Gloucestershire Archaeological Society*, 15 (1840), 28; 'Ancient Churchwardens' Accounts of a City Parish', *British Magazine and Monthly Register*, 33 (1848), 666.

some places the parish even subsidized the rector's income.[25] Priests could also be recompensed for more mundane services than their sacred duty of saying mass. These included playing or mending the church's organ, repairing the church clock, even washing the surplices.[26] Of course, control of the purse strings did not necessarily breed contempt. Sometimes parishes were sufficiently happy with their hired priests to make gifts to them. In 1545, for example, the churchwardens of Ludlow decided that Sir Richard Cupper should have a pair of gloves 'in a reward'.[27] At St Michael's, Spurriergate, York, in 1523, the parishioners agreed that Sir Thomas Werell could have his chamber rent-free 'for as long as he remaineth with us, and serveth Almighty God and doth us service'.[28] It would be facile to suggest that the accountability of many priests to corporate or individual lay employers inevitably undermined respect for the priesthood; it was precisely because priestly functions were valued so highly that such priests could find employment. None the less, the financial dependency of so many of the clergy upon the laity must have discouraged lay subservience in practical matters, and promoted a strong expectation of value for money.

THE POLITY OF THE PARISH

Relations between priests and people within the parish should have been marked by charity, respect, and mutual service. At times, perhaps, the ideal did not seem unattainable. When the magnificent spire of Louth

[25] 'Ancient Churchwardens' Accounts', ibid., 34 (1848), 681; B. R. Master and E. Ralph (eds.), *The Church Book of St Ewen's, Bristol, 1454–1584*, Bristol and Gloucestershire Archaeological Society Records Section, 6 (1967), pp. xxxiii–iv; F. R. Mercer (ed.), *Churchwardens' Accounts at Betrysden 1515–1573*, Kent Archaeological Society Records Branch, 5 (1982), 92, 94; Amphlett (ed.), *St Michael's in Bedwardine*, 14, 16.

[26] 'Ancient Churchwardens' Accounts', 34, p. 175; Mellows (ed.), *Peterborough Local Administration*, 104; F. Ouvry (ed.), 'Extracts from the Churchwardens' Accounts of the Parish of Wing in the County of Buckingham', *Archaeologia*, 36 (1855), 227; J. L. Glasscock (ed.), *The Records of St Michael's Parish Church, Bishop's Stortford* (1882), 46; C. Drew (ed.), *Lambeth Churchwardens' Accounts 1504–1645*, Surrey Record Society, 40 (1940), 23; Kerry (ed.), *St Lawrence, Reading*, 223; F. Somers (ed.), *Halesowen Churchwardens' Accounts 1487–1582*, Worcestershire Historical Society, 40 (1957), 60; R. C. Dudding (ed.), *The First Churchwardens' Book of Louth, 1500–1524* (Oxford, 1941), 27; Littlehales (ed.), *St Mary at Hill*, 269; North (ed.), *St Martin's, Leicester*, 7, 32; C. Cotton (ed.), 'Churchwardens' Accounts of the Parish of St Andrew, Canterbury, 1485–1557', *AC* 33 (1918–19), 2, 7; Glasscock (ed.), *St Michael's, Bishop's Stortford*, 23.

[27] Wright (ed.), *Churchwardens' Accounts of Ludlow*, 21.

[28] BIHR, PR Y/MS 4, fo. 35ʳ. See also North (ed.), *St Martin's, Leicester*, 9; Hanham (ed.), *Ashburton*, 34; Dudding (ed.), *Louth*, 187.

parish church was completed in 1515 and the weathercock fitted on top, the churchwardens recorded the scene in a passage which has become justifiably well-known:

there being William Ayleby, parish priest, with many of his brother priests there present, hallowing the said weathercock and the stone that it stands upon, and so conveyed upon the said broch, and then the said priests singing *Te Deum Laudamus* with organs. And then the kirk wardens gart ring all the bells and caused all the people there being to have bread and ale. And all to the loving of God, Our Lady, and all saints.[29]

Yet this idyll was all too easily disrupted. Within three years the Louth churchwardens were recording their expenses for taking to trial at Lincoln a priest who had broken into the parish treasure chest and purloined the contents.[30]

These two incidents from Louth suggest something of the pride which the laity of early sixteenth-century England took in their local church and its possessions, a circumstance which has much bearing on the day-to-day relations of priests and their parishioners. An intense parochial loyalty found its visible embodiment in the parish churches, many of which, like Louth, were being handsomely rebuilt in the years preceding the Reformation.[31] It is instructive that the only large-scale popular protest against the Henrician Reformation, the northern rebellions of 1536–7, seem to have been provoked not by Henry's assumption of Supreme Headship of the Church, and denial of papal authority, but in large measure by disturbing rumours that parishes were to be amalgamated and church treasures confiscated.[32] The laity's concern for the well-being of the parish church was usually expressed by their elected representatives, the churchwardens, who raised the money for the upkeep and repair of the nave, and were quick to complain to the authorities if the incumbent failed in his canonical obligation to maintain the fabric of the chancel.[33]

---

[29] Dudding (ed.), ibid. 181.   [30] Ibid. 191.

[31] G. H. Cook, *The English Medieval Parish Church* (1954), 55–9; Scarisbrick, *Reformation and the English People*, 12–i5; R. Whiting, *The Blind Devotion of the People* (Cambridge, 1989), 83–94; S. Brigden, *London and the Reformation* (Oxford, 1989), 23; MacCulloch, *Suffolk and the Tudors*, 140.

[32] C. S. L. Davies, 'Popular Religion and the Pilgrimage of Grace', in A. Fletcher and J. Stevenson (eds.), *Order and Disorder in Early Modern England* (Cambridge, 1985), 71.

[33] F. W. Ragg (ed.), 'Fragment of Folio Manuscript of the Archdeaconry Courts of Buckinghamshire, 1491–1495', *Records of Buckinghamshire*, 11 (1919–24), 341–2; M. Bowker, *The Secular Clergy in the Diocese of Lincoln, 1485–1520* (Cambridge, 1968), 127–36, 180; *Kentish Visitations*, 23, 135, 145, 255; Hale, *Precedents*, 112; S. Lander, 'Church Courts and the Reformation in the Diocese of Chichester, 1500–1558', in R. O'Day and F. Heal (eds.),

At no point was the parish church regarded as the private fiefdom of the clergy; they were at best tenants, and the most cursory examination of lay wills from this period will establish that gifts to the parish church far outnumbered bequests to the parish clergy.

This proprietorial attitude extended to the contents of the church: the chalices, vestments, and liturgical books which were the property of the parish, not of the priests who used them. In 1502 a chantry priest of Waltham in Kent was reported to the archdeacon for his repeated failure to lock the church door, thus exposing the church's treasures to the danger of theft.[34] The parishioners' anxiety was understandable, since the value and number of such items was sometimes considerable. A list of church goods drawn up by the churchwardens of Long Melford, Suffolk, in 1527 included fourteen chasubles and copes, six full sets of vestments, thirteen chalices, and a host of miscellaneous eucharistic and liturgical items, the wardens taking care to note which of these were 'in the keeping' of the chantry priest or parish priest.[35] When priests mistreated valuable parish property, they invariably aroused resentment. The chaplains and cantarists of St Nicholas's church, Newcastle, were said in 1501 to be tearing the newly repaired vestments and albs; a Kent priest who 'dealeth not fairly with the vestments when he putteth them on' was similarly reported in 1511.[36] Even worse was the rector of Worminghall in Buckinghamshire, who through negligence allowed two vestments to catch fire in the church.[37] A number of priests showed a propensity to hold on to items of parish property that was matched only by the determination of their parishioners to disgorge them, though there is a plaintive note in the charge brought by the churchwardens of Staple in 1511 that Sir John Russell was withholding a chalice 'the which we cannot get by no means'.[38] Squabbles over the possession of surplices and chalices seem very far from the high spiritual drama of the English Reformation. Yet these were matters of supreme importance to many of the lay men and women of the

---

Continuity and Change (Leicester, 1976), 62–71; J. F. Fuggles, 'The Parish Clergy in the Archdeaconry of Leicester, 1520–1540', *Leicestershire Archaeological and Historical Society Transactions*, 46 (1970–1), 38; C. E. Woodruff (ed.), 'An Archidiaconal Visitation of 1502', *AC* 47 (1935), 27.

[34] Woodruff (ed.), ibid. 41.

[35] D. Dymond and C. Paine (eds.), *The Spoil of Melford Church: The Reformation in a Suffolk Parish* (Ipswich, 1989), 10 ff.

[36] J. Raine (ed.), *The Injunctions and other Ecclesiastical Proceedings of Richard Barnes, Bishop of Durham, 1575–1582*, SS 22 (1850), pp. xxiv–xxv; *Kentish Visitations*, 224.

[37] *Lincoln Visitations*, i. 49. See also ibid. 62.

[38] W. M. Palmer, 'Fifteenth Century Visitation Records of the Deanery of Wisbech', *CAS* 39 (1940), 73, 74; *Lincoln Visitations*, i. 41, 122, 132, 135; *Kentish Visitations*, 110, 182.

time, and they serve to remind us of the many contextual layers that have to be peeled away to reveal the essential dynamics of the relationship between priests and people.

The belief, deeply held if not always articulately expressed, that the obedience and deference due to the parson and his assistants should be subsumed in a higher responsibility to corporate religious life, was reinforced by a strong sense that local matters should be regulated by tradition and parochial custom, rather than by clerical fiat. Towards the end of the fifteenth century there was considerable disquiet in the parish of Wisborough Green in Sussex when it was feared that the vicar planned to 'bring new customs and constructions among them'.[39] When disputes arose between priests and their parishioners, whether over tithes, or over some alleged dereliction on the part of the former, the latter would frequently claim that the priest was disregarding long-established and laudable custom.[40] By its very nature, custom is seldom codified, and is usually open to generous interpretation. No doubt it was often marshalled by those whose motives might not bear close inspection. None the less, it is clear that in matters concerning the government and regulation of parish affairs, few considered the opinion of the parson as a court of final appeal. He might sometimes indeed, as Diarmaid MacCulloch has acutely observed, be regarded as 'a temporary intruder into the unchanging structure of village life'.[41]

In doctrinal matters, few laypeople would have presumed to question the authority of the incumbent. Yet the functioning of a late medieval parish involved a number of areas in which his interests and those of his leading parishioners could easily come into conflict. Disputes sometimes centred on the position of the parish clerk, a functionary whose duties involved helping the priest in the performance of the divine office, as well as a host of more mundane duties about the church.[42] Essentially, the parish clerk was the assistant of the priest serving the cure, and many parishes were quick to insist that the incumbent should contribute to his salary.[43]

---

[39] Martin (ed.), 'Clerical Life in the Fifteenth Century', 363–4.

[40] OCRO, Dioc. MSS d. 14, 7ʳ, 11ʳ, 21ʳ⁻ᵛ, 34ʳ⁻ᵛ, 46ʳ, 189ʳ; PRO, Req. 2, 11/95; Req. 2, 12/54; C. 1, 746/36; C. 1, 900/34; C. 1, 929/9; *Kentish Visitations*, 100, 102, 112, 282; J. Raine (ed.), *The Fabric Rolls of York Minster*, SS 35 (1858), 271.

[41] MacCulloch, *Suffolk and the Tudors*, 142–3.

[42] P. Heath, *The English Parish Clergy on the Eve of the Reformation* (1969), 19–20; F. A. Gasquet, *Parish Life in Medieval England* (1906), 112–17.

[43] J. E. Binney and F. W. Weaver (eds.), *The Accounts of the Wardens of the Parish of Morebath, Devon, 1520–1573* (Exeter, 1904), 33–4; *Kentish Visitations*, 156, 220; *Lincoln Visitations*, i. 127; Hale, *Precedents*, 122.

On the other hand, there was in several places a marked unwillingness to allow the clerk to become an *ex officio* priestly lackey. In one London parish in the late fifteenth century, it was noted that the clerk had been admitted without the consent of the rector, and the ordinances drawn up for the parish clerks of Faversham in 1506 make it clear that they were to be responsible directly to the churchwardens, rather than to the incumbent.[44] Among the charges brought in 1535 against the curate of Harwich, Sir Thomas Calthorp, was that 'he had commanded the parish clerk to be sworn unto him'.[45] There were sometimes good reasons for the parish to insist upon accountability in the parish clerk. In 1529 the clerk of Beeston in Norfolk had become 'a man of ill-repute', and the parishioners wished to have him expelled from his post. The rector, however, informed them that 'I will keep him still in his office, and ask you no leave'.[46] It was this kind of petty yet imperious clericalism that cut most firmly against the assumptions of the respectable laity who expected to exercise a powerful, if not decisive say in the management of parochial affairs.

If the parish clerk often represented the anthropomorphic aspect of the contested no man's land between the claims of parson and churchwardens, its physical dimension was frequently found within the environs of the parish church. A regular source of lay disquiet was that rectors and vicars were pasturing beasts in the churchyard, and that these were fouling the place.[47] Despite the lament of the churchwardens of Coln Wake in Essex in 1540, that their churchyard was 'more like a pasture than a hallowed place', lay resentment was perhaps not in most cases directed against the quasi-sacrilege of the priest's husbandry.[48] Churchyards were, after all, used by the laity in this period for a variety of secular and communal purposes.[49] Rather, it may have been prompted by the recognition that, as the resting place of departed friends and kinsfolk, the churchyard was in a special sense the property of the community, and that the priest did wrong to attempt to arrogate it to his own private use.

---

[44] Hale, ibid. 6; F. F. Giraud (ed.), 'On the Parish Clerks and Sexton of Faversham, AD 1506–1593', *AC* 20 (1893), 206. [45] *LP* ix. 1059.

[46] *NCCD*, no. 396.

[47] *Lincoln Visitations*, i. 122, 126, 133, 134, 138; ii. 11; Moore, 'Proceedings of the Ecclesiastical Courts in the Archdeaconry of Leicester', 139, 193; W. S. Simpson (ed.), *Visitations of Churches Belonging to St Paul's Cathedral in 1297 and 1458*, CS NS 55 (1895), 105; *Kentish Visitations*, 176; A. G. Dickens, 'Early Protestantism and the Church in Northamptonshire', *Northamptonshire PP*, 8 (1983–4), 30; PRO, C. 1, 802/13; W. O. Ault, 'The Village Church and the Village Community in Medieval England', *Speculum*, 45 (1970), 205. [48] Hale, *Precedents*, 114.

[49] Cook, *English Medieval Parish Church*, 32–4; J. Bossy, *Christianity in the West, 1400–1700* (Oxford, 1985), 33; Raine (ed.), *Fabric Rolls of York Minster*, 256, 271.

This collision of interest often embraced the trees growing in the churchyard. The legal position here was delicate: any dead wood in the churchyard could be claimed by the rector, and he could fell living trees if the wood was to be used to repair the chancel. Parishioners were not entitled to such wood for the repair of the nave without the rector's permission, and sentence of excommunication could be passed on any who 'hew down violently . . . any trees in churchyard or in chapelyard'.[50] None the less, when the parish priest of Sutton-in-Ashfield in Nottinghamshire felled an ash tree growing in the churchyard, it was the parishioners, not the incumbent, who demanded to know by what authority he had acted.[51] At Croscombe in Somerset in around 1536, the rector and churchwardens both laid claim to the box tree in the churchyard. Significantly, it was the parish clerk, acting on the orders of the latter, who felled the tree, the boughs being used for palms on Palm Sunday, and the trunk being appropriated 'for the church use'. When the rector, William Bowreman, demanded its return, the churchwarden John Mydell replied defiantly that 'he was but a servant unto the parish, desiring the parson to ask it of the parish'.[52] Similar events took place at Church Langton in Leicestershire, where an impromptu parish meeting, summoned by the ringing of the church bells, led to the felling of fourteen or fifteen ash trees in the churchyard for the purpose of repairing the church roof. The parishioners, although perhaps mistaken, were firm in their belief that this 'was and is lawful for them to do'.[53] In such circumstances the laity manifested a robust independence of mind that was as far from the docility of a notional 'age of faith' as it was from the surly antisacramentalism of the Lollards. When, in 1538, the people of Shirland in Derbyshire were instructed by the rector's servant not to ring the bells on the now-abrogate feast-day of St Mark, a parishioner retorted that 'the parish might ring their bells, and ask the parson no leave'.[54]

Overt defiance of the incumbent's authority was, however, more probably exceptional than normative. As long as the priest did not behave in a grossly negligent or dictatorial way, the leading parishioners were usually happy to allow him a significant role in parish affairs. Early sixteenth-century churchwardens' accounts reveal rectors and vicars undertaking a

[50] Ault, 'Village Church and Village Community', 206; A. Brandeis (ed.), *Jacob's Well*, EETS 115 (1900), 26.					[51] PRO, STA. C. 2, 30/88.

[52] PRO, STA. C. 2, 18/301; G. Bradford (ed.), *Proceedings in the Court of Star Chamber in the Reigns of Henry VII and Henry VIII*, SRS 27 (1911), 232–9.

[53] PRO, STA. C. 2, 34/31. See also PRO, Req. 2, 17/85; STA. C. 3, 5/67; STA. C. 3, 5/81; R. S. Arrowsmith, *The Prelude to the Reformation* (1923), 52.

[54] PRO, STA. C. 2, 26/194.

variety of mundane yet important administrative tasks: disbursing church debts, overseeing the payment of alms, supervising workmen in the church, or writing the accounts themselves.[55] Generally, the rector's status as chief parishioner, or at least of *primus inter pares* seems to have been accepted. At St Andrew's, Canterbury, the final account was always made 'in the presence of Master Parson and the parishioners'.[56] At Stanford this was done 'before Sir John Fawkener and other of the honestest of the parish'.[57] At St Mary at Hill in London, the guild wardens reported to 'the right worshipful Mr Percy, parson of the said church, and other the worshipful of the parish'.[58]

Where there was any action to be taken which affected the interests of the whole community, priests might be expected to take a lead. When the parishioners of Meppershall in Bedfordshire found that a right of way had been blocked, it was Sir Humphrey Bynoe who made complaint to the Council 'in the name of all the inhabitants of the said town'.[59] If clerical initiative was to the forefront in the pursuit of minor local grievances, it is equally evident in protests of much greater moment, the popular rebellions which punctuate the history of early and mid-Tudor England. In the northern disturbances of 1536–7, the parish clergy appear to have played a vital role in fomenting and organizing revolt. The Lincolnshire rising of October 1536 was precipitated by a sermon from Thomas Kendall, vicar of Louth, claiming that the Church was in danger.[60] As the depositions of those who took part in the rising show, priests were deeply involved; spreading inflammatory rumours, providing food and money, urging resistance openly (and no doubt in confession as well), even summoning the commons by ringing church bells. Henry's vindictiveness towards the clerical rebels mirrored their importance in the revolt: none of those condemned to death were subsequently spared.[61] In

[55] Amphlett (ed.), *St Michael's in Bedwardine*, 10; North (ed.), *St Martin's, Leicester*, 51; J. M. Cowper (ed.), 'Churchwardens' Accounts of St Dunstan, Canterbury, 1484–1580', *AC* 17 (1887), 85, 92; Drew (ed.), *Lambeth Churchwardens' Accounts*, 16; Walters (ed.), 'Churchwardens' Accounts of Worfield', 113; Foster (ed.), *St Mary the Great, Cambridge*, 96; T. Wright (ed.), *Churchwardens' Accounts of the Town of Ludlow in Shropshire*, CS 102 (1869), 33; Binney and Weaver (eds.), *Accounts of Morebath*, 1.

[56] Cotton (ed.), 'St Andrew, Canterbury', 27.

[57] W. Haines (ed.), 'Stanford Churchwardens' Accounts (1552–1602)', *The Antiquary*, 98/17 (1888), 72. [58] Littlehales (ed.), *St Mary at Hill*, 325.

[59] PRO, STA. C. 2, 28/63. For similar examples, see PRO, STA. C. 2, 8/190–2; STA. C. 2 14/60; STA. C. 2, 20/356.

[60] Davies, 'Popular Religion and the Pilgrimage of Grace', 71.

[61] M. Bowker, 'Lincolnshire 1536: Heresy, Schism or Religious Discontent', in D. Baker (ed.), *SCH* 9 (Cambridge, 1972); M. Bowker, *The Henrician Reformation* (Cambridge, 1981), 152–6.

the Pilgrimage of Grace itself, priests were equally notable for their participation.[62] When, thirteen years later, disquiet at the direction of the government's religious policy once again spilled over in the South-Western 'Prayer Book' Rebellion, local priests were once again to the fore. The rebels' articles were almost certainly drawn up by the clergy, and in the aftermath of the revolt at least eight priests were executed.[63] The abortive rising that took place in Oxfordshire and Buckinghamshire at the same time was believed by Somerset to be 'by instigation of sundry priests . . . for these matters of religion'. After its suppression, four priests were put to death.[64] The parish clergy's notable lack of prominence in Ket's Rebellion should probably not be ascribed to its being an 'economic' rather than a 'religious' protest; no Tudor rebellion was entirely monocausal. More probably, the advance of Protestantism in East Anglia had done much to upset the delicate balance of expectation within the parishes, and the failure of the local clergy to provide a proper preaching ministry was a prominent feature of the rebels' demands.[65]

The idea that the conservative popular rebellions of 1536–7 and 1549 reveal an ignorant peasantry being manipulated by priests for their own ends is, however, almost certainly a false one. At Sampford Courtenay, epicentre of the revolt in Devon in 1549, the trouble began as a lay protest against clerical conformity in the use of the new Prayer Book.[66] During the Pilgrimage of Grace, tensions between lay and clerical participants surfaced at several points. At Kendal at the start of 1537, groups of laymen threatened the priest with a ducking if he refused to pray publically for the Pope, and at Carlisle, the reluctance of two prominent clerics to negotiate with the town authorities on behalf of the rebels led to the expression of the trenchant opinion that 'things would never be well until they had stricken off all the priests' heads'. Both incidents, as C. S. L. Davies has persuasively argued, point to a deep-seated fear of abandonment by the clergy in the tense atmosphere of the revolt.[67] The image of dutiful parishioners marshalled by zealous priests in defence of the old faith should probably be revised or discarded. None the less, it remains

---

[62] Davies, 'Popular Religion and the Pilgrimage of Grace', 69–70; C. Haigh, 'Anticlericalism and the English Reformation', in C. Haigh (ed.), *The English Reformation Revised* (Cambridge, 1987), 70; S. Brigden, 'The Northern Clergy in the Pilgrimage of Grace', University of Manchester BA thesis (1973).

[63] J. Cornwall, *The Revolt of the Peasantry, 1549* (1977), 201.

[64] A. Vere Woodman, 'The Buckinghamshire and Oxfordshire Rising of 1549', *Oxoniensia*, 22 (1957), 79, 81. [65] A. Fletcher, *Tudor Rebellions*, 3rd edn. (1983), 121–2.

[66] F. Rose-Troup, *The Western Rebellion of 1549* (1913), 131–4.

[67] Davies, 'Popular Religion and the Pilgrimage of Grace', 75, 84–5.

clear that, whatever the tensions engendered by clerical claims to an authority that could be questionable in both institutional and personal terms, in times of crisis the people wanted their priests to the fore, and expected them to provide a practical and moral leadership they were sometimes rather reluctant to assume.

PATTERNS OF NEIGHBOURLINESS

Priests stood *vis-à-vis* their parishioners as dispensers of grace in the sacraments, and as wielders of an accepted, if sometimes ill-defined, authority within the institutional life of the parish. That they also encountered lay men and women as individuals in a multitude of prosaic circumstances seems startlingly self-evident, but calls for comment none the less. The documentary sources on which the historian relies speak largely of disputes and disagreements between priests and their parishioners, but we have no reason to suppose this to have been normative, and a Henrician vicar of Dorking's reference to 'divers discrete and honest men which were then come to visit [him] . . . in his sickness' reveals the neighbourly concern which may often have been felt by laypeople for their curates.[68]

Where such laudable feelings existed, priests could reciprocate by performing a variety of useful services for lay friends and neighbours. Valuable goods and documents were sometimes deposited with priests for safe-keeping, and it was common for priests to act as mutually acceptable arbitrators in disputes.[69] When, for example, the Londoner Richard Lye was charged with having defamed William Shawdford by calling him a 'cut-purse', both parties agreed to remove the case from the commissary court and accept the arbitration of their parish priest.[70] Even outside the confessional, priests might be called upon to address the personal problems of their parishioners. In 1535 the curate of Slaley in County Durham, John Adamson, was approached in the churchyard by Anthony Howde, who had promised to marry one Marion Martyn despite a precontract with Janet Armstrong which invalidated the proposal. The

---

[68] PRO, STA. C. 2, 33/13.

[69] Moore (ed.), 'Ecclesiastical Courts in the Archdeaconry of Leicester', 651; Ragg (ed.), 'Archdeaconry Courts of Buckingham', 38, 46, 152; R. H. Helmholz (ed.), *Select Cases on Defamation to 1600*, Selden Society, 101 (1985), 22.

[70] R. M. Wunderli, *London Church Courts and Society on the Eve of the Reformation* (1981), 43.

hapless Howde sought the mediation of his curate: 'Sir John . . . I desire you to speak with the same Marion, to know her mind.'[71] How often priests undertook such services for their parishioners is impossible to say, but it is likely to have been often.

Another area where priests could be of service was in the drawing up and execution of last wills and testaments. There was clearly a pastoral and sacramental dimension here—the duty of visiting the sick and administering the last rites—but the extent to which priests were appointed as overseers and executors of wills suggests more than a perfunctory performance of duty. In the early sixteenth century, around one in ten wills named a priest as an executor, and nearly a third of the testators who desired an 'overseer' or 'supervisor' nominated a priest for the task. The involvement of priests in testamentary matters was not without its pitfalls. Priests were sometimes accused of making fraudulent wills, or of using guile to get themselves appointed as executor, and as executors they not infrequently found themselves involved in litigation with disappointed relatives.[72] Some contemporaries may have shared the suspicion of many modern historians that priests made for the death-bed, in part at least, to persuade vulnerable testators to remember the Church and the clergy in their last disposition of wealth.[73] One hopes there cannot have been many priests like Thomas Kyrkeby, chaplain of Halsall in Lancashire, who was reportedly in the habit of expelling the onlookers from the bedside of the sick, and urging the testator to remember his 'ghostly father'. If persuasion failed, he would write the will himself.[74] An examination of those wills which were witnessed by priests suggests, however, that behaviour like this was exceptional. It is true that wills witnessed by a cleric were more likely to leave a bequest for 'tithes forgotten', but this was only marginally so. In the first three decades of the sixteenth century, 58 per cent of wills naming a priest as a witness made such bequests, while 52 per cent of those not doing so made the same gesture. Priests would

---

[71] J. Raine (ed.), *Depositions and other ecclesiastical proceedings from the courts of Durham*, SS 21 (1845), 52.

[72] PRO, STA. C. 2, 17/137; 19/53; 25/294; 27/97; 30/38; 30/123; STA. C. 3, 1/77; Req. 2, 5/186; 5/337; 6/20; 9/45; 18/75; Fishwick (ed.), *Pleadings and Depositions in the Duchy Court of Lancaster*, ii. 21; *NCCD*, no. 35. It was to avoid this that one of John Colet's statutes for St Paul's forbade the vicars or deputies of the canons to be executors: J. H. Lupton, *Life of John Colet*, 2nd edn. (1909), 135–6.

[73] G. G. Coulton, 'Priests and People before the Reformation', in *Ten Medieval Studies*, 3rd edn. (Cambridge, 1930), 135; Arrowsmith, *The Prelude to the Reformation*, 58; Bowker, *Secular Clergy in the Diocese of Lincoln*, 113; Scarisbrick, *Reformation and the English People*, 10; M. Sheehan, *The Will in Medieval England* (Toronto, 1963), 181; W. K. Jordan, *The Charities of Rural England, 1480–1660* (1961), 364.

[74] Fishwick (ed.), *Pleadings and Depositions in the Duchy Court of Lancaster*, i. 199.

naturally, and legitimately, have reminded those eager to face their Maker with a light conscience of the possibilities for making recompense, but it seems unlikely that the self-interest of the clergy was the main reason either for their assiduity in attending upon the dying, or for the latter's propensity to make bequests to the Church. Most likely they were there because the testator had requested their presence, and because he valued the services the priest might undertake on his behalf.

At a person's birth, just as at his or her death, the priest had an essential cultic task to perform. But here as well his ability to render service extended beyond the purely sacramental. In the early sixteenth century, a considerable number of English parents seem to have requested priests to stand as godfathers to their children in baptism: nearly a quarter of the wills of parish clergy make bequests to godchildren, often to 'every godchild that I have'. That this formula might imply relatively large numbers is suggested by the will of Roger Leigh, rector of Lymm in Cheshire, who in 1551 made individual bequests to eight named godchildren, as well as providing a smaller sum for 'every other godchild' that he had in the parish.[75] It would appear that priests were quite frequently asked to become godparents by parishioners, but what motivated the latter to make this choice, and what degree of closeness it reflected between them and the priest who was to become their 'god-sib', is difficult to ascertain. It is not impossible that in some cases priests acted as sponsors simply because they were on hand at the baptism. In most cases the sums left by priests to their godchildren were relatively small, usually ranging from 2*d.* to 12*d.*, though some individual godsons and god-daughters were singled out for special favour. In 1518, a London priest, William Pontifex, left £9 6*s.* 8*d.* each to Thomas and William Gage, and 4*d.* to his other godchildren.[76] A Somerset priest left £6 6*s.* 8*d.* towards the marriage of a god-daughter in 1528, and a Lincolnshire vicar left a similar sum to a godson in 1530.[77] In such cases one can posit a firm bond of pre-existent amity between the priest and the parents which the artificial kinship created by baptism was designed to express and cement.[78] As a consequence of this relationship, priests might be called upon to make themselves useful

---

[75] G. J. Piccope (ed.), *Lancashire and Cheshire Wills and Inventories from the Ecclesiastical Court, Chester*, ChS 54 (1861), 48.

[76] I. Darlington (ed.), *London Consistory Court Wills, 1492–1547*, LoRS 3 (1967), 37.

[77] F. W. Weaver (ed.), *Somerset Medieval Wills, 1531–1558*, SRS 21 (1905), 4; C. W. Foster (ed.), *Lincoln Wills 1530–1532*, LRS 24 (1930), 33.

[78] John Bossy provides an intriguing sociological approach to the significance of late medieval and early modern godparenthood in 'Blood and Baptism: Kinship, Community and Christianity in Western Europe from the Fourteenth to the Seventeenth Centuries', in D. Baker (ed.), SCH 10 (Oxford, 1973), and in *Christianity in the West*, 15–18.

in practical ways. In 1533, for example, John Geldard of York bequeathed a substantial sum to his ward, Thomas Palisor, but requested that 'his godfather, Sir Thomas Werrell, have it in custody unto the said Thomas come to lawful age'.[79] In other instances, the bond of baptism was used to cement a natural kinship: godchildren were sometimes the nephews and nieces of their priestly sponsor.[80] Of course, some priests may have been selected merely to serve convenience, or out of unreflective conventionality, but even here the choice must have reflected a sense of the clergy's usefulness, and an awareness that a new relationship had been created. Natural children were denied to priests, but in baptism they could be presented with surrogates, and the man who was intended to be a 'ghostly father' to all his parishioners could fill a more overtly paternal role. Day-to-day involvement in the spiritual and material welfare of godchildren may sometimes have been minimal, yet a genuinely solicitous note is struck in the will of Robert Cock, priest of Ashton-under-Lyne, who in leaving small legacies to his several godchildren added 'my blessing'.[81] Such sentiments could be reciprocated: when the rector of Stratfield Saye in Hampshire died in December 1540, his godson, William Croft, claimed to have gone straight to the parsonage, 'intending there to pray for the soul of his said godfather'.[82] It would perhaps be tempting to leave the relationship of priests and laity upon this optimistic note, yet it is necessary here to turn to examine the counter-argument; that to some, perhaps many laypeople, the metaphors of paternal ministry could come to seem a fraud and a delusion, that proximity to priests could breed resentment and enmity as readily as regard.

[79] BIHR, Prob. Reg. 11, fo. 83ᵛ.
[80] PRO, PCC, Prob. 11, 10 Pynnyng (John Parker); 40 Pynnyng (Hugh Crompton); Piccope (ed.), *Lancashire and Cheshire Wills*, ChS os 51 (1860), 105.
[81] Piccope (ed.), ibid.   [82] PRO, STA. C. 2, 16/392.

8

The Priest as Enemy

AN 'ANTICLERICAL' LAITY?

In December 1529 the Imperial ambassador, Eustace Chapuys, penned a bleak report to his master, Charles V. It was now clear that Henry intended to abandon Charles's aunt, Katherine of Aragon, and to replace her as queen with Anne Boleyn. Moreover, Clement VII's revocation of the divorce case to Rome had angered the English ruling élite, and bred in them a determination to 'reform' the clergy and seize Church property. Their task would be the easier, Chapuys considered, 'as nearly all the people here hate the priests'.[1]

If Chapuys was right, this clearly has profound implications for our understanding of the English Reformation, and why it was ultimately able to triumph. That the English people on the eve of the Reformation were irredeemably anticlerical has long been asserted by historians, and the idea that priests and their privileges provoked widespread resentment among the laity has found a secure place in twentieth-century historical writing.[2] The most eminent proponent of this interpretation, A. G. Dickens, remarked over thirty years ago that 'the tide of anticlericalism enveloped devout and profane, Protestant and Catholic, rich and poor alike', and in his subsequent writings he has tenaciously held to the view that popular dissatisfaction with the clergy was a crucial element in the acceptance of the Reformation.[3] Other leading Tudor historians, such as G. R. Elton, M. C. Cross, and S. E. Lehmberg, have broadly endorsed

---

[1] *Calendar of letters, despatches, and state papers relating to the negotiation between England and Spain*, ed. P. De Gayangos (1879), iv (1). 367.

[2] See e.g. J. A. Froude, *History of England* (1893), i. 103; G. G. Coulton, 'Priests and People before the Reformation', in *Ten Medieval Studies*, 3rd edn. (Cambridge, 1930), 128.

[3] A. G. Dickens, *Lollards and Protestants in the Diocese of York* (1959), 12; 'Heresy and the Origins of English Protestantism', in *Reformation Studies* (1982); 'The Shape of Anticlericalism and the English Reformation', in E. I. Kouri and T. Scott (eds.), *Politics and Society in Reformation Europe* (1987); *The English Reformation*, 2nd edn. (1989), especially chs. 6 and 13.

the validity of this interpretation.[4] The most recent biographer of the
English clergy's staunchest lay defender, Thomas More, does not hesitate
to assert 'the general spirit of anticlericalism among the English people',
'the torrent of anticlerical feeling in the country', 'the sea of anticlericalism
rolling against the English Church', 'the almost ritual anticlericalism of
the English people'.[5]

Inevitably, this insistence on the importance and extent of anticlericalism
has invited a 'revisionist' response. In his Ford Lectures of 1982, J. J.
Scarisbrick argued for a general popular satisfaction with the services
offered by the late medieval Church, and 'a partnership between layman
and cleric'.[6] In an article first published in 1983, Christopher Haigh
suggested that the popular anticlericalism detected by historians was in
fact largely manifested by specific interest groups, and that the great
majority of laypeople on the eve of the Reformation seldom felt hostile
towards their pastors.[7] It is not the intention here to embark upon a
lengthy review of this controversy; indeed, it is hoped that the preceding
chapters have already thrown some light upon it. None the less, the
phenomenon of overt expressions of hostility towards priests and the
priesthood needs to be examined, placed in its proper context, and accounted for.

Three interrelated problems present themselves. In the first place,
there is the concept of 'anticlericalism' itself, its utility and deficiency as
a historical tool. Secondly, it is necessary to identify the contexts in which
hostility to the clergy surfaced, their extent and significance. Lastly, and
perhaps most importantly, critical or hostile attitudes towards priests
must be related to the progress of the English Reformation itself. It will
be argued here that the attitudes of the laity towards the clergy in the
early sixteenth century cannot be regarded simply as a 'cause' of the
Reformation, or as a constant which reconstructed itself quickly and
neatly under a new Protestant dispensation. Rather, the long-drawn-out
process of reform, which questioned long-held assumptions, tested political and religious loyalties, and upset delicately balanced social structures,

---

[4] G. R. Elton, *Reform and Reformation: England 1509–1558* (1977), 9–10, 53–6, 118–19;
C. Cross, *Church and People, 1450–1660* (1976), 43–5, 76–8; S. E. Lehmberg, *The Reformation Parliament, 1529–1536* (Cambridge. 1970), 5.

[5] R. Marius, *Thomas More* (1985), 312, 352, 360, 408.

[6] J. J. Scarisbrick, *The Reformation and the English People* (Oxford, 1984), 45, chs. 1–3
passim.

[7] C. Haigh, 'Anticlericalism and the English Reformation', in C. Haigh (ed.), *The English
Reformation Revised* (Cambridge, 1987). Haigh has recently restated his position, in *English
Reformations: Religion, Politics, and Society under the Tudors* (Oxford, 1993), 40–55.

engaged lay attitudes in an unremitting dialectic, within which perceptions of the clergy both acted upon and reacted against the forms of religious change.

The concept of 'anticlericalism' brings with it considerable interpretative difficulties, which have a tendency to intensify rather than resolve themselves as the evidence is subjected to closer scrutiny. These difficulties have, indeed, been recognized by historians. Christopher Haigh regards the notion of anticlericalism as a 'convenient fiction', and Professor Dickens admits that 'anticlericalism has become an unduly capacious word'.[8] Students of the past cannot, of course, even if it were desirable to do so, work entirely within the mental categories which were open to their subjects, but even so, 'anticlericalism' strikes one as more overtly anachronistic than many of the analytical tools at the historian's disposal. The term is more readily suggestive of Third Republic France than of late medieval England, and there appears to have been no equivalent expression available to early Tudor men and women. This in itself must be significant, and it is instructive to note that in Germany where, as most historians are agreed, instances of 'anticlericalism' were both more frequent and more violent than in England, the expression *Pfaffenhass* was used to denote intense antipathy to priests. In Germany, it has been suggested, anticlericalism acted as the motor of the early Reformation, binding together diverse forces in a determination to overthrow clerical privilege.[9] In England it is perhaps doubtful if antipathetic feelings towards the clergy ever possessed the coherence to take on this role, and a number of historians have recognized that if the expression is to retain any significant conceptual validity, 'anticlericalism' has to be broken down and examined in its component parts. C. S. L. Davies has described anticlericalism as 'a catch-all phrase', which could imply support for poor parochial curates alongside hostility to rich monastic appropriators of tithe.[10] In his classic biography of Henry VIII, J. J. Scarisbrick identified four distinct forms of early Tudor anticlericalism: unreflective resentment

---

[8] Haigh, 'Anticlericalism', 56; Dickens, 'The Shape of Anticlericalism', 379.

[9] H.-J. Goertz, *Pfaffenhass und gross Geschrei: Die reformatorischen Bewegungen in Deutschland, 1517–1529* (Munich, 1987), 52. See also F. R. H. Du Boulay, *Germany in the Later Middle Ages* (1983), 200–4; H. J. Cohn, 'Anticlericalism in the German Peasants' War, 1525', *PP* 83 (1979); R. W. Scribner, 'Anticlericalism and the German Reformation', in *Popular Culture and Popular Movements in Reformation Germany* (1987). Scribner's *For the Sake of Simple Folk: Popular Propaganda for the German Reformation* (Cambridge, 1981), reproduces many of the numerous anticlerical woodcuts which were conspicuously absent from Reformation England.

[10] C. S. L. Davies, 'Popular Religion and the Pilgrimage of Grace', in A. Fletcher and J. Stevenson (eds.), *Order and Disorder in Early Modern England* (Cambridge, 1985), 83.

of clerical wealth and power; the more theoretical secular anticlericalism epitomized by Thomas Cromwell; the idealistic 'Erasmian' reformism of those within the Church; and the more straightforward 'anticlericalism of heresy'.[11] Only in a very limited sense did these groups share a common cause; indeed their aims were often in direct conflict. There is a strong case for suggesting that real anticlericalism only becomes a possibility when the religious, ethical, and social values that the clergy uphold are rejected in favour of a perceptibly viable alternative. There is little difficulty in accepting the Lollards at their word in their contemptuous rejection of the Catholic priesthood as 'scribes and pharisees', 'enemies of Christ', 'disciples of antichrist'.[12] Similarly, their Protestant successors who, like Edward Hoppyng of Wakefield in May 1548, recognized 'none in heaven, neither in earth, to be my mediator between God and me, but [Christ] only', could afford to indulge a wholehearted detestation of the standard-bearers of the old religion.[13] The category might also include those few extreme Erasmians who envisaged a radically desacramentalized worship, and a thorough disendowment of the Church.

It does, however, seem somewhat perverse to lump these groups together with those 'anticlericals', many of them themselves priests, whose objective was a renewal of the clerical estate, and a revitalization rather than a diminution of its moral authority. John Colet, whose outlook has been described as 'clerical anticlericalism',[14] was as we have seen, a vocal proponent of high clerical status. The Chancellor of York, William Melton, similarly castigated abuses in order to uphold 'the honour of holy priesthood'.[15] Thomas More, who in his early career showed himself a persistent scourge of clerical ignorance and obscurantism, developed in the 1520s and 1530s into a vigorous, though by no means dewy-eyed defender of the clergy against the attacks of common lawyers and the first generation of English Protestants. It would be unwise to contend that there were absolutely no points of contact between orthodox and heterodox 'anticlericalism'; some Buckinghamshire Lollards are known to have attended Colet's sermons in the 1500s, and Dickens's contention that Protestant polemic could portray clerical shortcomings as the inevitably bad

---

[11] J. J. Scarisbrick, *Henry VIII* (1968), 243–4.

[12] D. P. Wright (ed.), *The Register of Thomas Langton, Bishop of Salisbury, 1485–1493*, CYS 74 (1985), 71–5.

[13] E. W. Crossley (ed.), *Halifax Wills 1545–1559* (Leeds, n.d.), 39.

[14] P. I. Kaufman, 'John Colet's *Opus de sacramentis* and Clerical Anticlericalism: The Limitations of "Ordinary Wayes" ', *JBS* 22 (1982).

[15] W. Melton, *Sermo exhortatorius cancellarii Eboracensis*, cited in A. G. Dickens and D. Carr (eds.), *The Reformation in England to the Accession of Elizabeth I* (1967), 16.

fruit of a theologically defective tree, seems a persuasive comment on how some English men and women may have edged their way towards Protestantism.[16] Sometimes Protestant and orthodox reformers used the same vocabulary: when mid-Tudor Protestants referred to the Catholic clergy as 'Baal's priests', they were merely echoing an expression used by late medieval preachers to castigate the unworthy.[17] Yet, as this example suggests, denunciation of clerical vice by educated priests had an extremely long pedigree by 1500, and to see it as feeding inexorably into lay and clerical theological revolt in the 1520s is surely to impose a false teleology that does not help to elucidate the origins of the Reformation.

If the concept of some kind of all-embracing anticlerical 'movement' is unsustainable, it remains inescapable that many individual laypeople left a record of their dislike for individual priests, and occasionally for the institution as a whole. Sometimes we can only guess at their reasons for doing so. In 1491 two Londoners were in trouble for calling priests 'whoresons' and 'whoremongers', and for wishing that 'there was never a priest in England'. A third, the tavern-keeper, John Oste, was said to rejoice at seeing priests in trouble.[18] Such men may have been influenced by Lollardy, or were driven to extreme statements by their vexation with a local priest. Certainly, personal quarrels could lead to the expression of a more general anticlericalism. When, in 1523, the Londoner Thomas Bukk fell out with the priest Thomas Caulond, he threatened him with violence 'that all other knave priests shall beware by thee'.[19] Such outbursts should perhaps not be taken entirely at face value. Court records ossify words which were spoken in passion. At moments of heightened tension there is a natural tendency to focus on the feature of an antagonist which is most distinctively 'other', and we cannot assume that Bukk or others like him were consistent enemies of the priesthood. In some recorded instances of lay criticism of priests the obverse reaction manifests itself, and the language is that of defeated expectation. In 1528, for example, the parishioners of Whitwick in Leicestershire complained of the moral and pastoral delinquency of their vicar, who did not 'do as other vicars and rectors'.[20] In 1542 the parishioners of Layer-de-la-Hay complained that

---

[16] Dickens, *The English Reformation*, 50–1; 'Shape of Anticlericalism', 404.

[17] P. Moone, *A short treatyse of certayne things abused in the popish church* (Ipswich, 1548), unpaginated; G. R. Owst, *Literature and Pulpit in Medieval England*, 2nd edn. (Cambridge, 1961), 257, 280; J. E. T. Rogers (ed.), *Loci e Libro Veritatum: Passages Selected from Gascoigne's Theological Dictionary* (Oxford, 1881), 188; PRO, SP 6/2, fo. 41ᵛ.

[18] Hale, *Precedents*, 27, 37–8.   [19] GLRO, DL/C/207, fo. 193ᵛ.

[20] A. P. Moore (ed.), 'Proceedings of the Ecclesiastical Courts in the Archdeaconry of Leicester, 1516–1535', *Associated Architectural Societies Reports and Papers*, 28 (1905), 193.

their priest celebrated mass at irregular times 'contrary to the usage of other curates'.[21] Such examples warn us to beware of assuming that clerical abuses must have generated anticlericalism.

There is difficulty too in deciding how representative those laypeople were, whose disagreements with clerics were severe enough to leave a mark in the records. Roger Harlakinden, a parishioner of Woodchurch in Kent, was reported in 1511 to 'check the parson and the priests that they cannot be [at] rest for him'. Yet Harlakinden was described by the churchwardens as 'a common oppressor of his neighbours, whom none loveth'.[22] At Kennington, the vicar had to endure the unremitting hostility of a group of four or five parishioners headed by Richard Ricard. These had assaulted the vicar, and spread a 'grievous and ungodly defamation' concerning him. Ricard was characterized as 'so infest against priests that he is ever talking of them, and ready to say the worst against them and their order'. It is conceivable that Ricard and his friends had Lollard sympathies; one of them was reported to have said that the images in the church were 'as good to roast meat with . . . as other wood'. Yet the report made to the archbishop's officials by the churchwardens included no direct charge of heresy, and rather sought to portray Ricard and his 'company' as antisocial elements. The complaints against him included homicide, assault, and multiple adultery, and the cause of his hatred for the vicar was said to be that the latter 'would not hold with him in his lewdness'.[23] There may well in some places have been a thuggish aspect to 'anticlericalism' that was occasioned neither by clerical misdemeanour nor by any positive spiritual aspirations, and that was condemned by the majority of lay men and women.

THE OCCASIONS AND CONTEXTS OF CONFLICT

A potent source of friction in some parishes was the question of tithes. As Susan Brigden has observed, 'nothing put the clergy and laity at odds so much as money'.[24] The right of all incumbents to extract from their parishioners a tenth of their income from all sources, and the rigidity with which that right was sometimes pursued, may have introduced a structural dysfunction into the ordinary operation of lay–clerical relations. Certainly, it is not hard to find cases where disputes over tithe

[21] Hale, *Precedents*, 119.   [22] *Kentish Visitations*, 160.   [23] Ibid. 203–5.
[24] S. Brigden, 'Tithe Controversy in Reformation London', *JEH* 33 (1982), 285.

boiled over into intense antagonism. The vicar of Linton in Kent claimed to have been 'almost strangled to death' by the wife and servant of a parishioner when he entered their house 'asking after a gentle manner the tithes and oblations'.[25] At Seasalter, a layman was reported to have 'laid violent hands upon his ghostly father for asking of his tithes'.[26] In some places, particularly in London where tithing arrangements were complicated, grievances could easily become communal as well as personal.[27] In the Oxfordshire parish of Swalcliffe in 1543, the parishioners clubbed together to pay the expenses of one of their number being sued for his tithes.[28]

With tithe disputes, as with other recorded occasions of lay–clerical conflict, there is, however, the danger of conflating the exceptional with the normative. A number of historians have pointed out that in many areas disputes in the courts over tithes were relatively infrequent: several dioceses might produce cases from fewer than 2 per cent of their parishes in a given year.[29] Of course, the paucity of tithe suits does not prove that where rectors did not resort to the courts payment always proceeded smoothly and without ill-will. It would be the ultimate *reductio ad absurdum* for a historian to suggest that every event of which we have a written record is by definition always atypical. None the less, it must be considered doubtful whether the irksome obligation to pay tithes was the crucial determinant of attitudes towards the clergy. The principle of tithing itself was virtually never questioned by orthodox laypeople, and disputes almost invariably centred on the interpretation of parish custom. Priests who encountered unwillingness to pay in full sometimes asserted how unusual such recalcitrance was.[30] Tithe-owners had, of course, an interest in claiming this, but occasionally parishioners conceded the point. A party in an Oxfordshire tithe suit in the 1540s accepted that in the past the rector had received the tithes and offerings of the parish and 'quietly

---

[25] PRO, C. 1, 748/15.   [26] *Kentish Visitations*, 85.

[27] Brigden, 'Tithe Controversy in Reformation London'; *London and the Reformation* (Oxford, 1989), 49–52, 167–8, 201–4; J. A. F. Thomson, 'Tithe Disputes in Later Medieval London', *EHR* 78 (1965). G. R. Elton paints a vivid picture of the tumult wrought in one Middlesex parish in 1530: 'Tithe and Trouble', in *Star Chamber Stories* (1958).

[28] OCRO, Oxf. dioc. MSS d. 14, fo. 21ʳ.

[29] C. Haigh, 'The Recent Historiography of the English Reformation', in Haigh (ed.), *The English Reformation Revised*, 23; 'Anticlericalism and the English Reformation', 68–9; J. F. Fuggles, 'The Parish Clergy in the Archdeaconry of Leicester, 1520–1540', *Leicestershire Archaeological and Historical Society Transactions*, 46 (1970–1), 39; N. P. Tanner, *The Church in Late Medieval Norwich, 1370–1532* (Toronto, 1984), 7; R. M. Wunderli, *London Church Courts and Society on the Eve of the Reformation* (1981), 110.

[30] PRO, STA. C. 2, 6/294; 11/55; STA. C. 3, 3/38.

possessed them without contradiction of any person'.[31] In another Oxfordshire tithe suit, several witnesses concurred that the defendant, Richard Walker, was 'an evil payer of his tithes' who 'doth not pay his tithes as he ought to do', and that 'everybody speaketh of it in the town'.[32] The three parishioners of Worlingworth in Suffolk who allegedly 'rebuked all other of the inhabitants . . . and call them fools in that they do pay any manner of tithes', seem likewise to have been unrepresentative of the mood of their parish.[33] It is not without significance either that a great many laypeople left bequests in their wills for 'tithes forgotten', more probably a gesture of pious convention than a confession of deliberate evasion. In short, the problems connected with the practice of tithing, vexing though they undoubtedly sometimes were, seem too shallow a foundation on which to erect the argument that resentment of the parish clergy was endemic and unremitting.

If 'anticlericalism' can be measured at all, it might seem that the most telling evidence would be that of violent attacks upon priests by laymen. These seem to have taken place, if not frequently, then at least with regularity.[34] In many cases it is not clear what had occasioned the assault, though quarrels over tithes were certainly prominent. Of early sixteenth-century Lancashire, Dr Haigh has written that 'there is no evidence that laymen attacked clergy *qua* clergy. Priests found themselves assaulted because they were often involved in conflicts, usually over fees and dues.'[35] While noting that they usually only became involved in these conflicts because they were priests, this seems a fair comment on the national picture. None the less, there is a sense in which physical aggression against priests cannot be considered simply as another manifestation of the ready resort to violence which is so marked a feature of late medieval society. Early Tudor laypeople should have been in no doubt that assaulting a priest was a very serious matter: excommunication was automatic for all

---

[31] OCRO, Oxf. dioc. MSS 14, fo. 34ʳ.   [32] Ibid. 80ᵛ–82ʳ.
[33] PRO, C. 1, 965/21.
[34] See e.g. J. A. F. Thomson, 'Clergy and Laity in London, 1376–1531', University of Oxford D.Phil. thesis (1960), 272; B. L. Woodcock, *Medieval Ecclesiastical Courts in the Diocese of Canterbury* (Oxford, 1952), 81; C. L. Kingsford (ed.), *Two London Chronicles*, Camden Miscellany, 12 (1910), 4; PRO, C. 1, 239/44; 375/39; Req. 2, 9/155; 10/251; STA. C. 2, 1/47; 3/199; 5/130; 7/149, 173, 215; 8/189; 14/114; 16/37; 17/86; 18/93, 290; 19/323; 21/168; 24/146, 428; 26/179, 194; 27/139; 28/63; 29/24, 40; 30/104; 31/120, 171; 33/57; STA. C. 3, 1/53; 4/74. It should be noted that Star Chamber litigants were perhaps prone to exaggerate the degree of violence they had suffered so as to bring their case within the purview of the court.
[35] C. Haigh, *Reformation and Resistance in Tudor Lancashire* (Cambridge, 1975), 57.

'that lay hand in violence on priest or on clerk'.[36] The unsuccessful attempt of John Baker, rector of Bowers Gifford, to avert an assault by an appeal to his priesthood has been remarked upon already, and when the London priest, Thomas Caulond, was manhandled in 1523 he told his attacker 'ye be accursed for to order a poor priest after this fashion'.[37] There was, the Church implied, a clear element of sacrilege in the maltreatment of the consecrated person of the priest, yet here again the disparity between what the priest was supposed to represent, and the imperfect way in which he exercised his ministry may have led some laypeople to exempt certain clerics from this prohibition. Undoubtedly, some assaults were perpetrated by those who would have been regarded by their contemporaries as simply vicious and irreligious, but for others a sense of outrage at clerical neglect or avarice may have prompted a more self-conscious, almost 'ritual' display of extreme disapprobation. E. W. Ives has recently remarked that 'anticlericalism in a Christian context is hostility, not to ministry but to an ethos among the clergy of caste rather than service'.[38] The two mentalities juxtaposed here are perhaps neither in theory nor in practice mutually exclusive, but it seems clear that where priests insisted on their status, rights, and privileges while neglecting their duties, violent antipathy might not be too far from the surface.

Nowhere was this more the case than with the clergy's self-assumed role as guardians and arbiters of religious orthodoxy. In the early sixteenth century it was often claimed, not without some justification, that priests tended to regard any criticism from the laity as *prima facie* evidence of heresy, despite the fact that vigorous censuring of their own order by clerical élites, and the promulgation of perhaps unrealistic standards had themselves helped to generate such criticism. Thomas More admitted, apropos of the case of Thomas Bilney, that it was widely believed that 'this name of a Lutheran serveth the clergy for a common cloak of a false crime', and that 'the people say that all this gear is done but only to stop men's mouths and to put every man to silence that would anything speak of the faults of the clergy'.[39] This view was certainly held by a London priest who in 1529 was reported to have said 'my lord of London will suffer no man to preach at Paul's Cross but flatterers and dissemblers, for they that say truth are punished as Bilney and Arthur was'.[40] The accusation

---

[36] Henderson (ed.), *Manuale et Processionale ad Usum Insignis Ecclesiae Eboracensis*, SS 63 (1874), 87.　　　　　　　　　　　　　　　　[37] GLRO, DL/C/207, fo. 205ʳ.
[38] Review of Brigden, *London and the Reformation*, *Historical Journal*, 34 (1991), 202.
[39] More, *Dialogue*, 30, 28.　　　[40] GLRO, DL/C/330, fo. 175ᵛ.

that priests would bring heresy charges against those who criticized the clergy was given wider currency by the repercussions of the Richard Hunne affair, Simon Fish alleging that if Hunne had not sued the praemunire, he would not have been taken as a heretic, a view shared by the London chronicler, Charles Wriothesley.[41] Fish's fellow Protestants Tyndale and Barlowe made similar charges, the latter alleging that

> Whosoever is so hardy
> To speak against priests' knavery,
> For an heretic they him take.[42]

Such accusations were not confined to the ranks of the Protestants. In 1529 a draft parliamentary bill charged that the bishops 'arrest and convent before them such as either doth preach, speak, or reason against their detestable and shameful living, and them in prison do keep under the colour and name of heresy'.[43] One of the members of the Reformation Parliament, the chronicler Edward Hall, remarked of the commons' grievances that 'these things before this time might in no wise be touched nor yet talked of by no man, except he would be made an heretic'.[44] This view was shared by Christopher St German,[45] and by the author of an anonymous *Dialogue between a clerke of convocacyon and a burges of the parlyament*. In this work, the burgess accuses the clerk that 'if I should contrary thine opinion, thou wilt call me an heretic, as many of you use to do when ye lack matter and learning to answer'.[46] In this context, the assault on the clergy's independent legislative power, such remarks served an obvious political purpose, yet the contemporary horror of the imputation of heresy was certainly genuine. The citizens of London were outraged when Bishop Fitzjames remarked that his chancellor could not be tried fairly in the city for his alleged part in the death of Richard Hunne, because the Londoners were so set 'in favour of depraved heresy'.[47] The members of the Reformation Parliament were equally incensed when

---

[41] S. Fish, *A Supplicacyon for the Beggars*, ed. F. J. Furnivall, EETS 13 (1871), 9; A. Ogle, *The Tragedy of the Lollards' Tower* (Oxford, 1949), 16.

[42] W. Tyndale, *An Answer to Sir Thomas More's Dialogue*, ed. H. Walter, PS (1850), 159; J. Barlow, *Burial of the Mass*, in E. Arber (ed.), *English Reprints* (1871), 123. See also J. M. Cowper (ed.), *Four Supplications, 1529–1553*, EETS es 13 (1871), 36.

[43] S. E. Lehmberg, *The Reformation Parliament, 1529–1536* (Cambridge, 1970), 87.

[44] E. Hall, *The Union of . . . Lancastre and Yorke* (1809), 765.

[45] C. St German, *A Treatise concernynge the division betwene the spirytualtie and temporaltie*, *CW* 9 (1979), 191.

[46] *A dyalogue betwene one Clemente a clerke of the convocacyon and one Bernarde a burges of the parlyament* (1532), sig. B.i^v.					[47] Ogle, *Tragedy of the Lollards' Tower*, 83.

Bishop Fisher remarked in the Lords that their proceedings seemed to him to be inspired 'by lack of faith only'.[48]

Such conflicts could also be played out at a more humble level. One can imagine the feelings of the parishioners of Waltham in Kent when their disreputable chantry priest referred to them as 'heretics, bastards and harlots', or of the Derbyshire man who was called 'whoreson Jew heretic' by his curate.[49] Such calumny invited laypeople to respond with a suit for slander. Indeed, Richard Hunne had instigated a defamation suit after being denounced by his parish priest in December 1512, claiming that his reputation and his business had been damaged.[50] No one was eager to trade with a heretic. When the vicar of Bosham in Sussex called one of his parishioners a heretic in 1507, the reaction of the parish forced the Bishop of Chichester to instigate proceedings for public defamation.[51] In Suffolk in the same year a priest and a layman were simultaneously counter-suing for defamation in the consistory court. The layman had reportedly accused the priest 'thou art a nought priest and a whoremonger', and the cleric had responded, predictably but unwisely, 'thou art a heretic'.[52] The instinctive response of many priests when confronted with lay censure was to fall back upon their assured position as the anointed people of God. This policy was to become increasingly dangerous as the religious and political upheavals set in motion after 1530 began to question that very position.

THE PRIESTHOOD AT BAY, 1530–1553

From the late 1520s onwards, an increasing number of English men and women were to be won over to the beliefs of Protestantism, and thereby acquire formal theological reasons for rejecting the Catholic priesthood. Yet it is likely that not until well into Elizabeth's reign did self-consciously Protestant believers cease to be a minority in England, and there are almost certainly other reasons why clerical–lay relations may have been

---

[48] Hall, *Union of . . . Lancastre and Yorke*, 766.

[49] C. E. Woodruff (ed.), 'An Archidiaconal Visitation of 1502', *AC* 47 (1935), 41; PRO, STA. C. 2, 26/194.

[50] R. J. Schoeck, 'Common Law and Canon Law in their Relation to Thomas More', in R. S. Sylvester (ed.), *St Thomas More: Action and Contemplation* (New Haven, Conn., 1972), 32.

[51] S. Lander, 'The Diocese of Chichester, 1508–1558: Episcopal Reform under Robert Sherburne and its Aftermath', University of Cambridge Ph.D. thesis (1974), 281.

[52] *NCCD*, no. 73.

becoming increasingly difficult in the years following Henry VIII's decision to separate from Katherine of Aragon. At Westminster, unprecedented events were taking place. In 1529 three parliamentary Acts were passed, restricting clerical pluralism and limiting the amounts paid by the laity in probate and mortuary fees.[53] This was followed by the King's forcing the clergy to surrender their independent legislative powers, and to recognize him, albeit in qualified manner, as Supreme Head of the Church.[54] In 1532 the House of Commons presented, with official approval, its *Supplication against the Ordinaries*, a comprehensive indictment of the English bishops and their officials.[55] At the court itself, attitudes were hardening, prompting Eustace Chapuys to make the observation with which this chapter opened. Henry's brother-in-law and intimate, Charles Brandon, Duke of Suffolk, opined that 'there was never legate nor cardinal that did good in England'.[56] Henry's second wife, Anne Boleyn, apparently refused to intercede for a young priest condemned to death for coining, on the grounds that there were too many priests in the country already. Ominously, the priest was hanged without first being degraded from his orders.[57]

The officially sponsored offensive on the privileged position of the clergy must have served to demoralize priests throughout the country. In September 1530, the Evesham monk, Robert Joseph, advised a young ordinand that though the priesthood was a great dignity, it is 'never so much trampled on and vilified as now'.[58] The parishes could not remain insulated from what was going on in London. In one Cornish village in 1530, the parishioners were being encouraged on the basis of reports from the capital in the quite erroneous belief that they were no longer bound to pay any mortuaries.[59] Before that date it had been almost universal in some parts of the country for those making wills to assign a specific item as a mortuary to their curate, despite the fact that these were in any case regulated by local custom. The Act of 1529 contained the provision that people could still voluntarily bequeath whatever they wanted, yet the old custom effectively collapsed, more or less overnight, in the wake of the new legislation. Across thirteen counties of northern and midland England,

---

[53] Lehmberg, *Reformation Parliament*, 81–102.

[54] J. A. Guy, *The Public Career of Sir Thomas More* (New Haven, Conn., 1980), 136–8, 147–51, 161–2, 185–201.

[55] H. Gee and W. J. Hardy (eds.), *Documents Illustrative of English Church History* (1896), 145–53.

[56] S. J. Gunn, *Charles Brandon, Duke of Suffolk, 1484–1545* (Oxford, 1988), 110.

[57] E. Ives, *Anne Boleyn* (Oxford, 1986), 194–5.

[58] R. Joseph, *Letter Book of Robert Joseph*, ed. H. Aveling and W. A. Pantin, Oxford Historical Society, NS 19 (1967), 107.   [59] PRO, C. 1, 666/8.

over 70 per cent of wills specified a mortuary before 1530, usually the best or second best animal, or the best item of clothing. After 1530 this fell to under 25 per cent, and in Edward's reign to only about 8 per cent, the few testators who still mentioned mortuaries usually saying that they wanted them to be paid 'according to the King's acts', a formulation which suggests that they may not have been sure exactly what the King's acts stipulated, but that they did not want to be out of line with officially sanctioned practice. It is not the intention here to suggest that the Reformation Parliament in some way released a flood of lay resentment and recrimination. It is notable that in 1530, the first year that mortuaries were no longer bound to be paid after the old fashion, the number of testators making bequests for 'tithes forgotten' rose very sharply, and many wills continued to bequeath the best beast under the heading of forgotten tithes.[60] Some laypeople clearly wished to cushion the financial blow the clergy had received. In 1529 Christopher Basse of South Witham bequeathed 'for my mortuary as the custom is, if it be lawful to be given; if not, I give to the parson of the church for the same 6s. 8d.'[61] In 1530, William Holden of Burton upon Stather defiantly left to his vicar 'in restitution of tithes forgotten, if any be, in discharge of my conscience, and for my mortuary, one cow, the statute to the contrary made notwithstanding'.[62] George Both of Dunham in Cheshire gave to the prior of Birkenhead in 1531 'my best horse to pray for me, in as much as there is a statute made that he can have no corpse present'.[63]

In the early 1530s the priesthood could still tap considerable reservoirs of goodwill. It is notable, for example, that though Parliament provided a scheme of rewards for reporting priests who breached the 1529 statutes, relatively few laypeople actually came forward to denounce clerical infringers.[64] None the less, the clear divergence of the purposes of Church and King involved unfamiliar and conflicting demands on the consciences of a people by and large deferential to authority in all its forms, and the spectacle of official proceedings being taken by King and Parliament against the clergy as a whole must have made a deep impression on the

[60] The percentage of testators in the sample making a bequest for forgotten tithes in 1529 was 31.2; in 1530 it rose to 47.5 per cent. These figures include bequests 'to the high altar', which seem to have been intended for this purpose.

[61] C. W. Foster (ed.), *Lincoln Wills, 1505–1530*, LRS 10 (1918), 126.

[62] Foster (ed.), *Lincoln Wills, 1530–1532*, LRS 24 (1930), 16.

[63] G. J. Piccope (ed.), *Lancashire and Cheshire Wills and Inventories from the Ecclesiastical Court, Chester*, ChS os 33 (1857), 93.

[64] Elton, *Reform and Reformation*, 139; Haigh, 'Anticlericalism and the English Reformation', 62; Brigden, *London and the Reformation*, 178.

English laity. Professor Elton has shown in his *Policy and Police* that a considerable number of priests were reported to the authorities in the 1530s for such offences as speaking against the King's marriage, praying for the Pope, failing to delete the Pope's name from service books, or insisting on traditional forms of abstinence during Lent. On the basis of these denunciations Elton has argued for a widespread devotion to the King and the realm in early Tudor England.[65] The action of the parishioners of Ashlower in Gloucestershire is revealing. They did not know whether their vicar had committed treason or not, but reported him to the authorities just in case.[66]

Doubtless many laypeople would have been shocked if their priest spoke against the King and his proceedings, yet it is possible that some protestations of loyalty may have been made disingenuously. There is an unmistakable trend in contemporary court material for traditional complaints about such matters as the quality of pastoral service in a parish to be accompanied by insinuations of treasonable attitudes on the part of the priest.[67] For example, when the churchwardens of Croscombe in Somerset reported that their rector was 'not the king's friend' because he had maintained a priest who had spoken in favour of the Pilgrimage of Grace, this was clearly their riposte to action the rector had taken against them for felling trees in the churchyard.[68] The break with Rome may therefore have permitted a shift in the balance of power in many parishes, providing disgruntled layfolk with a lever that they could use against traditionalist priests if the circumstances called for it, and it is possible that some charges may have been made maliciously and were unfounded.[69] After the break with Rome, every priest was potentially a traitor, just as before the Reformation every articulate or assertive layperson was, from the clergy's point of view, potentially a heretic. In the 1530s heresy was of less concern to the authorities than treason, and clerics of a traditionalist cast of mind may have had to learn to be more circumspect in their dealings with parishioners.

It was, however, on the parish clergy that the government relied for the implementation of religious change at the local level, and for explaining the vicissitudes of religious policy to their congregations. Few English priests abandoned their benefices for reasons of conscience in the sixteenth century, and in many parishes different doctrines would have been

[65] G. R. Elton, *Policy and Police* (Cambridge, 1972), 370.
[66] Haigh, *The English Reformation Revised*, 12.
[67] See e.g. PRO, STA. C. 2 3/149; 26/15; 31/61, 120; C. 1, 827/1; 1108/56.
[68] PRO, STA. C. 2, 18/301.   [69] See e.g. *LP* vii. 1440.

expounded at different times by the same man. Priests who had urged the observance of feast-days and Lenten fasts would, for example, have had to explain their abrogation. Priests who had regularly reminded their congregations of the absolute necessity of auricular confession would have had to accept that they had been mistaken, and after 1549, priests would have had to propound, with varying degrees of enthusiasm, the value of a communion service in English. In Mary's reign, the innovations had to be publicly renounced. None of this can have encouraged confidence in the teaching office of the clergy. Pleading against the introduction of the new book of homilies in 1547, Stephen Gardiner pointed out what seemed to him the absurdity of a curate reading on one Sunday from the *King's Book* of 1543, which condemned the doctrine of justification by faith alone, and the Sunday following reading the new homily on salvation which contradicted this teaching: 'And then one that list to quarrel with the priest, why he told them otherwise the last Sunday before. If the priest sayeth, "King Henry VIII bad him teach so"; "and was he", shall the other reply, "no true Christian man?" '[70]

One can only speculate as to how common this sort of reaction may have been, but it was a reproach to which many of the parish clergy must have been open. The tradition recorded by Thomas Fuller held that Simon Aleyn, vicar of Bray in Berkshire between 1540 and 1588, 'being taxed by one for being a turncoat and an unconstant changeling' retorted 'I have always kept my principle, which is this, to live and die the vicar of Bray.'[71] Robert Parkyn, curate of Adwick-le-Street in Yorkshire, was clearly no vicar of Bray. An articulate conservative, who read widely and compiled a polemical narrative of the Reformation, the drift of policy after 1547 must have involved him in agonies of conscience. Yet he, too, remained in office under Henry, Edward, Mary, and Elizabeth.[72] The conformism of some priests invited contemptuous rebuke from their parishioners. In Edward VI's reign, a priest was described as being a man 'more meet to have had the cure of some other trade and service, than to be a minister in the Church of Christ, the which he hath followed every way as the world cometh, not regarding nor respecting any religion thereat'.[73] William Horne, the vicar of St Petrock's in Exeter, had sworn after 1549 that he would rather be torn apart by wild horses than say mass again. Under Mary he conformed, remarking 'it is no remedy man, it is

---

[70] S. Gardiner, *Letters*, ed. J. A. Muller (Cambridge, 1933), 371.
[71] J. H. Bettey, *Church and Parish: A Guide for Local Historians* (1987), 86.
[72] A. G. Dickens, 'The Last Medieval Englishman' and 'Robert Parkyn's Narrative of the Reformation', in *Reformation Studies*.   [73] PRO, STA. C. 3, 9/19.

no remedy', to a reproachful Protestant parishioner.[74] In 1559 Marian Catholic priests faced an identical dilemma.

If the uncertain progress of the 'official' Reformation was putting more strain upon the relationship of priests and their parishioners, unwelcome economic developments did little to help. The severe inflation which England suffered in the 1540s reduced the income of incumbents in places where various tithes had been commuted for a cash payment. As rectors and vicars sought to overthrow such *modi decimandi* and reinstate payment in kind, tithe conflict intensified. At Lincoln, York, and elsewhere the number of tithe disputes rose dramatically from the 1540s.[75] Even before radical experiments in theology and liturgy questioned the assumptions which underpinned clerical status, the animosity of some laypeople towards priests may have been becoming a more marked feature of parish life.

It is, of course, impossible to establish this in absolute terms; the fuller documentation of the mid-sixteenth century may encourage an unduly pessimistic comparison with the pre-Reformation position. None the less, there is considerable evidence, as well as a growing consensus among historians, that this may have been the case. Christopher Haigh points to the marked rise in defamation suits instigated by Lancashire priests in the 1530s and 1540s.[76] Robert Whiting, in his recent study of the diocese of Exeter, has argued that verbal denigration of priests, physical assaults, and resistance to the clergy's financial demands were all growing from the 1530s, indicating 'a marked diminution of respect for the clergy in the Reformation years'.[77]

Perhaps the most telling evidence comes from the perceptions of contemporaries themselves: by the mid-1540s it had become commonplace to assert that the relationship between clergy and laity had deteriorated markedly within living memory. In 1545 Cuthbert Scott delivered a sermon at St Paul's Cross, taking for his theme the nature of the priesthood and the proper attitude towards it of the laity. He outlined in traditional manner the qualities required in a priest, while admitting that not all priests manifested these in their lives. The current attitude of the laity

[74] J. H. Bettey, *Church and Community: The Parish Church in English Life* (Bradford-on-Avon, 1979), 73–4.

[75] P. Heath, *The English Parish Clergy on the Eve of the Reformation* (1969), 152; C. Haigh, *Reformation and Resistance in Tudor Lancashire* (Cambridge, 1975), 25–6; Houlbrooke, *Church Courts and the People*, 147–8; J. S. Purvis (ed.), *Tudor Parish Documents of the Diocese of York* (Cambridge, 1948), 180; M. Bowker, *The Henrician Reformation* (Cambridge, 1981), 111, 135; J. Youings, *Sixteenth-Century England* (Harmondsworth, 1984), 191–2.

[76] Haigh, *Reformation and Resistance in Tudor Lancashire*, 56, 221, 242.

[77] Whiting, *Blind Devotion of the People*, 126–44.

was, however, entirely reprehensible. No group of men was wholly without fault, even the apostles had included a traitor in their midst, yet 'only the whole order of priesthood is therefore despised and condemned'. Laypeople were too apt to mark the mote, but neglect the plank in their own eye, and many of those who 'rail and cry out of priests' were themselves evil livers. Indeed, laypeople were themselves partly responsible for clerical failings, since patrons were apt to appoint to benefices priests who could 'flatter smoothly . . . [and] wink or rather laugh at your vices'. None the less, Scott was driven to conclude that 'the holy order of priesthood, which was wont to be had in great reputation as the worthiness of the thing doth require, is so run in contempt, that it is now nothing else but a laughing stock for the people'.[78]

There was undoubtedly an element of convention about this kind of outburst. The inveterate hostility of layman and priest had been something of a homilist's cliché ever since Boniface VIII had opened his bull *Clericos Laicos* in 1296 with the resounding declaration that 'the laity are always very hostile to the clergy'.[79] In 1487 Archbishop Morton had advanced the proposition in a speech to Canterbury Convocation, and in his famous address to the same body in February 1512 John Colet had alluded to the 'contradiction of the lay people'.[80] The alleged antipathy of clergy and laity could also be utilized for political purposes. Christopher St German gave full vent to his anticlerical leanings and proposals for curtailing the Church's jurisdiction in his ostensibly disinterested *eirenicon*, *A treatise concernynge the division betwene the spirytualtie and temporaltie*, the declared aim of which was to show 'how they may be brought to a unity'.[81] A parliamentary draft bill drawn up by St German in 1531 similarly alleged that relations were chronically bad, and sought to prohibit laypeople from saying 'that there is no good priest', and clerics from claiming that 'lay men love not priests'.[82] St German's real purpose was to advertise the occasions of lay grievance, and Thomas More seems justified in his mocking references to him as 'the Pacifier'.[83] The Queen's almoner, John Skip, made the familiar complaint in a sermon preached at court in 1536 that the clergy's detractors pointed to the faults of a single priest as if it were the fault of all.[84]

[78] W. Chedsay and C. Scott, *Two notable sermones lately preached at Pauls crosse* (1545), sigs. F.vii^r–G.v^v.
[79] G. G. Coulton, *Medieval Village, Manor, and Monastery*, paperback edn. (1960), 288.
[80] Wilkins, *Concilia*, iii. 618; J. H. Lupton, *Life of John Colet*, 2nd edn. (1909), 298.
[81] St German, *Treatise concernynge the division*, 177.
[82] J. A. Guy, *Christopher St German on Chancery and Statute*, Selden Society, suppl. ser. (1985), 131.   [83] T. More, *The Apology*, ed. J. B. Trapp, *CW* 9 (1979), *passim*.
[84] *LP* x. 615.

It does, however, seem to be the case that complaints of ill feeling between priests and laypeople appear with greater frequency and urgency from the 1540s onwards. The homilist Roger Edgeworth bemoaned the fact that even dutiful priests were now 'mocked and jested at' by 'light brained' laymen.[85] The Royal Injunctions of 1547 noted that 'many indiscreet persons do at this day uncharitably condemn and abuse priests and ministers of the Church', and the demand to know whether there were any such persons was repeated in Cranmer's Canterbury visitation articles of 1548 and Bishop Wakeman's articles for the diocese of Gloucester.[86] In November 1547 a royal proclamation complained of the 'many misorders by the serving men and other young and light persons and apprentices of London towards priests', and commanded that such persons should not 'use hereafter such insolence and evil demeanour towards priests, as reviling, tossing of them, taking violently their caps and tippets from them without just title or cause'.[87] As the proclamation recognized, attacks on priests were becoming more common in London in the late 1540s.[88] At Christmas 1545 the King himself addressed the problem. In a speech to Parliament he rebuked the assembled lay lords and commons: 'You of the temporalty be not clean and unspotted of envy; for you rail on bishops, speak slanderously of priests, and rebuke the taunt [i.e. haughty] preachers.'[89] Henry also charged the assembled clerics with lack of charity, and the purpose of the speech was to project the royal supremacy in terms of the King's stern yet caring fatherhood of the nation. None the less, the substance of the message was drawn from a commonplace of educated opinion. To Thomas Becon the mutual antagonism of priests and laity was practically proverbial: 'to whom is it unknown what dissension reigneth among the spiritualty and temporalty, as they are called now-a-days in many places? Seldom doth the one report well of the other. The layman hateth the priest, the priest again burneth not in charity.' Becon's diagnosis of the problem was predictably evangelical: 'priests are so little regarded at this day . . . because they hate knowledge, keep not the ways of our Lord God, nor endeavour themselves to feed Christ's

---

[85] J. Wilson, 'The Sermons of Roger Edgeworth: Reformation Preaching in Bristol', in D. Williams (ed.), *Early Tudor England: Proceedings of the 1987 Harlaxton Symposium* (Woodbridge, 1989), 239.

[86] *Visitation Articles*, ii. 129, 187; W. P. Kennedy (ed.), 'Bishop Wakeman's Visitation Articles for the Diocese of Gloucester, 1548', *EHR* 39 (1924), 255.

[87] P. L. Hughes and J. F. Larkin (eds.), *Tudor Royal Proclamations*, i. *The Early Tudors* (New Haven, Conn., 1964), 407.

[88] S. Brigden, 'Youth and the English Reformation', *PP* 95 (1982), 55–6. Because of the wealth and numbers of the clergy there, lay–clerical relations in London may have been consistently more strained than elsewhere. See Brigden, *London and the Reformation*, 47–8, 93, 115, 172.   [89] Scarisbrick, *Henry VIII*, 471.

flock with God's most blessed word'.[90] The aspirations of a growing body of English Protestants clearly contributed to the growing difficulties, but equally, if not more significant, may have been the disorientation of the great mass of theological unsophisticates, who had witnessed the clergy being attacked with impunity in the second half of Henry VIII's reign, and in Edward VI's were to see them forced to surrender the claims to exalted status which were posited upon celibacy and their sole custodianship of the keys of heaven.

The anecdotal and impressionistic evidence that lay regard for the institution of priesthood and its practitioners had declined significantly by the middle of the sixteenth century is supported by other sources which, while by no means definitive on this question, are more directly amenable to quantification. The level of recruitment to the clergy may, for example, represent at least a rough-and-ready barometer of the prestige priesthood enjoyed among the laity. In the late fifteenth century and early years of the sixteenth, large numbers were presenting themselves for ordination. At York an average of 187 secular priests were ordained every year between 1501 and 1527; at Lincoln 126 were ordained annually between 1514 and 1521.[91] Although demographic factors clearly played a role in this, there is no doubt that a career in the Church was attractive to a wide range of people; it has been pointed out that in the early sixteenth century there were more adult Englishmen in holy orders than in any other occupation bar agriculture.[92] The flood of vocations at this time perhaps meant that there were more priests in England than there was work for them to do, and at Lincoln and London recruitment slowed somewhat in the 1520s.[93] The figures took another downward turn with the beginning of the Reformation Parliament, and numbers began to fall heavily in most areas from the mid-1530s.[94] In Edward's reign, ordinations ceased altogether in the dioceses of York, Durham, and Chester, and in

[90] T. Becon, *Early Works*, ed. J. Ayre, PS (1843), 255; *Catechism of Thomas Becon*, ed. J. Ayre, PS (1844), 432.

[91] R. N. Swanson, *Church and Society in Late Medieval England* (Oxford, 1989), 35–6; V. Davis, 'Rivals for Ministry? Ordinations of Secular and Regular Clergy in Southern England *c*.1300–1500', in SCH 26 (Oxford, 1989), 104; J. A. H. Moran, 'Clerical Recruitment in the Diocese of York: Data and Commentary', *JEH* 34 (1983), 54; M. L. Zell, 'Economic Problems of the Parochial Clergy in the Sixteenth Century', in R. O'Day and F. Heal (eds.), *Princes and Paupers in the English Church, 1500–1800* (Leicester, 1981), 22.

[92] Youings, *Sixteenth-Century England*, 36.

[93] Ibid. 38; Zell, 'Economic Problems of the Parochial Clergy', 22.

[94] Haigh, 'Anticlericalism and the English Reformation', 71; M. Bowker, 'The Henrician Reformation and the Parish Clergy', *Bulletin of the Institute of Historical Research*, 50 (1977), 34; *The Henrician Reformation*, 125; Zell, 'Economic Problems of the Parochial Clergy', 22; J. C. H. Aveling, 'The English Clergy, Catholic and Protestant in the 16th and 17th Centuries', in W. Haase (ed.), *Rome and the Anglicans* (Berlin, 1982).

other dioceses only small numbers were ordained.[95] It is possible to adduce a strictly economic explanation for these developments, and to deny a connection with the status of the clergy as such. One can point to the increasing pressure of clerical taxation under Henry, the influx of former monks and friars on to the market for a benefice after the dissolution of the monasteries, and the further limiting of opportunities consequent upon the abolition of the chantries in 1547.[96] These factors cannot, of course, be discounted, but it seems unlikely that the decision to offer oneself for ordination was usually arrived at solely through a rational calculation of worldly advantage. At the beginning of the sixteenth century, most ordinands had little prospect of acquiring a rich benefice; the conclusion of Michael Zell is that 'thousands joined the ranks of the clergy with little prospect of job security or even a modicum of wealth'.[97] It could not surely have been merely naïve optimism that impelled them to do so. If prospective priests really were so sensitive to the laws of supply and demand, then ordinations should have been rising again in the Edwardian period when the pressure on benefices had diminished. In fact, this began to happen only after the accession of Mary and the abrogation of the Edwardian ordinal. At London, Oxford, Chester, and Exeter there seems to have been a backlog of candidates who were willing to be ordained only after the restoration of the old Catholic rite.[98] It seems likely that the fluctuation in recruitment to the priesthood was occasioned, to a greater or lesser extent, by the progressive demoralization of the clergy from 1529 onwards, culminating in a widespread suspicion of the Edwardian ordination services. A sense of genuine vocation, or at least a perception of the high prestige of the priesthood, may have been a stronger motive influencing the decision to enter the church than some historians have been prepared to allow.

The evidence of lay wills also reveals some apparently significant long-term trends, though it should not be forgotten that these are indicative only of the outlook of the comparatively well-to-do. In some respects the overall impression is that of continuity. Between 1500 and 1529, just over 20 per cent of the wills in the sample included a bequest to a secular priest that was not specifically in return for masses or other services. This

---

[95] S. Thompson, 'The Pastoral Work of the English and Welsh Bishops, 1500–1558', University of Oxford D.Phil. thesis (1984), 179, 184.

[96] J. J. Scarisbrick, 'Clerical Taxation in England, 1485–1547', *JEH* 11 (1960); Bowker, 'Henrician Reformation and the Parish Clergy', 35–6; M. L. Zell, 'The Personnel of the Clergy in Kent, in the Reformation Period', *EHR* 89 (1974), 517–18.

[97] Zell, 'Economic Problems of the Parochial Clergy', 40.

[98] Thompson, 'Pastoral Work of the English and Welsh Bishops', 187.

figure remained virtually constant throughout the rest of Henry VIII's reign and that of Edward VI. In so far as priests continued to be kinsmen and neighbours and to provide a pastoral service in the parishes, this is perhaps unsurprising and does not suggest a calamitous estrangement. In other respects, however, the testamentary evidence creates a contrary impression. Before the Reformation it had been common for those drawing up their wills to leave a small sum to their incumbent described as being for 'tithes forgotten'. This was in all probability not so much an indication that people were consciously and deliberately defaulting on their tithes, rather it argues for a desire in people to feel that they had done their duty by God and by their parson. It was not unusual for testators to leave money for forgotten tithes 'if any be', a formulation which does not suggest laxity or deliberate evasion. Though the most common form was to leave money for neglected tithes to the high altar of the parish church, a few testators made the bequest directly to 'Almighty God'. Between 1500 and 1529 nearly 56 per cent of the testators in the sample made provision for forgotten tithes, between 1530 and 1546 this fell to around 42 per cent, and in Edward's reign to just 15 per cent, despite the fact that there had been no substantial change to the law of tithe in this period. That there was a corresponding decline in the frequency with which mortuaries were bequeathed has already been remarked upon.

Also revealing is the changing role played by priests in the administration of laypeople's wills. To ensure a smooth progress through the courts, wills needed to name witnesses who could testify to the authenticity of the document, executors to carry out the provisions of the will, and also, although this was an optional precaution, supervisors or overseers to make sure the executors performed their duty conscientiously. In Henry VIII's reign, a priest was named as one of the witnesses to the will in over 70 per cent of cases, but between 1547 and 1553 this fell to around 50 per cent. Before 1530 about 10 per cent of wills nominated priests as executors; afterwards this fell to only 4 per cent. Similarly, in the thirty years before the Reformation Parliament met, over 30 per cent of the lay wills which named overseers or supervisors specified a priest. This later fell to around 20 per cent and after 1547 to 15 per cent. Overseers in particular were supposed to be men of standing and local influence, so the decline of priestly involvement here might seem particularly significant. Like the ordination figures, these statistics raise considerable interpretative problems. It has already been suggested, for example, that the decline in the number of wills being witnessed by priests after 1547 may reflect a growing rejection of the necessity for death-bed confession, rather than a lessened respect for priests *per se*, though the two motives are not, of course, entirely separable. It would be possible to suggest also that declining clerical involvement with this and other aspects of testamentary administration might point to the demise of the priest as sole parochial *literatus* in an increasingly literate society, though one may legitimately doubt whether so gradual and fundamental a social change could have been epitomized so quickly and dramatically. It is conceivable also that priests may have been appointed executors because of their familiarity with the details of the necessary exequies and that as masses for the dead came to be abolished it was no longer so pressing to appoint a clerical executor. This would not explain, however, why the decline in priestly executorship began as early as 1530. Of course, relative to the total population there would have been fewer priests in the middle of the sixteenth century than at its outset, but this in itself cannot account for the full extent of the changes, or for the fact that the downward trends generally predate the recruitment crisis of the late 1530s. The overall impression from a study of lay wills in the period 1500–53 is that of a steady disengagement and distancing of priests and laity. Taken together with the literary, forensic, and ordinal evidence, these developments seem to indicate, if not a rise in 'anticlericalism', then at least a conspicuous diminution of the status and prestige the priesthood had enjoyed before the Reformation, and of the perceived importance of priests in the lives, and deaths, of English Christians.

9

Conclusion

On 6 July 1553 the young King Edward VI was dead of tuberculosis. Within a fortnight Northumberland's attempt to install a puppet government under Lady Jane Grey had collapsed, and England's official experiment with Protestantism was, for the moment, at an end. In September a disconsolate Hooper noted that 'the altars are again set up throughout the kingdom' and that 'private masses are frequently celebrated'.[1] The restoration of Catholic sacramental worship which accompanied Mary's accession brought with it a traditional presentation of the role and function of the priest. The Latin mass was restored, along with mandatory auricular confession, and the campaign against married priests was carried through with a vigour which has shocked and impressed historians in equal measure.[2] The status of the clergy in the eyes of the laity was a pressing concern of the Marian authorities, and a number of homilists and theologians revived the arguments that had not been seen in print in England for many years: that priests wielded the keys of salvation, and that this raised their dignity high above that of other men.[3] A few Marian writers, notably Thomas Watson, attempted a more reasoned and persuasive justification of Catholic priesthood than had often previously been heard in England,[4] but for the most part the expectation was that the laity would once again recognize and respond to the exalted dignity of priests. In the circumstances of 1553, in a country deeply divided over religious

[1] H. Robinson (ed.), *Original Letters Relative to the English Reformation*, PS (1864), i. 100.

[2] W. H. Frere, *The Marian Reaction in its Relation to the English Clergy* (1896), 44–87; D. M. Loades, *The Reign of Mary Tudor*, 2nd edn. (1991), 106–7; H. Grieve, 'The Deprived Married Clergy in Essex, 1553–1561', *TRHS*, 4th ser., 22 (1940).

[3] E. Bonner, *A Profitable and Necessarye Doctryne* (1555), sig. Aa.ii^v–iv^v; J. Christopherson, *An exhortation to all menne to take hede and beware of rebellion* (1554), sig. T.iv^r–vi^v; R. Edgeworth, *Sermons* (1557), 167^r–170^v, 292^v–293^r; T. Watson, *Holsome and catholyke doctryne concerninge the seven sacraments* (1558), 115^{r-v}, 154^v–160^r; E. A. Macek, 'Richard Smith: Tudor Cleric in Defense of Traditional Belief and Practice', *Catholic Historical Review*, 72 (1986), 398. John Foxe provides a description of a sermon Bonner was claimed to have delivered to the convocation of 1554, 'setting forth the most incomparable and super-angelical order of priesthood', which follows closely the arguments of Sermon 111 in Herolt's *Sermones Discipuli*: Foxe, *Acts and Monuments*, vi. 433–4.

[4] Watson, *Holsome and catholyke doctryne*, 116^v, 153^v–158^v.

questions, the hope was an optimistic one. In the Cornish village of Linkinhorne at Christmas of that year, one parishioner coming home from mass rejoiced that he had 'seen that thing he saw not in four year', but his neighbour retorted, 'I would all priests were hanged.'[5]

The evidence we have noted for growing disrespect to the clergy in the later 1540s and early 1550s continues unabated into Mary's reign. In London, verbal and physical attacks on priests seem to have been common, and from Colchester a cleric complained to his bishop that 'the ministers of the Church are hemmed at in the open streets and called knaves'.[6] The Queen's chaplain, John Christopherson, was driven to conclude that priests would be better off 'among the Turks and Saracens' than among the heretics who mocked and despised them.[7] As with earlier denunciations of lay wilfulness and ingratitude there was an element of ritual in such declarations, yet there seems little doubt that in the middle years of the sixteenth century the task of the parish clergy in disciplining, instructing, and redeeming their flock had become increasingly difficult. Some English men and women now entertained clearly incompatible views of the nature and proper function of the priesthood, and the religious and political tergiversations of the 1540s and 1550s had probably done much to dislocate the perceptions and expectations both of the laity and of the parish clergy themselves. In requiring married priests to perform public penance before their congregations, the Marian Church did little to improve the situation, and the desperate shortage of parish clergy in the 1550s and 1560s probably bears witness to some kind of crisis of confidence.

Yet to suggest, as, for example, Christopher Haigh has done, that anticlericalism was a clear 'result' of the Reformation is perhaps to misrepresent the case.[8] That defensive clericalism could co-exist with a reformed conception of clerical ministry is beyond question: many Elizabethan and Jacobean ministers continued to insist on the high dignity of their calling and to complain that they were not receiving their due from the laity.[9] Yet the claims of these men were predicated not upon

---

[5] A. L. Rowse, *Tudor Cornwall*, 2nd edn. (1969), 304–5.

[6] S. Brigden, *London and the Reformation* (Oxford, 1989), 598–600; Wilkins, *Concilia*, iv. 96; *Visitation Articles*, ii, 347, 350; Foxe, *Acts and Monuments*, viii. 383.

[7] Christopherson, *An exhortation to beware of rebellion*, sig. T.iv[r].

[8] C. Haigh, 'Anticlericalism and the English Reformation', in C. Haigh (ed.), *The English Reformation Revised* (Cambridge, 1987), 74.

[9] P. Lake, 'Richard Kilby: A Study in Personal and Professional Failure', in W. J. Sheils and D. Wood, *The Ministry, Clerical and Lay*, SCH 26 (Oxford, 1989); *Moderate Puritans and the Elizabethan Church* (Cambridge, 1982), 16–17, 88, 130–1; P. Collinson, *The Religion of Protestants* (Oxford, 1982), 111–14; J. W. Blench, *Preaching in England in the Late Fifteenth and Sixteenth Centuries* (Oxford, 1964), 301–2.

the recognition of their ordination, but upon their assiduity in preaching the Word of God. The pre-Reformation priesthood, by contrast, sited its status in its assured capacity to dispense sacramental grace. In so far as the mechanisms of absolution and mediation controlled by priests gave to the bulk of the laity the nearest thing on offer to a promise of eternal salvation, demands that they should be adjudged superior to all temporal and celestial beings were scarcely hyperbole. Yet the implications of the concept of sacramental priesthood seem to have required a leap of imagination of which relatively few among the clergy and laity of early Reformation England showed themselves capable. Christopher St German identified the problem with disarming frankness in 1533: if priests were mistreated by the laity, surely they only had themselves to blame 'if it be well considered how much good priests be beloved and cherished of lay men'.[10] The fact that wicked, or even mundane and mediocre men might be the prime instruments of divine grace was in itself a paradox, and one that contemporaries from all walks of life often found difficult to resolve. By allowing or encouraging its spokesmen to disseminate an arch-clericalist world-view, which had no place for fallible ministers, the Church created a currency of inflated expectation, and was repaid by the laity in that same coin. In dress, demeanour, conduct, many laypeople hoped to recognize in the priest those tokens of sanctity which would serve to guarantee the spiritual gifts the clergy claimed to be able to bestow.

Thomas Watson, the Marian Bishop of Lincoln, claimed in 1558 to detect a double reason for laypeople to respect and obey the ministers of the Church: 'they be not only our neighbours, whom for that respect we ought to love as ourselves, but also they be the causes of our spiritual life.'[11] In fact, Watson had unwittingly hit upon the crux of his Church's clericalist dilemma; many laypeople found it understandably difficult that the neighbour who so often shared the preoccupations of the community's secular life was also the source of its spiritual life, and much of the evidence for what has traditionally been regarded as 'anticlericalism' may reflect this antinomy, and the attempt to resolve it by demanding higher clerical standards. The tension that was thus always implicit in the relationship of priest and parishioner was exacerbated by the Reformation changes, as doubts and confusion as to the religious role of the priest and his reciprocal obligations to his parishioners followed upon liturgical, doctrinal, and devotional 'reforms', imposed by the authority of Church and State, and welcomed by a growing minority at the parish level.

---

[10] C. St German, *Salem and Bizance*, in J. Guy *et al.* (eds.), *The Debellation of Salem and Bizance*, *CW* 10 (1987), 381.   [11] Watson, *Holsome and catholyke doctryne*, 160ʳ.

Conflicting ideas about the nature and tasks of the clerical ministry were to remain thereafter a permanent feature of the English religious scene, and if widespread dissatisfaction with the theory and practice of priesthood had relatively little to do with the initial causes of the 'English Reformation', the complex of political, social, and religious change comprehended by that expression did much to expose and exacerbate the contradictions inherent in English parochial life.

In his treatise on the Seven Penitential Psalms, the Henrician martyr John Fisher had lamented that while in apostolic times there had been no golden chalices, but many golden priests, 'now be many chalices of gold, and almost no golden priests'.[12] The unflattering comparison between the golden priests of the past and the wooden priests of the present age was by Fisher's time a familiar adage,[13] and it may well be doubted whether at any stage of the Church's existence the golden priests have not been hugely outnumbered by the wooden, and are always likely to be so. It was unfortunate, but perhaps unavoidable, that so many in sixteenth-century England were encouraged to expect rough but serviceable wood to emulate glittering and unattainable gold.

[12] J. Fisher, *The English Works*, ed. J. E. B. Mayor, EETS es 27 (1876), 181.

[13] E. R. Harvey, 'The Ymage of Love', in More, *Dialogue*, 740 ff.; Foxe, *Acts and Monuments*, iv. 259; G. Marc'hadour, 'Golden Priests and Chalices of Gold', *Moreana*, 6 (1969); 'Fisher and More: A Note', in B. Bradshaw and E. Duffy (eds.), *Humanism, Reform and the Reformation* (Cambridge, 1989); E. Cameron, *The European Reformation* (Oxford, 1991), 47.

Bibliography

PRIMARY SOURCES

Manuscripts

1. *Public Record Office*

Early Chancery Proceedings	C. 1, 239/44; 240/26; 253/27; 346/77; 365/39; 375/39; 377/22; 441/36; 458/3; 469/54; 475/3; 487/22; 533/3; 649/25; 659/6; 666/8; 746/36; 748/15; 802/13; 827/1; 867/72; 900/34; 929/9; 945/31; 965/21, 25; 1044/69; 1068/80; 1069/63; 1093/11; 1108/51, 56; 1201/15; 1275/52; 1309/73
Proceedings in the Court of Star Chamber, Henry VIII	STA. C. 2, 1/47, 82–3, 90; 2/154, 267; 3/149, 199–200; 4/202; 5/130; 6/294; 7/149, 173, 215; 8/189, 190–2; 9/63, 137; 10/153; 11/55; 12/196; 14/60, 114, 152; 15/139; 16/37, 91, 216, 392; 17/26, 86, 88, 137; 18/93, 290, 301; 19/53, 323; 20/356; 21/160, 168; 24/20, 66, 146, 359, 428; 25/294, 333; 26/15, 179, 194, 251, 454; 27/41, 97, 139; 28/63, 105; 29/24, 46, 49, 78, 83, 121, 149, 181; 30/38, 88, 104, 114, 123; 31/60, 61, 120, 155, 171, 178; 32/20; 33/1, 13, 57; 34/31; 35/68, 74
Proceedings in the Court of Star Chamber, Edward VI	STA. C. 3, 3/38, 81; 4/74; 5/16, 48, 67, 81; 6/68
Proceedings in the Court of Requests	Req. 2, 3/293; 5/186, 337; 6/20, 101; 7/38; 9/45, 155; 10/68, 251; 11/95, 115; 12/54; 17/85; 18/42, 75; 27/38
State Papers, Henry VIII	SP 1/83; 100
Theological Tracts	SP 6/2; 4; 11
Prerogative Court of Canterbury, Registers of wills	Prob. 11, 'Blamyr', 'Moone', 'Holgrave', 'Bennett', 'Holder', 'Maynwaring', 'Porch', 'Jankyn', 'Hogen', 'Alenger', 'Pynnyng', 'Bucke'

2. *Greater London Record Office*

Consistory Court Deposition Books, 1510–16, 1521–4, 1529–33	DL/C/206; 207; 208
Vicar-General's Book ('Foxford'), 1521–39	DL/C/330

3. *Guildhall Library, London*

Register of Bishop Fitzjames 1506–22	MS 9531/9

4. *Hampshire Record Office*

Consistory Court Deposition Book, 1531–47	C. 3/1

5. *Oxfordshire County Record Office*

Ecclesiastical Court Deposition Book, 1540s	Oxf. Dioc. MSS d. 14

6. *Balliol College, Oxford*

Commonplace Book of Richard Hill	MS 354

7. *Borthwick Institute of Historical Research, York*

Churchwardens' Book of St Michael Spurriergate, 1518–48	BI PR Y/MS 4
Dean and Chapter Act Book, 1387–1494	D/C AB 1
Dean and Chapter Cause Papers	D/C CP 1524/13; 1528/5; 1533/4; 1536/2; 1538/3; 1539/1; 1542/1; 1547/3
Dean and Chapter, Miscellaneous	D/C Misc.
Exchequer and Prerogative Courts of York, will registers	Prob. Reg. 11
Letters Testimonial	Ord. 1554/1/2–9, 28; 1555/1/10–16, 22; 1556/1/17–21, 23–6, 29; 1557/1/30–40; Adm. 1557/7, 30
Registers of Archbishop Thomas Wolsey 1514–28, and Archbishops Holgate and Heath 1547–57	Reg. 27
Sixteenth-Century Cause Papers	CP G 11/1504; 166/1522; 273/1540; 338/1545; 423/1550

Printed Sources

ADDY, S. O. (ed.), 'Wills at Somerset House Relating to Derbyshire', *Journal of the Derbyshire Archaeological and Natural History Society*, 45 (1923).

AMPHLETT, J. (ed.), *The Churchwardens' Accounts of St Michael's in Bedwardine, 1539–1603 . . . [and] St Helen, Worcester, 1519–1529*, Worcestershire Historical Society, 6 (1896).

AMYOT, T. (ed.), 'Transcript of an Original Manuscript Containing a Memorial from George Constantyne to Thomas Lord Cromwell', *Archaeologia*, 23 (1831).

'Ancient Churchwardens' Accounts of a City Parish, St Andrew Hobard, Eastcheap', *British Magazine and Monthly Register*, 33 (1848).

AQUINAS, THOMAS, *Summa Theologica*, English tr. (New York, 1948).

The assaute and co[n]quest of heven, Berthelet (1529).

AUDELAY, J., *Poems*, ed. E. K. Whiting, EETS 184 (1931).

BAILEY, F. A. (ed.), *The Churchwardens' Accounts of Prescot, Lancashire, 1523–1607*, Lancashire and Cheshire Record Society, 104 (1953).

BAKER, J. H. (ed.), *The Reports of Sir John Spelman*, Selden Society, 94 (1978).

BALE, J., *The Acts of Englysh Votaryes* (1560), facsimile edn. (Amsterdam, 1979).

—— (?), *An answere to a papystycall exhortacyon*, in H. Huth and W. C. Hazlitt (eds.), *Fugitive Tracts* (1875).

—— *The Vocacyon of Johan Bale to the Bishoprick of Ossorie in Irelande* (1553).

BANNISTER, A. T. (ed.), *Registrum Thome Spofford, Episcopi Herefordensis, 1422–1448*, CYS 23 (1914).

BARLOW, J., *The Burial of the Mass*, in E. Arber (ed.), *English Reprints* (1871).

BARNES, R., *The Reformation Essays of Dr Robert Barnes*, ed. N. S. Tjernagel (1963).

BECON, T., *Early Works*, ed. J. Ayre, PS (1843).

—— *The Catechism of Thomas Becon*, ed. J. Ayre, PS (1844).

—— *Prayers and Other Pieces*, ed. J. Ayre, PS (1844).

BELL, P. (ed.), *Bedfordshire Wills, 1480–1519*, Bedfordshire Historical Record Society, 45 (1966).

BENTON, G. M. (ed.), 'Essex Wills at Canterbury', *Transactions of the Essex Archaeological Society*, 21 (1937).

BERKOWITZ, D. S. (ed.), *Humanist Scholarship and Public Order: Two Tracts against the Pilgrimage of Grace by Sir Richard Morison* (Washington, 1984).

BESTALL, J. M., and FOWKES, D. V. (eds.), *Chesterfield Wills and Inventories, 1521–1603*, Derbyshire Record Society, 1 (1977).

BETTENSON, H. (ed.), *Documents of the Christian Church* (Oxford, 1943).

BINNEY, J. E., and WEAVER, F. W. (eds.), *The Accounts of the Wardens of the Parish of Morebath, Devon, 1520–1573* (Exeter, 1904).

BLAKE, N. F. (ed.), *Quattuor Sermones printed by William Caxton*, Middle English Texts, 12 (Heidelberg, 1975).

BLUNT, J. H. (ed.), *The Myroure of Oure Ladye*, EETS ES 19 (1873).

The Boke of the Ghostly Father, de Worde (c.1521).

BONDE, W., *The Pylgrymage of Perfeccyon*, de Worde (1531).

BONNER, E., *A profitable and necessarye doctryne* (1555).

BOWKER, M. (ed.), *An Episcopal Court Book for the Diocese of Lincoln, 1514–1520*, LRS, 61 (1967).

BRADFORD, G. (ed.), *Proceedings in the Court of Star Chamber in the Reigns of Henry VII and Henry VIII*, SRS 27 (1911).

BRADFORD, J., *The Writings of John Bradford . . . Letters, Treatises, Remains*, ed. A. Townsend, PS (1853).

BRANDEIS, A. (ed.), *Jacob's Well*, EETS 115 (1900).

BRIGG, W., and LUMB, G. D. (eds.), *Testamenta Leodensia*, Thorseby Society, 4, 9, 11, 15, 19, 27 (1893–1919).

BRINKLOW, H., *The Complaynt of Roderyck Mors . . . & the Lamentacyon of a Christen Agaynst the Cyte of London*, ed. J. M. Cowper, EETS ES 22 (1874).

BROWN, W. (ed.), *Yorkshire Star Chamber Proceedings*, vols. i, iii, YAS, 41, 51, (1909–14).

Calendar of letters, despatches, and state papers relating to the negotiation between England and Spain, ed. P. De Gayangos (1879).

CATHERINE OF SIENA, *The Orchard of Syon*, tr. Dane James (1519).

CHANDOS, J. (ed.), *In God's Name: Examples of Preaching in England from the Act of Supremacy to the Act of Uniformity, 1534–1662* (1971).

CHAUCER, G., *The Canterbury Tales*, ed. N. F. Blake (1980).

CHEDSAY, W., and SCOTT, C., *Two notable sermones lately preached at Pauls crosse* (1545).

CHRISTOPHERSON, J., *An exhortation to all menne to take hede and beware of rebellion* (1554).

'Churchwardens' Accounts of the Parish of St Margaret Pattens, London', *The Sacristy*, 1 (1871).

CIGMAN, G. (ed.), *Lollard Sermons*, EETS 294 (1989).

CIRKET, A. F. (ed.), *English Wills, 1498–1526*, Bedfordshire Historical Record Society, 37 (1956).

CLARK, A. (ed.), *Lincoln Diocese Documents, 1450–1544*, EETS 149 (1914).

CLAY, J. W. (ed.), *North Country Wills . . . at Somerset House and Lambeth Palace, 1383 to 1558*, SS 116 (1908).

——and CROSSLEY, E. W. (eds.), *Halifax Wills, 1389–1544* (Halifax, 1904).

COBB, C. S. (ed.), *The Rationale of Ceremonial, 1540–1543*, ACC 18 (1910).

COLE, R. E. G. (ed.), *Chapter Acts of the Cathedral Church of St Mary of Lincoln, AD 1520–1536*, LRS 12 (1915).

COLLINS, F. (ed.), *Wills and Administrations from the Knaresborough Court Rolls*, vol. i SS 104 (1902).

COOK, R. B. (ed.), *Wills of Leeds and District*, Thoresby Society, 22, 24 (1915–19).

——(ed.), *Early Pontefract Wills*, Thoresby Society, 26 (1924).

——(ed.), *Wills of the Parishes of Rothwell, Saxton, Sherburn in Elmet, Swillington, Thorner, Whitkirk and Woodkirk*, Thoresby Society, 33 (1935).

COOKE, A. M. (ed.), *Act Book of the Ecclesiastical Court of Whalley, 1510–1538*, ChS 44 (1901).

COTTON, C. (ed.), 'Churchwardens' Accounts of the Parish of St Andrew Canterbury, 1485–1557', *AC* 32–4 (1917–20).

COVERDALE, M., *Writings and Translations*, ed. G. Pearson, PS (1844).

——*Remains*, ed. G. Pearson, PS (1846).

COWPER, J. M. (ed.), *Four Supplications, 1529–1553*, EETS ES 13 (1871).

——(ed.), 'Churchwardens' Accounts of St Dunstan, Canterbury, 1484–1580', *AC* 17 (1887).

CRANMER, T., *Writings and Disputations . . . Relative to the Sacrament of the Lord's Supper*, ed. J. E. Cox, PS (1844).

——*Miscellaneous Writings and Letters*, ed. J. E. Cox, PS (1846).

CROSSLEY, E. W. (ed.), *The Testamentary Documents of Yorkshire Peculiars*, YAS (RS) 74 (1929).

——(ed.), *Halifax Wills, 1545–1559* (Leeds, n.d.).

CROWLEY, R., *Select Works*, ed. J. M. Cowper, EETS ES 15 (1872).

—— *The Confutation of xiii articles wherunto N. Shaxton subscribed*, J. Day and W. Seres (1548).

Cura Clericalis (1532).

CUTHBERT, E. G., and ATCHLEY, F. (eds.), 'On the Mediaeval Parish Records of the Church of St Nicholas, Bristol', *Transactions of the St Paul's Ecclesiological Society*, 6 (1906–10).

DALTON, J. N. (ed.), *The Manuscripts of St George's Chapel, Windsor Castle* (Windsor, 1957).

DARLINGTON, I. (ed.), *London Consistory Court Wills, 1492–1547*, LoRS 3 (1967).

DAVIS, N. (ed.), *Paston Letters and Papers of the Fifteenth Century* (Oxford, 1971).

DEARMER, P. (ed.), *Dat Boexken van der Missen*, ACC (1903).

DICKENS, A. G. (ed.), *Tudor Treatises*, YAS 125 (1959).

——(ed.), *Clifford Letters of the Sixteenth Century*, SS 172 (1962).

——and CARR, D. (eds.), *The Reformation in England to the Accession of Elizabeth I* (1967).

DIONYSIUS CARTHUSIANUS, *The Lyfe of Prestes* (*c*.1533).

Dives and Pauper (1534).

DREW, C. (ed.), *Lambeth Churchwardens' Accounts, 1504–1645*, Surrey Record Society, 40 (1940).

DUDDING, R. C. (ed.), *The First Churchwardens' Book of Louth, 1500–1524* (Oxford, 1941).

A dyalogue betwene one Clemente a clerke of the convocacyon, and one Bernarde a burges of the parlyament, J. Rastell (*c*.1532).

DYBOSKI, R. (ed.), *Songs, Carols and other Miscellaneous Poems from the Balliol MS 354: Richard Hill's Commonplace-Book*, EETS ES 101 (1908).

DYMOND, D., and PAINE, C. (eds.), *The Spoil of Melford Church: The Reformation in a Suffolk Parish* (Ipswich, 1989).

EARWAKER, J. P. (ed.), *Lancashire and Cheshire Wills and Inventories at Chester with an Appendix of Abstracts of Wills now lost or destroyed*, ChS NS 3 (1884).

——(ed.), *Lancashire and Cheshire Wills and Inventories 1572 to 1696 now preserved at Chester with an appendix of Lancashire and Cheshire Wills and Inventories proved at York or Richmond, 1542 to 1649*, ChS NS 28 (1893).

EDGEWORTH, R., *Sermons* (1557).

ELLIS, H. (ed.), *Original Letters Illustrative of English History*, 3 vols., 3rd ser. (1846).

ELVEY, E. M. (ed.), *The Courts of the Archdeaconry of Buckingham, 1483–1523*, Buckinghamshire Record Society, 19 (1975).

ERASMUS, D., *Collected Works*, tr. R. A. Mynors, ed. B. G. Bietenholz (Toronto, 1987).

ESHILBY, H. D. (ed.), 'Some Wills from the Richmond Registry', *The Northern Genealogist*, 3 (1900).

Exornatorium Curatorum, de Worde (1520).

FISH, S., *A Supplicacyon for the Beggars*, ed. F. J. Furnivall, EETS 13 (1871).

FISHER, J., *The English Works*, ed. J. E. B. Mayor, EETS ES 27 (1876).

——*The Defence of the Priesthood*, tr. P. E. Hallett (1935).

FISHWICK, H. (ed.), *Pleadings and Depositions in the Duchy Court of Lancaster*, Lancashire and Cheshire Record Society, 32, 35, 40 (1896–9).

The floure of the commaundementes of god, tr. A. Chertsey, de Worde (1521).

FOSTER, C. W. (ed.), *Lincoln Wills Registered in the District Probate Registry at Lincoln, 1271–1532*, LRS, 5, 10, 24 (1914–30).

FOSTER, J. E. (ed.), 'Churchwardens' Accounts of St Mary the Great Cambridge', CAS 35 (1905).

FOWLER, J. T. (ed.), *Acts of the Chapter of the Collegiate Church of Ripon, 1452–1506*, SS 64 (1875).

FOX, R., *Letters of Richard Fox, 1486–1527*, ed. P. S. and H. M. Allen (Oxford, 1929).

FOXE, J., *Acts and Monuments*, ed. S. R. Cattley and G. Townsend, 8 vols. (1837–41).

FRERE, W. H. (ed.), *Exposition de la messe*, ACC 2 (1899).

——and KENNEDY, W. P. (eds.), *Visitation Articles and Injunctions of the Period of the Reformation*, ii, ACC (1910).

FRY, G. S. (ed.), *Walthamstow Wills (1335–1559)*, Walthamstow Antiquarian Society Official Publication, 9 (1921).

FURNIVALL, F. J. (ed.), *Ballads from Manuscripts*, Ballad Society (1868–72).

FYLLOL, J., *Agaynst the possessyons of the clergye*, J. Skot (1537).

GAIRDNER, J. (ed.), 'Bishop Hooper's Visitation of Gloucester', *EHR* 19 (1904).

GARARD, FRIAR, *The Interpretacyon and Sygnyfycacyon of the Masse* (1532).

GARDINER, S., *The Letters of Stephen Gardiner*, ed. J. A. Muller (Cambridge, 1933).

GATTY, A. S. (ed.), 'Churchwardens' Accounts, 1520–1546', in *Registers of Ecclesfield Parish Church, Yorkshire* (1878).

GEE, H., and HARDY, W. J. (eds.), *Documents Illustrative of English Church History* (1896).

GIBBONS, A. (ed.), *Ely Episcopal Records* (1890).

GIBSON, E. C. (ed.), *The First and Second Prayer Books of Edward VI* (1910).

GIRAUD, F. F. (ed.), 'On the Parish Clerks and Sexton of Faversham, AD 1506–1593', *AC* 20 (1893).

GLASSCOCK, J. L. (ed.), *The Records of St Michael's Parish Church, Bishop's Stortford* (1882).

GRAY, D. (ed.), *The Oxford Book of Late Medieval Verse and Prose* (Oxford, 1985).

GRIFFITHS, J. (ed.), *The Two Books of Homilies* (Oxford, 1859).

HAINES, W. (ed.), 'Stanford Churchwardens' Accounts (1552–1602)', *The Antiquary*, 98/17 (1888).

HALE, W. H. (ed.), *A Series of Precedents and Proceedings in Criminal Causes* (1847).

HALL, E., *The Union of the two Noble and Illustre Famelies of Lancastre and Yorke* (1809).

HANHAM, A. (ed.), *Churchwardens' Accounts of Ashburton, 1479–1580*, Devon and Cornwall Record Society, NS 15 (1970).

HARINGTON, W., *The Comendacions of Matrymony*, J. Rastell (1528).

HAZLITT, W. C. (ed.), *Remains of the Popular Poetry of England* (1864).

——(ed.), *A Select Collection of Old English Plays*, 4th edn. (1874).

HEATH, P. (ed.), *Medieval Clerical Accounts* (York, 1964).

HELMHOLZ, R. H. (ed.), *Select Cases on Defamation to 1600*, Selden Society, 101 (1985).

HENDERSON (ed.), *Manuale et Processionale ad Usum Insignis Ecclesiae Eboracensis*, SS 63 (1874).

HEROLT, J., *Sermones Discipuli* (1510).

HEYWOOD, J., *Works and Miscellaneous Short Poems*, ed. B. A. Milligan, Illinois Studies in Language and Literature (Urbana, Ill., 1956).

HILARIE, H., *The Resurrecion of the Masse* (Strasbourg, 1554).

HILSEY, J., *The manual of prayers, or the prymer in Englysh & Laten, set forth by Ihon Bysshope of Rochester at the comaundemente of Thomas Cromwell*, J. Wayland (1539).

HINDE, G. (ed.), *The Registers of Cuthbert Tunstal, Bishop of Durham 1530–1559, and James Pilkington, Bishop of Durham, 1561–1576*, SS 161 (1952).

HOBHOUSE, E. (ed.), *Churchwardens' Accounts of Croscombe, Pilton, Yatton, Tintinhull, Morebath, and St Michael's, Bath, 1349–1560*, SRS 4 (1890).

HOCCLEVE, T., *The Minor Poems*, ed. F. J. Furnivall, EETS ES 61 (1892).

HODGSON, J. C. (ed.), *Wills and Inventories from the Registry at Durham, part III*, SS 112 (1906).

HOLLAND, W., and RAVEN, J. J. (eds.), *Cratfield Parish Papers* (1895).

HOOPER, J., *Early Writings*, ed. S. Carr, PS (1843).

HUGGARDE, M., *The displaying of the Protestants* (1556).

HUGHES, P. L., and LARKIN, J. F. (eds.), *Tudor Royal Proclamations*, i. *The Early Tudors* (New Haven, Conn., 1964).

HUSSEY, A. (ed.), *Kent Chantries*, Kent Archaeological Society Records Branch, 12 (1936).

HUTCHINSON, R., *The Image of God, or laie man's boke* (1560).

IRVINE, W. F. (ed.), *A Collection of Lancashire and Cheshire Wills not now to be found in any Probate Registry, 1301–1752*, Lancashire and Cheshire Record Society, 30 (1896).

JENKINSON, H., and FOWLER, G. H. (eds.), *Some Bedfordshire Wills at Lambeth and Lincoln*, Bedfordshire Historical Record Society, 14 (1931).

JEWEL, J., *Works*, ed. J. Ayre, PS (1847).

JOSEPH, R., *The Letter Book of Robert Joseph*, ed. H. Aveling and W. A. Pantin, Oxford Historical Society, NS 19 (1967).

KEMPE, M., *The Book of Margery Kempe*, ed. S. B. Meech, EETS 212 (1940).

KENNEDY, W. P. (ed.), 'Bishop Wakeman's Visitation Articles for the Diocese of Gloucester, 1548', *EHR* 39 (1924).

KINGSFORD, C. L. (ed.), *Two London Chronicles*, Camden Miscellany, 12 (1910).

KITCHING, C. J. (ed.), *The Royal Visitation of 1559*, SS 187 (1975).

——(ed.), *London and Middlesex Chantry Certificates 1548*, LoRS 16 (1980).

KITTO, J. V. (ed.), *St Martin-in-the-Fields, the Accounts of the Churchwardens, 1525–1603* (1901).

KLEIN, E. J. (ed.), *The Imitation of Christ from the First Edition of an English Translation Made c.1530 by Richard Whitford* (New York, 1941).

LACEY, T. A. (ed.), *The King's Book, 1543* (1895).

LANCASHIRE, I. (ed.), *Two Tudor Interludes* (Manchester, 1980).

LANGFORDE, *Meditatyons for goostly exercyse in the tyme of the masse*, in J. Wickham Legg (ed.), *Tracts on the Mass*, Henry Bradshaw Society, 27 (1904).

LANGLAND, W., *Piers the Ploughman*, ed. J. F. Goodridge (Harmondsworth, 1966).

LATIMER, H., *Sermons*, ed. G. E. Corrie, PS (1844).

——*Sermons and Remains*, ed. G. E. Corrie, PS (1845).

LEACH, A. F. (ed.), *Visitations and Memorials of Southwell Minster*, CS NS 48 (1891).

LE ROY LADURIE, E., *The Territory of the Historian*, tr. B. and S. Reynolds (Hassocks, 1979).

Letters and Papers, Foreign and Domestic, of the Reign of Henry VIII, ed. J. S. Brewer, J. Gairdner, and R. H. Brodie, 21 vols. (1862–1932).

LEVER, T., *Sermons 1550*, ed. E. Arber, English Reprints (1870).

LISTER, J., *Yorkshire Star Chamber Proceedings, vol. iv*, YAS 70 (1927).

LITTLEHALES, H. (ed.), *The Medieval Records of a London City Church (St Mary at Hill), 1420–1559*, EETS 125, 128 (1904–5).

LLOYD, C. (ed.), *Formularies of Faith put Forth by Authority during the Reign of Henry VIII* (Oxford, 1825).

LOUIS, C. (ed.), *The Commonplace Book of Robert Reynes of Acle: An Edition of Tanner MS 407* (New York, 1980).

LOVE, N., *The Mirror of the Blessed Life of Jesu Christ*, ed. by a monk of Parkminster (1926).

LUMB, G. D. (ed.), *Testamenta Leodiensia*, Thoresby Society, 19 (1911–13).

LUMBY, J. R. (ed.), *Ratis Raving and other Moral and Religious Pieces*, EETS 41 (1876).

LUTHER, M., *Luther's Works*, ed. J. Pelikan *et al.* (Philadelphia, 1955–   ).

LYDGATE, J., *Minor Poems*, ed. H. N. MacCracken, EETS 107 (1911).

LYNDWOOD, W., *Provinciale*, ed. J. V. Bullard and H. C. Bell (1929).

McCALL, H. B. (ed.), *Yorkshire Star Chamber Proceedings, vol. ii*, YAS 45 (1911).

McGREGOR, M. (ed.), *Bedfordshire Wills Proved in the Prerogative Court of Canterbury, 1383–1548*, Bedfordshire Historical Record Society, 58 (1979).

MACLEAN, J., 'Notes on the Accounts of the Procurators, or Churchwardens, of the Parish of St Ewen's, Bristol', *Transactions of the Bristol and Gloucestershire Archaeological Society*, 15 (1840).

MCNEILL, J. T., and GAMER, H. M. (eds.), *Medieval Handbooks of Penance* (1938).

MANDER, G. P. (ed.), *A Register of Stafford and other Local Wills*, William Salt Archaeological Society, 50 (1926).

MARCOURT, A., *A Declaration of the Masse*, tr. from French (1547).

MARDY, J., *A breife recantacion of maystres missa* (1548).

MARTIN, C. T. (ed.), 'Clerical Life in the Fifteenth Century, as Illustrated by Proceedings of the Court of Chancery', *Archaeologia*, 60 (1907).

MARTIN, T., *A Treatise declaring and plainly provyng, that the pretensed marriage of priestes . . . is no marriage* (1554).

MASTER, B. R., and RALPH, E. (eds.), *The Church Book of St Ewen's Bristol, 1454– 1584*, Bristol and Gloucestershire Archaeological Society Records Section, 6 (1967).

MELANCHTHON, P., *A godly defense . . . defending the mariage of preists*, tr. G. Joye (Antwerp, 1541).

MELLOWS, W. T. (ed.), *Peterborough Local Administration: Parochial Government before the Reformation*, Northamptonshire Record Society, 9 (1937).

MELTON, W., *Sermo exhortatorius cancellarii Eboracensis hiis qui ad sacros ordines petunt promoveri* (c.1510).

MERCER, F. R. (ed.), *Churchwardens' Accounts at Betrysden, 1515–1573*, Kent Archaeological Society Records Branch, 5 (1982).

MIRC, J., *Instructions for Parish Priests*, EETS 131 (1868).

——*Festial*, ed. T. Erbe, EETS ES 96 (1905).

MONTE ROCHERII, G. DE, *Manipulus Curatorum*, de Worde (1509).

MOONE, P., *A short treatyse of certayne things abused in the popish church* (Ipswich, 1548).

MOORE, A. P. (ed.), 'Proceedings of the Ecclesiastical Courts in the Archdeaconry of Leicester, 1516–1535', *Associated Architectural Societies Reports and Papers*, 28 (1905).

MORE, T., *Utopia*, ed. E. Surtz, S. J. and J. H. Hexter, *CW* 4 (1963).

——*A Dialogue Concerning Heresies*, ed. T. M. C. Lawler, G. Marc'hadour, and R. C. Marius, *CW* 6 (1981).

——*Letter to Bugenhagen, Supplication of Souls, Letter against Frith*, ed. F. Manley, G. Marc'hadour, R. Marius, and C. H. Miller, *CW* 7 (1990).

——*The Apology*, ed. J. B. Trapp, *CW* 9 (1979).

——*The Debellation of Salem and Bizance*, ed. J. Guy, R. Keen, C. H. Miller, and R. McGugan, *CW* 10 (1987).

——*The Answer to a Poisoned Book*, ed. S. Foley and C. H. Miller, *CW* 11 (1985).

——*Treatise on the Passion, Treatise on the Blessed Body, Instructions and Prayers*, ed. G. E. Haupt, *CW* 13 (1976).

——*De Tristitia Christi*, ed. C. H. Miller, *CW* 14 (1976).

MORE, T., *The Workes of Sir Thomas More Knyght . . . wrytten by him in the Englysh tonge* (1557).

——*St Thomas More: Selected Letters*, ed. E. F. Rogers (New Haven, Conn., 1961).

MUNBY, L. M. (ed.), *Life and Death in King's Langley: Wills and Inventories, 1498–1659*, King's Langley Local History and Museum Society (1981).

NICHOLS, J. G. (ed.), *Chronicle of the Grey Friars of London*, CS OS 53 (1851).

——(ed.), *Narratives of the Days of the Reformation*, CS 77 (1859).

NORTH, T. (ed.), *The Accounts of the Churchwardens of St Martin's, Leicester, 1489–1844* (Leicester, 1884).

OESTERLEY, H. (ed.), *Shakespeare's Jest Book* (1866).

The Ordinary of crysten men, de Worde (1506).

OUVRY, F. (ed.), 'Extracts from the Churchwardens' Accounts of the Parish of Wing in the County of Buckingham', *Archaeologia*, 36 (1855).

PAGE, W. (ed.), *Yorkshire Chantry Surveys*, SS 91 (1894).

PAGE-TURNER, F. A. (ed.), *The Bedfordshire Wills and Administrations Proved at Lambeth Palace and in the Archdeaconry of Huntingdon*, Bedfordshire Historical Record Society, 2 (1914).

PEACOCK, E. (ed.), 'Extracts from the Churchwardens' Accounts of the Parish of Leverton, in the County of Lincoln', *Archaeologia*, 41 (1867).

——(ed.), 'Extracts from Lincoln Episcopal Visitations in the Fifteenth, Sixteenth and Seventeenth Centuries', *Archaeologia*, 48 (1885).

PICCOPE, G. J. (ed.), *Lancashire and Cheshire Wills and Inventories from the Ecclesiastical Court, Chester*, ChS OS 33, 51, 54 (1857–61).

PILKINGTON, J., *Works*, ed. J. Scholefield, PS (1852).

POCOCK, N. (ed.), *Records of the Reformation* (Oxford, 1870).

——(ed.), *Troubles Connected with the Prayer Book of 1549*, CS NS 37 (1884).

PONET, J., *A defence for mariage of priests* (1556).

Prymer of Salysbury Use (Paris, 1531).

PURVIS, J. S. (ed.), *Tudor Parish Documents of the Diocese of York* (Cambridge, 1948).

——(ed.), *A Medieval Act Book with Some Account of Ecclesiastical Jurisdiction at York* (York, 1943).

RAGG, F. W. (ed.), 'Fragment of Folio Manuscript of the Archdeaconry Courts of Buckinghamshire, 1491–1495', *Records of Buckinghamshire*, 9 (1919–24).

RAINE, A. (ed.), *York Civic Records*, iii, YAS (RS) 106 (1942).

RAINE, J. (ed.), *Wills and Inventories Illustrative of the History, Manners, Language, Statistics &c. of the Northern Counties of England from the Eleventh Century Downwards*, SS 2 (1835).

——(ed.), *Depositions and other ecclesiastical proceedings from the courts of Durham*, SS 21 (1845).

——(ed.), *The Injunctions and other Ecclesiastical Proceedings of Richard Barnes, Bishop of Durham, 1576–1587*, SS 22 (1850).

——(ed.), *Wills and Inventories from the Registry of the Archdeaconry of Richmond*, SS 26 (1853).

——(ed.), *The Fabric Rolls of York Minster*, SS 35 (1858).

——(ed.), *Testamenta Eboracensia*, vols. iv–vi, SS 53, 79, 106 (1869–1902).

——(ed.), *English Miscellanies Illustrating the History and Language of the Northern Counties of England*, SS 85 (1890).

RAMSEY, J., *A Plaister for a galled horse* (1548).

RAWLINS, S. W., and FITZROY JONES, I. (eds.), *Somerset Wills from Exeter*, SRS 62 (1952).

RIDLEY, N., *Works*, ed. H. Christmas, PS (1843).

ROBINSON, H. (ed.), *Original Letters Relative to the English Reformation*, PS (1846–7).

ROGERS, J. E. T. (ed.), *Loci e Libro Veritatum: Passages Selected from Gascoigne's Theological Dictionary* (Oxford, 1881).

ROSS, W. O. (ed.), *Middle English Sermons*, EETS 209 (1940).

ROYE, G. DE, *The Doctrinal of Sapyence*, Caxton (1489).

ST CLARE BYRNE, M. (ed.), *The Lisle Letters* (Chicago, 1981).

ST GERMAN, C., *A treatise concernynge the division betwene the spirytualtie and temporaltie*, in *CW* 9 (1979).

——*Salem and Bizance*, in J. Guy, R. Keen, C. H. Miller, and R. McGugan (eds.), *The Debellation of Salem and Bizance*, *CW* 10 (1987).

SALTER, H. (ed.), 'A Visitation of Oxfordshire in 1540', *Oxford Archaeological Society Reports*, 75 (1930).

SHILTON, D. O., and HOLWORTHY, R. (eds.), *Medieval Wills from Wells*, SRS, 40 (1925).

SIMMONS, T. F. (ed.), *The Lay Folk's Mass Book*, EETS 71 (1879).

——and NOLOTH, H. E. (eds.), *The Lay Folk's Catechism*, EETS 118 (1901).

SIMPSON, W. S. (ed.), *Visitations of Churches Belonging to St Paul's Cathedral in 1297 and 1458*, CS NS 55 (1895).

SKAIFE, R. H. (ed.), *The Register of the Guild of Corpus Christi in the City of York*, SS 57 (1872).

SKELTON, J., *The Complete English Poems*, ed. J. Scattergood (Harmondsworth, 1983).

SMITH, R., *A Defence of the Blessed Masse* (1546).

——*A briefe treatys settyng forth divers truthes* (1547).

——*Of Unwritten Verities* (1548).

SNEYD, C. A. (ed.), *A Relation or Rather a True Account of the Island of England . . . about the Year 1500*, CS, 1st ser., 37 (1847).

SOMERS, F. (ed.), *Halesowen Churchwardens' Accounts, 1487–1582*, Worcestershire Historical Society, 40 (1957).

STAPLETON, T. (ed.), *Plumpton Correspondence*, CS OS 4 (1839).

STARKEY, T., *A Dialogue between Pole and Lupset*, ed. T. F. Mayer, CS, 4th ser., 37 (1989).

Statutes of the Realm, 11 vols. (1830–52).

Stella Clericorum, de Worde (1531).

STEWART-BROWN, R. (ed.), *Lancashire and Cheshire Cases in the Court of Star Chamber*, Lancashire and Cheshire Record Society, 71 (1916).

STONE, E. D., and COZENS-HARDY, B. (eds.), *Norwich Consistory Court Deposi-tions, 1499–1512 and 1518–1530*, Norfolk Record Society (1938).

SWAYNE, H. F. (ed.), *Churchwardens' Accounts of S. Edmund and S. Thomas Sarum, 1443–1702*, Wiltshire Record Society (1896).

The Storie of the Masse, in J. de Voragine, *The Golden Legend*, Caxton (1483).

THOMPSON, A. H. (ed.), *Visitations in the Diocese of Lincoln, 1517–1531*, LRS, 33, 35 (1940–4).

THOMPSON, C. H. (ed.), 'Chantry Priests at Plymouth', *Devon and Cornwall Notes and Queries*, 18 (1935).

The Traytte of Good Lyvyng and Good Deying (Paris, 1503).

TURNER, W., *A new Dialogue wherein is conteyned the examinatio[n] of the Messe and of that kind of priesthode whiche is ordeyned to say messe*, J. Day and W. Seres (1548).

TYMMS, S. (ed.), *Wills and Inventories from the Registers of the Commissary of Bury St Edmund's and the Archdeacon of Sudbury*, CS OS 49 (1850).

TYNDALE, W., *Doctrinal Treatises*, ed. H. Walter, PS (1848).

—— *The Practice of Prelates*, ed. H. Walter, PS (1849).

—— *An Answer to Sir Thomas More's Dialogue*, ed. H. Walter, PS (1850).

Valor Ecclesiasticus temp. Henrici VIII, ed. J. Caley and J. Hunter, Record Com-mission (1810–34).

VERGIL, P., *The Anglia Historia of Polydore Vergil AD 1485–1537*, ed. D. Hay, CS 74 (1950).

VERON, J., *Certayne litel treatises set forth . . . for the erudition and learnyng, of the symple & ignorant peopell*, H. Powell (1548).

Vertue of Y^e Masse, de Worde (*c.*1520).

VORAGINE, J. DE, *The Golden Legend*, Caxton (1483).

WADLEY, J. P. (ed.), *Notes or Abstracts of the Wills contained in the volume entitled the Great Orphan Book and Book of Wills in the Council House at Bristol*, Bristol and Gloucestershire Archaeological Society (1886).

WALTERS, H. B. (ed.), 'The Churchwardens' Accounts of the Parish of Worfield, 1500–1572', *Shropshire Archaeological and Natural History Society*, 3rd ser., 3–9 (1903–9).

WARREN, F. E. (ed.), *The Sarum Missal in English* (1911).

WATKIN, A. (ed.), *Dean Cosyn and Wells Cathedral Miscellanea*, SRS 56 (1941).

WATSON, T., *Holsome and catholyke doctryne concerninge the seven sacraments* (1558).

WEATHERLEY, E. H. (ed.), *Speculum Sacerdotale*, EETS 200 (1936).

WEAVER, F. W. (ed.), *Some Early Wills at Wells District Probate Registry, reprinted from the Downside Review* (1895).

—— (ed.), *Somerset Medieval Wills, 1383–1558*, SRS, 16, 19, 21 (1901–5).

—— (ed.), *Wells Wills (Serel Collection)*, Somersetshire Archaeological and Natural History Society Proceedings, 4th ser., 1 (1916).

WEAVER, J. R. H., and BEARDWOOD, A. (eds.), *Some Oxfordshire Wills Proved in the Prerogative Court of Canterbury, 1393–1510*, Oxfordshire Record Society (1958).

WHITFORD, R., *A Werke for Housholders* (1530).

—— *The Pype or Tonne of the Lyfe of Perfection* (1532).

—— *A dialogue or communicacion bytwene the curate or ghostly father & the parochiane or ghostly chyld for a due preparacion unto howselynge* (1537).

WICKHAM LEGG, J. (ed.), *The Clerk's Book of 1549*, Henry Bradshaw Society (1903).

—— (ed.), *The Sarum Missal* (1916).

WILKINS, D. (ed.), *Concilia Magnae Britaniae et Hiberniae* (1737).

WILLIAMS, J. F. (ed.), *The Early Churchwardens' Accounts of Hampshire* (1913).

WOOD-LEGH, K. L. (ed.), *Kentish Visitations of Archbishop William Warham and his Deputies, 1511–1512*, Kent Records (1984).

WOODRUFF, C. E. (ed.), 'Extracts from Original Documents Illustrating the Progress of the Reformation in Kent', *AC* 31 (1915).

—— (ed.), 'An Archidiaconal Visitation of 1502', *AC* 47 (1935).

WOOLEY, R. M. (ed. and tr.), *The York Provinciale put forth by Thomas Wolsey* (1931).

WRIGHT, D. P. (ed.), *The Register of Thomas Langton, Bishop of Salisbury, 1485–93*, CYS 74 (1985).

WRIGHT, T. (ed.), *Three Chapters of Letters Relating to the Suppression of the Monasteries*, CS 26 (1843).

—— (ed.), *Churchwardens' Accounts of the Town of Ludlow in Shropshire from 1540 to the End of the Reign of Queen Elizabeth*, CS 102 (1869).

WRIOTHESLEY, C., *A Chronicle of England during the Reigns of the Tudors, from AD 1485 to 1559*, vol. i, ed. W. D. Hamilton, CS NS 11 (1875).

SECONDARY SOURCES

Printed Books and Articles

ADDLESHAW, G. W., and ETCHELLS, F., *The Architectural Setting of Anglican Worship* (1948).

ARIÈS, P., *The Hour of Our Death*, tr. H. Weaver (Harmondsworth, 1981).

ARROWSMITH, R. S., *The Prelude to the Reformation* (1923).

ASTON, M., *Lollards and Reformers, Images and Literacy in Late Medieval Religion* (1984).

—— *England's Iconoclasts: Laws Against Images*, i (Oxford, 1988).

AULT, W. O., 'The Village Church and the Village Community in Medieval England', *Speculum*, 45 (1970).

AVELING, J. C. H., 'The English Clergy, Catholic and Protestant, in the 16th and 17th Centuries' in W. Haase (ed.), *Rome and the Anglicans* (Berlin, 1982).

BAGCHI, D., ' "Eyn Mercklich Unterscheyd": Catholic Reactions to Luther's Doctrine of the Priesthood of all Believers', in W. J. Sheils and D. Wood (eds.), *The Ministry: Clerical and Lay*, SCH 26 (Oxford, 1989).

BARRON, C. M., 'The Parish Fraternities of Medieval London' in C. M. Barron and C. Harper-Bill (eds.), *The Church in Pre-Reformation Society* (Woodbridge, 1985).

BELLAMY, J. G., *Criminal Law and Society in late Medieval and Tudor England* (Gloucester, 1984).

BENEDICT, P., *Rouen during the Wars of Religion* (Cambridge, 1981).

BERNARD, G. W., *War, Taxation and Rebellion in early Tudor England* (1986).

BETTEY, J. H., *Church and Community: The Parish Church in English Life* (Bradford-on-Avon, 1979).

——*Church and Parish: A Guide for Local Historians* (1987).

BICKNELL, E. J., *A Theological Introduction to the Thirty-Nine Articles of the Church of England*, 3rd edn. (1955).

BLENCH, J. W., *Preaching in England in the late Fifteenth and Sixteenth Centuries* (Oxford, 1964).

BOSSY, J., 'Blood and Baptism: Kinship, Community and Christianity in Western Europe from the Fourteenth to the Seventeenth Centuries', in D. Baker (ed.), SCH 10 (Oxford, 1973).

——'The Social History of Confession in the Age of the Reformation', *TRHS*, 5th ser., 25 (1975).

——'The Mass as a Social Institution 1200–1700', *PP* 100 (1983).

——*Christianity in the West, 1400–1700* (Oxford, 1985).

BOWKER, M., 'Non-Residence in the Lincoln Diocese in the Early Sixteenth Century', *JEH* 15 (1964).

——*The Secular Clergy in the Diocese of Lincoln, 1485–1520* (Cambridge, 1968).

——'Lincolnshire 1536: Heresy, Schism or Religious Discontent', in D. Baker (ed.), SCH 9 (Cambridge, 1972).

——'The Henrician Reformation and the Parish Clergy', *Bulletin of the Institute of Historical Research*, 50 (1977).

——*The Henrician Reformation: The Diocese of Lincoln under John Longland, 1521–1547* (Cambridge, 1981).

BOYLE, L. E., 'The *Oculus Sacerdotis* and some other Works of William of Pagula', *TRHS*, 5th ser., 5 (1955).

BRIGDEN, S., 'Tithe Controversy in Reformation London', *JEH* 33 (1982).

——'Youth and the English Reformation', *PP* 95 (1982).

——'Religion and Social Obligation in Early Sixteenth-Century London', *PP* 103 (1984).

——*London and the Reformation* (Oxford, 1989).

BRILIOTH, Y., *Eucharistic Faith and Practice, Evangelical and Catholic*, tr. A. G. Herbert (1961).

BROOKE, C., 'Chaucer's Parson and Edmund Gonville: Contrasting Roles of Fourteenth-Century Incumbents', in D. M. Smith (ed.), *Studies in Clergy and Ministry in Medieval England* (York, 1991).

BROOKS, F. W., 'The Social Position of the Parson in the Sixteenth Century', *Journal of the British Archaeological Association*, 3rd ser., 10 (1945–7).

BROSNAN, J. B., 'Episcopacy and Priesthood According to St Thomas', *American Ecclesiastical Review*, 121 (1949).

BROWE, P., *Die eucharistischen Wunder des Mittelalters* (Breslau, 1938).

——*Die Verehrung der Eucharistie im Mittelalter*, new edn. (Freiburg im Breisgau, 1967).

BROWN, S., *The Medieval Courts of the York Minster Peculiar* (York, 1984).

BURGESS, C., '"A fond thing vainly invented": An Essay on Purgatory and Pious Motive in Later Medieval England', in S. Wright (ed.), *Parish, Church and People: Local Studies in Lay Religion, 1350–1750* (1988).

BUTTERWORTH, C. C., and CHESTER, A. G., *George Joye 1495?–1553* (Philadelphia, 1962).

CAMERON, E., *The European Reformation* (Oxford, 1991).

CARLSON, E. J., 'Clerical Marriage and the English Reformation', *JBS* 31 (1992).

CHADWICK, O., *The Reformation* (Harmondsworth, 1972).

CLARK, F., *Eucharistic Sacrifice and the Reformation*, new edn. (Chulmleigh, 1981).

CLARK, P., *English Provincial Society from the Reformation to the Revolution: Religion, Politics and Society in Kent, 1500–1640* (Hassocks, 1977).

CLEBSCH, W. A., *England's Earliest Protestants, 1520–1535* (New Haven, Conn., 1964).

COHN, H. J., 'Anticlericalism in the German Peasants' War, 1525', *PP* 83 (1979).

COLLINSON, P., *The Religion of Protestants: The Church in English Society, 1559–1625* (Oxford, 1982).

——*The Birthpangs of Protestant England* (1988).

——'Shepherds, Sheepdogs, and Hirelings: The Pastoral Ministry in Post-Reformation England', in W. J. Sheils and D. Wood (eds.), *The Ministry: Clerical and Lay*, SCH 26 (Oxford, 1989).

COOK, G. H., *The English Medieval Parish Church* (1954).

——*Medieval Chantries and Chantry Chapels* (1963).

COOKE, B., *Ministry to Word and Sacraments: History and Theology* (Philadelphia, 1977).

COOPER, J. P., 'The Supplication against the Ordinaries Reconsidered', *EHR* 72 (1957).

CORNWALL, J. C., *The Revolt of the Peasantry, 1549* (1977).

——*Wealth and Society in Early Sixteenth-Century England* (1988).

COULTON, G. G., *The Medieval Village* (Cambridge, 1926).

——'Priests and People before the Reformation', in *Ten Medieval Studies*, 3rd edn. (Cambridge, 1930).

——*Medieval Village, Manor, and Monastery*, paperback edn. (1960).

COX, J. C., *Churchwardens' Accounts* (1913).

——and FORD, C. B., *Parish Churches* (1961).

CREHAN, J. H., 'Medieval Ordinations', in C. Jones, G. Wainwright, and E. Yarnold (eds.), *The Study of Liturgy* (1978).

CRESSY, D., *Literacy and the Social Order* (Cambridge, 1980).

CROSS, C., *Church and People, 1450–1660*, paperback edn. (1976).

——'Lay Literacy and Clerical Misconduct in a York Parish during the Reign of Mary Tudor', *York Historian* (1980).

CROSS, C., 'Priests into Ministers: The Establishment of Protestant Practice in the City of York', in P. N. Brooks (ed.), *Reformation Principle and Practice* (1980).

CRUICKSHANK, C., *Henry VIII and the Invasion of France* (Stroud, 1990).

CUTTS, E. L., *Parish Priests and their People in the Middle Ages in England* (1898).

—— *Scenes and Characters of the Middle Ages*, 6th edn. (1926).

DAVIES, C. S. L., 'Popular Religion and the Pilgrimage of Grace', in A. Fletcher and J. Stevenson (eds.), *Order and Disorder in Early Modern England* (Cambridge, 1985).

DAVIS, J. F., 'Lollardy and the Reformation in England', *ARG* 73 (1982).

—— *Heresy and Reformation in the South-East of England, 1520–1559* (1983).

DAVIS, V., 'Rivals for Ministry? Ordinations of Secular and Regular Clergy in Southern England *c*.1300–1500', in W. J. Sheils and D. Wood (eds.), *The Ministry: Clerical and Lay*, SCH 26 (Oxford, 1989).

DELUMEAU, J., *Catholicism between Luther and Voltaire*, tr. J. Moiser (1977).

DERRETT, J. D. M., 'The Affairs of Richard Hunne and Friar Standish', in J. B. Trapp (ed.), *The Apology, CW* 9 (1979).

DICKENS, A. G., *Lollards and Protestants in the Diocese of York* (1959).

—— *Reformation Studies* (1982).

—— 'Early Protestantism and the Church in Northamptonshire', *Northamptonshire, PP* 8 (1983–4).

—— 'The Shape of Anticlericalism and the English Reformation' in E. I. Kouri and T. Scott (eds.), *Politics and Society in Reformation Europe* (1987).

—— *The English Reformation*, 2nd edn. (1989).

DITTES, J. E., 'The Symbolic Value of Celibacy for the Catholic Faithful', *Concilium*, 8 (1972).

DOUGLAS, M., *Purity and Danger: An Analysis of the Concepts of Pollution and Taboo*, paperback edn. (1984).

DRURY, T. W., *Confession and Absolution: The Teaching of the Church of England as Interpreted and Illustrated by the Writings of the Reformers of the Sixteenth Century* (1903).

—— *Elevation in the Eucharist* (Cambridge, 1907).

DU BOULAY, F. R. H., *Germany in the Later Middle Ages* (1983).

DUFFY, E., *The Stripping of the Altars: Traditional Religion in England, 1400–1580* (New Haven, Conn., 1992).

DUGGAN, L. G., 'The Unresponsiveness of the late Medieval Church: A Reconsideration', *SCJ* 9 (1978).

—— 'Fear and Confession on the Eve of the Reformation', *ARG* 75 (1984).

DUGMORE, C. W., *The Mass and the English Reformers* (1958).

ELIADE, M., *The Sacred and the Profane*, tr. W. R. Trask (New York, 1959).

—— (ed.), *The Encyclopedia of Religion* (New York, 1987).

ELLIOT, J. H., *Imperial Spain, 1469–1716* (Harmondsworth, 1970).

ELTON, G. R., 'The Commons' Supplication of 1532: Parliamentary Manœuvres in the Reign of Henry VIII', *EHR* 66 (1951).

—— 'Tithe and Trouble' in *Star Chamber Stories* (1958).

——*Policy and Police: The Enforcement of the Reformation in the Age of Thomas Cromwell* (Cambridge, 1972).

——*Reform and Reformation: England 1509–1558* (1977).

——'Politics and the Pilgrimage of Grace', in B. C. Malament (ed.), *After the Reformation* (Manchester, 1980).

FAIRFIELD, L. P., *John Bale: Mythmaker for the English Reformation* (West Lafayette, Ind., 1976).

FINES, J., *A Biographical Register of Early English Protestants . . . 1525–1558* (1981).

FISHER, R. M., 'The Reformation of Clergy at the Inns of Court 1530–1580', *SCJ* 12 (1981).

FLETCHER, A., *Tudor Rebellions*, 3rd edn. (1983).

FRERE, W. H., *The Marian Reaction in its Relation to the English Clergy* (1896).

FROUDE, J. A., *History of England* (1893).

FUGGLES, J. F., 'The Parish Clergy in the Archdeaconry of Leicester, 1520–1540', *Leicestershire Archaeological and Historical Society Transactions*, 46 (1970–1).

GASQUET, F. A., *The Eve of the Reformation* (1900).

——*Parish Life in Medieval England* (1906).

GINZBURG, C., *The Cheese and the Worms*, tr. J. and A. Tedeschi (1980).

GOERTZ, H.-J., *Pfaffenhass und gross Geschrei: Die reformatorischen Bewegungen in Deutschland 1517–1529* (Munich, 1987).

GOGAN, B., *The Common Corps of Christendom: Ecclesiological Themes in the Writings of Sir Thomas More* (Leiden, 1982).

GRIEVE, H., 'The Deprived Married Clergy in Essex', *TRHS*, 4th ser., 22 (1940).

GUNN, S. J., *Charles Brandon, Duke of Suffolk, 1484–1545* (Oxford, 1988).

GUY, J. A., *The Public Career of Sir Thomas More* (New Haven, 1980).

——*Christopher St German on Chancery and Statute*, Selden Society, suppl. ser. (1985).

HAIGH, C., *Reformation and Resistance in Tudor Lancashire* (Cambridge, 1975).

——'Some Aspects of the Recent Historiography of the English Reformation', in W. J. Mommsen, P. Alter, and R. W. Scribner (eds.), *Stadtbürgertum und Adel in der Reformation* (1979).

——'The Church of England, the Catholics and the People', in C. Haigh (ed.), *The Reign of Elizabeth I* (1984).

——'Anticlericalism and the English Reformation', in C. Haigh (ed.), *The English Reformation Revised* (Cambridge, 1987).

——*English Reformations: Religion, Politics, and Society under the Tudors* (Oxford, 1993).

HARDISON, O. B., *Christian Rite and Christian Drama in the Middle Ages* (Baltimore, 1965).

HARDWICK, C., *A History of the Articles of Religion* (1890).

HARPER-BILL, C., 'A Late Medieval Visitation: The Diocese of Norwich in 1499', *Proceedings of the Suffolk Institute of Archaeology and History*, 34 (1977).

——'Dean Colet's Convocation Sermon and the Pre-Reformation Church in England', *History*, 73 (1988).

HARPER-BILL, C., *The Pre-Reformation Church in England, 1400–1530* (1989).

HARVEY, E. R., 'The Ymage of Love', in More, *Dialogue*.

HAY, D., *Europe in the Fourteenth and Fifteenth Centuries* (1970).

HEAL, F., 'Economic Problems of the Clergy', in F. Heal and R. O'Day (eds.), *Church and Society in England, Henry VIII to James I* (1977).

——'The Parish Clergy and the Reformation in the Diocese of Ely', *CAS* 66 (1977).

——*Hospitality in Early Modern England* (Oxford, 1990).

HEATH, P., *The English Parish Clergy on the Eve of the Reformation* (1969).

HODGETT, G. A. J., *Tudor Lincolnshire* (Lincoln, 1975).

HOULBROOKE, R., *Church Courts and the People during the English Reformation* (Oxford, 1979).

HUDSON, A., 'A New Look at the Lay Folk's Catechism', *Viator*, 16 (1985).

——*The Premature Reformation* (Oxford, 1988).

HUGHES, J., 'The Administration of Confession in the Diocese of York in the Fourteenth Century', in D. M. Smith (ed.), *Studies in Clergy and Ministry in Medieval England*, Borthwick Studies in History, 1 (York, 1991).

HUGHES, P., *The Reformation in England, i. The King's Proceedings* (1956).

HUGHES, P. E., *The Theology of the English Reformers* (1965).

IVES, E., *Anne Boleyn* (Oxford, 1986).

——Review of S. Brigden, *London and the Reformation*, in *Historical Journal*, 34 (1991).

JANELLE, P., *L'Angleterre catholique à la veille du schisme* (Paris, 1935).

JONES, D., *The Church in Chester, 1300–1540*, ChS (1957).

JONES, W. R. D., *William Turner: Tudor Naturalist, Physician and Divine* (1988).

JORDAN, W. K., *The Charities of Rural England, 1480–1660* (1961).

JUNG, C. G., 'Transformation Symbolism in the Mass', in J. Campbell (ed.), *Pagan and Christian Mysteries*, tr. R. Manheim and R. F. C. Hull (New York, 1963).

JUNGMANN, J. A., *The Mass of the Roman Rite*, tr. F. A. Brunner (New York, 1951).

KAUFMAN, P. I., 'John Colet's *Opus de sacramentis* and Clerical Anticlericalism: The Limitations of "Ordinary Wayes" ', *JBS* 22 (1982).

KELLY, M., 'The Submission of the Clergy', *TRHS*, 5th ser., 15 (1965).

KERRY, C., *A History of the Municipal Church of St Lawrence, Reading* (Reading, 1883).

KING, J. N., *English Reformation Literature* (Princeton, NJ, 1982).

KREIDER, A., *English Chantries: The Road to Dissolution* (Cambridge, Mass., 1979).

KURTSCHEID, B., *A History of the Seal of Confession*, tr. F. A. Marks (1927).

LAKE, P., *Moderate Puritans and the Elizabethan Church* (Cambridge, 1982).

——'Richard Kilby: A Study in Personal and Professional Failure', in W. J. Sheils and D. Wood, *The Ministry: Clerical and Lay*, SCH 26 (Oxford, 1989).

LANDER, J. R., *Government and Community, England, 1450–1509* (Cambridge, Mass., 1980).

LANDER, S., 'Church Courts and the Reformation in the Diocese of Chichester,

1500–58' in R. O'Day and F. Heal (eds.), *Continuity and Change: Personnel and Administration of the Church in England, 1500–1642* (Leicester, 1976).

LEA, H. C., *A History of Auricular Confession and Indulgences in the Latin Church* (1896).

—— *History of Sacerdotal Celibacy in the Christian Church*, 3rd edn. rev. (1907).

LECLERCQ, J., 'The Priesthood in the Patristic and Medieval Church', in N. Lash and J. Rhymer (eds.), *The Christian Priesthood* (1970).

LEFF, G., *Heresy in the Later Middle Ages* (Manchester, 1967).

LEHMBERG, S. E., *The Reformation Parliament, 1529–1536* (Cambridge, 1970).

LLOYD, C., *The Queen's Pictures* (1991).

LOACH, J., 'Reformation Controversies', in J. McConica (ed.), *The History of the University of Oxford*, iii (Oxford, 1986).

LOADES, D. M., *The Reign of Mary Tudor*, 2nd edn. (1991).

LUPTON, J. H., *Life of John Colet*, 2nd edn. (1909).

MACCULLOCH, D., *Suffolk and the Tudors* (Oxford, 1986).

—— and BLATCHLY, J., 'Pastoral Provision in the Parishes of Tudor Ipswich', *SCJ* 22 (1991).

MACEK, E. A., 'Richard Smith: Tudor Cleric in Defense of Traditional Belief and Practice', *Catholic Historical Review*, 72 (1986).

MCFARLANE, K. B., *Wycliffe and English Non-Conformity* (Harmondsworth, 1972).

MCHARDY, A. K., 'Careers and Disappointments in the Late Medieval Church: Some English Evidence', in W. J. Sheils and D. Wood (eds.), *The Ministry: Clerical and Lay*, SCH 26 (Oxford, 1989).

MACLURE, M., *The Paul's Cross Sermons, 1534–1642* (Toronto, 1958).

MANNING, B., *The People's Faith in the Time of Wyclif* (Hassocks, 1975).

MARC'HADOUR, G., 'Golden Priests and Chalices of Gold', *Moreana*, 6 (1969).

—— 'Fisher and More: A Note', in B. Bradshaw and E. Duffy (eds.), *Humanism, Reform and the Reformation: The Career of Bishop John Fisher* (Cambridge, 1989).

MARIUS, R., *Thomas More* (1985).

MARTOS, J., *Doors to the Sacred* (1981).

MAYHEW, G. J., 'The Progress of the Reformation in East Sussex, 1530–1559: The Evidence from Wills', *Southern History*, 5 (1983).

MESSENGER, E. C., *The Reformation, the Mass and the Priesthood* (1936).

MILLER, H., *Henry VIII and the English Nobility* (Oxford, 1986).

MORAN, J. A. H., 'Clerical Recruitment in the Diocese of York: Data and Commentary', *JEH*, 34 (1983).

—— *The Growth of English Schooling, 1340–1548* (Princeton, NJ, 1985).

MULLER, J. A., *Stephen Gardiner and the Tudor Reaction* (1926).

MURRAY, A., 'Confession as a Historical Source in the Thirteenth Century', in R. H. C. Davis and J. M. Wallace-Hadrill (eds.), *The Writing of History in the Middle Ages* (Oxford, 1981).

NICHOLS, A., *Holy Order: The Apostolic Ministry from the New Testament to the Second Vatican Council* (Dublin, 1990).

NICHOLS, A. E., 'The Etiquette of Pre-Reformation Confession in East Anglia', *SCJ* 17 (1986).

O'DAY, R., *The English Clergy: The Emergence and Consolidation of a Profession, 1558–1642* (Leicester, 1979).

—— *The Debate on the English Reformation* (1986).

——'The Anatomy of a Profession: The Clergy of the Church of England', in W. Prest (ed.), *The Professions in Early Modern England* (Beckenham, 1987).

OGLE, A., *The Tragedy of the Lollards' Tower* (Oxford, 1949).

OWEN, D. M., 'Synods in the Diocese of Ely in the latter Middle Ages and the Sixteenth Century' in G. J. Cuming (ed.), SCH 3 (1966).

—— *Church and Society in Medieval Lincolnshire* (Lincoln, 1971).

OWST, G. R., *Preaching in Medieval England* (Cambridge, 1926).

—— *The Destructorium Viciorum of Alexander Carpenter* (1952).

—— *Literature and Pulpit in Medieval England*, 2nd edn. (Cambridge, 1961).

OXLEY, J. E., *The Reformation in Essex to the Death of Mary* (Manchester, 1965).

OZMENT, S. E., 'Marriage and the Ministry in the Protestant Churches', *Concilium*, 8 (1972).

—— *The Reformation in the Cities* (New Haven, Conn., 1975).

PALLISER, D. M., *The Reformation in York 1534–1553* (York, 1971).

——'Popular Reactions to the Reformation during the Years of Uncertainty, 1530–70', in F. Heal and R. O'Day (eds.), *Church and Society in England: Henry VIII to James I* (1977).

PALMER, W. M., 'Fifteenth-Century Visitation Records of the Deanery of Wisbech', *CAS* 39 (1940).

PANTIN, W. A., *The English Church in the Fourteenth Century* (Cambridge, 1955).

——'Instructions for a Devout and Literate Layman', in J. G. Alexander and M. T. Gibson (eds.), *Medieval Learning and Literature* (Oxford, 1976).

PARKER, T. M., *The English Reformation to 1558* (Oxford, 1950).

PENDRILL, C., *Old Parish Life in London* (Oxford, 1937).

PLATT, C., *The English Medieval Town* (1976).

POCOCK, N., 'The Condition of Morals and Religious Belief in the Reign of Edward VI', *EHR* 39 (1895).

PORTER, H. C., 'The Gloomy Dean and the Law: John Colet, 1466–1519', in G. V. Bennett and J. D. Walsh (eds.), *Essays in Modern English Church History* (1966).

POSCHMANN, B., *Penance and the Anointing of the Sick*, tr. F. Courtney (Freiburg, 1964).

POUND, J., 'Clerical Poverty in Early Sixteenth-Century England: Some East Anglian Evidence', *JEH* 37 (1986).

POWER, D. N., *Ministers of Christ and His Church: The Theology of the Priesthood* (1969).

PROCTER, F., and FRERE, W. H., *A New History of the Book of Common Prayer*, 3rd edn. (1905).

REX, R., *The Theology of John Fisher* (Cambridge, 1991).

ROSE-TROUP, F., *The Western Rebellion of 1549* (1913).

ROWSE, A. L., *Tudor Cornwall*, 2nd edn. (1969).

RUBIN, M., *Corpus Christi: The Eucharist in Late Medieval Culture* (Cambridge, 1991).

RUPP, E. G., *Studies in the Making of the English Protestant Tradition* (Cambridge, 1947).

SCARISBRICK, J. J., 'Clerical Taxation in England, 1485–1547', *JEH* 11 (1960).

—— *Henry VIII* (1968).

—— *The Reformation and the English People* (Oxford, 1984).

—— 'Fisher, Henry VIII and the Reformation Crisis', in B. Bradshaw and E. Duffy (eds.), *Humanism, Reform and the Reformation: the Career of Bishop John Fisher* (Cambridge, 1989).

SCHOECK, R. J., 'Common Law and Canon Law in their Relation to Thomas More', in R. S. Sylvester (ed.), *St Thomas More: Action and Contemplation* (New Haven, Conn., 1972).

SCRIBNER, R. W., 'Anticlericalism and the German Reformation' in *Popular Culture and Popular Movements in Reformation Germany* (1987).

—— *For the Sake of Simple Folk: Popular Propaganda for the German Reformation* (Cambridge, 1981).

SHEEHAN, M., *The Will in Medieval England* (Toronto, 1963).

SHEILS, W. J., and WOOD, D. (eds.), *The Ministry: Clerical and Lay*, SCH 26 (Oxford, 1989).

SIMON, J., *Education and Society in Tudor England* (Cambridge, 1966).

SKEAT, W. W., and MAYHEW, A. L. (eds.), *A Glossary of Tudor and Stuart Words* (Oxford, 1914).

SLOYAN, G., 'Biblical and Patristic Motives for Celibacy of Church Ministers', *Concilium*, 8 (1972).

SMITH, H. M., *Pre-Reformation England* (1938).

SMITH, L. B., *A Tudor Tragedy: The Life and Times of Catherine Howard* (1961).

SPIELMANN, R. M., 'The Beginning of Clerical Marriage in the English Reformation: The Reigns of Edward and Mary', *Anglican and Episcopal History*, 56 (1987).

STEVENS BENHAM, L. M., 'The Durham Clergy, 1494–1540: A Study of Continuity and Mediocrity among the Unbeneficed', in D. Marcombe (ed.), *The Last Principality: Politics, Religion and Society in the Bishopric of Durham, 1494–1660* (Nottingham, 1987).

STOREY, R. L., 'A Fifteenth-Century Vicar of Laxton', *Transactions of the Thoroton Society of Nottinghamshire*, 88 (1984).

STRYPE, J., *Ecclesiastical Memorials*, 6 vols. (Oxford, 1822).

SURTZ, E., *The Works and Days of John Fisher* (Cambridge, Mass., 1967).

SWANSON, R. N., *Church and Society in Late Medieval England* (Oxford, 1989).

—— 'Problems of the Priesthood in pre-Reformation England', *EHR* 417 (1990).

TANNER, N. P., *The Church in Late Medieval Norwich, 1370–1532* (Toronto, 1984).

TANNER, N. P., 'The Reformation and Regionalism: Further Reflections on the Church in Late Medieval Norwich', in J. A. F. Thomson (ed.), *Towns and Townspeople in the Fifteenth Century* (Gloucester, 1988).

TENTLER, T. N., 'The Summa for Confessors as an Instrument of Social Control', in C. Trinkaus and H. A. Oberman (eds.), *The Pursuit of Holiness in Late Medieval and Renaissance Religion* (Leiden, 1974).

——*Sin and Confession on the Eve of the Reformation* (Princeton, NJ, 1977).

THOMAS, K., *Religion and the Decline of Magic*, paperback edn. (1978).

THOMPSON, A. H., *The English Clergy and their Organization in the Later Middle Ages* (Oxford, 1947).

THOMSON, J. A. F., 'Tithe Disputes in Late Medieval London', *EHR* 78 (1963).

——*The Later Lollards* (Oxford, 1965).

——'Piety and Charity in Late Medieval London', *JEH* 16 (1965).

THURSTON, H., 'The Elevation', *The Tablet* (2 Nov. 1907).

TILLEY, M. P., *A Dictionary of the Proverbs in England in the Sixteenth and Seventeenth Centuries* (Ann Arbor, Mich., 1950).

TUDOR, P., 'Religious Instruction for Children and Adolescents in the Early English Reformation', *JEH* 36 (1985).

TYLER, P., 'The Status of the Elizabethan Parochial Clergy', in G. J. Cuming (ed.), SCH 4 (Leiden, 1967).

VASELLA, O., *Reform und Reformation in der Schweiz* (Münster, 1965).

VERE WOODMAN, A., 'The Buckinghamshire and Oxfordshire Rising of 1549', *Oxoniensia*, 22 (1957).

WESTLAKE, H. F., *The Parish Gilds of Medieval England* (1919).

WHITING, R., ' "For the Health of my Soul": Prayers for the Dead in the Tudor South-West', *Southern History*, 5 (1983).

——*The Blind Devotion of the People: Popular Religion and the English Reformation* (Cambridge, 1989).

WILLIAMS, G., 'Two Neglected London-Welsh Clerics: Richard Whitford and Richard Gwent', *Transactions of the Honourable Society of Cymmrodorion* (1961).

——*The Welsh Church from Conquest to Reformation* (1962).

WILLIAMS, J. F., 'The Married Clergy of the Marian Period', *Norfolk Archaeology*, 32 (1961).

WILSON, J., 'The Sermons of Roger Edgeworth: Reformation Preaching in Bristol', in D. Williams (ed.), *Early Tudor England: Proceedings of the 1987 Harlaxton Symposium* (Woodbridge, 1989).

WOODCOCK, B. L., *Medieval Ecclesiastical Courts in the Diocese of Canterbury* (Oxford, 1952).

WOOD-LEGH, K. L., *Perpetual Chantries in Britain* (Cambridge, 1965).

WUNDERLI, R. M., *London Church Courts and Society on the Eve of the Reformation* (1981).

YOST, J. K., 'The Reformation Defence of Clerical Marriage', *Church History* (1981).

Youings, J., 'The South-Western Rebellion of 1549', *Southern History*, 1 (1979).
——*Sixteenth-Century England* (Harmondsworth, 1984).
Zell, M. L., 'The Personnel of the Clergy in Kent in the Reformation Period', *EHR* 89 (1974).
——'The Use of Religious Preambles as a Measure of Religious Belief in the Sixteenth Century', *Bulletin of the Institute of Historical Research*, 50 (1977).
——'Economic Problems of the Parochial Clergy in the Sixteenth Century', in R. O'Day and F. Heal (eds.), *Princes and Paupers in the English Church, 1500–1800* (Leicester, 1981).

Unpublished Works

Ball, R. M., 'The Education of the English Parish Clergy in the Later Middle Ages, with Particular Reference to the Manuals of Instruction', University of Cambridge Ph.D. thesis (1976).
Barratt, D. M., 'The Condition of the Parish Clergy between the Reformation and 1660, with Special Reference to the Dioceses of Oxford, Worcester and Gloucester', University of Oxford D.Phil. thesis (1949).
Brigden, S., 'The Northern Clergy in the Pilgrimage of Grace', University of Manchester BA thesis (1973).
Garrity, A., 'The Parish Clergy in the Deanery of Holderness, 1475–1550', University of York MA thesis (1981).
Harper-Bill, C., 'An Edition of the Register of John Morton, Archbishop of Canterbury, 1486–1500', University of London Ph.D. thesis (1977).
Lander, S. J., 'The Diocese of Chichester, 1508–1558: Episcopal Reform under Robert Sherburne and its Aftermath', University of Cambridge Ph.D. thesis (1974).
Marshall, P., 'Attitudes of the English People to Priests and Priesthood, 1500–1553', University of Oxford D.Phil. thesis (1990).
Rhodes, J., 'Private Devotion in England on the Eve of the Reformation', University of Durham Ph.D. thesis (1974).
Spencer, H. L., 'English Vernacular Preaching in the Late Fourteenth and Fifteenth Century', University of Oxford D.Phil. thesis (1982).
Stevens, L. M., 'The Durham Clergy of the Early Sixteenth Century, 1494–1540', University of Durham MA thesis (1979).
Thompson, S., 'The Pastoral Work of the English and Welsh Bishops, 1500–1558', University of Oxford D.Phil. thesis (1984).
Thomson, J. A. F., 'Clergy and Laity in London, 1376–1531', University of Oxford D.Phil. thesis (1960).
Tudor, P., 'Changing Private Belief and Practice in England: Devotional Literature c.1475–1550', University of Oxford D.Phil. thesis (1984).

Index

ABC against the Spiritualty 104
Abell, Robert 62
Aberford (Yorks.) 157
absenteeism, *see* non-residence
abuse of priests 128–9, 136–7, 147–8, 226, 228
Acts of Englysh Votaryes 164
Adamson, John 207
Adeson, John 8
Adwick-le-Street (Yorks.) 225
Alcock, John, Bishop of Lincoln 134
Alen, Richard 128, 131
Aleyn, John, layman 137
Aleyn, John, priest 195
Aleyn, Richard 195
Aleyn, Simon, vicar of Bray 225
Alfreton (Derby.) 67
Amalarius, Bishop of Metz 36
Ambrose, St 116
Amicable Grant (1525) 136, 189
Anabaptism 49
Annes, William 109
anointing of the sick 175, 182, 192
Answer to a Poisoned Book 71
Answer to the Commoners of Devonshire and Cornwall 169
'anticlericalism' 2, 124, 125, 133, 148 n., 211–16, 219, 232, 235–6
Appledore (Kent) 58, 130
Aquinas, Thomas 13, 20, 109, 116
Ardleigh (Essex) 152
Ariès, Philippe 3
Armstrong, Janet 207
Arthur, Thomas 219
Articles of Faith 7, 29, 30, 88, 91, 92, 101–2
Arundel, Earl of 84
Arundel (Sussex) 149
Ash (Kent) 189
Ashburton (Devon) 172
Ashlower (Glos.) 224
Ashton-under-Lyne 210
Ashwell (Herts.) 91
Audley, Thomas 26
Augustine, St 117

Ave Maria 29
Axminster (Devon) 122
Aylesbury (Bucks.) 105
Aylesford (Kent) 100
Aylet, Richard 58
Aylond, Richard 193

Bache, William 132
Baily, William 129
Baker, Joan 87
Baker, John 137, 219
Bale, John 35, 145–6, 164
Banbury (Oxon.) 136
baptism 122, 175, 181–2
Barford (War.) 14
Barfreston (Kent) 191
Barlowe, Jerome 87, 104, 121–2, 220
Barnby Moor (Notts.) 152
Barnes, Robert 146, 164, 166
Baron, James 149
Barton, William 67, 68, 180
Basse, Christopher 223
Basset, James 111 n., 130
Baxter, Edward 111
Becon, Thomas 32, 35, 38, 60, 64, 75, 82, 86, 87, 107, 140, 228
Bedyll, Thomas 24
Beeston (Norfolk) 203
benefit of clergy 108, 222
Benet, Anthony 131
Bennet, Thomas 104, 164
Bennett, Richard 151
Benson, Richard 16
Benson, Robert 131
Bentworth (Hants.) 151
Beresford, Edward 183
Bernadino of Siena 89 n.
bible 28, 89, 102, 104–7, 169
Biddenham (Beds.) 112
Bigod, Francis 98
Billingborough (Lincs.) 154, 163
Bilney, Thomas 219
Bird, Christopher 178
Bishophill (Yorks.) 90
Bishops' Book (1537) 115–17

Black Bourton (Oxon.) 157
Blackfriars Council (1382) 48
Black Notely (Essex) 13, 185
Blunham (Beds.) 14
Boke of the Ghostly Father 7, 10, 15
Boleyn, Anne 123, 222
Bolton, John 22
Bonde, William 36, 37
Boniface VIII 227
Bonner, Edmund, Bishop of London 93,
    133, 190, 233 n.
Book of C mery Talys 42, 149
Book of Common Prayer:
    (1549) 30, 76–7, 78, 79–80, 85, 206
    (1552) 77–8, 80, 85
Book of Homilies (1547) 93–4, 106, 225
Bora, Katharina von 165
Borowe, Richard 152
Bosham (Sussex) 221
Bossy, John 182
Boswel, Thomas 130
Boswell, James 75
Botefeld, Thomas 84
Both, George 223
Bowden, Peter 131, 179
Bowers Gifford (Essex) 137, 219
Bowker, Margaret 103, 159, 178
Bowreman, William 204
Bozen, Nicole 90
Bradford, John 31, 50, 97
Bradley, Christopher 147
Brandon, Charles, Duke of Suffolk 222
Brasbrigge, Robert 147
Brekenden, Richard 124
Brentford (Middx.) 147, 155
Bridge (Kent) 187
Brigden, Susan 216
Bringhurst (Leics.) 152
Brinklow, Henry 21, 24, 99, 139
Bristol 11, 95
Broadwell (Oxon.) 190
Brogden, William 171
Broke, Reginald 62, 67
Bromfyld, John 28
Bromyard, John 90
Browne, Henry 161
Browne, Richard 194
Browning, Agnes 136
Buckburge, Robert 154
Bucke, Alison 152
Buckingham, Duke of 21 n.
Bucknall (Lincs.) 17
Budworth (Ches.) 151

Bukk, Thomas 215
Buknall, Agnes 111
Buknall, Henry 111
Buknall, Robert 111
Bullak, Edmund 67
Burial of the Mass 21, 81–2
Burton, Gilbert 123
Burton upon Stather (Yorks.) 223
Bury St Edmunds 58
Bynoe, Humphrey 205

Calais 45 n.
Caldbeck (Cumb.) 8
Calthorp, Thomas 203
Cambridge 94
canon law 18, 22 n., 23, 56, 60, 88, 101,
    142, 190
Canterbury 94, 205
Cantlowe, Geoffrey 112
Carder, Richard 24, 60
Carleton 24
Carlisle 170, 206
Carlson, E. J. 173 n.
Carpenter, William 85
Carter, John 66
Caulond, Thomas 215, 219
Cayling, Elizabeth 18
Cecil, William 172
celibacy, clerical 111, 132, 142–73 *passim*, 229
    see also concubinage; immorality,
    clerical; marriage of clergy
Challock (Kent) 152
chantry priests 12, 15, 50–5, 58, 67, 95,
    100, 128, 154, 157, 162, 179, 190,
    198, 201
chaplains, private 92, 126–7, 135, 197–8
Chapuys, Eustace 211, 222
Charing (Kent) 27
charity 19, 27, 61–2, 116, 177, 185–6,
    190–1
Charles d'Orleans 16
Charlton (Kent) 191
Chaucer, Geoffrey 191
Chester 159
Cheyney, John 130
Chillington (Beds.) 27, 157
Chipping (Lancs.) 195
Christopherson, John 234
church courts 12, 14, 22, 27, 62, 84, 89,
    122, 128, 147–8, 149, 154, 207
Church Langton (Leics.) 204
churchwardens 12, 162, 187, 199, 200,
    203–4, 224

churchyards 203–4, 224
Claryngbole, Alice 152
Clayhidon (Devon) 131
Cleasby (Yorks.) 197
Clericos Laicos (1296) 227
Clerk, John 110
Clerke, Agnes 153
Clere, Sir John 155
Clifford, Lord 97
Cobbe, Alison 149
Cochlaeus 72
Cock, Robert 210
Colaton Raleigh (Devon) 128, 131
Colchester 234
Colet, John 45, 46, 72, 108, 121, 125, 126, 127, 160, 191, 214, 227
Coll, Agnes 155
Collard, Thomas 73
Collinson, Patrick 32
Coln Wake (Essex) 203
Colyer, Richard 134
Colyns, Roger 186
Combes, Thomas 149
communion, *see* Eucharist
concubinage, clerical 60, 147, 148, 150–3, 157, 158–9
confession 5–34 *passim*, 48, 60–1, 80, 90, 109, 116, 118, 122, 174, 225
  choice of confessors 13–16
  at deathbed 16–18, 33, 231–2
  failure to administer 12–13
  failure to confess 11–12, 14
  Protestant critique of 9, 31–3, 99
  and religious instruction 29–30
  and sedition 28–9
  seal of confession 19–23, 27
  women and 23–6
  see also 'ghostly fathers'
conformism of clergy 224–6
Confutation of Unwritten Verities 146
Constable, Leonard 67, 68
Constantine, George 101
convocation 45, 108, 121, 125, 227
Conyng, Robert 43
Cooper, Thomas 49
Copleston, Henry 128
Corbett, William 22
Cornwallis, Thomas 24, 157
Cosyn, John 157
Cotton (Suffolk) 191
Court of Chancery 16, 109
Court of Requests 60
Court of Star Chamber 67, 84, 127

Coventry 84
Coverdale, John 135
Coverdale, Miles 9, 21, 49, 138, 162
Cowfold (Sussex) 131
Cowley, Thomas 106
Cowper, Janet 147
Crabbe, Thomas 122
Cranbrook (Kent) 134
Crane, Anne 24
Crane, Robert 24, 157
Cranmer, Thomas, Archbishop of
  Canterbury 75, 76, 93, 138, 146, 168
Crispin, Dr 102
Croft, William 210
Cromwell, Thomas 28, 111, 132, 151, 168, 214
Croscombe (Som.) 204, 224
Cross, Claire 99, 211
Croucaer, Robert 29
Crowley, Robert 97, 175
Culpeper, Thomas 29
Cupper, Richard 199
Cura Clericalis 114
Curtop, John 134

Dalton, William 123
Darcy, Lord 190
Darell, John 129
Dartford (Kent) 55
Davies, C. S. L. 206, 213
Dawson, Bertram 95
Day, John 42 n.
Deal (Kent) 31, 106
death, priests' role in 16, 17, 33, 124, 182–3, 192
Denton (Kent) 157, 185
Denton (Oxon.) 191
Derfield (Yorks.) 130
De Tristitia Christi 56
Dialogue between a clerke . . . and a burges 220
Dialogue between Pole and Lupset 97
Dialogue Concerning Heresies 9, 47, 56, 104–5, 146
Dialogue or familiar talk between two neighbours 42
Dialogue . . . unto howselynge 16
Dichaunte, Roger 138
Dickens, A. G. 167, 211, 213, 214
Digby, Sir John 58
Dives and Pauper 37, 38, 88, 134, 142, 159, 160, 183, 186
Doctrinal of Sapyence 48, 118, 125, 160

'donatism' 10–11, 47–59, 75, 99–100, 116, 125–6, 158, 159–63
Doncaster (Yorks.) 13
Dorking (Surrey) 207
Dormi Secure (sermon collection) 87
Dover 180
Down St Mary (Devon) 27, 190
dress, clerical 114, 126, 130, 133–6
Dunham (Ches.) 223
Durham 54
Dutton, Thomas 197
Dymchurch (Kent) 178

East Chinnock (Som.) 181
Easter 12, 14, 19, 24, 27, 62, 64, 68, 79, 179, 185, 186, 198
Eck, Johan 72
Ecleston, Edmund 147
Edgeworth, Roger 91, 134, 228
education of clergy 52, 82, 96–101, 103–4, 112
    graduates 96–7, 98, 99, 106
    ignorance 97–9
    teaching by clergy 100–1, 102–3
Edward VI 76, 233
Edwarde, James 197
Eliot, T. S. 41
Ellesborough (Bucks.) 179
Elsenham (Essex) 187
Elton, G. R. 32, 211, 224
Erasmus, Desiderius 46, 91–2, 144
Erle, Jane 151
Eston (Hants.) 53
Eucharist 19, 29, 30, 61, 64, 66, 76, 78, 80
    denial of 185–8
    refusal to receive 62
    spiritual reception of 70–1
    see also Book of Common Prayer; mass
Evenley (Northants.) 130
Eversholt (Beds.) 183
Everston, Thomas 100
Everyman 118
'Evil May Day' (1517) 95
Ewell (Surrey) 112
Examination of the Masse 65, 104
Exeter 225
Exornatorium Curatorum 90, 113

Faccombe (Hants.) 124
families of clergy 194–6
Fastelinge, Agnes 21
Faversham (Kent) 25, 28, 203
Fawkener, John 205

Festial 47, 87, 94, 103
Fieldhouse, Margaret 157
Fish, Simon 20, 220
Fisher, John, Bishop of Rochester 108 n., 117, 120–1, 143, 165, 175, 221, 236
Fitzjames, Sir John 55
Fitzjames, Richard, Bishop of London 220
Flint, Thomas 130
Floure of the commaundements of god 84
Foliambe, Sir Godfrey 135
foreign priests 123, 128–9
Forest, John, Friar 28
Fourth Lateran Council (1215) 11, 13
Fox, Richard, Bishop of Winchester 21, 88, 151
Fox, Richard, Essex curate 122
Foxe, John 43, 65, 66, 73, 167, 233 n.
Franston (Suffolk) 157
fraternity priests 12, 15, 128, 198
Freston (Suffolk) 24
friars 14, 15, 27, 51, 52, 96, 100, 146, 163, 184, 186, 230
Frost, Walter 134
Froude, J. A. 46
Fuller, Thomas, antiquary 225
Fuller, Thomas 91

Gallampton, John 23, 62, 128–9
Gammon, Philip 122
Gardiner, Stephen, Bishop of Winchester 64, 76, 93–4, 165 n., 225
Garford, Richard 152
Garsington, William 135
Geldard, John 210
General Sentence 91
Germany 26, 213
'ghostly fathers' 14, 16, 18, 21, 26, 32, 217
Gilbard, John 137
Gilbert, Thomas 123
Gislingham (Suffolk) 135
Glastonbury 17
Gloys, James 127
Godffrey, Michael 109
Godfrey, Eleanor 73
Godmersham (Kent) 106
godparenthood, clerical 209–10
Godwyn, John 76
Gold, Henry 92, 105
Golden Legend 65, 73, 87, 94
Graffham (Sussex) 136
Grant, Richard 26
Gravesend (Kent) 95

Grayingham (Lincs.) 43
Grayme, George 170–1
Great Brickhill (Bucks.) 75
Great Marlow (Bucks.) 73
Grey, Lady Jane 233
Grey Friars Chronicle 74
guild priests, *see* fraternity priests

Habram, Agnes 151
Haigh, Christopher 151, 212, 213, 218, 226, 234
Halifax (Yorks.) 190
Hall, Edward 220
Hall, Richard 17
Hallington (Lincs.) 152
Halsall (Lancs.) 61, 136, 189
Halsall, Richard 189
Hampden, William 43
Hampton, Roger 27
Hancock, Thomas 75, 170
Hanson, Thomas 18
Harbledown (Kent) 178–9
Harbotell, William 178
Hareby (Lincs.) 152
Harlakinden, Roger 216
Harlow (Essex) 161
Harman, Roger 106
Harper, William 78
Harrison, James 123
Hart, William 75
Hartwell (Bucks.) 43
Harwich (Essex) 203
Harvey, Friar 17
Harvey, Richard 106–7
Hatche, Elyn 27, 131
Haverhill (Suffolk) 12, 154
Hawrigge (Bucks.) 180
Hayes (Middx.) 92, 105
Heal, Felicity 81, 190
Heath, Peter 150, 184
Hemstead, Robert 122
Henry VII 21
Henry VIII 1, 76, 115, 116, 167, 225, 228
heresy, accusations of 219–21
Herolt, Johannes 89
Heron (Kent) 110
Heywood, John 30
Hickscorner 120, 148–9
Hilarie, Hugh 35, 82
Hill, Richard 32
Hilman, Richard 84, 87
Hilsey, John, Bishop of Rochester, 72
Hoccleve, Thomas 61

Hogg, John 177
Holden, William 223
Holdsworth, John 111
Holdsworth, Richard 112
Holgate, Robert, Archbishop of York 139, 171
Holme, Edward 110
Holme, John 52
Holme, Wilfrid 87
holy orders 109, 110, 111, 113–17, 118, 128, 138–41, 233, 235
'honest priests' 51–3, 58, 132–3, 162–3
see also 'donatism'
Hooper, John, Bishop of Gloucester 31, 81, 107, 139, 168–9, 192, 233
Hoppyng, Edward 214
Horne, William 225
hospitality, clerical duty of 175, 188–90, 191
Houghton Conquest (Beds.) 26
Howard, Katharine 29 n.
Howde, Anthony 207
Howden, Thomas 112
Huchyns, Elizabeth 149
Huggarde, Miles 171
Hugh of St Victor 114
Hull 4
Hunne case 108, 128, 187 n., 220, 221
Husee, John 130
Hussey, Lord 123
Hutten, Ulrich von 144
Hutton Wandesley (Yorks.) 67

ignorance of clergy, *see* education of clergy
Ilande, Thomas 112
Ilande, Christopher 112
Imitation of Christ 45, 46, 71
immorality, clerical 38–9, 132, 144–50, 153–63
see also concubinage
Inglepage, John 14
injunctions:
    (1536) 92
    (1538) 29, 92, 106
    (1547) 92, 228
    episcopal 29, 190
Interlude of Youth 61
Interpretacyon and Sygnyfycacyon of the Masse 36, 44, 55, 57, 58, 64, 74
Ipswich 21
Iver (Bucks.) 24, 60
Ives, E. W. 219
Ivychurch (Kent) 178

Jackson, William 31
James, Anne 170
Janelle, Pierre 52 n.
Jeffrason, Thomas 147
Jencyll, James 130
Jersey 153
Johnson, Samuel 75
Joseph, Robert 119, 222
Joyce, James 118 n.
Joye, George 145
Jungmann, J. A. 41

Katherine of Aragon 123
Kelvedon (Essex) 107, 149
Kempe, Margery 10, 130
Kendal (Cumb.) 206
Kendall, Thomas 95, 205
Kennington (Kent) 216
Ket's Rebellion (1549) 102–3, 206
Kidderminster, Richard, Abbot of
    Winchcombe 108
King's Book (1543) 70, 115–17, 225
Kingsdown (Kent) 178
Kingston, Edmund 8
Kirkby Malzeard (Yorks.) 101
Knolles, Dr 185
Kyrkeby, Thomas 61, 136, 208
Kyrkham, Thomas 161

Lammot, John 16
Lamsyn, Thomas 110
Lander, J. R. 59
Lanteglos (Corn.) 156
Latimer, Hugh 31, 79, 86, 94, 97–8, 107,
    132, 139, 169
Layer Breton (Essex) 194
Layer-de-la-Hay (Essex) 216
Lay Folk's Catechism 113
Lay Folk's Mass Book 59
lay patronage 197–9
Lea, H. C. 20
Lee, Edward, Archbishop of York 96, 190
Lee, Rowland, Bishop of Coventry and
    Lichfield 14, 133
Leeds 147
Lehmberg, S. E. 211
Leigh, Roger 209
Leigh (Som.) 130
Leke, Richard 54
Lent 12, 13, 14, 23, 25, 28, 29, 103, 225
Lentham, Henry 130–1
Le Roy Ladurie, E. 26 n.
letters testimonial 132–3

Lever, Thomas 98
Levyt, Giles 96
Liber Officialis 36
Life of Pico 119
Lincolnshire Rebellion (1536) 95, 123,
    200, 205
Linkinhorne (Corn.) 234
Linton (Kent) 217
Lisle, Lord 111 n., 130
litigiousness of priests 131, 136, 191
Littlebourne (Kent) 190
Little Chart (Kent) 129
Little Plumstead (Norfolk) 186
Little Tey (Essex) 180
localism of clergy 195–6
Lollards, Lollardy 10, 23, 48–9, 62, 84–5,
    87–8, 113, 122, 138, 158, 161, 214,
    215, 216
London 14, 41, 73, 76, 128, 147, 149, 168,
    195, 217, 228, 234 parishes: All
    Hallows on the Wall 22; St Andrew
    Eastcheap 161; St Botolph
    Aldgate 89; St Botolph
    Aldersgate 187; St Botolph
    Billingsgate 73; St Christopher-next-
    the-Stocks 157, 162; St Clement's
    Eastcheap 137; St Giles
    Cripplegate 73, 153, 162; St Mary at
    Hill 198, 205; St Mary
    Woolchurch 13; St Martin
    Outwich 74; St Michael
    Queenhithe 148; St Mildred Bread
    St 73; St Olave Old Jewry 67; St
    Stephen's Colman St 157; St Thomas
    the Apostle 74
Longford, George 52
Longland, John, Bishop of Lincoln 94,
    131, 143
Long Melford (Suffolk) 201
Loose, Richard 62
Loughborough (Leics.) 182–3
Louth (Lincs.) 95, 199–200, 205
Love, Nicholas 48
Lowes, George 32
Lowthorpe (Yorks.) 8
Ludlow 193, 199
Ludolph of Saxony 8
Lush, Dr 105
Luther, Martin 45, 48, 86, 165
Lybbe, William 27
Lydgate, John 61, 70
Lydgolde, Thomas 147, 155–6
Lydgolde, Katherine 156

Lye, Richard 207
Lyfe of Prestes 120, 134, 142, 160, 189
Lymm (Ches.) 209
Lytchett Maltravers (Dorset) 67
Lytell, John 95
Lytell geste how the plowman lerned his pater noster 30

MacCulloch, Diarmaid 202
Maidstone (Kent) 150
Man, Robert 66
Man, Thomas 88
Manipulus Curatorum 71, 114
Mapledurham (Berks.) 17
Maplisden, George 134
Marbecke, John 75
Mardy, John 82
Marius, Richard 165 n.
marriage of the clergy 162, 163–73, 233, 234
marriage, sacrament of 143, 175
Marshall, James 154
Marshall, John 153
Marshall, Robert 106–7
Martin, Thomas 164, 165 n., 171, 172, 173
Martock (Som.) 95
Marton, William 149
Martyn, Marion 207
Martyr, Peter 170
Masham (Yorks.) 177
mass 35–85 *passim*, 88–9, 92, 96, 99, 104, 107, 109, 113–4, 115–16, 122, 126, 140, 159–63, 174, 180–1, 216, 233
    allegory in 35–40, 74
    elevation in 40, 41–3, 62, 74, 75, 77–8, 81, 167
    final blessing in 43–4, 77
    for the dead 50–6, 129, 130, 161–3
    laity's role in 59, 64–6, 73–4, 77, 79
    'meeds of the mass' 83
    neglect of 101
    prayers in 57–9, 105, 126
    Protestant critique of 35, 63–6, 71, 73–5, 76–8, 79–80
    see also 'donatism'; Eucharist; obits; trentals
Mastall, Henry 27, 131
Matthew, John 147
Mawnford, Michael 89
Mayler, John 73
Melton, William 191, 214
Mendlesham (Suffolk) 167–8
Menheniot (Corn.) 102
Meppershall (Beds.) 205

Meryng, Dame Anne 67
Millet, William 55
Minster Lovell (Oxon.) 43
Mirc, John 7, 10, 103
Modus Confitendi 7, 10
monks 14, 15, 96, 110, 111, 124, 184, 230
Mont, Christopher 168
Mordaunt, Lord 28
Moore (Oxon.) 128
More, Thomas 9, 20, 22–3, 47, 56, 59, 71, 91, 104–5, 111, 117, 119, 121, 143, 144, 146–7, 151, 157, 163, 164, 165, 197, 212, 214, 219, 227
Moreman, Dr 102
Morison, Richard 150
morrow-mass priests 12
Morton, John, Cardinal Archbishop of Canterbury 21, 125, 227
Morton, Richard 76
mortuaries 18, 186–7, 222–3
Murner, Thomas 72
Mydell, John 204
Mynstreley, William 45 n.
Myroure of oure Ladye 69, 70
Myrows, Gilbert 129

Nepomuk, St John 20
Ness (Salop) 84
Nether Fonthill (Wilts.) 84
Nevill, George, Archbishop of York 88
Newbury (Berks.) 85, 122
Newcastle 111, 138, 183, 201
Newchurch (Kent) 178
Newington (Kent) 62, 67
'New Learning' 28
Newman, Kentish tanner 25
New Testament, *see* bible
Newton (Cambs.) 170
Nichols, Philip 24, 25, 169
non-residence 99, 177–9, 183–4
Norfolk, Duke of 76
North Kilworth (Leics.) 195
Northumberland, Duke of 172, 233
Northumberland, Earl of 197
North Waltham (Hants.) 123
Norton Davy (Northants) 136
Norwich 55
Norwich, Simon 135
Nowell, John 106
Nuffield (Oxon.) 136

Oakham (Leics.) 135
obits 51, 54

Oculus Sacerdotis 115
O'Day, Rosemary 174
Ombersley (Worcs.) 119
Orchard of Syon 119, 125, 160
Order of Communion (1548) 30, 76
Ordinary or crysten men 20
Ordinals, Edwardian 140, 230
ordination, *see* holy orders; recruitment to priesthood
Ospringe (Kent) 180
Oste, John 215
Oswestry (Salop) 195
Oxford 54, 91, 170, 181
Oxfordshire Rising (1549) 206
Ozment, Steven 9, 26

Page, Andrew 100
Palisor, Thomas 210
Palmes, John 151
Palsgrave, John 155–6
papacy, *see* pope
Parham, William 67
parish clerks 202–3
parish custom 202–4, 217
Parker, Geoffrey 112
Parker, Thomas 197
Parkyn, Robert 162, 167, 172, 225
Paston, Margaret 144
Paston, Walter 144
Paston, Sir William 155
Pater Noster 28, 29, 30, 69, 92, 102
Pattiswick (Essex) 178
Patrixbourne (Kent) 152
Paul's Cross 88, 94, 108, 125, 219, 226–7
Pawlett (Som.) 23, 62, 128, 184
Payntour, Robert 155
Peckham, John, Archbishop of Canterbury 88
Peerson, Anthony 74
Pembury (Kent) 22
Pendle (Lancs.) 13
Penrith (Cumb.) 101
Pers, John 124
Perry, Joyce 110
'Peter's Pence' 187
Peythe, Thomas 17
Pfaffenhass 213
Philcock, John 22
Philippes, John 53
Philips, Thomas 47
Pierson, William 155
Pilgrimage of Grace (1536) 28, 101, 190, 200, 206, 224

Pilton, (Northants) 149
Plaister for a galled horse 74, 160–1
Pluckley (Kent) 178
Plumpton, Robert 104
Plumpton, William 178
pluralism 177, 222
Plymouth 12
Ponet, John, Bishop of Winchester 93, 165 n.
Pontefract 59
Pontifex, William 209
Poole (Dorset) 75, 170
pope 28, 92, 116, 131, 206, 224
Potation for Lent 32
Practice of Prelates 21
Pratt, William 100
preaching 33, 74, 82–3, 86–96, 98, 101, 102, 105–6, 107, 115–16, 140, 192, 228–9, 235
priesthood, theology of, *see* holy orders; confession; mass
priesthood of all believers 138, 173, 175
'priestliness' 129–37
primers 18, 72
purgatory 16 n., 50–1, 54, 55, 79, 163, 181
Pycke, Alice 17
Pykering, Christopher 197
Pykering, Thomas 17
Pykes, William 95
Pykyll, Thomas 153

Quattuor Sermones 88, 113–14
Queenborough (Kent) 95

Ramsey, John 74, 160–1
Rastell, John 42, 149
Rationale of Ceremonial 65, 69
Recantacion of maystres missa 82
recruitment to priesthood 109–10, 112, 229–30
Reculver (Kent) 179, 190
Rede, Simon 191
Reformation Parliament 220, 222, 223, 229
religious instruction 29–30, 101–3
Resurrecion of the Masse 82
Reve, John 22
Revel, Tristram 111
Revell, John 62
Revell, Robert 92
Reynes, Robert 115
Ricard, Richard 216
Richardson, Richard 186
Ridley, Nicholas, Bishop of London 31, 49, 79, 94, 138, 190

Ringwood (Hants) 89
Ripon (Yorks.) 143
Roberde Abbey (Sussex) 124
Robyns, Edmund 58, 130
Roff, Robert 193
Roke, Isabell 185
Roke, James 185
Roo, John 156–7
Rosthone (Ches.) 182
Rowkshaw, William 8
Runcorn (Lancs.) 151
Rushton, Henry 130–1
Russell, John 201
Rycket, Robert 156
Rymyngton, William de 160

Sacombe (Herts.) 178
sacraments 7, 88, 93, 99, 113–14, 115–16,
  125, 179–85, 188, 192
  see also anointing of the sick; baptism;
  confession; Eucharist; holy orders;
  marriage; mass
Sadler, John 62
St German, Christopher 47, 121, 135, 177,
  188, 197–8, 220, 227, 235
St Margaret at Cliffe (Kent) 183
Salisbury, Countess of 21 n.
Samborne, Nicholas 17
Sampford Courtney (Devon) 78, 206
Sampson, Elizabeth 49
Savile, Henry 53
Scandella, Domenico 11 n.
Scarisbrick, J. J. 116, 212, 213
Scott, Cuthbert 226–7
Scott, Walter 1
Seasalter (Kent) 128, 217
sedition 28–9, 170, 224
Selling (Kent) 179
Seman, Richard 124
Sermones Discipuli 8, 87, 89, 117–18, 233 n.
Sermones Parati 87
servants, priests as 110, 127, 197–8
  see also chaplains
Seven Deadly Sins 7, 9, 15, 32, 88
Sevill, William 137
Sevington (Kent) 30
Sezincote (Glos.) 101, 179
Shakerston (Leics.) 22
Shakyll, Alice 154
Shawdford, William 207
Shawell (Leics.) 152
Shaxton, Nicholas, Bishop of
  Salisbury 144

Sherborne (Hants) 95
Sherburne, Robert, Bishop of
  Chichester 131, 221
Shipton-under-Wychwood (Oxon.) 155
Shirland (Derby.) 62, 204
Short Treatise . . . of Christ's Blessed Body 48
Shoter, Robert 131, 158, 179, 187
'Shriving pew' 6
Simnel, Lambert 128
simony 186–7
Sittingborne (Kent) 130
Six Articles (1539) 25, 28, 71, 73, 153,
  167, 168
Skelton, John 97
Skip, John 227
Slaley (Durham) 207
Smelt, William 128
Smith, Henry Maynard 150
Smith, James 17
Smith, Richard, theologian 105
Smith, Richard 194
social status of clergy 127–8, 196–9, 204–5
Somerton (Suffolk) 129
Southfleet (Kent) 100
Southwell (Northants) 8
South-Western Rebellion (1549) 25, 29,
  78–9, 102, 107, 168, 181, 206
South Witham (Lincs.) 223
Spalding (Lincs.) 99
Speculum Sacerdotale 60
Spire, James 95
Spire, Thomas 136
Sprent, Thomas 23, 62, 184
Stagg, Alexander 170–1
Stanard, Thomas 27, 186
Stanley, Edward, Lord Monteagle 95
Stanton, John 9 n.
Staple (Kent) 201
Starkey, Thomas 97
Steeple Bumpstead (Essex) 122
Stella Clericorum 125
Stendhal 197
stipendiary priests 12, 100, 127, 196
Stoker, Gerard 186
Storie of the Mass 65, 69
Stratfield Saye (Hants) 210
Strauss, Jacob 26
Streatley (Beds.) 66
Streteham, Edmund 106–7
Stubys, Nicholas 159
Sturry (Kent) 180
Sulgrave (Northants) 136
Summa Angelica 8

Summa Anthonini 8
Supplication against the Ordinaries (1532) 188, 222
Supplicacyon for the Beggars 20
Supplication of Souls 146
Supplication of the Poore Commons 106
Sutton-in-Ashfield (Notts.) 204
Swalcliffe (Oxon.) 217
Swanne, William 100
Swynnerton (Staffs.) 106
Syon Abbey 15, 69

Taillour, Simon 12, 154
Tailor, Henry 157–8
Tailour, Thomas 122
Talbot, Nicholas 58
Tankard, Henry 191
Tanner, Norman 55
Tarrington (Herts.) 162, 186
Taynton (Oxon.) 154
Ten Articles (1536) 92
Ten Commandments 7, 9, 15, 29, 30, 32, 92, 101
Tendring (Essex) 62
Tenterden (Kent) 112, 193
Tentler, T. N. 8, 11
testamentary involvement of priests 208–9, 231–2
Testwood, Robert 74
Tewkesbury (Glos.) 12
Thanington (Kent) 184
Thimbelby (Lincs.) 111
Thoresby, John, Archbishop of York 113
Thormanton (Glos.) 197
Thornham Magna (Suffolk) 135
Thornton (Bucks.) 154
Thorpe, William 42
Thrower, Thomas 22
Thurlbie, Robert 149
Ticehurst (Sussex) 106
tithes 18, 62, 84, 130–1, 135, 158, 172, 179, 186, 189–90, 191, 196, 213, 216–18, 226
'tithes forgotten' 208, 218, 223, 231
Toller, Catherine 161
tonsure 109, 114, 136–7, 139
Townstal (Devon) 191
Traytte of Good Lyvyng and Good Deying 56, 90, 114
Treatise concernynge the division 227
Treatise on the Passion 71
trentals 16 n., 51, 54, 55, 95, 124
Trevyhan, John 156

Turner, Roger 16
Turner, William 35, 65, 104
Twickenham 27, 186
Tyball, John 122
Tyndale, William 9, 15, 21, 31, 45, 97, 104, 111, 139, 151, 163, 164, 169, 182, 220
Tyngle, William 154
Tyrell, Thomas 135
Tyting, Nicholas 186

'unwritten verities' 105

Vergil, Polydore 94, 128
Vertue of the Masse 38, 60, 61, 70, 84
vestments 37–9, 77, 78, 109 n., 195, 201
Veysey, John 67, 68, 84
violence:
    against priests 67, 84, 137, 181, 215, 217, 218–19, 228, 234
    by priests 130–1, 148
visitations 90–1, 92–3, 99, 101, 144–5, 152, 176, 180
visiting the sick 131, 182, 191, 193
vocation 110–11, 112, 132–3, 230

Wadhurst (Sussex) 195
Waghen (Yorks.) 177–8
Wakefield (Yorks.) 140, 185, 214
Waldershare (Kent) 128
Waldyng, Thomas 59
Wales 150
Walker, Richard 218
Wallay, George 24
Waltham (Kent) 221
Warde, Thomas 137
Warham, William, Archbishop of Canterbury 91, 136, 144, 181
Warner, William 193
Warrington (Ches.) 171
Watson, Thomas, Bishop of Lincoln 233, 235
Warthill (Yorks.) 149
Wastyll, Thomas 193
Wayd, Robert 68
Weber, Max 55
Wedon, Robert 52 n.
Wellflett, George 195
Wells 12
Wembury (Devon) 184
Werell, Thomas 199, 210
West, John 89
West, Nicholas, Bishop of Ely 88
Westwell (Oxon.) 91

Wharram Percy (Yorks.) 154
Whitford, Richard 10, 15–16, 25, 46, 70,
    88–9, 111, 143
Whiting, Robert 226
Whitwick (Leics.) 215
Whyghtt, Thomas 75
Whytt, Robert 67
Witdecombe, John 95
Willett, Ralph 62
Williams, Glanmor 150
Windsor (Berks.) 25
Wingfield (Wilts.) 74
Winksworth (Derby.) 183
Wisborough Green (Sussex) 202
Wiseman, Sir John 135
Wissett (Suffolk) 62
Wodde, Michael, *see* Day, John
Wolsey, Thomas Cardinal 21, 81, 111, 36,
    151

women 23–6, 39, 92, 148, 150, 157–8,
    168 n., 171, 181
Woodchurch (Kent) 216
Wooton (Kent) 41, 180
Wooton (Oxon.) 47
Works of Mercy 7, 32
Worminghall (Bucks.) 201
Wrawby (Leics.) 99
Wren, Geoffrey 179
Wriothesley, Charles 167, 220
Wyche, William 162
Wyclif, John 48, 125
Wyllestrop, Sir Oswald 68
Wyllet, Ralph 155

York 41, 95, 99, 166, 199
Youings, Joyce 79

Zell, Michael 230

DATE DUE

DEC 31 '98			
MAY 3 0 2003			
			Printed in USA